The
Strange
Death
of
Republican
America

The Strange Death of Republican America

CHRONICLES OF A COLLAPSING PARTY

By Sidney Blumenthal

UNION SQUARE PRESS
An imprint of Sterling Publishing Co., Inc.

New York / London
www.sterlingpublishing.com

STERLING and the distinctive Sterling logo are registered
trademarks of Sterling Publishing Co., Inc.

Library of Congress Cataloging-in-Publication Data
Blumenthal, Sidney, 1948-
The strange death of Republican America : chronicles of a collapsing
party / by Sidney Blumenthal.
    p. cm.
ISBN-13: 978-1-4027-5789-1
ISBN-10: 1-4027-5789-1
1. United States—Poliltics and government—2001- 2. United States—
Foreign relations—2001- 3. Conservatism—United States. 4.
Radicalism—United States. 5. Republican Party (U.S. : 1854-) 6.
Political corruption—United States. 7. Bush, George W. (George Walker),
1946- 8. Bush, George W. (George Walker), 1946—-Friends and associ-
ates. I. Title.
E902.B585 2008
973.93—dc22
                                                    2007045348

2   4   6   8   10   9   7   5   3   1

Published by Sterling Publishing Co., Inc.
387 Park Avenue South, New York, NY 10016
© 2008 by Sidney Blumenthal
Distributed in Canada by Sterling Publishing
c/o Canadian Manda Group, 165 Dufferin Street
Toronto, Ontario, Canada M6K 3H6
Distributed in the United Kingdom by GMC Distribution Services
Castle Place, 166 High Street, Lewes, East Sussex, England BN7 1XU
Distributed in Australia by Capricorn Link (Australia) Pty. Ltd.
P.O. Box 704, Windsor, NSW 2756, Australia

Sterling ISBN-13: 978-1-4027-5789-1
ISBN-10: 1-4027-5789-1

For information about custom editions, special sales, premium and
corporate purchases, please contact Sterling Special Sales
Department at 800-805-5489 or specialsales@sterlingpublishing.com.

For Sean Wilentz

Books by Sidney Blumenthal

*The Permanent Campaign: Inside the World
of Elite Political Operatives* (1980)

*The Rise of the Counter-Establishment:
The Conservative Ascent to Political Power*
(originally published in 1986, republished in 2008)

The Reagan Legacy (coeditor with Thomas Byrne Edsall) (1988)

*Our Long National Daydream: A Political Pageant
of the Reagan Era* (1988)

Pledging Allegiance: The Last Campaign of the Cold War (1990)

The Clinton Wars (2003)

How Bush Rules: Chronicles of a Radical Regime (2006)

CONTENTS

Introduction:
The Strange Death
of Republican America

On May 3, 2007, ten Republican candidates aspiring to succeed George W. Bush as president debated at the Ronald W. Reagan Library, where they mentioned Reagan twenty-one times and Bush not once. By raising the icon of Reagan, they hoped to dispel the shadow of Bush. Reagan himself had often invoked magic—"the magic of the marketplace" was among his trademark phrases and he had been the TV host at the grand opening of Disneyland, "the Magic Kingdom," in 1955. Evoking his name was an act of sympathetic magic in the vain hope that its mere mention would transfer his success to his pretenders and transport them back to the heyday of Republican rule.

Bush's second term has witnessed the great unraveling of the Republican coalition. His radicalism has pushed conservatism to extreme claims on executive power, preemptive war, the rule of law, a one-party state, hostility to science, suppression of career staff professionals in the departments and agencies, and the hollowing out of the federal government. In my first volume on this unique presidency, *How Bush Rules: Chronicles of a Radical Regime*, I described and analyzed the period from the zenith of Bush's hubris immediately after "mission accomplished" was proclaimed in Iraq through the early part of his second term, when he hypercharged his radical agenda by attempting to privatize Social Security; asserted presidential power in the Terri Schiavo case; and pursued a military solution to the war in Iraq against the pleadings of his commanders in the field. Finally, Hurricane Katrina blew away the façade of the decisive self-proclaimed "war president."

This book, *The Strange Death of Republican America: Chronicles of a Collapsing Party*, continues the story as the Republican Party, after nearly two generations of political dominance, rapidly disintegrates under the

1

stress of Bush's failures and the Republicans' scandals and disgrace.

On September 10, 2001, Bush was at the lowest point in public approval of any president that early in his term. It was a sign that he seemed destined to join the list of previous presidents who had gained the office without popular majorities and served only one term. After the terrorist attacks of September 11, Bush's fortunes were reversed, and he was no longer seen as drifting but masterful. Reflecting the tenor of the Washington press corps, David Broder, the chief political columnist for the *Washington Post*, after hearing Bush declare, "God is not neutral," pronounced, "The rhetoric is Lincolnian, and so are the tragic forces that have forged the conviction in this president's words."[1] (Lincoln, of course, had never presumed to penetrate the motives of God; his characteristic insight, delivered in his second inaugural address, was, "The Almighty has His own purposes.")

Despite the portentous rhetoric of his speechwriters and the fractured history of the pundits, Bush overnight assumed a superior position politically. Now he appeared to take his place in the long line of Republican presidents who had preceded him. He acted as though his astronomical popularity in the aftermath of September 11 ratified whatever radical course he might take in international affairs and vindicated whatever radical policies and politics he might follow at home.

Vice President Dick Cheney assumed control of concentrating unfettered executive power, a project to which he had been devoted since he had served as the assistant to presidential counselor Donald Rumsfeld in the Nixon White House. (Cheney's involvement with neoconservatism has been continuous for more than three decades, beginning in the Ford White House, when he was deputy chief of staff to Rumsfeld and then chief of staff, as I document in the introduction to the new edition of my book, *The Rise of the Counter-Establishment*.) Karl Rove, the president's chief political strategist, took charge of subordinating federal departments and agencies to the larger political goal of achieving a permanent Republican realignment through a one-party state—another Nixonian objective, run by another Nixonian. (Rove had been among the youngest of the dirty tricksters involved in the broad Watergate scandal and was questioned by the FBI.) Cheney and Rove's complementary efforts gave the substance to the radical theory of the "unitary executive."

---

[1] David Broder, "Bush's Speech—Echoes of Lincoln," *Grand Rapids Press*, Sept. 23, 2001.

In 2004, Bush swaggered through his reelection campaign, still swept along on the momentum from September 11. He and Rove did not consider the perverse and unprecedented illogic of *Bush v. Gore* as anything but a rightful decision. They did not see the means by which he became president as artificial, making his position inherently weak and unstable. Bush took occupying the office itself and September 11 as tantamount to a resounding mandate for his radicalism. Nor did Bush or Rove view Bush's steady and precipitous decline in popularity as cause to reconsider their preconceptions. After the Afghanistan invasion, Bush's numbers tumbled until he ramped up the campaign for the invasion of Iraq, after which his standing dived again, only to spike once more after the capture of Saddam Hussein, only to fall again. Nonetheless, Rove drew no lessons from these warnings, except that war and terror served as indispensable political weapons to sustain Bush. On this rock, Rove proposed to build a reigning party.

After the invasion of Iraq, Dick and Lynne Cheney sent out their 2003 Christmas card embossed with a suggestion offered by Benjamin Franklin, a Deist, for a nonsectarian prayer to open the Constitutional Convention, but it was now infused with a more martial meaning: "If a sparrow cannot fall to the ground without His notice, is it probable that an empire can rise without His aid?" After the 2004 election victory, Rove's former political deputy and Republican National Committee chairman Ken Mehlman said, "If there's one empire I want built, it's the George Bush empire."[2]

The Bush administration was reinforced in its political mission by a press corps that admired its power, refused to recognize its radicalism, and sought to project its rule far into the future. The press had served as an essential instrument for the disinformation campaign to establish the rationale for the war in Iraq and would almost utterly misunderstand its own role in the fallout occurring during the investigation and trial of Cheney's chief of staff, I. Lewis "Scooter" Libby, covered in detail in these pages.

On the eve of his second inauguration, *Newsweek* published a cover story about Bush that portrayed him as a commanding, deeply informed, intellectually curious, and probing president: "Whether he's remaking his team or plotting his second-term policies, Bush's leadership style belies his caricature as a disengaged president who is blindly loyal, dislikes dissent and

[2] Tom Hamburger and Peter Wallsten, *One Party Country: The Republican Plan for Dominance in the 21st Century* (Hoboken, NJ: John Wiley & Sons, Inc., 2006) p. 102.

covets his own downtime. In fact, Bush's aides and friends describe the mirror image of a restless man who masters details and reads avidly, who chews over his mistakes and the failings of those around him, and who has grown ever more comfortable pulling the levers of power."[3]

A week after the 2004 election, David Broder knowingly assured readers in the *Washington Post* that "before throwing yourself over a cliff or emigrating to Sweden," they should understand that Bush had appointed moderate White House aides and the Republican Congress would act as a moderating force. "Checks and balances are still there. The nation does not face 'another dark age,' unless you consider politics, with all its trade-offs and bargaining, a black art."[4]

Perhaps the most considered, comprehensive, and boldest analysis after the 2004 election came from two English journalists, writers for *The Economist* magazine, John Micklethwait and Adrian Wooldridge. In their book, *The Right Nation*, they conflated Bush's unilateralism, the religious right, and the conservative counter-establishment of think tanks and foundations with American exceptionalism. "Today, thanks in large part to the strength of the Right Nation, American exceptionalism is reasserting itself with a vengeance."

They categorically declared that the realignment Rove was seeking had at last appeared. Bush's reelection was the crowning moment of the entire Republican era, setting it on a firm foundation for a generation to come. "Who would have imagined that the 2004 presidential election would represent something of a last chance for the Democrats?" they wrote. "But conservatism's progress goes much deeper than the gains that the Republican Party has made over the past half century or the steady decline in Democratic registration. The Right clearly has ideological momentum on its side in much the same way that the Left had momentum in the 1960s."[5]

The Economist's correspondents were Tories in search of a promised land after the Labour Party became the natural party of government in Britain with the post-Thatcher crackup of the Conservatives. The United States was a fantastic canvas for their thwarted dreams. They were delirious to discover that while conservatism had fallen from grace and favor

[3] Richard Wolffe, "Window of Opportunity," *Newsweek*, Jan. 24, 2004.
[4] David Broder, "Darkness? Hardly," *Washington Post*, Nov. 14, 2004.
[5] John Micklethwait and Adrian Wooldridge, *The Right Nation: Conservative Power in America* (New York: Penguin, 2005) pp. 382, 380.

in Britain it held every lever of national power in the New World. "Thatcher could never rely on a vibrant conservative movement to support her (unless you regard a couple of think tanks as a movement) while American conservatism has been going from strength to strength for decades," they wrote with undisguised envy.[6]

At least in one way the Republican triumph in 2004 echoed British political history, resembling that of the British Liberal Party in 1910. "From that victory they never recovered," wrote George Dangerfield in *The Strange Death of Liberal England*.[7] But the strange death of Republican America, the supposed "Right Nation," cannot be attributed to the same reasons as the decline of Liberal England, a complacent faith of good intentions bypassed and trampled by events that it presumed to understand as it drifted into the dark passage of world war.

Bush willfully and heedlessly tempted the fates. He built a grand palace of Republican dreams that crashed down upon his party. Casting aside all caution, he believed that he could reorder the entire Middle East; imagined he could invade Iraq and remake it in his image; spread democracy easily through the region; settle the Israeli-Palestinian conflict with no peace process; forge a one-party state at home; replace professionals throughout the federal government with political appointees regardless of the legal, practical, or human impact (as was seen in Hurricane Katrina); regard the rule of law as an obstacle to a commander in chief who presumed the right by fiat to make, obey, or disobey any law he wished, including the right to order torture (which he euphemistically called "enhanced interrogation techniques"); and hold facts, evidence, and reality in contempt as though they would never have consequences. An anonymous senior White House aide, apparently Karl Rove, explained the administration's credo to journalist Ron Suskind, writing in *The New York Times Magazine*: "We're an empire now, and when we act, we create our own reality. And while you're studying that reality—judiciously, as you will—we'll act again, creating other new realities, which you can study too, and that's how things will sort out. We're history's actors . . . and you, all of you, will be left to just study what we do."[8]

---

[6] Ibid., p. 411.
[7] George Dangerfield, *The Strange Death of Liberal England* (New York: Capricorn Books, 1961) p. 6.
[8] Ron Suskind, "Faith, Certainty and the Presidency of George W. Bush," *The New York Times Magazine*, October 17, 2004.

Much of the Washington press corps seemed to agree. The guiding assumption of American politics was that Bush's presidency was girded by a stable conservative consensus and that politics would operate on this consensus into the foreseeable future. In this view, Bush became not only the most recent expression of Republican supremacy but also its strongest. It was a curious refraction of the consensus school of the 1950s that envisioned American politics as an unbroken thread of liberalism.

According to the consensus school, the dissimilarities between American and European politics—ravaged in the twentieth century by wars and totalitarian movements—suggested an essential consensus predating the creation of the nation rooted in the thought of John Locke. "The American community is a liberal community," wrote the historian Louis Hartz in his highly influential *The Liberal Tradition in America*, published in 1955.[9] That same year, William F. Buckley, Jr., launching the modern conservative movement in the first issue of *National Review*, wrote that conservatism "stands athwart history, yelling Stop." By 2004, after Bush's victory, conservatives were triumphalist. "The 2004 election was about as clear a vindication as we could have hoped for . . ." wrote Micklethwait and Wooldridge, ". . . that conservatism is the dominant force in American politics and that conservatism explains why America is different."[10] Turning the old consensus thesis on its head, they argued that the American community is a conservative community.

For long periods of time, political alignments shift incrementally and slowly. But our politics also has a volatile history, not always placid, erupting suddenly and sharply through cataclysms, and often as a result of violence. The Civil War, the Great Depression, and the Vietnam War and the civil rights revolution were earthquakes that abruptly overturned long-settled arrangements. When Herbert Hoover was elected in 1928, his landslide victory was universally seen as the peak of Republican Party consolidation, the culmination of the party's progress since the Civil War. Similarly, when Lyndon Johnson was elected in 1964, his landslide was interpreted as the apotheosis of the New Deal. For two generations the Republicans have been running on the themes and infrastructure developed since the Democratic collapse in 1968, as chronicled in *The Rise of the Counter-Establishment*.

[9] Louis Hartz, *The Liberal Tradition in America* (New York: Harcourt Brace & Co., 1955) p. 3.
[10] Micklethwait and Wooldridge, *The Right Nation: Conservative Power in America* (New York: Penguin, 2005) p. 400.

The scale of the Bush disaster is larger than any cataclysm since then. Whether or not there is a powerful geopolitical analogy between the war in Iraq and the Vietnam War, as Bush at first insistently denied, then vehemently argued, there is a pertinent domestic political analogy. Vietnam ended a Democratic era as definitively as Iraq is closing a Republican one.

Republicanism at its pinnacle—during the Reagan years—had been an easy identity for adherents to wear. With the recession of 1982 a memory, tax rates, especially for the wealthy, drastically lowered, and the country at peace amid the Cold War, President Reagan demanded no sacrifice or pain. His carefree attitude disdained the Protestant ethic, with banker's hours that conveyed there was no relationship between hard work and reward. His sunny disposition had removed the scowl of Richard Nixon and the stain of Watergate from the party. Yet Reagan's landslide of forty-nine states in 1984 echoed Nixon's landslide of forty-nine states in 1972. One famous victory was built on the other, one Californian paving the way for another. Nixon's work of realignment as well as his self-destruction made possible the rise of Reagan, who had been his rival for the Republican nomination in 1968.

Conservatives prefer to date the origins of the Republican ascent to the candidacy of Barry Goldwater in 1964. But it was his defeat followed by the shattering of the Johnson presidency over Vietnam that cleared the path for the resurrection of Richard Nixon, who was the main progenitor of the Republican rise. Only on the ruins of the Goldwater debacle was Nixon able to capture the Republican nomination in 1968. He was the author of the project for an imperial presidency. Watergate, a concatenation of plots, was an emanation of that grand design, both to create an unaccountable executive and harness the federal government into a political machine for what Nixon first called a "New Majority." The 1974 "Final Report of the Select Committee on Presidential Campaign Activities" documented the Senate Watergate Committee's investigation into Nixon's effort to use "the powers of incumbency" through programs such as "the Responsiveness Program," created to "redirect Federal moneys to specific administration supporters and to target groups and geographic areas to benefit" his campaign. [11]

[11] John W. Dean, "Will a Dark Cloud Follow Karl Rove Back to Texas?: Congress Is Still Investigating Serious Criminal Abuses of Executive Powers," FindLaw, http://writ.news.findlaw.com/dean/20070824.html, Aug. 24, 2007.

If Nixon had succeeded in his plan, the U.S. government and politics would have taken very different forms. But his resignation shattered the center in the Republican Party, and Nixon made possible not only Jimmy Carter but also Ronald Reagan. The traditional Republican center attempted to hold under Gerald Ford, but it could not cohere, even within Ford's own White House, where his successive chiefs of staff, Donald Rumsfeld and Dick Cheney, undermined it.

The Republican fall parallels the previous decline of the Democrats. From 1968 through 1988, the story of the Democratic Party had been its internal disintegration and reduction to its base.

The Republican Party dominance was not illusory, mere smoke and mirrors, though it did have superior image-making, too. After the enfranchisement of black voters in the South in the mid-1960s, whites deserted the Democratic Party and flocked to the Republican Party, eventually creating a GOP Solid South, as Lyndon Johnson had feared when he told his youthful press secretary Bill Moyers upon signing civil rights legislation, "We have lost the South for a generation." The Republicans turned many urban and suburban ethnic Catholics, who had been at the core of the New Deal, into Republicans, by exploiting strategies of racial fear around issues of crime, education, taxation, and housing and by appealing to cultural traditionalism on issues such as abortion and women's rights generally.

The Republicans also won over formerly progressive Western states, through an anti-government states' rights Sagebrush Rebellion on behalf of local extractive industries. Running for governor in 1966, Reagan tipped California, which had been balanced for decades between liberal Democrats and liberal Republicans, toward the conservative wing of his party. The movement of California into the Republican column signaled the shift of geopolitical equilibrium to the Sun Belt, a new alliance of West and South, and consolidated the Republican Party coalition.

Kevin Phillips, a strategist for the Nixon campaign in 1968, wrote in his seminal book, *The Emerging Republican Majority* (published the following year), that Nixon's victory "bespoke the end of the New Deal Democratic hegemony and the beginning of a new era in American politics. . . . Today the interrelated Negro, suburban and Sun Belt migrations have all but destroyed the New Deal coalition." Phillips described how the alignment of the Democratic Party with civil rights ("many Negro demands") provoked a reaction. "The South, the West and the Catholic sidewalks of New York were the focal points of conservative opposition to the welfare liberalism of the federal government . . ."[12]

Even as he planned to wind down the Vietnam War, Nixon painted anti-war critics and Democrats as unpatriotic and hostile to national security, and for decades the Democrats could not escape the stigma. In defense of his Vietnam policy, Nixon conjured up a "Silent Majority" in opposition to the antiwar movement. This constituency transmuted a decade later into the so-called "Reagan Democrats" included many of the same former Democrats who had defected to Nixon's banner. A host of domestic and foreign policy motives drove them: resentment against liberal elites and minorities over social welfare policy; antagonism to the youthful university-based counterculture undermining traditionalism; and liberal softness against Communism supposedly weakening the will to win in Vietnam.

None of these themes, including the anti-Communist one, lost their vitality even after the end of the Vietnam War. Nixon's resignation over Watergate gave the Democrats an opening, but Jimmy Carter's presidency proved a spectacle of Democratic infighting and provided the Republican right the chance to seize control of the party in 1980 by running on an agenda against economic mismanagement and Soviet adventurism. By now, conservatism was transformed from a cranky backward-looking isola-tionist fringe into a vigorous, politically skillful movement that had cap-tured and held the commanding heights of the Republican Party.

In 1984, the Democrats nominated Carter's vice president, who, unfairly or not, bore the burden of past ineptitude, to compete with Reagan at a time of peace and prosperity. By August 1984, Gallup found that on the question of "increasing respect for the U.S. overseas," Reagan led Walter Mondale 48 to 33 percent. Reagan's reelection affirmed the Republican era, its national coalition and lock on the presidency.

The Republicans were the dominant political party, even when the par-ties appeared momentarily and evenly matched in public opinion or when the Democrats controlled one or both houses of the Congress. Democrats invariably bore the burden of defending themselves from past errors, real or imagined, and on positions from gun control to abortion Republicans used "wedge issues" to splinter the Democratic coalition and fuse the Republican one.

---

[12] Kevin Phillips, *The Emerging Republican Majority* (New Rochelle, NY: Arlington House, 1969) pp. 25, 39, 37.

The exposure of the Iran-contra scandal during Reagan's second term brought his domestic programs to a grinding halt. This bizarre scandal involved a convoluted effort to create a parallel, secret, and illegal U.S. foreign policy, offshore and underground, evading the Congress and the usual channels of the national security apparatus. In 1987, the congressional hearings into the scandal and the Senate's rejection of Reagan's far-right nominee to the Supreme Court, Robert Bork, who as Nixon's hatchet man in the "Saturday Night Massacre" had fired the Watergate special prosecutor, had a further radicalizing effect on the right. Meanwhile, Reagan revived his moribund presidency by reversing his course, negotiating an arms control treaty with Soviet leader Mikhail Gorbachev and proclaiming the end of the Cold War. Though Republicans from both the right and the center criticized him as a naive utopian, his demarche lifted his fallen popularity and that of his vice president, making possible his election.

The political career of George H. W. Bush illustrates the contradictions of Republicanism and the growing radicalism of the party that his son would later push to an extreme. His difficulties reflected the radicalization of the party going back to 1964 and his circuitous route in navigating its currents. As much as he was overwhelmed by events, the elder Bush was also undermined by his inability to sustain a viable Republican center post-Reagan. For every gesture he made toward fiscal prudence, a traditional Republican virtue, his party punished him. In 1992, former Nixon speechwriter and conservative firebrand Patrick Buchanan challenged Bush for the Republican nomination, capturing 38 percent of the vote in New Hampshire, a humiliation for the incumbent president. Buchanan's insurgency and the right's obstreperousness made it necessary for Bush to lend them the stage of the Republican National Convention in Houston, a disaster for him that contributed to his loss in the general election.

The principal lesson the son absorbed from his father's political failure was to avoid having enemies on the right. George W. Bush became what his father never could, a radical conservative, transcending the problems that had plagued the father throughout his career. The son systematically abandoned the father's respect for fiscal responsibility, individual rights, the separation of church and state, the Congress, constitutional checks and balances, and a realistic and bipartisan foreign policy. George W. Bush saw Reagan more than his father as his model, but he was as little like Reagan as he was like his father. Bush's radicalism has provided a vantage point for historical revisionism, causing his Republican predecessors, judged to be avatars of conservatism in their day, as more moderate in perspective. Reagan's pragmatic willingness to negotiate with congressional Democrats on such matters as Social Security, for example, takes on another aspect. But the inexorable movement to the right is inarguable as a historical pattern.

Every time the conservative Republican period seemed to be exhausted it gained new impetus through openings created by Democratic fractious-ness and incompetence in politics and governing. With each cycle, conser-vatism reemerged more radicalized—a steady march further to the right. After Nixon's disgrace in Watergate came Reagan; after the conservative crackup that engulfed George H. W. Bush came the radical Congress elected in 1994, led by Newt Gingrich and Tom DeLay; and then came George W. Bush.

Bill Clinton's presidency served as an interregnum that might have broken the Republican era for good had his vice president Al Gore been permitted to assume the office he won by a popular majority. But the conservative bloc on the Supreme Court ultimately thwarted him from occupying it. When the court in *Bush v. Gore* handed the presidency to Bush it gave him an extra-ordinary and unnatural chance to extend Republican power.

Only through the will to power in the Florida contest, the deus ex machina of the Supreme Court, and the tragedy of September 11 was Bush able to gain and hold the presidency. But he and the Republicans have been living on borrowed if not stolen time.

Karl Rove believed he could engineer a political realignment by re-creating his work in Texas where he marshaled money and focused cam-paign technology in order to destroy the Democrats. But the analogy of the nation as Texas writ large was faulty from the start. In Texas he had the wind at his back, regardless of how elaborate and clever his machinations. The transformation of Texas in the 1980s and 1990s into a Republican state was a delayed version of Southern realignment. Yet Rove came to Washington believing that the example of Texas could be transferred to the national level. With the attacks of September 11, this seasoned architect of realignment believed he possessed the impetus to enact his theory. It apparently never occurred to Rove or Bush that using Iraq to lock in the political impact of September 11 would ever backfire. In his first inaugural address, Bush spoke of an "angel in the whirlwind," but the whirlwind was of his own making. For all intents and purposes Rove could not have done more damage to the Republican Party than if he had been the control agent for the Manchurian Candidate.

The cataclysm has consumed Rove's theory, his president, his party, and not only the prospects for a Republican majority, but the hope that the Republicans will become more than a remnant of what they once were. The Republicans may take years if not decades to re-create their party, but that project will have to be on a wholly different basis.

The radicalization of the Republican Party is not at an end, but may only be entering a new phase. Loss of the Congress in 2006 is not accepted as reproach. Quite the opposite, it is understood by the Republican right as the result of lack of will and nerve, failure of ideological purity, errant immorality by members of Congress, and betrayal by the media and moderates within their own party. They may never recover from the election of 2004, when they believed their agenda received majority support and they ecstatically thought they were "the Right Nation."

Herbert Hoover did not transform his party but became its avatar through failure. By contrast, Bush has remade the Republican Party, turning it into a minority party as a consequence of his radicalism. Bush's discredited Republicanism has further provoked the radicalization of its base where religious right and nativist elements are increasingly dominant. The party is in the grip of an intolerant identity politics—white male semirural fundamentalist Protestant—that seems only to alienate women, suburbanites, Hispanics, and young people. By the end of his presidency, Bush had achieved the long conservative ambition of remaking the Republican Party without an Eastern moderate wing. Once a national coalition, embracing New York and California, Alabama and Illinois, the Republican Party has retreated into the Deep South and Rocky Mountains.

If the Republicans lose the presidential election of 2008 they may well be a rump party, captive of the conservatives. As a minority within the Congress, rather than proposing a positive agenda, they would most likely act as a negative force, trying to block progressive legislation. Republican cadres would use their skills honed in the partisan wars to attempt to demonize a new Democratic president, hoping that piling up negative ratings will be enough to drag down that president's popularity, regain the Congress and eventually the White House. Republicans will not get electoral traction again until the Democrats falter or collapse. In short, the Republicans are now strictly the party of reaction.

In 1952, the originator of the notion of realignment, political scientist Samuel Lubell, wrote in his seminal work, *The Future of American Politics*, American politics is not a contest of "two equally competing suns, but a sun and a moon. It is within the majority party that the issues of the day are fought out; while the minority party shines in the reflected radiance of the heat thus generated."[13] When Lubell wrote this, even as Dwight Eisenhower was about to win the presidency resoundingly, the Democrats were the sun and the Republicans the moon. Only after Nixon did the parties exchange place in the political solar system. Now after George W. Bush a new Copernican revolution is occurring.

The endless Republican invocation of Reagan really harkens back to the glory days of 2004. In the fallen house of cards they imagine they are still rightful owners of the White House, a fantasy of restoration that may grip them for a long time to come.

But the Democrats have not yet reached their full majority or solidified their new party. They are on the eve of becoming a majority national party for the first time in their history without conservative Southerners at their core. The Democrats can only consolidate their future coalition once in government and through successful governing. Then they will be the sun. In Bush's final days, a new era has not yet dawned, but an old one is setting.

[13] Samuel Lubell, *The Future of American Politics* (New York: Harper and Row, 1952) p. 200.

PART ONE

Implosion: From Stephen Colbert's Monologue to Mark Foley's Emails

The Fool

The most scathing public critique of the Bush presidency and the complicity of a craven press corps yet was delivered at the annual black-tie White House Correspondents' Association dinner on Saturday night by a comedian. President Bush was reported afterward to be seething, while the press corps responded to the zingers with stone cold silence, playing the classic straight man. Subsequently, many news reports of the event airbrushed out the joker.

Stephen Colbert plays a crank conservative commentator in a parody on Comedy Central four nights a week. Performing his routine within ten yards of Bush's hostile stare and before 2,600 members of the press and their celebrated guests, Colbert's offense of lèse-majesté affronted the amour propre of the embedded audience. After his mock praise of Bush as a rock against reality, Colbert censured the press by flattering its misfeasance. "Over the last five years you people were so good—over tax cuts, WMD intelligence, the effect of global warming. We Americans didn't want to know, and you had the courtesy not to try to find out . . . Here's how it works: The president makes decisions. He's 'the decider.' The press secretary announces those decisions, and you people of the press type those decisions down. Make, announce, type. Just put 'em through a spell-check and go home . . . Write that novel you got kicking around in your head. You know, the one about the intrepid Washington reporter with the courage to stand up to the administration. You know—fiction!" (Silence)

Perhaps ironically, on the day after Colbert's performance, *The New York Times* published a front-page story on the latest phase of the administration's war on the press. Now Bush is weighing "the criminal prosecution of reporters under the espionage laws." Since the *Washington Post* exposed the existence of CIA "black site" prisons holding untold numbers of detainees without due process of law and *The New York Times* disclosed the president's order to the National Security Agency to engage in domestic surveillance

17

without court warrants, the administration has applied new draconian methods to clamp down.

"Has *The New York Times* Violated the Espionage Act?" reads the title of a lengthy article in the neoconservative journal *Commentary*, by senior editor Gabriel Schoenfeld, laying out the case for prosecution. "What *The New York Times* has done is nothing less than to compromise the centerpiece of our defensive efforts in the war on terrorism," he writes. When the *Post* and the *Times* won Pulitzer Prizes for their stories, William Bennett, a former Republican Cabinet secretary and now a commentator on CNN of the sort satirized by Colbert, declared, "What they did is worthy of jail."

At Bush's orders, dragnets are being conducted throughout the national security bureaucracy in search of press sources. Government officials have been subjected to lie detector tests and interrogations. Within a week of the awarding of the Pulitzer Prizes, CIA analyst Mary McCarthy was fired for having had an "unauthorized" contact with a member of the press. At the same time, the FBI subpoenaed four decades of files accumulated by recently deceased investigative journalist Jack Anderson in an attempt to exhume old classified material.

Bush takes a different attitude on his own leaking of secrets for political purposes. Dozens of selective National Security Council documents were leaked to journalist Bob Woodward for his 2002 encomium, *Bush at War*. Vice President Cheney and his staff leaked disinformation to reporters to make the case that Saddam Hussein possessed weapons of mass destruction. And Bush and Cheney authorized Cheney's then chief of staff I. Lewis "Scooter" Libby to leak portions of the National Intelligence Estimate on Iraq's WMD to sympathetic reporters in an effort to discredit a critic, former ambassador Joseph Wilson.

In January, two officials of the American Israel Public Affairs Committee (the so-called *Israel lobby*) were indicted for receiving classified material from a Pentagon official who was later sentenced to prison. The AIPAC officials are being prosecuted as if they were reporters receiving leaks, and if convicted under the 1917 Espionage Act, the precedent would be ominous for journalists. "Why should persons at the *Times* not be treated in the same manner?" writes Schoenfeld.

Some in the press understand the peril posed to the First Amendment by an imperial president trying to smother the constitutional system of checks and balances. For those of the Washington press corps who reproved a court jester for his irreverence, the game of status is apparently more urgent than the danger to liberty. But it's no laughing matter.

May 4, 2006

Coup at the CIA

The moment that the destruction of the Central Intelligence Agency began can be pinpointed to a time, a place, and even a memo. On August 6, 2001, CIA Director George Tenet presented to President Bush his Presidential Daily Briefing, a startling document titled "Bin Laden Determined to Strike in U.S." Bush did nothing, asked for no further briefings on the issue, and returned to cutting brush at his Crawford, Texas, compound.

In Bush's denial of responsibility after the September 11 terrorist attacks, the search for scapegoats inevitably focused on the lapse in intelligence and therefore on the CIA, though it was the FBI whose egregious incompetence permitted the plotters to escape apprehension. Bush's intent to invade Iraq set up the battle royal that followed.

Tenet, an inveterate staff careerist held over from the Clinton administration, had ingratiated himself with the new White House tenant with salty stories, but it was in his eagerness to please Bush on Iraq that he ensured his tenure and made himself indispensable. At first, Tenet opposed including in the president's speech of October 2002 the disinformation that Iraq was seeking to build nuclear weaponry using yellow cake uranium Saddam Hussein supposedly sought to purchase in Niger, and the reference was knocked out. Yet, having already been discredited, the falsehood was inserted into the president's State of the Union address of January 2003, becoming the now infamous "sixteen words."

Tenet reassured Bush that the case for Saddam's possession of WMD was a "slam-dunk." At CIA headquarters in Langley, Virginia, Tenet promised then Secretary of State Colin Powell that for Powell's February 5, 2003, speech before the U.N. Security Council, the information that would be used to prove Saddam had WMD was ironclad. Powell insisted that Tenet be seated behind him while he spoke, as visual reinforcement of his statement's unimpeachable character. Yet every piece of it was false, and the humiliated Powell later said he had been "deceived." Tenet resigned on June 4, 2004, and shortly thereafter was awarded the Presidential Medal of Freedom.

After the brief interim appointment of CIA professional John McLaughlin, on August 10, 2004, almost three years to the day after the August 6 Presidential Daily Briefing on bin Laden, Bush named Porter Goss the new director of Central Intelligence. The president was looking for someone to rid him of the troublesome agency. In Goss, he thought he had discovered the perfect man for the bloody job, but the nature of the task undid Goss, and in his unraveling another scandal unfolded.

In the absence of any reliable evidence, CIA analysts had refused to put their stamp of approval on the administration's reasons for the Iraq war. Vice President Dick Cheney and his chief of staff, I. Lewis "Scooter" Libby, personally came to Langley to intimidate analysts on several occasions. Secretary of Defense Donald Rumsfeld and his then deputy secretary, Paul Wolfowitz, constructed their own intelligence bureau, called the Office of Special Plans, to sidestep the CIA and shunt disinformation corroborating the administration's arguments directly to the White House. "The administration used intelligence not to inform decision-making, but to justify a decision already made," Paul Pillar, then the chief Middle East analyst for the CIA, writes in the March–April issue of *Foreign Affairs*. "The process did not involve intelligence work designed to find dangers not yet discovered or to inform decisions not yet made. Instead, it involved research to find evidence in support of a specific line of argument—that Saddam was cooperating with Al-Qaeda—which in turn was being used to justify a specific policy decision."

But despite urgent pressures to report to the contrary, the CIA never reported that Saddam presented an imminent national security threat to the United States, that he was near to developing nuclear weapons, or that he had any ties to Al-Qaeda. Moreover, analysts predicted a protracted insurgency after an invasion of Iraq. Tenet, despite the lack of cooperation from the CIA's Directorate of Intelligence, acted as backslapper for the administration's policy.

The White House was in a fury. The CIA's professionalism was perceived as political warfare, and the agency apparently was seen as the center of a conspiracy to overthrow the administration. Inside the offices of the president, the vice president, and the secretary of defense, the CIA was referred to as a treasonous enemy. "If we lived in a primitive age, the ground at Langley would be laid waste and salted, and there would be heads on spikes," wrote neoconservative columnist David Brooks in *The New York Times* on November 13, 2004, citing White House officials and "members of the executive branch" as his sources. Reflecting their rage, he called on Bush to "punish the mutineers . . . If the C.I.A. pays no price for its behavior, no one will pay a price for anything, and everything is permitted. That, Mr. President, is a slam-dunk."

Goss combined the old-school tie with cynical zealotry. A graduate of Hotchkiss and Yale (class of 1960) and married to a Pittsburgh heiress, he had served as a CIA operative, left the agency for residence on Sanibel Island, Florida, a resort for the wealthy, bought the local paper, sold it for a fortune, and was elected to the House of Representatives in 1988. There he struck up an alliance with Newt Gingrich and his band of radicals. And after they captured the House in 1994, Goss used his CIA credential to become chairman of the Intelligence Committee.

In that position, he proved his bona fides to the Bush administration time and again. "Those weapons are there," he declared after David Kay, head of the Iraq Survey Group, reported that there were no WMD. He blocked investigations into detainee abuse at Abu Ghraib and into prewar disinformation churned by the neoconservatives' favorite Iraqi exile, Ahmed Chalabi. "I would say that the oversight has worked well in matters relating to Mr. Chalabi," Goss said. He also derided the notion of investigating the outing of covert CIA operative Valerie Plame Wilson: "Somebody sends me a blue dress and some DNA, I'll have an investigation." Goss was onboard with the cavalier way in which Plame was outed, a breach that revealed ingrained contempt for the agency as well as the supremacy of political objectives over national security.

On April 21, 2005, his mission dictated by Bush's political imperatives, Goss became CIA director. Immediately, he sent a memo to all employees, ordering them to "support the administration and its policies in our work." He underscored the supremacy of the party line: "As agency employees we do not identify with, support, or champion opposition to the administration or its policies."

He installed four political aides to run the agency from his offices on the seventh floor at Langley. Within weeks, an exodus of professionals began and then turned into a flood. In the Directorate of Operations, he lost the director, two deputies, and more than a dozen department and division directors and station chiefs out in the field. In the Directorate of Intelligence, dozens took early retirement. Four former operations chiefs, horrified by the carnage, sought to meet with Goss, but he refused.

As a result of hectoring by the 9/11 Commission, Bush established the position of national director of intelligence, a new layer of bureaucracy, but one that lacked operational or intelligence resources of its own. Suddenly, the CIA's preeminence was shattered. Since its creation by the National Security Act of 1947 at the onset of the Cold War, the CIA had dominated the intelligence community. But now the "central" part of the CIA was handed off to the new NDI [National Director of Intelligence], whose lines of authority and power were untested and uncertain.

The "global war on terror," meanwhile, was a boon to the concentration of power within the Pentagon, and that department gained control of more than 80 percent of the total budget for intelligence. Without its assigned place at the top of the pyramid, the CIA became disoriented and ever more peripheral. That suited Rumsfeld's empire building. And the CIA's plight was aggravated by the power grabs of the first NDI, John Negroponte (coincidentally an old Yale classmate of Goss's). Without natural functions of its own, Negroponte's office seized them from the CIA.

Acting on the president's charge, Goss in effect purged the CIA. He was even conducting lie detector interrogations of officers to root out the sources of stories leaked to the press—to the *Washington Post*, for example, in its Pulitzer Prize–winning exposé of CIA "black site" prisons where detainees are jailed without any due process, Red Cross inspection, or Geneva Conventions protection. Last month, a CIA agent, Mary McCarthy, was fired for her contact with a reporter. Like others subjected to questioning, she was asked her political affiliation.

But Goss's purging weakened the agency and his own inherent bureaucratic strength in relation to his voracious rivals at the Directorate of National Intelligence and the Pentagon. The more he served as the president's loyalist, the less was his power. By fulfilling his mission, he diminished himself. The butcher's defense of the integrity of the CIA from the directorate and the Pentagon lacked all conviction.

Goss's attempt to run the CIA through his own band of loyalists proved his ultimate undoing. It turned out that the "gosslings," as they were known at

Langley (after "quislings"), had unsavory connections that trailed them into the agency. An unintended consequence of Goss's dependence on his team of political hatchet men was that his future was dependent on their past.

As Goss parried with Negroponte and Rumsfeld, federal investigators began to close in on his third-ranked official, in charge of contracting, Kyle "Dusty" Foggo, for possibly granting illegal contracts to Brent Wilkes, the military contractor named as "co-conspirator No. 1" in the indictment of convicted former Republican Representative Randy "Duke" Cunningham, now serving eight years in prison for accepting $2.4 million in bribes. Wilkes, who gave $630,000 in cash and favors to Cunningham, remains under investigation by prosecutors. Cunningham has confessed to accepting a $100,000 bribe from "co-conspirator No. 1." Wilkes's business associate, Mitchell Wade, has pleaded guilty to bribing Cunningham.

For years, Wilkes hosted "hospitality suites" at the Watergate Hotel for House members and other associates that involved poker games and, allegedly, prostitutes. That, too, is under investigation. Foggo has admitted his presence, but "just for poker." At least six House members, unnamed so far, are alleged to have participated. Goss has denied attending as CIA director, but not as an elected representative. Yet another hand at the poker table has been identified as Brant Bassett, aka "Nine Fingers." Bassett was Goss's staff director on the House Intelligence Committee and was hired as a consultant to the CIA's Directorate of Operations.

Foggo and Wilkes are best friends going back to high school in suburban San Diego. They were roommates at San Diego State, where they were members of the Young Republicans, were best men at each other's weddings, and named their sons after each other. Wilkes pays for a joint wine locker for them at The Capital Grille steak house favored by lobbyists and Republican legislators.

The White House announcement of Goss's resignation was incredibly abrupt, without advance warning or a named successor. White House aides frenetically briefed the press that the sole reason was an internecine conflict between Goss and Negroponte. But such an internal controversy could have been managed for a smooth transition. Something else appeared to be at work.

Indeed, in March, the CIA's inspector general had launched an investigation into Foggo's relationship with Wilkes, who had received CIA contracts in Iraq. Three days after Goss left, Foggo quit, too. In a highly unusual development, two days later, on Wednesday, the special agent in charge of the Defense Criminal Investigative Service's investigation in the "Duke" Cunningham case, Rick Gwin, spoke publicly: "This is much bigger and wider than just Randy 'Duke' Cunningham," he told Southern California's *North County Times*. "All that has just not come out yet, but it won't be much longer and then you will know just how widespread this is."

President Bush has nominated General Michael Hayden, the former director of the National Security Agency and currently Negroponte's deputy, as the new CIA director. He has distinguished himself as a loyalist to the administration by using his uniform as a shield against the heat generated by the revelation of illegal domestic surveillance by the NSA.

Regardless of anodyne assurances offered in his forthcoming congressional testimony, Hayden will preside over the liquidation of the CIA as it has been known. The George H. W. Bush CIA headquarters building in Langley will of course remain standing. But the agency will be chipped apart, some of its key parts absorbed by other agencies, with the Pentagon emerging as the ultimate winner.

The militarization of intelligence under Bush is likely to guarantee military solutions above other options. Uniformed officers trained to identify military threats and trends will take over economic and political intelligence for which they are untrained and often incapable, and their priorities will skew analysis. But the bias toward the military option will be one that the military in the end will dislike. It will find itself increasingly bearing the brunt of foreign policy and stretched beyond endurance. The vicious cycle leads to a downward spiral. And Hayden's story will be like a dull shadow of Powell's—a tale of a "good soldier" who salutes, gets promoted, is used and abused, and is finally discarded.

No president has ever before ruined an agency at the heart of national security out of pique and vengeance. The manipulation of intelligence by political leadership demands ever tightened control. But political purges provide only temporary relief from the widening crisis of policy failure.

May 11, 2006

The Nativist Revolt

President Bush's nationally televised address on immigration Monday night was intended as a grand gesture to revive his collapsing presidency, but instead he has plunged the Republican Party into a political centrifuge that is breaking it down into its raw elements, which are colliding into each other, triggering explosions of unexpected and ever greater magnitude.

The nativist Republican base is at the throat of the business community. The Republican House of Representatives, in the grip of the far right, is at war with the Republican Senate. The evangelical religious right is paralyzed while the Roman Catholic Church has emerged as a mobilizing force behind the mass demonstrations of millions of Hispanic immigrants. Every effort Bush makes to hold a nonexistent Republican center is generating an opposing effect within his party.

Bush's victory in 2004 depended upon the calibrated management of highly volatile constituencies. The religious right was shepherded by referendums against gay marriage in sixteen swing states. The Catholic hierarchy was carefully split so that conservatives using the abortion issue were raised to the pulpit while progressive-minded bishops concerned with a broader agenda were isolated. The fevered imaginations of nativists were captivated by hosts of enemies who appeared in the whirlwind of September 11.

Bush's political handlers were determined to suppress immigration as an issue. Coming from Texas and hardly uninformed about the future of American demographics, they understood the immense significance of the Hispanic vote. Though Hispanic voter participation falls far below eligibility—at 14 percent of eligible voters in 2004, they made up only 6 percent of voters—the number voting among a group that will soon constitute about 20 percent of the population is increasing in every election cycle. Bush's ability to capture 5 percent more of the Catholic vote and 10 percent more of the Hispanic vote in 2004 than he did in 2000 on the basis of social issues like gay marriage was one of the most decisive factors giving him a second term.

But as his presidency has weakened, Bush has lost his grip on his party. As Bush's neoconservative foreign policy has been discredited, a virulent form of isolationist nationalism, always lurking beneath the surface, has filled the vacuum. Bush successfully exploited fear arising from the September 11, 2001, attacks and conflated them with Iraq. But the public has turned against the Iraq War. Fear of the Other is being displaced onto the traditional nativist target: immigrants. It need not be said that they are Catholic and dark-skinned. From the Know-Nothing Party of the 1850s to the Ku Klux Klan of the 1920s, American politics has been racked by cycles of nativism, appearing in periods of conservative reaction.

The House has approved a bill that would make it a felony to hire or even help undocumented workers. On the right, this is considered a condition for the eventual deportation of the more than 11 million such workers, and anything short of this solution is branded a treasonous "amnesty."

Bush's modest proposal for allowing undocumented workers to stay in the country and eventually be granted citizenship has incited nothing but anger and contempt on the right. His rhetorical sops—his risible opposition to the singing of the national anthem in Spanish, for example—have only galvanized and legitimized the nativists. And his planned dispatch of six thousand National Guard troops to the two-thousand-mile border with Mexico has inspired widespread ridicule—a "Band-Aid," derided California Republican Governor Arnold Schwarzenegger.

Meanwhile, the U.S. Conference of Catholic Bishops has identified the church, body and soul, as the moral guardian of immigrants and a proponent of offering them social services and citizenship. The future of the church in the Western Hemisphere, in the pews and the priesthood, pressed by evangelical missionaries, rests with the growth of the Hispanic population. For the church, defense of the human rights of immigrants is a salient moral cause and a matter of survival. It is also the oldest heritage and bulwark of the American church.

Last month, when a prominent organization of the religious right, the Family Research Council, attempted to summon support for the House bill, the National Hispanic Christian Leadership Conference warned that it would break away, and the stunned leaders of the religious right were stymied.

The Republican Party as a whole is recapitulating the self-destruction of the California Republican Party. In 1994, Republican Governor Pete Wilson advocated Proposition 187, which threatened to deny social services, health care, and education to undocumented workers, and it aroused the Hispanic sleeping giant. From that moment, in national elections, California became one of the safest Democratic states, and only an anomaly like Schwarzenegger, an immigrant, could emerge as a viable statewide candidate.

Ronald Reagan's party is a thing of the past.

The delicate coalition Bush put together in 2004 has shattered. But in losing control of the debate on immigration, which reflects his loss of control of the political debate in general, he has lost something more—the capacity to speak for the American idea. In 1938, President Franklin D. Roosevelt confidently spoke before the convention of the nativist Daughters of the American Revolution. "Remember, remember always," he said, "that all of us, and you and I especially, are descended from immigrants and revolutionists."

May 18, 2006

Defeat Through Victory

When new Iraqi Prime Minister Nouri Kamel al-Maliki unveiled his government last week, five months after his country's elections, and was unable to appoint ministers of defense and interior, President Bush hailed it as a "turning point." And that was just one month after Maliki's mentor, former Prime Minister Ibrahim al-Jafaari, to whom he had been loyal deputy, installed in the position through the support of radical Shiite cleric Muqtada al-Sadr, was forced to relinquish his office through U.S. pressure.

Bush has been proclaiming Iraq at a turning point for years. "Turning point" is a frequent and recurring talking point, often taken up by the full chorus of the president ("We've reached another great turning point," November 6, 2003; "A turning point will come in less than two weeks," June 18, 2004), vice president ("I think about when we look back and get some historical perspective on this period, I'll believe that the period we were in through 2005 was, in fact, a turning point," February 7, 2006), secretary of state, and secretary of defense, and ringing down the echo chamber.

This latest "turning point" reveals an Iraqi state without a social contract, a government without a center, a prime minister without power, and an American president without a strategy. Each sectarian group maintains its own militia. Each leader's influence rests on these armed bands, separate armies of tens of thousands of men. The militias have infiltrated and taken over key units of the Iraqi army and local police, using them as death squads, protection rackets, and deterrent forces against enemies. Reliable statistics are impossible, but knowledgeable reporters estimate there are about forty assassinations a day in Iraq. Ethnic cleansing is sweeping the country. From Kirkuk in the north to Baghdad in the middle to Basra in the south, Kurds are driving out Turkmen and Arabs, Shiites are killing Sunnis, and the insurgency enjoys near unanimous support among Sunnis.

Contrary to Bush's blanket rhetoric about "terrorists" and constant reference to the insurgency as "the enemy," "foreign fighters are a small component of the insurgency," according to Anthony H. Cordesman of the Center for Strategic and International Studies.

Patrick Cockburn, one of the most accurate and intrepid journalists in Iraq, wrote last week in *The Independent* of London that "the overall security situation in Iraq is far worse than it was a year ago. Baghdad and central Iraq, where Shia, Sunni and Kurd are mixed, is in the grip of a civil war fought by assassins and death squads. As in Bosnia in 1992, each community is pulling back into enclaves where it is the overwhelming majority and able to defend itself."

While Prime Minister Maliki has declared his intention to enforce an unused militia-demobilization decree proclaimed by the now disbanded Coalition Provisional Authority in 2004, he has made no gesture beyond his statement, and no Iraqi leader has volunteered to be the first test case of demobilization. *The New York Times* Wednesday cited an American official on the absence of action on this front: "'They need to begin by setting examples,' an American official in Baghdad said of the Iraqi government. 'It is just very noticeable to me that they are not making any examples.' 'None,' the official said. 'Zero.'"

Maliki's inability to fill the posts of minister of defense and minister of the interior reflects the control of the means of violence by factions and sects unwilling to cede it to a central authority. Inside the new government, ministries are being operated as sectarian fiefdoms. The vacuum at the defense and interior ministries represents a state of civil war in which no one can be vested with power above all.

In his speech on Monday referring to another "turning point," President Bush twice spoke of "victory." "Victory" is the constant theme he has adopted since last summer, when he hired public opinion specialist Peter Feaver for the National Security Council. Feaver's research claims that the public will sustain military casualties so long as it is persuaded that they will lead to "victory." Bush clings to this P.R. formula to explain, at least to himself, the decline of his political fortunes. "Because we're at war, and war unsettles people," he said in an interview with NBC News last week. To make sense of the disconcerting war, he imposes his familiar framework of us versus them, "the enemy" who gets "on your TV screen by killing innocent people" against himself.

In his Monday speech, Bush reverted yet again to citing September 11, 2001, as the ultimate justification for the Iraq War. Defiant in the face of terrorists, he repeated whole paragraphs from his 2004 campaign stump speech. "That's just the lessons of September the 11th that I refuse to forget," he said. Stung by the dissent of the former commanders of the U.S. Army in Iraq who have demanded the firing of Secretary of Defense Donald Rumsfeld, Bush reassured the audience that he listens to generals. "I make my mind up based not upon politics or political opinion polls, but based upon what the commanders on the ground tell me is going on," he said.

Yet, currently serving U.S. military commanders have been explicitly telling him for more than two years, and making public their view, that there is no purely military solution in Iraq. For example, General John Abizaid, the U.S. commander, said on April 12, 2004: "There is not a purely U.S. military solution to any of the particular problems that we're facing here in Iraq today."

Newsweek reported this week that the U.S. military, in fact, is no longer pursuing a strategy for "victory." "It is consolidating to several 'superbases' in hopes that its continued presence will prevent Iraq from succumbing to full-flown civil war and turning into a failed state. Pentagon strategists admit they have not figured out how to move to superbases, as a way of reducing the pressure—and casualties—inflicted on the U.S. Army, while at the same time remaining embedded with Iraqi police and military units. It is a circle no one has squared. But consolidation plans are moving ahead as a default position, and U.S. Ambassador Zalmay Khalilzad has talked frankly about containing the spillover from Iraq's chaos in the region."

Yet Bush continues to declare as his goal (with encouragement from his polling expert on the NSC) the victory that the U.S. military has given up on. And he continues to wave the banner of a military solution against "the enemy," although this "enemy" consists of a Sunni insurgency whose leadership must eventually be conciliated and brought into a federal Iraqi government and of which the criminal Abu Musab al-Zarqawi faction and foreign fighters are a small part.

Bush's belief in a military solution, moreover, renders moot progress on a political solution, which is the only potentially practical approach. His war on the Sunnis simply agitates the process of civil war. The entire burden of progress falls on the U.S. ambassador, whose inherent situation as representative of the occupying power inside the country limits his ability to engage in the international diplomacy that might make his efforts to bring factions together possible. Washington, in any case, shut down Khalilzad's tentative outreach to Iran. Secretary of State Condoleezza Rice, for her part, finds herself in Bulgaria, instead of conducting shuttle diplomacy in Amman, Jordan; Riyadh, Saudi Arabia; Ankara, Turkey; and Tehran. The diplomatic vacuum intensifies the power vacuum in Iraq, exciting Bush's flights of magical thinking about victory: I speak, therefore it is.

Bush doesn't know that he can't achieve victory. He doesn't know that seeking victory worsens his prospects. He doesn't know that the U.S. military has abandoned victory in the field, though it has been reporting that to him for years. But the president has no rhetoric beyond "victory."

Bush's chance for a quick victory in Iraq evaporated when the neoconservative fantasy collapsed almost immediately after the invasion. But the "make-believe" of "liberation" that failed to provide basic security set in motion "fratricidal violence," as Nir Rosen writes in his new book, *In the Belly of the Green Bird: The Triumph of the Martyrs in Iraq*, based on firsthand observation of the developing insurgency in the vacuum created by U.S. policy.

Indeed, Bush's nominee for director of the CIA, General Michael Hayden, former director of the National Security Agency, in his confirmation hearings, acknowledged the neoconservative manipulation of intelligence to make the case for the Iraq war and disdained it. Asked by Senator Carl Levin, D-Michigan, about the administration's efforts to tie Saddam Hussein to Al-Qaeda, Hayden replied: "Sir, I—as director of NSA, we did have a series of inquiries about this potential connection between Al-Qaeda and the Iraqi government. Yes, sir."

The exchange continued:

Levin: Now, prior to the war, the undersecretary of defense for policy, Mr. [Douglas] Feith, established an intelligence analysis cell within his policy office at the Defense Department. While the intelligence community was consistently dubious about links between Iraq and Al-Qaeda, Mr. Feith produced an alternative analysis, asserting that there was a strong connection. Were you comfortable with Mr. Feith's office's approach to intelligence analysis?

Hayden: No, sir, I wasn't. I wasn't aware of a lot of the activity going on, you know, when it was contemporaneous with running up to the war. No, sir, I wasn't comfortable.

Hayden then explained at length the difference between working from the facts and trying to cherry-pick data to support a hypothesis. He made clear that the administration had engaged in the latter. Levin asked: "Now, I believe that you actually placed a disclaimer on NSA reporting relative to any links between Al-Qaeda and Saddam Hussein. And it was apparently following the repeated inquiries from the Feith office. Would you just tell us what that disclaimer was?"

Hayden answered: "Yes, sir. SIGINT [SIGnals INTelligence] neither confirms nor denies—and let me stop at that point in the sentence so we can stay safely on the side of unclassified. SIGINT neither confirms nor denies, and then we finished the sentence based upon the question that was asked. And then we provided the data, sir." In the language of the agency, in other words, Hayden would not lend support to the Bush's administration's twisting of intelligence.

On May 15, Karl Rove, Bush's chief political advisor, gave a speech revealing one of his ideas about politics. "I think," he said, "there's also a great utility in looking at game changers. What are the things that will allow us to fundamentally change people's behavior in a different way?" Since September 11, Rove has made plain that terrorism and war are the great game changers for Bush.

But while war may be the game changer for Bush's desire to put in place a one-party state, forge a permanent Republican majority, redefine the Constitution and the relationships of the branches of the federal government, and concentrate power in the executive, Bush has only the rhetoric of "victory." He has not stated what would happen the day after "victory." Although a victory parade would be his political nightmare, now the absence of victory is his nightmare. With every proclaimed "turning point," "victory" becomes ever more evanescent. He has no policy for victory and no politics beyond victory.

May 25, 2006

The War Paradigm

Something that senior officials call the "war paradigm" is the Bush administration's central organizing principle. They do not use the phrase publicly, just among themselves, but they bend policy to serve it. After September 11, 2001, they instantly adopted the war paradigm without any internal discussion. George W. Bush, who proclaimed, "I'm a war president" and insisted that he made decisions "with war on my mind," assumed the war paradigm as his natural state and right. According to its imperatives, the president in his wartime capacity as commander in chief makes and enforces laws as he sees fit, in effect as a sovereign, overriding the constitutional system of checks and balances. Some of the paradigm's expressions include Bush's fiats on the treatment of "war on terror" detainees, domestic surveillance, and international law and treaties, and his more than 750 signing statements appended to laws enacted by Congress that he claims he can implement as he chooses.

In the beginning, the elements of the war paradigm appeared to be expediencies, conceived as a series of emergency measures in the struggle against Al-Qaeda. But, in fact, their precepts were developed in law review articles before September 11 by John Yoo, promoted to deputy assistant attorney general in the Office of Legal Counsel at the Department of Justice, where Vice President Cheney's office assigned him to write key secret memos on torture, surveillance, and executive power. Once Bush approved them, the clerisy of neoconservative lawyers, at least as tightly knit as Opus Dei, put them into effect. The war paradigm is Bush's "Da

Vinci Code," the difference being that its high priests acknowledge in private that it is real.

They fervently believe that the Constitution is fatally flawed and must be severely circumscribed. The Bush administration's "holy grail," another phrase officials use in private, is to remove suspects' rights to due process, speedy trial, and exculpatory evidence. The war paradigm, which they contrast with a caricatured "law enforcement paradigm," is to be constantly strengthened to conduct a permanent war against terror, which can never be finally defeated. There is no exit strategy from emergency.

Tony Blair's worthy words at Georgetown University in Washington last week about "interdependence" and a "new international institutional architecture" were an irrelevancy. Bush soaks up encouragement for the war paradigm while paying no attention to gestures of wishful and unrequited sentimentality. If Blair is pleased to offer such niceties that have no bearing on Bush, Bush is pleased, too. This special relationship is dramatically unlike those Margaret Thatcher conducted in speaking her coruscating mind freely to presidents, occasionally to their benefit.

In the short run, Bush's defense of his war paradigm could precipitate three potential constitutional crises. In the first, freedom of the press would be at issue. On May 21, Attorney General Alberto Gonzales announced the "possibility" that *The New York Times* would be prosecuted under the 1917 Espionage Act for publishing its Pulitzer Prize–winning article on the administration's warrantless domestic surveillance. "It can't be the case," he said, that the First Amendment "trumps" the "right" of the government "to go after criminal activity"—and he then defined the *Times*'s printing of its story as "criminal activity."

In the second case, the administration could assert that a wartime executive is above the law. Last week, in a federal court filing, Special Prosecutor Patrick Fitzgerald, who has charged the vice president's former chief of staff, I. Lewis "Scooter" Libby, with perjury and obstruction of justice, made plain his intention to summon Cheney to the witness stand in order to impeach Libby's credibility or else commit perjury himself. Will the administration defend the "war vice president" by fighting the subpoena as an infringement on the "unitary executive," who should be immune from such distractions in wartime?

In the third case, if either house of Congress should fall to the Democrats in the November midterm elections, the oversight suppressed during one-party rule would be restored. Would the administration then refuse congressional requests for documents, as it did when the short-lived Democratic Senate in Bush's first year asked for those pertaining to Cheney's energy task force—whose members reportedly included Enron CEO Ken Lay, last week convicted on numerous counts of fraud?

One year after Cheney declared the Iraqi insurgency "in the last throes," the Marine Corps is investigating the revenge murders of at least twenty-four Iraqi civilians by Marines in Haditha—and the murders' coverup—and among the daily carnage in Iraq two members of a CBS News crew were recently killed in an ambush while a CBS News correspondent is in critical condition. "The U.S. military has become just another militia," said journalist Nir Rosen.

Bush does not contemplate the slightest retreat from the war paradigm, which he embraces as his reason for being, regardless of the war's unpopularity. After his 2004 victory, he claimed he had had his "accountability moment." But the Constitution is an intricate mechanism of checks and balances that creates constant accountability. The question at the heart of Bush's politics is whether that can be indefinitely suspended and in the meantime the Constitution radically revised.

June 1, 2006

The Bush Way of War

Former president George H. W. Bush waged a secret campaign over several months early this year to remove Secretary of Defense Donald Rumsfeld. The elder Bush went so far as to recruit Rumsfeld's potential replacement, personally asking a retired four-star general if he would accept the position, a reliable source close to the general told me. But the former president's effort failed, apparently rebuffed by the current president. When seven retired generals who had been commanders in Iraq demanded Rumsfeld's resignation in April, the younger Bush leaped to his defense. "I'm the decider and I decide what's best. And what's best is for Don Rumsfeld to remain," he said. His endorsement of Rumsfeld was a rebuke not only to the generals but also to his father.

The elder Bush's intervention was an extraordinary attempt to rescue simultaneously his son, the family legacy, and the country. The current president had previously rejected entreaties from party establishment figures to revamp his administration with new appointments. There was no one left to approach him except his father. This effort to pluck George W. from his troubles is the latest episode in a recurrent drama—from the drunken young man challenging his father to go "mano a mano," to the father pulling strings to get the son into the Texas Air National Guard and helping salvage his finances from George W.'s mismanagement of Harken Energy. For the father, parental responsibility never ends. But for the son, rebellion continues. When journalist Bob Woodward asked George W. Bush if he had consulted his father before invading Iraq, he replied, "He is the wrong father to appeal to in terms of strength. There is a higher father that I appeal to."

The former president, a practitioner of foreign policy realism, was intruding on the president's parallel reality. But the realist was trying to shake the fantasist in vain. "The president believes the talking points he's given and repeats on progress in Iraq," a Bush administration national security official told me. Bush redoubles his efforts, projects his firmness, in the conviction that the critics lack his deeper understanding of Iraq that allows him to see through the fog of war to the Green Zone as a city on a hill.

Just as his father cannot break Bush's enchantment with "victory," so the revelation of the Haditha massacre does not cause him to change his policy. For him, the alleged incident is solely about the individual Marines involved; military justice will deal with them. It's as though the horrific event had nothing to do with the war. Haditha, too, exists in a bubble.

Before the Iraq War, the administration received and dismissed warnings of the dangers of a prolonged occupation from the State Department, the CIA, and the military. A month before the invasion, in February 2003, the Army War College's Strategic Studies Institute published a paper by a team of its experts, "Reconstructing Iraq: Insights, Challenges, and Missions for Military Forces in a Post-Conflict Scenario." Civil war, sectarian militias, anarchy, suicide bombers, and widespread insurgency—if there was a lengthy occupation—were predicted: "Ethnic, tribal, and religious schisms could produce civil war or fracture the state after Saddam is deposed . . . The longer a U.S. occupation of Iraq continues, the more danger exists that elements of the Iraqi population will become impatient and take violent measures to hasten the departure of U.S. forces." But the Bush administration simply ignored this cautionary analysis. Among the report's cogent warnings was that insurgents could incite violence to provoke repression, forcing U.S. troops into an uncontrollable "action-reaction cycle." Nearly three years after the invasion, the Marines in Haditha were apparently caught up in that whirlwind.

On November 19, 2005, a roadside bomb blew up an armored vehicle of Kilo Company of the 3rd Battalion, 1st Marine Regiment, patrolling in the upper Euphrates Valley, and Lance Corporal Miguel Terrazas was killed. For hours afterward, members of the unit apparently murdered twenty-four civilians, including women, children, and old people, in cold blood. Kilo Company was on its third tour of duty and had engaged in the battle of Fallujah, in which the city of 300,000, held by insurgents, was leveled.

The coverup at Haditha reportedly began instantly. However, an Iraqi journalism student shot a video the day after of the bloodstained and bullet-riddled houses where the massacre had occurred. That video made its way to an Iraqi human rights group and finally to a correspondent from *Time* magazine. When *Time* made its first queries, the Marine spokesman, Captain Jeffrey S. Pool, who had issued the first statement on Haditha as an action against terrorists months earlier, told reporters that they were falling for Al-Qaeda propaganda. "I cannot believe you're buying any of this," he wrote in an e-mail. Nonetheless, word reached Lieutenant General Peter W. Chiarelli, the second-highest-ranking U.S. military officer in Iraq, that there had been no investigation and he ordered one immediately.

Chiarelli, as Thomas E. Ricks reported in the *Washington Post*, "is an unusual general in today's Army, with none of the 'good old boy' persona seen in many other top commanders. He had praised an article by a British officer that was sharply critical of U.S. officers in Iraq for using tactics that alienated the population. He wanted U.S. forces to operate differently than they had been doing."

The article that influenced Chiarelli was published in the U.S. Army's *Military Review*, in its November–December 2005 issue, and was written by British Brigadier Nigel Aylwin-Foster, a deputy commander training the Iraqi military. In it he wrote that U.S. officers showed "cultural insensitivity" that "arguably amounted to institutional racism" and "fueled the insurgency." Aylwin-Foster also argued that the U.S. doctrine of "too kinetic" war fighting was part and parcel of its "cultural insensitivity," accelerating the alienation of Iraqis and stimulating the insurgency. "In short," he wrote, "the U.S. Army has developed over time a singular focus on conventional warfare, of a particularly swift and violent style, which left it ill-suited to the kind of operation it encountered as soon as conventional warfighting ceased to be the primary focus in OIF (Operation Iraqi Freedom)." He concluded that the prevailing notion of military victory was self-undermining, contributing to failure, and that the United States in Iraq needed to rethink its fundamental doctrine: "The realization that all military activity is subordinate to political intent, and must be attuned accordingly: mere destruction of the enemy is not the answer."

Aylwin-Foster's article appeared at about the same time as the incident at Haditha, providing a broader analysis of the problems that underlay it than simply battlefield stress, though that, too, was obviously an important factor. His article was one of many red flags. He even quoted a U.S. colonel: "If I were treated like this, I'd be a terrorist!"

On May 30, the new Iraqi ambassador to the United States, Samir Sumaidaie, appeared on CNN, where he claimed that U.S. Marines had murdered his young cousin in Haditha, in an incident that occurred before the massacre. "Well, they said that they shot him in self-defense. I find that hard to believe because A) he is not at all a violent—I mean, I know the boy. He was [in] a second-year engineering course in the university. Nothing to do with violence. All his life has been studies and intellectual work. Totally unbelievable. And, in fact, they had no weapon in the house . . . I believe he was killed intentionally. I believe that he was killed unnecessarily. And unfortunately, the investigations that took place after that sort of took a different course and concluded that there was no unlawful killing. I would like further investigation."

The next day, May 31, Iraqi Prime Minister Nouri al-Maliki said that U.S. attacks against civilians had become a "daily phenomenon" by troops who "do not respect the Iraqi people. They crush them with their vehicles and kill them just on suspicion. This is completely unacceptable." Maliki's outburst revealed that opposition to the occupation has become the basis of political legitimacy in Iraqi politics. Haditha brought this reality boiling to the surface.

The Bush way of war has been ahistorical and apolitical, and therefore warped strategically, putting absolute pressure on the military to provide an outcome it cannot provide—"victory." From the start, Bush has placed the military at a disadvantage, and not only because he put the U.S. Army in the field in insufficient numbers, setting it upon a task it could not accomplish. U.S. troops are trained for conventional military operations, not counterinsurgency, which requires the utmost restraint in using force. The doctrinal fetish of counterterrorism substitutes for and frustrates counterinsurgency efforts.

Conventional fighting takes two primary forms: chasing and killing foreign fighters as if they constituted the heart of the Sunni insurgency and seeking battles like Fallujah as if any would be decisive. Where battles don't exist, assaults on civilian populations, often provoked by insurgents, are misconceived as battles. While this is not a version of some video game, it is still an illusion.

Many of the troops are on their third or fourth tour of duty, and 40 percent of them are reservists whose training and discipline are not up to the standards of their full-time counterparts. Trained for combat and gaining and holding territory, equipped with superior firepower and technology, they are unprepared for the disorienting and endless rigors of irregular warfare. The Marines, in particular, are trained for "kinetic" warfare, constantly in motion, and imbued with a warrior culture that sets them apart from the army. Marines, however well disciplined, are especially susceptible because of their perpetual state of high adrenaline to the inhuman pressures of irregular warfare.

As Bush's approach has stamped failure on the military, he insists ever more intensely on the inevitability of victory if only he stays the course. Ambiguity and flexibility, essential elements of any strategy for counterinsurgency, are his weak points. Bush may imagine a scene in which the insurgency is conclusively defeated, perhaps even a signing ceremony, as on the USS *Missouri*, or at least an acknowledgment, a scrap of paper, or perhaps the silence of the dead, all of them. But his infatuation with a purely military solution blinds him to how he thwarts his own intentions. Jeffrey Record, a prominent strategist at a U.S. military war college, told me: "Perhaps worse still, conventional wisdom is dangerously narcissistic. It completely ignores the enemy, assuming that what *we* do determines success or failure. It assumes that only the United States can defeat the United

States, an outlook that set the United States up for failure in Vietnam and for surprise in Iraq."

Haditha is a symptom of the fallacy of Bush's military solution. The alleged massacre occurred after the administration's dismissal of repeated warnings about the awful pressures on an army of occupation against an insurgency. Conflating a population that broadly supports an insurgency with a terrorist enemy and indoctrinating the troops with a sense of revenge for September 11 easily leads to an erasure of the distinction between military and civilian targets. Once again, a commander in chief has failed to learn the lessons of Algeria and Vietnam.

Bush's abrogation of the Geneva Conventions has set an example that in this unique global war on terror, in order to combat those who do not follow the rules of war, we must also abandon those rules. This week a conflict has broken out in the Pentagon over Rumsfeld's proposed revision of the Army Field Manual for interrogation of prisoners, which would excise Common Article Three of the Geneva Conventions that forbids "humiliating and degrading treatment." And, this week, Senator Carl Levin, D-Michigan, proposed a bill that would make the administration provide "a full accounting on any clandestine prison or detention facility currently or formerly operated by the United States Government, regardless of location, where detainees in the global war on terrorism are or were being held," the number of detainees, and a "description of the interrogation procedures used or formerly used on detainees at such prison or facility and a determination, in coordination with other appropriate officials, on whether such procedures are or were in compliance with United States obligations under the Geneva Conventions and the Convention Against Torture." The administration vigorously opposes the bill.

Above all, the Bush way of war violates the fundamental rule of warfare as defined by military philosopher Carl von Clausewitz: War is politics by other means. In other words, it is not the opposite of politics, or its substitute, but its instrument, and by no means its only one. "Subordinating the political point of view to the military would be absurd," wrote Clausewitz, "for it is policy that creates war. Policy is the guiding intelligence and war only the instrument, not vice versa."

Rumsfeld's Pentagon, meanwhile, reinforces Bush's rigidity as essential to "transformational" warfare; by now, however, the veneer has been peeled off to reveal sheer self-justification. Rumsfeld is incapable of telling the president that there is no battle, no campaign, that can win the war. Saving Rumsfeld is Bush's way of staying the course. But it also sends a signal of unaccountability from the top down. The degradation of U.S. forces in Iraq is a direct consequence of the derangement of political leadership in Washington. And not even the elder Bush can persuade the president that his way of war is a debacle.

June 8, 2006

"Mission Accomplished" in a Business Suit

Months before Abu Musab al-Zarqawi was killed by a U.S. airstrike, American military commanders and intelligence officers in Iraq battled Secretary of Defense Donald Rumsfeld and the White House to "degrade" the terrorist's dramatically inflated image, while Rumsfeld and the White House resisted, ultimately for "domestic political reasons," as a military source involved in this internal controversy told me. In the end, the military lost.

President Bush's June 8 statement on Zarqawi's death the night before described him as "the operational commander of the terrorist movement in Iraq," "one of its most visible and aggressive leaders," and his death as "a severe blow to Al-Qaeda." But the president said, "we can expect the terrorists and insurgents to carry on without him." Superficially sober, Bush's remarks conflated the lone wolf Zarqawi not only with Al-Qaeda—though Zarqawi had seized on the Al-Qaeda label as self-proclaimed grandiosity and Al-Qaeda leader Ayman al-Zawahiri had earlier denounced his extreme tactics—but also with the entire Sunni insurgency, with which Zarqawi had been in conflict and which well might have been responsible for betraying him. Bush's rhetorical account was an implicit dismissal of U.S. intelligence.

If Zarqawi's killing was a new version of Saddam Hussein's capture ("We got him!"), Bush's surprise visit to Baghdad on Tuesday was "Mission

Accomplished" in a business suit. Six months after the Iraqi election, with Prime Minister Nouri al-Maliki at last having appointed defense and interior ministers amid sectarian civil war, Bush declared, "They themselves have to get some things accomplished." One thing Bush was attempting to accomplish was a reversal of his own political fortunes. Zarqawi's death had provided a convenient platform for the unfolding of his scripted theater featuring a two-day Camp David retreat of his war cabinet, the midnight flight to Baghdad, and repeated references to September 11, but no broad new initiatives for a political solution.

President Bush, in a speech on October 7, 2002, making the case for invading Iraq, first introduced Zarqawi to the world as Exhibit A in Saddam's "links to international terrorist groups . . . We know that Iraq and Al-Qaeda have had high-level contacts that go back a decade." (A CIA report made public in October 2004 found no evidence of any "links" between Saddam and Zarqawi, who in any case did not operate in Iraq until after his release from a seven-year sentence in a Jordanian prison in 1999.)

Since the rise of the Iraqi insurgency, U.S. military intelligence had been directed to build up Zarqawi's profile as its leader through a psychological warfare ("psy-op") effort. On April 10, the *Washington Post* reported on internal military documents it obtained about this psy-op: "The documents explicitly list the 'U.S. Home Audience' as one of the targets of a broader propaganda campaign." According to talking points in a 2004 briefing, the goal was: "Villainize Zarqawi/leverage xenophobia response." One military intelligence officer involved stated that Zarqawi's followers were "a very small part of the actual numbers" of insurgents, but this had little bearing on the program. Another officer concluded, "The Zarqawi PSYOP program is the most successful information campaign to date."

The depth and breadth of the insurgency are depicted in a new documentary, *Meeting Resistance*, that has not been publicly released. The film's directors are Molly Bingham, an American journalist who was briefly jailed in Abu Ghraib by Saddam's regime at the onset of the U.S. invasion, and Steve Connors, a British journalist. It is the single most astonishing documentary yet on the Iraq War, portrays a full range of insurgents, from fighters to spies to imams, speaking in their own voices, explaining their motives and actions, from the first days of the insurgency onward. "I began to see something, that we had become an occupied country," says one who became a warrior. It is as though The Battle of Algiers had been shot from the inside, from the point of view of the insurgents, and not played by actors. Among other revelations, insurgents express their hostility in 2004 to Zarqawi as an obstacle to unity against the occupation but not as an impediment to the insurgency's popular growth. "So now," says an insurgent, "whether Zarqawi is captured dead or alive has no impact."

Bush's latest effort to foster belief in a "turning point" may trap him within his own psy-op. Unless Bush successfully includes the Sunnis in the political process and creates a new internationalized diplomacy, he will remain narrowly circumscribed by the consequences of his accumulated failures. Burdened by years of misjudgment, disinformation, and delusion, Bush has again risked committing the blunder of raising expectations followed by deeper disillusionment within the "U.S. Home Audience."

June 15, 2006

Surrealpolitik

On the night of June 12, shortly after Karl Rove received an e-mail from his attorney, Robert Luskin, informing him he would not be indicted by Special Prosecutor Patrick Fitzgerald, the president's chief political advisor advisor appeared before a New Hampshire Republican Party group to deliver a call to arms for the midterm elections. Rove defined the theme for the upcoming contest, the last one of the Bush presidency, as the same one he had set after September 11, 2001, when he ordered Republicans to polarize the country on the issue of terrorism and war. Democrats were weak and soft, he said; Republicans, strong and tough. Now, with Bush's popularity at low ebb, Rove instructed the party to taint the Democrats as favoring "cutting and running" in Iraq.

The following week, on cue, the Republicans introduced a resolution in the House of Representatives against any "timetable" for a withdrawal of U.S. forces from Iraq. Overnight the divided and dispirited Republicans turned the tables on the Democrats. Even as the Democrats issued a program calling for a "new direction," their own version of the 1994

Republican Contract with America, which carefully did not mention Iraq, they scattered in different directions upon mention of the war. Instilling discipline in their ranks would be a forbidding task even for a pack leader like Cesar Millan, the "dog whisperer." It was just as Rove had reckoned.

The House resolution passed easily last week and has moved on to the Senate, where Democratic divisions have once again been highlighted. The resolution has no binding authority, but instead is a purely political contrivance. No hearings have been held. Indeed, Congress as a body enforcing its constitutional mandate of oversight is virtually defunct. The Senate Foreign Relations Committee is passive in its being trampled. The Senate Select Committee on Intelligence has put out a distorted report casting blame solely on the CIA for intelligence failures on the absence of weapons of mass destruction in Iraq. The Senate Armed Services Committee refuses to summon for testimony the commanding generals in Iraq who have called for the resignation of Secretary of Defense Donald Rumsfeld. The Republican Senate this week voted against investigating the abuses of contractors in Iraq. Yet the Republicans are desperate to stage a symbolic vote on the war.

The Iraq resolution is above all a manifesto of articles of faith. We face "an adversary that is driven by hatred of American values"—not an insurgency against an occupation or a sectarian civil war. Then, "by early 2003," Saddam Hussein "supported terrorists"—suggesting nonexistent links to Al-Qaeda. Now, "the terrorists have declared Iraq to be the central front in their war"—suggesting that the effect is its own cause, not that terrorism has emerged in reaction against the U.S. occupation. Finally, we "will prevail in the Global War on Terror, the noble struggle to protect freedom from the terrorist adversary." Thus we battle one enemy despite his many faces, like Satan, and our goal is nothing mundane like stability or a political solution but "freedom." Inserted into this credo is the tactical twist against a "timetable"—though General George Casey, the top U.S. military commander in Iraq, submitted a plan, a timetable, in November 2005 to Rumsfeld, at his insistence, for withdrawal of tens of thousands of troops this year. None dare call it "cut and run."

The Republicans' tone of theological certainty covers their anxious expediency. In the clarifying polarization of Congress the lethal netherworld of Iraq is held at bay. The politics of the Iraq resolution are the congressional analogue of Bush's recent five-hour visit to the Green Zone intended to present an upbeat message, leaving unacknowledged, for example, a twenty-three-point cable sent at the same time from the U.S. embassy to the State Department chronicling the descent of Iraqi embassy employees into sectarian strife and fundamentalist Islamic strictures, putting their "objectivity, civility, and logic" under relentless siege.

For the White House, the killing of Abu Musab al-Zarqawi on June 8 became a platform for retailing old talking points, claims of eventual victory, and strained appeals to history. Some perspective was provided at the beginning of this week's debate on the Senate's Iraq resolution with the publication of a new book, *The One Percent Doctrine: Deep Inside America's Pursuit of Its Enemies Since 9/11*, by Ron Suskind. Its facts cast light on the basic operations of the Bush White House, though facts have a discounted value in the current environment.

On June 14, the Pentagon dispatched a document titled "Iraq Floor Debate Prep Book" to Republicans in the House. A Pentagon public affairs officer admitted to the *Washington Post* that the seventy-four-page document originated in the White House but was repackaged as a Pentagon publication. It is a cut-and-paste rush job to refute advocates of "cut and run." It is also a representative document of the Bush administration: Evidence is cherry-picked, slogans substitute for facts, falsehoods are sold as truth, and "victory" is promised. Connections between Al-Qaeda and Iraq are slyly hinted at. The old accusations against Jose Padilla as the "dirty bomber," no longer being pressed against him, reappear. The Pentagon document, eagerly seized upon by congressional Republicans as a treasure trove of talking points, accurately gauges the White House's estimate of their ability to assess information on their own.

On the day the Pentagon talking points were sent to the House Republicans, Bush reformulated compassionate conservatism to demonstrate his concern for the continuing loss of life in Iraq. "I'm like most Americans, it is—death affects my way of thinking."

On June 18, White House press secretary Tony Snow attempted to put recent events in historical perspective: "The president understands people's impatience—not impatience, but how a war can wear on a nation. He understands that. If somebody had taken a poll in the Battle of the Bulge, I daresay people would have said, 'Wow, my goodness, what are we doing here?' But you cannot conduct a war based on polls." Snow's analogy was the latest effort to compare Bush and his troubles to the difficulties of previous presidents, from Lincoln to Truman. His reference to the Battle of the Bulge was an original contribution. In that battle, fought in December 1944, Hitler concentrated his remaining forces on the western front for a final desperate assault to break the inevitable Allied drive across the Rhine, and failed. In fact, there are polls available from that time. The American people were not impatient. They knew victory was coming. And their support for President Franklin D. Roosevelt, who had been reelected to his fourth term a month before, increased to 72 percent.

On Tuesday, Vice President Dick Cheney, in a speech at the National Press Club, defended his statement of May 2005 that the Iraqi insurgency was in its "last throes." "I don't think anybody anticipated the level of violence that we've encountered," he added. His comment, besides strangely echoing Bush's on Hurricane Katrina ("I don't think anybody anticipated the breach of the levees"), belied precise warnings from the CIA, the Army War College, and seventy experts gathered by the National Defense University who sent a report before the war to the administration but never received acknowledgment of receipt. But for the moment at least, Cheney's restatement of optimism or obliviousness expresses regained political confidence.

The Republican resolution on Iraq, the Pentagon's "Iraq Floor Debate Prep Book," Snow's fractured knowledge of history and Cheney's last "last throes" all fall back on a seamless but warped account of current events that is fabricated out of manipulated intelligence, filtered through ideological blinders, and held to no tests by a deliberately unaccountable presidency.

Ron Suskind, a former Pulitzer Prize–winning reporter for *The Wall Street Journal* and the author of *The Price of Loyalty: George W. Bush, the White House, and the Education of Paul O'Neill*, provides new details in this ongoing story in his new book, *The One Percent Doctrine*, published this week.

Suskind begins at the briefing of President Bush at his Crawford, Texas, homestead on August 6, 2001, about a CIA memo titled "Bin Laden Determined to Strike in U.S." Upon listening to the CIA briefer, Bush says, "All right, you've covered your ass, now." He asks no more questions.

The week after September 11, Cheney asked CIA Director George Tenet, who was grateful he had not been fired and was eager to please, to establish the link between the terrorist attacks and Saddam Hussein by putting the CIA imprimatur on a meeting of one of the hijackers, Mohammed Atta, with an Iraqi intelligence agent in Prague, Czech Republic, early in

2001. "We'll get right on it, Mr. Vice President," Tenet said. On September 21, he reported: "Our Prague office is skeptical about the report. It just doesn't add up." Two weeks after that, at Cheney's instigation, Rumsfeld created a parallel intelligence operation called the Policy Counterterrorism Evaluation Group, headed by neoconservative Undersecretary of Defense Douglas Feith. This operation funneled unevaluated intelligence and disinformation directly into the White House through Cheney's national security staff.

Shortly after September 11, Brent Scowcroft, George H. W. Bush's former national security advisor and his closest associate, whom George W. Bush appointed chairman of the President's Foreign Intelligence Advisory Board, met with Cheney. Scowcroft told him that the intelligence community required reorganization and in particular that much of the Pentagon's intelligence operations should be transferred to the CIA. But that would have divested Cheney and Rumsfeld of much of their bureaucratic empire. Scowcroft's recommendation was the beginning of the end of his influence. He never met with Cheney again. Secretary of State Colin Powell was also systematically cut out and trampled. The elder Bush was not consulted.

Prince Bandar bin Sultan, then the Saudi ambassador, with long ties to the Bush family, observed that the relationship between the forty-first and forty-third presidents was, as Suskind writes, "cool and distant, not even what one would expect of a father and son; that the son didn't consult the father—even though he was, quite possibly, the most valuable advisor presented by modern history."

Cheney took it upon himself to withhold crucial information from the president on the theory that fostering Bush's ignorance was a defensive wall of "plausible deniability." Cheney's thinking ran back to Nixon in Watergate. "He [Nixon] was accountable, and that doomed his presidency," writes Suskind. Cheney created an unaccountable executive, who subsisted on information given him on a "need to know" basis determined by the vice president and "could essentially be 'deniable' about his own statements." At first, Cheney acted as a visible regent. "Bush asked Cheney not to offer him advice in crowded rooms. Do that privately. Cheney did."

Cheney decided not to give Bush the entire National Intelligence Estimate on WMD in Iraq, but only a one-page summary of "key findings," which excluded caveats, including statements from the Energy Department and the State Department Bureau of Intelligence and Research that the aluminum tubes that Cheney and the neoconservatives insisted were proof of Saddam's ongoing nuclear weapons program "more likely are intended for conventional weapons." Bush read or skimmed what he was handed and asked no questions. He was the perfect "deniable" president.

Suskind's Bush is a familiar figure, a mixture of bluster and cluelessness. He loves being briefed by groups of men talking tough. "They all start talking like operators, no matter what's being reported. These are men who, on balance, never experienced the bracing effects . . . of military action. The few who have, like Powell, and his deputy Rich Armitage, smooth over these disparities . . . by joining in the tough talk that they know, from experience, is hollow at its core."

At one briefing in 2002, Suskind writes, Bruce Gephardt, deputy director of the FBI, told Bush that a group of men of "Middle Eastern descent" in Kansas had been discovered offering "cash for a large storage facility." "Middle Easterners in Kansas," said Bush. "We've got to get on this, immediately." Bush is reported to like barking orders, almost at a shout. The next day, he demanded a report. "Mr. President, the FBI has Kansas surrounded!" "That's what I like to hear," Bush replied. But it turned out that the men of Middle Eastern descent were operators of flea markets, not would-be terrorists. The diligent FBI had closed in on their accumulated piles of old clothing and Sinatra records.

At a December 13, 2002, year-end review of the war on terror for the president in the Cabinet Room conducted by two dozen senior officials, Bush had some difficulty following the complex details and lack of a simple story line. When Kenneth Dam, deputy secretary of the Treasury, informed him, "Mr. President, the majority of the funders for Al-Qaeda are Saudis," Bush "looked at Dam, perplexed, as though he either hadn't read the handout in front of him, or was somehow surprised—though this was all but common knowledge." "That's enough for today," said the president.

At other moments, the president who proudly relied on his "gut" for decision making, raised a pertinent question. "Do some of these harsh methods really work?" he asked at one point about the torture of detainees. But he never followed up. Meanwhile, Cheney developed the "rules." Action was liberated from evidence. Even a "1 percent chance" that some conjectured terrorist threat would materialize was good enough for a preemptive strike.

In March 2002, a CIA and FBI team in Pakistan captured Abu Zubaydah, touted as a top Al-Qaeda commander. Bush was prompted to call him "chief of operations" for Al-Qaeda, naming him as "No. 3" to bin Laden. Dan Coleman, one of FBI's top agents on Al-Qaeda, was assigned to read Zubaydah's diary. In it, he writes in three incoherent voices, reflecting different personalities, writes Suskind. "The CIA had long suspected that the ubiquitous Zubaydah was involved in the August 1998 bombings of the U.S. embassies in Africa. He [Coleman] looked for entries in the summer of 1998 in Zubaydah's diary. Nothing . . . nothing but nonsense." Coleman reported to an FBI official: "This guy is insane, certifiable, split personality."

Bush was briefed. "I said he was important," the president complained to Tenet. "You're not going to let me lose face on this, are you?" "No sir, Mr. President." So Zubaydah became the first experiment in the new rules on torture in which the Geneva Conventions did not apply. Over at CIA headquarters in Langley, Virginia, a CIA official told Suskind, "Around the room a lot of people just rolled their eyes when we heard comments from the White House. I mean, Bush and Cheney knew what we knew about Zubaydah. The guy had psychological issues. He was, in a way, expendable. It was like calling someone who runs a company's in-house travel department the COO."

But the decision was made to "torture a mentally disturbed man and then leap, screaming, at every word he uttered." He was "waterboarded," simulating drowning. Zubaydah babbled about terrorist threats to shopping malls, nuclear power plants, supermarkets, and about Al-Qaeda plans to build a nuclear device. The administration sounded alerts on every unconfirmed threat. In May 2002, New York City was put on high alert over Zubaydah's torture-incited ravings that the Brooklyn Bridge and the Statue of Liberty were targets. Cheney went on *Larry King Live* to defend the alerts: "We now have a large number of people in custody, detainees, and periodically as we go through this process we learn more about the possibility of future attacks."

Throughout 2002, Cheney directly pressured the CIA's Directorate of Intelligence to assert both that Saddam was connected to Al-Qaeda and the 9/11 attacks and that Saddam was seeking yellow cake uranium for his nuclear weapons program. But the agency determined through numerous sources that these claims were false. Yet Cheney's operation and Rumsfeld's jerry-rigged intelligence shop kept insisting that the CIA put its seal of approval on the Atta-in-Prague story and the yellow cake uranium one, too.

On January 10, 2003, Stephen Hadley, then deputy national advisor, called Jami Miscik, deputy director of the CIA's Directorate of Intelligence, from the office of Cheney's chief of staff, I. Lewis "Scooter" Libby, demanding that Miscik appear in Libby's office that afternoon. According to Suskind, Miscik told Tenet, "If I have to go back to hear their crap and rewrite this goddamn report . . . I'm resigning, right now." So the report was not rewritten. As a result, U.S. intelligence sources could not be cited and the disinformation had to be attributed elsewhere. Thus Bush, in his 2003 State of the Union address, delivered his infamous sixteen words: "The British government has learned that Saddam Hussein recently sought significant quantities of uranium from Africa." Bush's falsehoods were an accomplishment of Cheney's "deniable" presidency. Inside the CIA, Cheney was nicknamed "Edgar," after ventriloquist Edgar Bergen.

In place of regular policy deliberation there was a series of vacuums. Every morning, after reading his Bible, eating breakfast, and working out, Bush received his briefing from the CIA and FBI directors, which was repackaged to him orally by Cheney or Condoleezza Rice. "What Bush knew before, or during, a key decision remained largely a mystery. Only a tiny group . . . could break this seal." "There was never any policy process to break, by Condi or anyone else," Suskind quotes Deputy Secretary of State Armitage as saying. "There was never one from the start. Bush didn't want one, for whatever reason. One was never started."

On October 29, 2004, Osama bin Laden released his "October surprise," an eighteen-minute tape attacking Bush. The CIA analyzed the tape and concluded that "bin Laden's message was clearly designed to assist the president's reelection." That day, at a meeting at the CIA, acting director John McLaughlin remarked, "Bin Laden certainly did a nice favor today for the president." Miscik presented analysis that bin Laden felt challenged by the rise of the thuggish Zarqawi, who called himself commander of Al-Qaeda in Iraq, and that bin Laden was refocusing attention through his tape on his cosmic and continuing one-on-one battle with Bush. "Certainly," she said, "he would want Bush to keep doing what he's doing for a few more years."

After the presidential election, in mid-November 2004, Suskind writes, Cheney directly pressured Miscik to leak a distorted part of a CIA report to "prove" that the war in Iraq was quelling, not inciting, terrorism. Cheney intended to declassify it and have the CIA make it public. But Miscik knew that the report "concluded nothing of the sort," and refused to take part in leaking false information. She was told that the new CIA director, Porter Goss, had said, "Saying no to the vice president is the wrong answer." "Actually," she replied, "sometimes saying no to the vice president is what we get paid for." Within a few weeks, she was forced out. Soon much of the CIA's top echelon was purged for adhering to its residual professional standards.

The passage of the Republican congressional resolution on Iraq stands on the wreckage of those standards. (The Pentagon talking points refer to Zubaydah as "bin Laden's field commander.") The continuing primacy of apparatchiks Cheney and Rumsfeld reflects the conquest of their conception of the executive. And Rove's exploitative strategies subordinate a potential political solution in Iraq to the paramount importance of a political solution in the midterm elections. Call it the triumph of surrealpolitik.

June 22, 2006

The Avoiding of the President

President Bush's effectiveness as a domestic president is ending not with a bang but with a whimper. Almost four months before the midterm elections, congressional Republicans fear an association with him might alienate their constituencies and result in a loss of the House of Representatives. They hold the House by only fifteen seats and suddenly even previously safe districts are at risk. Just a month ago Bush delivered a nationally televised address on immigration, urging Congress to provide for eventual citizenship for the more than 12 million illegal immigrants in the country (the pro-business position). He convinced the Senate, but the House refused to budge from its punitive position to criminalize any assistance to illegal immigrants.

The White House had hoped that the killing of terrorist Abu Musab al-Zarqawi would reverse Bush's slide in popularity. Indeed, there was a slight bump upward of several points. But this is a classic epiphenomenon that has already started to wither.

From the vantage point of Capitol Hill, the most salient factor is that Bush's evanescent Zarqawi "recovery" has failed to cast any glow onto Republican prospects. Enforcing party discipline for a purely political congressional vote last week that endorsed Bush's policy in Iraq, such as it is, has barely quelled panic. Even as Bush briefly nudged up ever so slightly from the low to mid-thirties, Republican candidates fell further behind in the polls. For Republicans, Bush has become cement shoes.

Two recent near-death experiences have desperately frightened Republicans. In a June 6 by-election to fill the seat of the corrupt and imprisoned Republican Congressman Randy "Duke" Cunningham in suburban San Diego, one of the safest Republican districts in the country, the Republican narrowly held on only through demagogic appeals against immigrants. Then, in Utah, in an even safer Republican district, the state party denied endorsement to Representative Chris Cannon, a Republican with a 100 percent American Conservative Union voting record, because he had made the mistake of supporting Bush's immigration plan. On Tuesday, Cannon edged out a primary challenge from an anti-immigrant activist who insisted he was battling "Satan."

Southern Republicans picked this moment to stall the extension of the 1965 Voting Rights Act that had been enacted after a century of African-American disenfranchisement in the South. Their ringleader, Representative Lynn Westmoreland of Georgia, is also the sponsor of bills that would require the display of the Ten Commandments in the House and Senate as well as of amendments to the Constitution to justify these sorts of displays. On June 14, he ventured forth to explain his proposals on Comedy Central, where comedian-interviewer Stephen Colbert asked him a trick question, "What are the Ten Commandments?" "You mean all of them?" Westmoreland stammered. "Um. Don't murder. Don't lie. Don't steal. Um. I can't name them all."

In the Senate on Tuesday, Republicans staged a daylong debate on a constitutional amendment to ban flag burning. Senate Majority Leader Bill Frist proclaimed the issue nothing less than a "crisis": "Enemies of American freedom abroad are well aware of the ideals emblemized by the American flag." The measure failed by one vote to attain the necessary two-thirds majority.

So far this year, according to the Citizens Flag Alliance, there have been four incidents of flag burning, whose evildoers have been not a single Al-Qaeda suspect but the usual rowdy small-town teenagers. One of the most notable cases of 2005 occurred last July 4, after midnight, when an eighteen-year-old in Maryville, Tennessee (population 23,000, located in Frist's native state), burned a flag in a neighbor's yard and was arrested after the police detected "beer cans 'all over the property and in the street,'" according to the local newspaper. The Associated Press reported, "His father said the teenager 'has no reason for anger against the United States' and could easily have ignited a garbage can instead of a flag." The lad was jailed for nine days.

While the Senate was consumed debating the flag-burning amendment, Representative Mark Kennedy, the Republican Senate candidate in Minnesota, was removing every mention and likeness of Bush from his campaign literature and advertising. As the Republican cultural warriors march into the midterm elections, they are unfurling nativism and jingoism as their banners, and some are even raising the shadow of Jim Crow. The unpopular conservative president is the emblem they seek to hide. Only by suffering slights from Republicans can Bush hope to escape a Congress led by Democrats that would cast sunlight on his remarkably secretive and unaccountable administration.

June 29, 2006

Judgment Day

The Supreme Court ruling in the case of *Hamdan v. Donald Rumsfeld, Secretary of Defense, et al.*, on June 29 did far more than settle the limited question of whether alleged terrorist detainees can be tried before secret military tribunals. By declaring Bush's position unconstitutional, the court in effect judged his concept of his presidency and his methods in his "global war on terror" illegitimate. In his majority opinion, Justice John Paul Stevens's strategic capitalization emphasized the larger point: "The Executive," he wrote, "is bound to comply with the Rule of Law."

Inside the Bush administration, senior legal authorities refer to their novel framing of the law as the "war paradigm." Its origins can be traced to

Vice President Dick Cheney's experience with the thwarting of Richard Nixon's imperial presidency and Cheney's subsequent decades-long effort to re-create it on a new basis. The attacks of September 11 provided the casus belli for the concentration of power in an executive unfettered by checks and balances. Legal doctrines developed by neoconservative theorists, who happened to be appointed to key posts in the Justice Department's Office of Legal Counsel, were applied.

Instantly, the war paradigm became operational. Cheney and his then legal counsel and current chief of staff David Addington, directed John Yoo, deputy assistant director in the OLC, to write the key memos detailing the new imperial presidency. The first principle is that president as commander in chief can set or obey laws as he wishes. From that flowed Bush's dismissal of the Geneva Conventions, denigrated as "quaint" by then White House legal counsel Alberto Gonzales, now U.S. attorney general. On February 2, 2002, Bush signed a directive unilaterally withdrawing enforcement of the Geneva Conventions, specifically Common Article 3, which prohibits torture. He has also evaded the Foreign Intelligence Surveillance Court, ordering the National Security Agency to engage in warrantless eavesdropping on Americans; invested his vice president with presidential powers over classified intelligence; and imprisoned thousands of alleged terrorists without due process of law.

The political dimension of the war paradigm is inextricably linked to its legal one. It has the advantage of serving polarizing politics. "Either you are with us or you are with the terrorists," Bush said repeatedly after 9/11. Against the war paradigm Bush's warriors propped up a straw man they call the "law-enforcement paradigm." The efficacy of law enforcement or the ineffectiveness of waging "war" is beside the point. Those for "war" are true patriots and strong, but those for "law enforcement" are weak and wimpy. "One is sort of a crime-solving approach, a law-enforcement approach, and the other is a national strategy, military, intelligence, wartime approach," Cheney said.

But even more than Cheney, Karl Rove, Bush's chief political advisor, has been the public advocate of the war paradigm as political wedge issue. Speaking before the Conservative Party of New York state last year, Rove said, "Perhaps the most important difference between conservatives and liberals can be found in the area of national security. Conservatives saw the savagery of 9/11 and the attacks and prepared for war; liberals saw the savagery of the 9/11 attacks and wanted to prepare indictments and offer therapy and understanding for our attackers." In the demonized politics and legal netherworld of the war paradigm, the rule of law is for sissies.

And yet Hamdan's case moved through the courts. Salim Ahmed Hamdan, believed to be a driver and bodyguard of Osama bin Laden, was captured in Afghanistan in 2001 and jailed at the Guantánamo prison camp. The Bush administration held him for a year without charges and then declared he would be tried at some unspecified time before a secret military commission on unspecified crimes of "conspiracy." In this kangaroo court, Hamdan was not entitled to be present, or to see or learn any accusations or evidence against him. Hearsay would be admissible, though he'd never know what it might be. So Hamdan filed a suit challenging the legality of the tribunal and claiming he had rights under military and international law.

Now the Supreme Court's decision has thrown Bush's war paradigm into profound crisis. As the Republicans nervously approach midterm elections, Bush, through Rove, is prompting the Republican Congress to uphold his discredited position in order to continue demonizing Democrats. But transforming the issue into another Manichaean battle of "us" versus "the terrorists" will not make his position any more constitutional.

"We conclude," reads the court's opinion, "that the military commission convened to try Hamdan lacks power to proceed because its structure and procedures violate both the UCMJ [Uniform Code of Military Justice] and the Geneva Conventions." The ruling is sweeping in its rejection of Bush's claims; it leaves none of the precepts of his war paradigm standing. In its wake his imperial presidency, at least before the majesty of the law, is a ruin.

The court dismisses Bush's insistence that the congressional Authorization for the Use of Military Force is the basis of his authority as commander in chief to assume bottomless extraordinary powers. In the Hamdan case, his use of the congressional authorization to justify military commissions is also discarded. But Bush has also cited the authorization for many of his dubious actions, from holding detainees without due process to domestic spying. The court's opinion is that the authorization cannot serve to "expand or alter the authorization" that Congress initially intended. The president's war powers, the court reminds him, does not contravene the Congress' war powers.

Nor does the president's fiat override the Uniform Code of Military Justice or the Geneva Conventions. In the case of the UCMJ, according to the court, the president cannot suppress due process. In the case of the Geneva Conventions, he cannot withdraw from an international treaty of which the United States is a signatory. Justice Stevens, writing for the majority, said, "The UCMJ conditions the President's use of military commissions on compliance not only with the American common law of war, but also with the rest of the UCMJ itself, insofar as applicable, and with the 'rules and precepts of the law of nations.'"

Bush's designation of Hamdan and other detainees as "enemy combatants," a vague category of stateless persons not granted the international protections of prisoners of war, is tossed out. Stevens cites Common Article 3 of the Geneva Conventions, but without elaborating its substance. That article, in fact, forbids torture—"cruel treatment and torture [and] outrages upon personal dignity, in particular humiliating and degrading treatment." Here, therefore, the court rejects Bush's torture policy. (And, as we shall see, Anthony Kennedy raises Common Article 3 with possibly explosive consequences.)

Whether Hamdan is associated with a power that signed or didn't sign the Geneva Conventions is irrelevant, despite Bush's argument that the issue is central. "Common Article 3, then, is applicable here" and, Stevens goes on, citing the court's collective opinion, "requires that Hamdan be tried by a 'regularly constituted court affording all the judicial guarantees which are recognized as indispensable by civilized peoples.'"

Stevens's conclusion does not show any sympathy for Hamdan, or suggest that he has been unjustly imprisoned, or that he should be released. Contrary to Rove's earlier insinuations, he does not offer "therapy" or "understanding." Stevens, however, does wear his heart on his sleeve on "law enforcement." "We have assumed, as we must, that the allegations made in the Government's charge against Hamdan are true," he writes. "We have assumed, moreover, the truth of the message implicit in that charge—viz., that Hamdan is a dangerous individual whose beliefs, if acted upon, would cause great harm and even death to innocent civilians, and who would act upon those beliefs if given the opportunity. It bears emphasizing that Hamdan does not challenge, and we do not today address, the Government's power to detain him for the duration of active hostilities in order to prevent such harm. But in undertaking to try Hamdan and subject him to criminal punishment, the Executive is bound to comply with the Rule of Law that prevails in this jurisdiction."

Justices Stephen Breyer and Anthony Kennedy added to the impact of Stevens's opinion with important concurrences. Breyer underlined the point that the congressional authorization cannot be used by Bush to rationalize whatever action he chooses. "The Court's conclusion," he writes, "ultimately rests upon a single ground: Congress has not issued the Executive a 'blank check.'" Breyer's citation of the phrase "blank check" is his way of evoking the justice who has just retired, Sandra Day O'Connor, and her opinion in *Hamdi v. Rumsfeld*, a case in 2004 that foreshadowed the Hamdan decision. The court ruled in that case that a U.S. citizen, held as an "enemy combatant" in Guantánamo, could not be detained indefinitely without the right to challenge his imprisonment and the right to counsel. O'Connor wrote, "A state of war is not a blank check for the President."

When O'Connor was on the court, she was considered to be the key swing vote. Now that pivotal spot belongs to Anthony Kennedy. His opinion is worthy of intense interest, however, for more than that reason. Kennedy ventures into territory where others have not. His disdain for Bush's position is palpable. He cites Justice Robert Jackson's famous opinion in the 1952 Youngstown case: "When the President takes measures incompatible with the expressed or implied will of Congress, his power is at its lowest ebb." But Kennedy quotes Jackson not simply to expose the depth to which Bush has sunk. He is building toward another conclusion—those who violate the Geneva Conventions can be prosecuted for war crimes.

The Geneva Conventions, after all, constitute an international treaty, enacted by the Congress. "By Act of Congress, moreover," Kennedy writes, "violations of Common Article 3 are considered 'war crimes,' punishable as federal offenses, when committed by or against United States nationals and military personnel. See 18 U.S.C. §2441. There should be no doubt, then, that Common Article 3 is part of the law of war as that term is used in §821."

Kennedy moves on to discuss why Bush's military commissions do not meet the "general standards" of "civilized peoples." He has left dangling the open question of war crimes. But the opinion of a justice of the Supreme Court speaking in the majority is not merely a theory. Of all the justices, Kennedy, the swing moderate, has raised the most potentially volatile issue.

But Bush, Cheney, Rumsfeld, et al., need not worry that they will soon find themselves in the dock. There is little chance that the Justice

Department under Gonzales will ever pursue Kennedy's logic, let alone develop a convoluted argument for why it shouldn't apply.

Indeed, Gonzales expressed dismay at the Supreme Court's decision. On cue and on message, he said, "What this decision has done is, it's hampered our ability to move forward with a tool which we had hoped would be available to the president of the United States in dealing with terrorists." Nonetheless, he said that the administration would work with the Republican Congress "to look at legislation" and he was "hopeful that we will have the ability to try people through military commissions."

Within hours of the Supreme Court ruling, House Majority Leader John Boehner of Ohio circulated a memo, obviously already prepared, among Republican members that provided them with talking points: The court had given "special privileges to terrorists" and the Democrats were weak on terrorism. "There is a clear choice between Capitol Hill Democrats who celebrate offering special privileges to violent terrorists, and Republicans who want the president to have the necessary tools to prosecute and achieve victory in the global war on terror," the memo stated.

Though the Hamdan decision devastates the legitimacy of Bush's war paradigm, his instinct is to rally around it. Those legal minds in the administration behind the memos from which sprang the far-flung system of prisons holding droves of detainees without due process in Iraq and elsewhere—possibly numbering in the tens of thousands, according to Lawrence Wilkerson, a chief of staff to former secretary of state Colin Powell—have proposed no gesture of transition. That is despite the immense damage done to American prestige. Instead, Rove has been given license to gin up reaction to the court decision as another opportunity for activating the Republican base.

Senior leadership in the military has long opposed Bush's war-paradigm policies. From the start the Judges Advocate General vehemently resisted the abrogation of legal standards. Then Powell, the former chairman of the Joint Chiefs of Staff, spoke for much of the military in his opposition. But they were ignored. Last year, the general counsel of the U.S. Navy, Alberto Mora, and Matthew Waxman, deputy assistant secretary of defense for detainee policy, strongly argued for adherence to Common Article 3. But Cheney, Rumsfeld, and Addington suppressed them.

For the national security career professionals, Kennedy's opinion may provide a useful retort. CIA personnel, assigned control of secret detainee prisons, or "black sites," may wonder if there might ever be circumstances in which they could be subject to war-crimes prosecution. In the unseen bureaucratic politics post-Hamdan, Kennedy's opinion may give them a handhold of resistance.

For Rove, Bush's political spearhead, everything is short-term. Nothing matters but the midterm elections. A new issue that can be twisted to polarize and stir up Republicans is welcomed as a godsend. Through Rove's machinations and a one-party Republican Congress, Bush is attempting to create political immunity from constitutional wreckage.

But the decision stands in history. Hamdan is a bookend on the imperial presidency; the decision in *United States v. Nixon* is the other. In his presentation to the Supreme Court, Nixon's attorney, James St. Clair, argued, "The President wants me to argue that he is as powerful a monarch as Louis XIV, only four years at a time, and is not subject to the processes of any court in the land except the court of impeachment." On July 24, 1974, Chief Justice Warren Burger, speaking for the court, ruled that there was nothing in the Constitution to "sustain an absolute, unqualified Presidential privilege of immunity from judicial process under all circumstances." Nixon was forced to give up his incriminating White House tapes, and he resigned on August 9. In Nixon's fall began Cheney's dream. There are many monuments to presidents in Washington, but there is no Nixon memorial, only the Vietnam War Memorial. If there is ever a Bush Monument, it may be a cage surrounded by barbed wire, above which is engraved in marble the lasting judgment of Justice Stevens: "THE EXECUTIVE IS BOUND TO COMPLY WITH THE RULE OF LAW."

July 6, 2006

A Pantomime Presidency

President Bush was against diplomacy before he was for it. But with the collapse of U.S. foreign policy from the Middle East to North Korea, he claims to have become a born-again realist. "And it's, kind of . . . painful . . . for some to watch, because it takes a while to get people on the same page," he said at his July 7 press conference, adding, in an astonished tone, "Not everybody thinks the exact same way we think. Different words mean different things to different people."

Two years ago at the Republican convention he boasted of his "swagger, which in Texas is called walking." But in the face of the consequences of his failures, he has swaggered into a corner.

In a befuddled response to Israel's reoccupation of Gaza and bombing of Lebanon, the secretary of state, Condoleezza Rice, asked for restraint while the president offered support. Bush has regressed to embracing no policy, just as he did when he first entered office. His failure to give the Palestinian president, Mahmoud Abbas, any tangible gains to show his electorate helped Hamas win. Now the U.S.'s abandonment of any peace process is yielding a downward spiral of mutual recrimination in the region.

Similarly, on Iraq, Bush has returned to mouthing inane platitudes about "victory." He promises to "defeat" the enemy while ignoring his generals' admonition that a political solution is critical as Iraq descends into civil war.

What the president doesn't know and when he didn't know it remain pertinent. In January 2003 Bush met three prominent Iraqi dissidents who, in discussing scenarios of post-Saddam Hussein Iraq, "talked about Sunnis and Shi'ites. It became apparent to them that the president was unfamiliar with these terms." Peter Galbraith, who was involved in Iraqi diplomacy as a Senate aide for decades, carefully sources this anecdote in his new book, *The End of Iraq: How American Incompetence Created a War Without End.*

Bush's policy toward North Korea is paralyzed, reduced to kowtowing to China in the forlorn hope that it would implore the hermit kingdom to forswear developing nuclear weapons and firing test missiles. But the Chinese have declared they will veto any U.S.–initiated sanctions in the U.N. Security Council.

When Bush was president-elect, Bill Clinton's national security team had a treaty with North Korea essentially wrapped up. The incoming secretary of state, Colin Powell, was enthusiastic. As president, Bush cut off diplomacy and humiliated Powell and the South Korean president, Kim Dae-Jung, for seeking to continue the process associated with Clinton. In Bush's vacuum—a series of empty threats—North Korea predictably reacted with outrageous violations intended to capture US attention. Then undersecretary of state, John Bolton constantly subverted the U.S. negotiator, Charles "Jack" Pritchard.

After Pritchard quit in 2003, Bush sent a new negotiator to the six-party talks in 2004 but prohibited him from meaningful negotiation. The North Koreans responded with extreme gestures, and Bush has answered that he will not speak to them directly. "By not talking with North Korea," Pritchard wrote last month in the *Washington Post*, "we are failing to address missiles, human rights, illegal activities, conventional forces, weapons of mass destruction, terrorism and anything else that matters to the American people. Isn't it about time we actually tried to solve the problem rather than let it fester until we blow it up?"

The North Korea debacle shows that Bush's ruinous approach began before the Iraq invasion, indeed before 9/11. His latest pantomimes of policies recall Gertrude Stein's description of Oakland, California: "there is no there there."

July 18, 2006

The Emperor's New Veto

President Bush's first veto marks the first time he has lost control of the Republican Congress. But it is significant for more than that. Until now, the president has felt no need to assert his executive power over the legislative branch. Congress was whipped into line to uphold his every wish and stifle nearly every dissent. Almost no oversight hearings were held. Investigations into the Bush administration's scandals were quashed.

Potentially troublesome reports were twisted and distorted to smear critics and create scapegoats, like the Senate Select Intelligence Committee's report on faulty intelligence leading into the Iraq War. Legislation, which originates in the House of Representatives, was carefully filtered by imposition of an iron rule that it must always meet with the approval of the majority of the majority. By employing this standard, the

Republican House leadership, acting as proxy for the White House, managed to rely on the right wing to dominate the entire congressional process.

The extraordinary power Bush has exercised is unprecedented. Bill Clinton issued thirty-seven vetoes, George H. W. Bush forty-four, and Ronald Reagan seventy-eight. To be sure, they had to contend with Congresses led by the opposing party. Nonetheless, all presidents going back to the 1840s, and presidents before them, used the veto power, even when their parties were in the congressional majority. Just as the absence of any Bush vetoes has highlighted his absolute power, so his recourse to the veto signals its decline.

The vote in the Senate on Tuesday in favor of federal support for medical research using embryonic stem cells, which have the potential to cure many diseases and disabilities, while short of the two-thirds required to override a veto, was an overwhelming break with Bush, sixty-three to thirty-seven. The administration has struck back with false claims made by Karl Rove (assuming the role of science advisor) that adult stem cells are equivalent to embryonic ones, and with the accusation, made by White House press secretary Tony Snow, that using the thousands of routinely discarded embryos for research would amount to "murder." On Wednesday, Bush declared that the bill "crosses a moral boundary that our decent society needs to respect. So I vetoed it."

One-party congressional rule has been indispensable to Bush's imperial presidency. Its faltering reflects Republican panic in anticipation of the midterm elections, the disintegration of Bush's authority, and of his concept of a radical presidency. As the consequences of Bush's rule bear down on the Republicans, the right demands that he recommit to the radicalism that has entangled him in one fiasco after another. Bush's latest crisis is also a crisis of the paranoid style that has been instrumental in sustaining Republican ascendancy.

The first principle underlying the Bush presidency was never more succinctly articulated than at the July 12 hearing called by the Senate Judiciary Committee. The Supreme Court had ruled two weeks earlier, in *Hamdan v. Rumsfeld*, that the administration's detainee policy was in violation of the Geneva Conventions and without a legal basis. Steven Bradbury, the acting assistant attorney general in charge of the Office of Legal Counsel at the Department of Justice, appeared to defend not only the discredited policy but also the notion that as commander in chief Bush has the authority to make or enforce any law he wants—the explicit basis of the infamous torture memo of 2002. Senator Patrick Leahy, D-Vermont, asked Bradbury about the president's bizarre claim that the Supreme Court's Hamdan decision in fact "upheld his position on Guantánamo."

"Was the president right or was he wrong?" asked Leahy. "It's under the law of war—," said Bradbury. Leahy repeated his question: "Was the president right or was he wrong?" Bradbury then delivered his immortal reply: "The president is always right."

Bradbury meant more than that Bush personally is "always right." He had condensed into a phrase the legal theory of presidential infallibility. In his capacity of commander in chief, the president can never be wrong, simply because he is president. Despite the Supreme Court's ruling in Hamdan that presidential powers in foreign policy do not override or supplant those that the Constitution assigns to Congress, Bradbury instinctively fell back on the central dogma of the Bush White House. According to the doctrine, the rule of law is just an expression of executive fiat. He can suspend due process of detainees, conduct domestic surveillance without warrants, and decide which laws and which parts of laws he will enforce by appending signing statements to legislation at will. The president becomes an elective monarch who should be above checks and balances.

On Tuesday, Attorney General Alberto Gonzales appeared before the Senate Judiciary Committee, where he reiterated his belief in presidential infallibility. Under questioning, he admitted that Bush himself had denied security clearances to the Justice Department's Office of Professional Responsibility, thereby thwarting its investigation into whether government lawyers had acted properly in approving and overseeing the National Security Agency's warrantless domestic surveillance, ordered by the president to evade the Foreign Intelligence Surveillance Court. Never before in its thirty-one-year history has the OPR been denied clearances, much less through the direct intervention of the president. But Gonzales insisted that the president cannot do wrong. "The president of the United States makes decisions about who is ultimately given access," he said. And he is always right. Case closed.

Bush's coverup—legitimate because he says it is, and Gonzales's defense, smug in his certitude—are only the latest wrinkles in his radical presidency. "The president and vice president, it appears," writes John W. Dean, the former counsel to President Nixon, in his new book, *Conservatives Without Conscience*, "believe the lesson of Watergate was not to stay within the law, but rather not to get caught. And if you do get caught, claim that the president can do whatever he thinks necessary in the name of national security."

The metastasizing of conservatism under Bush is a problem that has naturally obsessed Dean. His part in the Watergate drama as the witness who stepped forward to describe a "cancer on the presidency" has given him an unparalleled insight into the roots of the current presidency's pathology. He recalls the words of Charles Colson, Nixon's counselor and overseer of dirty tricks: "I would do anything the president of the United States would ask me to do, period." This vow of unthinking obedience is a doctrinal forerunner of Bush's notion of presidential infallibility.

Dean, moreover, was close to Barry Goldwater, progenitor of the conservative movement and advocate of limited government. Dean was the high school roommate of Barry Goldwater, Jr., and became close to his father. In his retirement, the senator from Arizona, who had been the Republican presidential nominee in 1964, had become increasingly upset at the direction of the Republican Party and the influence of the religious right. He and Dean talked about writing a book about the perverse evolution away from conservatism as he believed in it, but his illness and death prevented him from the task.

Now, Dean has published *Conservatives Without Conscience*, whose title is a riff on Goldwater's creedal *Conscience of a Conservative*, and intended as an homage.

Conservatism, as Dean sees it, has been transformed into authoritarianism. In his book, he revives an analysis of the social psychology of the right that its ideologues spent decades trying to deflect and discourage. In 1950, Theodor Adorno and a team of social scientists published *The Authoritarian Personality*, exploring the psychological underpinnings of those attracted to Nazi, fascist, and right-wing movements. In the immediate aftermath of Senator Joseph McCarthy's rise and fall, the leading American sociologists and historians of the time—Daniel Bell, David Riesman, Nathan Glazer, Richard Hofstadter, Seymour Martin Lipset, and others—contributed in 1955 to *The New American Right*, examining the status anxieties of reactionary populism. The 1964 Goldwater campaign provided grist for historian Hofstadter to offer his memorable description of the "paranoid style" of the "pseudo-conservative revolt."

While Dean honors Goldwater, he picks up where Hofstadter left off. "During the past half century," he writes, "our understanding of authoritarianism has been significantly refined and advanced." In particular, he cites the work of Bob Altemeyer, a social psychologist at the University of Manitoba, whose studies have plumbed the depths of those he calls "right-wing authoritarians." They are submissive toward authority, fundamentalist in orientation, dogmatic, socially isolated and insular, fearful of people different from themselves, hostile to minorities, uncritical toward dominating authority figures, prone to a constant sense of besiegement and panic, and punitive and self-righteous. Altemeyer estimates that between 20 and 25 percent of Americans might be categorized as right-wing authoritarians.

According to Dean's assessment, "Nixon, for all his faults, had more of a conscience than Bush and Cheney . . . Our government has become largely authoritarian . . . run by an array of authoritarian personalities," who flourish "because the growth of contemporary conservatism has generated countless millions of authoritarian followers, people who will not question such actions."

But it is Bush's own actions that have produced a political crisis for Republican one-party rule. In their campaign to retain Congress, Republicans are staking their chips on the fear generated by the war on terror and the culture war, doubling and tripling their bets on the paranoid style. To that end, House Republicans have unveiled what they call the "American Values Agenda." Despite the defeat of key parts of the program—constitutional amendments against gay marriage and flag burning—and the congressional approval of embryonic stem cell research, the Republicans hope that these expected setbacks only inflame the conservative base. Their strategy is to remind their followers that enemies surround them and that the president is always right.

July 20, 2006

Splitting the Republican Cell

Nearly five years and an epoch ago, on August 9, 2001, George Bush delivered his first nationally televised speech on "an issue that is one of the most profound of our time"—stem cell research. Three days earlier, on August 6, an anxious CIA briefer had presented to him an urgent Presidential Daily Brief entitled "Bin Laden Determined to Strike in U.S.," warning of "patterns of suspicious activity in this country consistent with preparations for hijackings." "All right," the president replied. "You've covered your ass, now." He asked no questions and returned to his elaborate preparation for his big speech on stem cells.

For days, Bush had built dramatic tension, flying into his Crawford, Texas, homestead a parade of experts, leaking to the traveling press corps the difficulty of the decision he was pondering, and quietly assuring leaders of the religious right that they would be satisfied with the outcome. One thing that would not distract him from the first important political event of his presidency intended to solidify his conservative base was an intelligence report about some hypothetical threat.

In his speech Bush declared that he was banning federal support for embryonic stem cell research, but permitting research on sixty lines of adult stem cells, which are far less malleable and productive by nature. One month later, on September 11, Al-Qaeda terrorists staged terrorist attacks in New York and Washington, and the stem cell issue receded into the background. But five months before the 2006 midterm elections it has reemerged, splitting Republican ranks and setting the Republican Congress, erstwhile faithful servant of the president but now frightened of losing the control it has held since 1995, against Bush.

On July 19, he felt compelled to issue the first veto of his presidency against a bill authorizing embryonic stem cell research that passed both the previously compliant House of Representatives and Senate by large margins. Dozens of Republicans rushed to cosponsor the measure Bush vetoed.

Standing in the East Room of the White House, surrounded by young children associated with a group called Nightlight Christian Adoptions who were adopted when they were still frozen embryos originally prepared for in vitro fertilization, he said, "these boys and girls are not spare parts." But he did not explain that only 10 percent of such embryos are adopted and the rest of the infinitesimal 150 cell blastocysts, hundreds of thousands of them, are routinely discarded as waste. By his fiat they will remain unused to develop cures for a host of diseases—cancer, heart, Parkinson's, Multiple Sclerosis, Alzheimer's, spinal cord injuries, and others. Nor did Bush explain that of the sixty adult stem cells initially provided for research, which are always far less promising than embryonic ones, all are now contaminated and unavailable for work on human disorders.

Bush's veto is more than his latest exercise in faith-based assertion contrary to empirical evidence. The political calculation is to arouse right-wing followers to turn out at the polls in November in order to retain a Republican congressional majority. It is so compelling as an issue that it inspired Bush's chief political strategist, Karl Rove, to pose as a scientific expert. A week before Bush's action, Rove held forth to the *Denver Post* editorial board that there is "far more promise from adult stem cells than from embryonic stem cells." Unfortunately, Rove's statement was disinformation—"just not true," Dr. Michael Clarke, the associate director of the Institute for Stem Cell Biology at Stanford University and the world's leading researcher on adult stem cells, told the *Chicago Tribune.*

Despite Bush's machinations, the White House strategy has not operated according to expectations. Bush's approach is opposed by even a majority of Republican voters, divided the Republican party, roiled politics from California to Missouri, and pushed conservative senators and members of the House onto the defensive.

Bush should have sensed early on that the issue was fraught with peril. In 2004, as Ronald Reagan, stricken with Alzheimer's, was dying, his wife, Nancy Reagan, made a heartfelt plea: "Science has presented us with a hope called stem cell research, which may provide our scientists with many answers that for so long have been beyond our grasp. I just don't see how we can turn our backs on this. We have lost so much time already. I just really can't bear to lose any more." But Bush turned a deaf ear to her.

After Reagan's death, his native California overwhelmingly voted in favor of a referendum, supported by Republican Governor Arnold

Schwarzenegger, that established the right to stem cell research in the state constitution and provided $3 billion in funding. About 50 percent of the nation's biomedical research capacity is located in California. Bush's veto, which prevents use of any facility that receives federal support, effectively stymies the will of the voters there. But the day after the veto, Governor Schwarzenegger authorized a $150 million loan to the state's new stem cell research institute, saying, "I remain committed to advancing stem cell research in California, in the promise it holds for millions of our citizens who suffer from chronic diseases and injuries that could be helped as a result of stem cell research."

Meanwhile, Republicans in the key swing state of Missouri have been thrown into turmoil over stem cells. A referendum similar to the one in California is on the ballot and opinion polls show two-thirds support for it. Over the past five years, Republicans have gained control of the governorship and the legislature for the first time since the 1920s, and both senators are Republicans. Members of the anti-abortion movement, the conservative wing of the Roman Catholic Church, and the Southern Baptist Convention have served as indispensable soldiers in the party's march to power. But the Republican governor, Matt Blunt, sensing a turning of the tide, has endorsed the stem cell referendum. Republican U.S. Senator Jim Talent, a stalwart of the religious right, up for reelection this year, has taken positions that have offended every conceivable constituency. He has declared himself to be neutral on the state referendum, opposed to criminalizing research, and voted in the Senate to uphold Bush's veto. His Democratic opponent, state auditor Claire McCaskill, who is in favor of the referendum, has vaulted into the lead.

The most eminent Republican in the state, former Senator John Danforth, an ordained Episcopal priest, heir to the Ralston Purina fortune, and an old friend of George H. W. Bush, is among the most outspoken advocates of the referendum. In an article he wrote for *The New York Times* last year, Danforth lamented that the Republican Party "has gone so far in adopting a sectarian agenda that it has become the political extension of a religious movement." And he rebuked those opposed to embryonic stem cell research, saying they seek to "punish people who believe it is their religious duty to use science to heal the sick."

In the beginning of his presidency, Bush adopted stem cell research as both a signature issue of higher morality and a vicious wedge issue that would divide Democrats. Its return at Republican instigation marks their panic over Bush's political decline and a reversal of fortune not only for Bush and this element of his polarizing social agenda but also of his promise of a monolithic Republican party.

July 21, 2006

Birth Pangs

Once again the Bush administration is floating on a wave of euphoria. Israel's offensive against Hezbollah in Lebanon has liberated anew the utopian strain of neoconservatism that had been traduced by the Iraqi sectarian civil war. And Secretary of State Condoleezza Rice has propelled herself forward as chief cheerleader. "What we're seeing here," she said, "are the birth pangs of a new Middle East." At every press conference she repeats the phrase "a new Middle East" as though its incantation were magical. Her jaunt to the region is intended to lend the appearance of diplomacy in order to forestall it.

In Rome Wednesday, the U.S. scuttled a proposal by European and Arab nations for an immediate cease-fire in Lebanon. As explained to me by several senior State Department officials, Rice is entranced by a new "domino" theory: Israel's attacks will demolish Hezbollah; the Lebanese will blame Hezbollah and destroy its influence; and the backlash will extend to the Palestinians' Hamas, which will collapse. From the administration's point of view, the Israel-Lebanon conflict is a proxy war with Iran (and Syria) that will inexplicably help turn around Iraq. "We will prevail," Rice says nearly as often as she refers to a "new Middle East."

The Bush administration has traditionally engaged in promiscuous threat conflation—Al-Qaeda with Saddam Hussein, North Korea, and Iran in "the axis of evil," and now inferentially the Shiite Hezbollah with the Sunni Iraqi insurgency. By asserting "we" before "will prevail" Rice is engaging in national-interest conflation. According to the Rice doctrine, the United States has now deserted its historical role as ultimate guarantor of

Israel's security by acting as the honest broker among all parties. Rather than emphasize the paramount importance of Lebanese sovereignty, presumably a matter of concern to an administration that had made a nation's sovereignty Exhibit A in the spread of democracy in a "new Middle East," Rice has downplayed or ignored it in favor of an uncritical endorsement of Israel's offensive against Hezbollah, which has destroyed much of Lebanon's infrastructure, made refugees of about 20 percent of the Lebanese, and treated the Lebanese government as a contemptible irrelevance. Rice's trip was calculated to interpose the influence of the United States to prevent a cease-fire and to give Israel at least another week of unimpeded military action.

To the Bush administration the conflagration has appeared as a deus ex machina to rescue it from the Iraq quagmire. That this is patently absurd does not dawn on those who remain in thrall to the same pattern of thought that imagined the invaders of Iraq would be greeted with flowers in the streets of Baghdad. Denial is the basis of repetition. New and irrefutable revelations of the administration's disastrous consequences are brushed off like lint.

This week has also seen the publication of *Fiasco: The American Military Adventure in Iraq*, by Thomas E. Ricks, the military correspondent of the *Washington Post*, a book devastating in its factual deconstruction. The Iraqi invasion, he writes, was "based on perhaps the worst war plan in American history." The policy making at the Pentagon was a "black hole," with the U.S. Army adamantly opposed to "the optimism," and resistance by the staff of the Joint Chiefs of Staff to disinformation linking Iraq to September 11 dismissed. ("How the hell did a war on Iraq become part of the war on terrorism?" demanded one officer summarizing the general reaction of the Joint Chiefs' staff.) Orders that "smacked of politicized military leadership" suppressed internal debate; commanders who raised questions were cashiered. After the absence of a plan for postwar Iraq, blunder upon blunder fostered the insurgency. These errors combined with "ignorance of long-held precepts of counter-insurgency warfare," leading to a "descent into abuse" and torture.

In one of its unintentionally ironic curiosities, the Bush White House has created an Office of Lessons Learned, complete with director and deputies. But the thinking that made possible the catastrophe in Iraq is not a subject of this office. Instead, the delusional mind-set went underground only to surface through the crack of the current crisis. There have been no lessons learned about the blowback from Iraq—about Iraq's condemnation of Israel and its sympathy for Hezbollah—or about the United States' unwillingness to deal with the Palestinian Authority that made inevitable the rise of Hamas, or about the counterproductive repudiation of direct contact with Syria and Iran.

Indeed, Rice's "new Middle East" doctrine is one in which the United States is distrusted and even hated by traditional Arab allies, and the U.S. ability to restrain Israel while negotiating on behalf of its security has been relinquished and diminished. Since Rice became secretary of state she has been in search of what she has called "transformational diplomacy." At last, she has discovered the transformation by abandoning the diplomacy.

July 27, 2006

Ring of Fire

The National Security Agency is providing signal intelligence to Israel to monitor whether Syria and Iran are supplying new armaments to Hezbollah as it fires hundreds of missiles into northern Israel, according to a national security official with direct knowledge of the operation. President Bush has approved the secret program.

Inside the administration, neoconservatives on Vice President Dick Cheney's national security staff and Elliott Abrams, the neoconservative senior director for the Near East on the National Security Council, are prime movers behind sharing NSA intelligence with Israel, and they have discussed Syrian and Iranian supply activities as a potential pretext for Israeli bombing of both countries, the source privy to conversations about the program says. (Intelligence, including that gathered by the NSA, has been provided to Israel in the past for various purposes.) The neoconservatives are described as enthusiastic about the possibility of using NSA intelligence as a lever to widen the conflict between Israel and Hezbollah and Israel and Hamas into a four-front war.

Secretary of State Condoleezza Rice is said to have been "briefed" and to be "on board," but she is not a central actor in pushing the covert neoconservative scenario. Her "briefing" appears to be an aspect of an internal struggle to intimidate and marginalize her. Recently she has come under fire from prominent neoconservatives who oppose her support for diplomatic negotiations with Iran to prevent its development of nuclear weaponry.

Rice's diplomacy in the Middle East has erratically veered from initially calling on Israel for "restraint," to categorically opposing a cease-fire, to proposing terms for a cease-fire guaranteed to conflict with the European proposal, and thus to thwarting diplomacy, prolonging the time available for the Israeli offensive to achieve its stated aim of driving Hezbollah out of southern Lebanon. But the neocon scenario extends far beyond that objective to pushing Israel into a "cleansing war" with Syria and Iran, says the national security official, which somehow will redeem Bush's beleaguered policy in the entire region.

In order to try to understand the neoconservative road map, senior national security professionals have begun circulating among themselves a 1996 neocon manifesto against the Middle East peace process. Titled "A Clean Break: A New Strategy for Securing the Realm," its half-dozen authors included neoconservatives highly influential with the Bush administration—Richard Perle, first-term chairman of the Defense Policy Board; Douglas Feith, former undersecretary of defense; and David Wurmser, Cheney's chief Middle East aide.

"A Clean Break" was written at the request of incoming Likud Party Prime Minister Benjamin Netanyahu and intended to provide "a new set of ideas" for jettisoning the policies of assassinated Israeli Prime Minister Yitzhak Rabin. Instead of trading "land for peace," the neocons advocated tossing aside the Oslo agreements that established negotiations and demanding unconditional Palestinian acceptance of Likud's terms, "peace for peace." Rather than negotiations with Syria, they proposed "weakening, containing, and even rolling back Syria." They also advanced a wild scenario to "redefine Iraq." Then King Hussein of Jordan would somehow become its ruler; and somehow this Sunni monarch would gain "control" of the Iraqi Shiites, and through them "wean the south Lebanese Shia away from Hezbollah, Iran, and Syria."

Netanyahu, at first, attempted to follow the "clean break" strategy, but under persistent pressure from the Clinton administration he felt compelled to enter into U.S.–led negotiations with the Palestinians. In the 1998 Wye River accords, concluded through the personal involvement of President Clinton and a dying King Hussein, the Palestinians agreed to acknowledge the legitimacy of Israel and Netanyahu agreed to withdraw from a portion of the occupied West Bank. Further negotiations, conducted by his successor Ehud Barak, that nearly settled the conflict ended in dramatic failure, but potentially set the stage for new ones.

At his first National Security Council meeting, President George W. Bush stunned his first secretary of state, Colin Powell, by rejecting any effort to revive the Israeli-Palestinian peace process. When Powell warned that "the consequences of that could be dire, especially for the Palestinians," Bush snapped, "Sometimes a show for force by one side can really clarify things." He was making a "clean break" not only with his immediate predecessor but also with the policies of his father.

In the current Middle East crisis, once again, the elder Bush's wise men have stepped forward to offer unsolicited and unheeded advice. (In private they are scathing.) Edward Djerejian, a former ambassador to Israel and Syria and now the director of the James Baker Institute at Rice University, urged on July 23, on CNN, negotiations with Syria and Iran. "I come from the school of diplomacy that you negotiate conflict resolution and peace with your enemies and adversaries, not with your friends," he said. "We've done it in the past, we can do it again."

Charles Freeman, the elder Bush's ambassador to Saudi Arabia, remarked, "The irony now is that the most likely candidate to back Hezbollah in the long term is no longer Iran but the Arab Shiite tyranny of the majority we have installed in Baghdad." Indeed, when Iraqi Prime Minister Nouri al-Maliki came to Washington in the last week of July he preceded his visit with harsh statements against Israel. And in a closed meeting with U.S. senators, when asked to offer criticism of Hezbollah, he steadfastly refused.

Richard Haass, the Middle East advisor on the elder Bush's National Security Council and President Bush's first-term State Department policy planning director, and now president of the Council on Foreign Relations, openly scoffed at Bush's Middle East policy in an interview on July 30 in the *Washington Post*: "The arrows are all pointing in the wrong direction. The biggest danger in the short run is it just increases frustration and alienation from the United States in the Arab world. Not just the Arab world, but in

Europe and around the world. People will get a daily drumbeat of suffering in Lebanon and this will just drive up anti-Americanism to new heights." When asked about the president's optimism, he replied, "An opportunity? Lord, spare me. I don't laugh a lot. That's the funniest thing I've heard in a long time. If this is an opportunity, what's Iraq? A once-in-a-lifetime chance?"

The same day that Haass's comments appeared, Brent Scowcroft, the elder Bush's national security advisor and still his close friend, published an op-ed in the *Washington Post* written more or less as an open letter to his erstwhile and errant protégé Condoleezza Rice. Undoubtedly, Scowcroft reflects the views of the former President Bush. Adopting the tone of an instructor to a stubborn pupil, Scowcroft detailed a plan for an immediate end to the Israel-Hezbollah conflict and for restarting the Israeli-Palestinian peace process, "the source of the problem." His program is a last attempt to turn the president back to the ways of his father. If the elder Bush and his team were in power and following the Scowcroft plan, a cease-fire would have been declared. But Scowcroft's plan resembles that of the Europeans, already rejected by the Bush administration, and Rice is the one offering a counterproposal that has put diplomacy into a stall.

Despite Rice's shunning of the advice of the Bush I sages, the neoconservatives have made her a convenient target in their effort to undermine all diplomatic initiatives. "Dump Condi," read the headline in the right-wing *Insight* magazine on July 25. "Conservative national security allies of President Bush are in revolt against Secretary of State Condoleezza Rice, saying that she is incompetent and has reversed the administration's national security and foreign policy agenda," the article reported. Former House Speaker Newt Gingrich, a member of the Defense Policy Board, was quoted: "We are sending signals today that no matter how much you provoke us, no matter how viciously you describe things in public, no matter how many things you're doing with missiles and nuclear weapons, the most you'll get out of us is talk."

A month earlier, Perle, in a June 25 op-ed in the *Washington Post*, revived an old trope from the height of the Cold War, accusing those who propose diplomacy of being like Neville Chamberlain, the British prime minister who tried to appease Hitler. "Condoleezza Rice," wrote Perle, "has moved from the White House to Foggy Bottom, a mere mile or so away. What matters is not that she is further removed from the Oval Office; Rice's influence on the president is undiminished. It is, rather, that she is now in the midst of and increasingly represents a diplomatic establishment that is driven to accommodate its allies even when (or, it seems, especially when) such allies counsel the appeasement of our adversaries."

Rice, agent of the nefarious State Department, is supposedly the enemy within. "We are in the early stages of World War III," Gingrich told *Insight*. "Our bureaucracies are not responding fast enough. We don't have the right attitude."

Confused, ineffectual, and incapable of filling her office with power, Rice has become the voodoo doll that Powell was in the first term. Even her feeble and counterproductive gestures toward diplomacy leave her open to the harshest attacks from neoconservatives. Scowcroft and the Bush I team are simply ignored. The sustained assault on Rice is a means to an end—restoring the ascendancy of neoconservatism.

Bush's rejection of and reluctance to embrace the peace process concluded with the victory of Hamas in the Palestinian elections. This failure was followed by a refusal to engage Hamas, potentially splitting its new governmental ministers from its more radical leadership in Damascus. Predictably, the most radical elements of Hamas found a way to lash out. And Hezbollah seized the moment by staging its own provocation.

Having failed in the Middle East, the administration is attempting to salvage its credibility by equating Israel's predicament with the U.S. quagmire in Iraq. Neoconservatives, for their part, see the latest risk to Israel's national security as a chance to scuttle U.S. negotiations with Iran, perhaps the last opportunity to realize the fantasies of "A Clean Break."

By using NSA intelligence to set an invisible tripwire, the Bush administration is laying the condition for regional conflagration with untold consequences—from Pakistan to Afghanistan, from Iraq to Israel. Secretly devising a scheme that might thrust Israel into a ring of fire cannot be construed as a blunder. It is a deliberate, calculated, and methodical plot.

August 3, 2006

Axis of Failure

On Monday, the day the cease-fire was imposed on Israel's war in Lebanon against Hezbollah, and just days after the London terrorists were arrested, President Bush strode to the podium at the State Department to describe global conflict in neater and tidier terms than any convoluted conspiracy theory. Almost in one breath he explained that events "from Baghdad to Beirut," and Afghanistan, and London, are linked in "a broader struggle between freedom and terror"; that far-flung terrorism is "no coincidence," caused by "a lack of freedom"—"We saw the consequences on September the 11th, 2001"—and that all these emanations are being combated by his administration's "forward strategy of freedom in the broader Middle East," and that "that strategy has helped bring hope to millions." If there was any doubt about "coincidence," he concluded a sequence stringing together Lebanon, Iraq and Iran by defiantly pledging, "The message of this administration is clear: America will stay on the offense against Al-Qaeda." Thus Bush's unified field theory of fear, if it is a theory.

Then, once again, Bush declared victory. Hezbollah, he asserted, had gained nothing from the war, but had "suffered a defeat."

At the moment that Bush was speaking an Israeli poll was released that revealed the disintegration of public opinion there about the war aims and Israeli leadership. Fifty-two percent believed that the Israeli army was unsuccessful, and 58 percent believed Israel had achieved none of its objectives. The disapproval ratings of Prime Minister Ehud Olmert and Defense Minister Amir Peretz skyrocketed to 62 percent and 65 percent, respectively.

The war has left Israel's invincible image shattered and moral authority tarnished, while leaving Hezbollah standing on the battlefield, its reputation burnished in the Arab street "from Baghdad to Beirut." Virtually the entire Israeli political structure has emerged from the ordeal discredited. When the war against Hezbollah ended, the war of each political and military leader against every other one began.

"You cannot lead an entire nation to war promising victory, produce humiliating defeat and remain in power," wrote Ari Shavit, a columnist for *Haaretz*, which published his call for the replacement of Olmert on its front page. As the political leaders accused one another of blunders, and beat their breasts in a desperate effort to survive (Olmert confessed "deficiencies"), the military commanders attacked and counterattacked. General Udi Adam, head of the Israel Defense Forces Northern Command, who had been ousted as the offensive turned sour, gave a newspaper interview blaming the government for confusion and errors. Dan Halutz, the IDF chief of staff, issued an order forbidding all army personnel from giving press interviews, just as the newspapers were filled with the shocking exposé that Halutz had sold a stock portfolio within hours of learning of the Hezbollah kidnapping of two Israeli soldiers but before the Israeli government announced a response. The Knesset began an investigation. "We simply blew it," ran the headline on another column in *Haaretz*.

Israel's strategic debacle was a curiously warped and accelerated version of the U.S. misadventure in Iraq. It used mistaken means in pursuit of misconceived goals, producing misbegotten failure. Rather than seek the disarmament of Hezbollah, Israel sought to eliminate it permanently. If the aim had been to disarm it, in line with United Nations Resolution 1559, Israel might have initiated a diplomatic round, drawing in Saudi Arabia, Jordan, and Egypt, to help with the Lebanese government. But, encouraged by the Bush administration, Israel treated Lebanese sovereignty as a fiction. With U.S. support, Israeli unilateralism was unfurled. The possible consequences of anything less than stunning and complete triumph in a place where Israel had long experienced disaster were dismissed.

After having withdrawn in 2000 from its occupation of Lebanon, achieving few of the aims declared in the 1982 invasion, the Israeli government launched an air campaign that would supposedly extirpate Hezbollah. The wishful thinking behind the air campaign was similar to that of the Bush administration in its invasion of Iraq. Upon the liberators' entry into Baghdad, Vice President Cheney explained beforehand, the population would greet them with flowers. In Lebanon, the idea was that the more destruction wreaked by Israel, the more the population would blame Hezbollah. Of course, as common sense and every previous historical example should have dictated, the opposite occurred. When the air campaign obviously failed, the army was thrown into the breach, sent to relive

Israel's 1982 agony. Cautions about repeating the past were ignored, and the past was repeated.

Israel's national security has never been so damaged and endangered. And none of it would have been possible without the Bush administration's incitement and backing at every calamitous turn. The further erosion of U.S. credibility has also been severe.

As Bush made clear in his Monday press conference, the administration conceived of the Israeli offensive in Lebanon as a third front in his global war on terror, after Iraq and Afghanistan. Opening this new front, Secretary of State Condoleezza Rice said, was part of the "birth pangs" of "a new Middle East." With the third front, Bush redoubled his bets on his entire policy. Some in the administration hoped that it might open fourth and fifth fronts in Syria and Iran.

The administration used diplomacy to forestall diplomacy. It became Bush's instrument for giving the Israeli offensive free rein. As administration officials encouraged the Israelis in their strategy, they reinforced the Israeli government's illusionary belief that air power alone could rapidly bring about a wondrous victory.

After deliberately dallying, Rice belatedly made her way to the region, where she conducted feckless discussions in order to give the Israelis more time. She had already made her separate peace with Cheney and his covey of neoconservatives, and she was inclined to believe whatever the Israelis said. She was heedless of the analysis of State Department experts and the urgent warnings of her erstwhile mentor, Brent Scowcroft, the elder Bush's national security advisor.

Instead of recognizing that the Israelis were encountering difficulties, Rice served as the stalwart enabler of the collapsing strategy. But the limitations of her utility were exposed when the Israelis neglected to inform her of the bombing of the town of Qana, where at least twenty-six civilians, including sixteen children, were killed. The fig leaf of her influence was removed.

No administration official has suffered more collateral damage from the Lebanon war than Rice. Her flights to and fro have exposed her as vacillating and reckless, fretful and compliant, opportunistic but myopic, and in every guise ineffective. She wound up as the cheerleader on the rubble.

It can be said with a high degree of certainty, not simply tragic precedent, that the Bush administration engaged in this latest fiasco by ignoring the caveats and worst-case scenarios that must have been produced by the intelligence community. It is inconceivable that there was no intelligence assessment of Hezbollah's military, social, and political capabilities, along with a range of potential outcomes. Unquestionably, such documents exist. One of them might well have taken the form of a Presidential Daily Brief, which would have been presented to Bush by National Intelligence Director John Negroponte. It is also inevitable to conclude that having been briefed, Bush heard only what he wanted to hear.

Afterward, as the Israelis tore at one another, Bush proclaimed victory, following his Iraq P.R. formula. While his phrases might be a tonic to his political base, the rest of the world, especially now the Israelis, receive it as the empty rhetoric it is. The more Bush declares success when there is failure, the more U.S. credibility is tattered.

Perhaps the most important and unanswerable question is whether Bush believes his own propaganda. Whether he believes what he says is beside the point, because the only thing that matters is that he acts on it. The propaganda may be false and distorted. It may be historically and analytically meaningless, like Bush's recent adoption of the neoconservative ideological code words "Islamic fascism," lacking in any significant empirical value. But such pejorative phrases are helpful in stymieing public debate by evoking connotations of Hitler and Mussolini, who never dreamed of restoring a mythical caliphate. Bush's propaganda is his policy. And with every failure, it seems a new front is opened.

On the day Bush declared the defeat of Hezbollah in Lebanon, he had an unusual lunch at the Pentagon with four experts on Iraq, only one of whom was a neoconservative. According to their accounts, Bush was perturbed and baffled by the demonstrations of Iraqi Shiites in support of Hezbollah. "I do think he was frustrated about why 10,000 Shiites would go into the streets and demonstrate against the United States," one participant told *The New York Times*. Yet another expert, Carole O'Leary, a professor at American University and a State Department consultant, observed that Bush stressed that "the Shia-led government needs to clearly and publicly express the same appreciation for United States efforts and sacrifices as they do in private."

Bush's demand for expressions of gratitude from the Iraqis is not a new one. In his memoir, L. Paul Bremer III, head of the ill-fated Coalition Provisional Authority, records that above all other issues, Bush stressed the need for an Iraqi government to declare its thanks. "It's important to have someone who's willing to stand up and thank the American people for their sacrifice in liberating Iraq," Bush told Bremer three times in one meeting. Puzzled by expressions of Shiite solidarity with Hezbollah, Bush's demand for gratitude remains unchanged.

This week Bush broke from his usual long summer vacation at his Crawford, Texas, homestead for a press conference and meetings in Washington. The week before, while the Lebanon war was still raging, Bush invited Reuters correspondent Steve Holland to join him on an hour and a half bicycle ride in one-hundred-degree heat. (Bush holds contests for his staff at Crawford to belong to his "100-Degree Club." When the temperature hits one hundred degrees, they run three miles while the president rides his bike alongside them, urging them to run faster. "You can do it! Come on!" At the end, they receive T-shirts and pose for pictures with Bush.) "Bush does not ride quietly, constantly shouting out in his Texas twang the names of trees and geographic features and yelling at himself to pedal faster," Holland wrote. As Bush rode up a hill, leading an entourage of sweating Secret Service agents and the reporter, he shouted to no one in particular: "Air assault!"

August 17, 2006

Father and Son

Every Bush presidency is unhappy in its own way. George W. Bush has contrived to do the opposite of his father, as if to provide evidence for a classic case of reaction formation. Rather than halt the U.S. Army before Baghdad, he occupied the whole country. Rather than pursue a Middle East peace process that dragged along a recalcitrant Israeli government, he cast the process aside.

"Frustrated?" President Bush volunteered in his Monday press conference. "Sometimes I'm frustrated." His crankiness has deeper sources than having truncated his usual monthlong summer vacation in sweltering

Crawford, Texas. "Rarely surprised," he continued, extolling his world-weary omniscience. "Sometimes I'm happy," he plunged on, but thought better than to elaborate. "This is—but war is not a time of joy. These aren't joyous times. These are challenging times, and they're difficult times, and they're straining the psyche of our country." Then he decided he would indicate he was a calming influence, so he added, "I understand that."

But Bush is trapped in a self-generated dynamic that eerily recalls the centrifugal forces that spun apart his father's presidency. George H. W. Bush, a World War II fighter pilot, was unfairly said by the media to suffer from "the wimp factor," "emasculated by the office of vice president," according to a notorious *Newsweek* cover story in 1987. (George W., acting as enforcer, his then favorite role, cut *Newsweek*'s reporters off from further access.) It was not until the Gulf War that the public became convinced that the elder Bush was a strong leader and not the wimp he was stereotypically depicted as. But then almost immediately afterward came a recession. Bush's feeble response was not seen as merely an expression of typical Republican policy but as a profound character flaw. If Bush was strong, why didn't he solve the problem? The public concluded he was indifferent, and its view of him curdled into anger. Outdoing the father by subduing "the wimp factor," the son has not grasped that it was the father's presumed strength and not his weakness that undid him in the end.

President Bush's staggering mismanagement of the Iraqi occupation, making the old colonial "savage wars of peace" appear by comparison as case studies for modern business schools of benign competence, has until recently served his purpose of seeming to defy the elements of chaos he himself has aroused. By stringing every threat together into an immense plot that justifies a global war on terrorism, however, he has ultimately made himself hostage to any part of the convoluted story line that goes haywire.

Because Bush has told the public that Iraq is central to the war on terror, the worse things go in Iraq, the more the public thinks the war on terror is going badly. Asked at his press conference what invading Iraq had to do with September 11, Bush seemed so dumbfounded that at first he answered directly. "Nothing," he said, before sliding into a falsely aggrieved self-defense—"except for it's part of—and nobody has ever suggested in this administration that Saddam Hussein ordered the attack."

Asked about sectarian violence in Iraq, Bush's voice suddenly went passive. "You know, I hear a lot of talk about civil war." Indeed, he might have heard it from his top generals, John Abizaid and Peter Pace, who testified before the Senate on August 3, seriously off-message from Bush's P.R. campaign of relentlessly stressing "victory." As Abizaid said, "Sectarian violence is probably as bad as I have seen it."

All the stopgap strategies have failed to halt it—eliminating Abu Musab al-Zarqawi, mobilizing the civil action teams, building up the police, concentrating forces in Baghdad. Asked three times what his strategy is, or whether he has a new one, Bush tried to fend off the question with words like "dreams" and "democratic society." "That's the strategy," he said. Then Bush confused having a strategy with being in Iraq. "Now, if you say, are you going to change your strategic objective," he struggled to explain, "it means you're leaving before the mission is complete." Finally, as always, he asserted that if the United States withdrew, "the enemy would follow us here," forgetting that London is "here." Or is it? "Here" dissolved into abstraction, too.

Perhaps Bush's bizarre summer reading, according to his press office, of Albert Camus's *The Stranger* is responsible for his mélange of absurdities, appeal to an existential threat, and erratic point of view, veering from aggressor to passive observer. Would a staff aide have the audacity to suggest that he read B. H. Liddell Hart's military classic, *Strategy*? "Self-exhaustion in war," wrote Liddell Hart, "has killed more States than any foreign assailant." It was a lesson in restraint the father understood when he stopped short of Baghdad.

August 24, 2006

Remembrance of Things Past

President Bush declared a National Day of Remembrance on August 29, the day of Hurricane Katrina's landfall—not on September 2, the day the federal government finally responded to the disaster. He has begun commemorating highlights of his presidency as though he were a guide leading visitors through the wonders of the George W. Bush

Presidential Library. His dissociation is one element in the continuity of his methods.

The population of New Orleans is about half of the 455,000 it was when the storm hit, reduced to the size it was in 1880. Here the Bush administration has built a bridge to the nineteenth century. Along the Mississippi coast, fewer than 5 percent of the wrecked homes are being rebuilt. The $17 billion in federal community development block grants has only now slowly begun trickling in. Little of it will go to low-income home owners and none to renters, who constitute about half of those displaced.

On his Remembrance tour, his thirteenth visit to the region since Katrina, Bush arrived first, on Monday, in Mississippi. "It's a sense of renewal here," he proclaimed, gesturing out at the beach. "You know, each visit, you see progress. I was struck by the beauty of the beaches. The beaches were pretty rough after the storm, as you know. Today they are pristine and they're beautiful. They reflect a hopeful future, as far as I'm concerned."

The next day he came to New Orleans to herald "progress." "We're addressing what went wrong," he declared in a voice that quickly trailed from bravado into passivity. Later he perked up, after calling the storm "biblical," offering his own King James Version of Katrina rebuilding: "There will be a momentum, a momentum will be gathered. Houses will begat jobs, jobs will begat houses."

Katrina week is an ordeal he must weather before 9/11 week, which will begat the Republicans' midterm elections campaign. Even on the day Bush was obliged to stage what appears will be his annual Groundhog Day in New Orleans until the end of his term, Secretary of Defense Donald Rumsfeld previewed the fall season's political line. At the American Legion convention, he attacked "some who argue for tossing in the towel . . . some seem not to have learned history's lessons . . . quitters . . . the Blame America First mentality." In Iraq, and everywhere else for that matter, "fascists" are the enemy, failure to support the administration is appeasement, and the press is subverting the struggle by reporting stories like those about torture at Abu Ghraib.

Rumsfeld did not mention the clash the day before between units of the Iraqi army and Muqtada al-Sadr's Mahdi army (Sadr is Prime Minister Nouri al-Maliki's most important political ally), in which twenty-eight were killed, including an Iraqi general and more than a dozen soldiers, beheaded in a town square after they ran out of ammunition. In July, Rumsfeld had ridiculed the notion that sectarian strife in Iraq bears any resemblance to civil war. "If you think of our Civil War, this is really very different," he said. The metrics would seem to be satisfied when large-scale military units battle, but Rumsfeld retreated from bloody facts on the ground to higher rhetoric. "Can we truly afford to believe that, somehow or someway, vicious extremists could be appeased?" he charged, and went on without describing the "vicious extremists" (Muqtada al-Sadr?), except as "fascists."

Making his escape from New Orleans, Bush laid preparations for a Churchillian reenactment during the upcoming 9/11 week. In his press conference last week Bush had upset his past innuendoes by conceding that the relationship of Saddam Hussein to the terrorist attacks of 9/11 was "nothing." But in an interview with NBC News anchor Brian Williams on Tuesday, Bush scrambled to repackage his all-inclusive unified field theory. "They—they weren't—no, I agree, they weren't Iraqis, nor did I ever say Iraq ordered that attack, but they're a part of—Iraq is part of the struggle against the terrorists . . . I personally do not believe that Saddam Hussein picked up the phone and said, 'Al-Qaeda, attack America.'" Thus Bush remembered a story no one had ever suggested before he did in his interview; and in refuting his own concocted tale he hinted once again at dark liaisons between Saddam and Al-Qaeda.

Bush could hardly wait to put remembrance of Katrina behind him. He rushed to the American Legion convention on Thursday to begin a series of speeches on the stakes in the war on terror and Iraq that will climax with his commemoration of September 11. Framed by the tragic date, Bush hopes to recapture his image as the president holding the bullhorn while standing on the rubble of the World Trade Center. His idea of memory is the erasure of almost everything that has followed his heroic moment. He wishes to remember the past so long as most of it is forgotten.

Bush's remembrances of 9/11 only point to the opportunities that he has squandered. When he stood on the ruins of the World Trade Center virtually the whole world had declared its solidarity with the United States, Al-Qaeda had lost almost all sympathy throughout Muslim communities, and even Syria and Iran offered to help the United States destroy the terrorist threat. Now Bush stands on the rubble of his policy and reminds us by his presence what he has not built.

Even the recent indictments in London of members of a terrorist ring there, achieved through effective law enforcement techniques, underline

Bush's continued denigration of law enforcement and the rule of law and militarization of policy. The London plot also glaringly but silently carries the suggested possibility that 9/11 might well have been preventable.

Five years later, the Day of Remembrance for September 11 should properly begin on August 6 to recall the Presidential Daily Brief that Bush received in 2001, titled "Bin Laden Determined to Strike in U.S.," which he ignored, dismissing his CIA briefer: "Well, you've covered your ass now." Before then, the administration had shunted aside the terrorist issue as something tainted by association with Bill Clinton. Counterterrorism chief Richard Clarke was ignored and demoted, pushed off the National Security Council Principals Committee. Despite Clarke's urgent entreaties, the Principals Committee discussed terrorism only once, deciding at Rumsfeld's behest not to fly Predator drones for surveillance over Osama bin Laden's camps in Afghanistan. Bush's final dismissal of the threat warning on August 6 meant that the CIA and FBI and other agencies were under no pressure from above to coordinate or even to be on the alert for terrorist plots.

In the aftermath of the derelict approach before 9/11, incompetent bungling has been compounded. By now the history is all too sadly familiar: allowing bin Laden to escape at Tora Bora by failing to commit U.S. troops; draining personnel and resources from Afghanistan in the run-up to the invasion of Iraq; contempt for our alliances and disregard of world opinion; and the incredible accumulation of blunders in Iraq that have produced the present and ever-widening crisis, which has restored and sustained prestige for terrorism from Baghdad to London, constantly replenishing a potential reservoir of able and willing terrorists. To that extent, Bush has transformed his initially false conflation of Iraq and terror into a fact, though terror has become a more universal tactic than he allows, deployed in Iraq by Shiite militias (sometimes operating as police or army) and Sunni insurgents alike.

On the day Bush visited New Orleans, Attorney General Alberto Gonzales appeared in Baghdad to meet with Iraqi officials on detainee and interrogation policy. As White House counsel, Gonzales had notoriously referred to the Geneva Conventions on torture as "quaint" and helped preside over Bush's abrogation of them. He has also overseen Bush's policy of appending signing statements to bills enacted by Congress, declaring that the president alone will decide which laws and parts of laws he will enforce or not enforce—including those regarding torture techniques—a general policy that the American Bar Association last month stated was "contrary to the rule of law." On Wednesday, in Baghdad's Green Zone, Gonzales memorably explained the limits of permissible methods of torture: "It's difficult to decide what is appropriate and what is allowed under law."

Bush's ratcheting up of his ahistorical analogies since "Mission Accomplished" in Iraq has always been in inverse relationship to crises produced by his absence of strategy. Rumsfeld's phantasmagorical séance summoning the specters of Adolf Hitler and Neville Chamberlain, apart from the transparency of his deluded grandiosity, should also be understood as the deliberate substitution of fever for strategy. With the Bush administration, the more heated the rhetoric, the emptier the policy.

Each disaster of Bush's presidency triggers remembrance of another. Bush's neglectful behavior before Katrina recalls his studious indifference to terrorism on the eve of 9/11. His refusal to respond to the briefing by Max Mayfield, director of the National Hurricane Center, that the levees would likely be breached eerily repeated his administration's dismissive attitude toward Clarke's warnings and the August 6 PDB on bin Laden. From 9/11 to Katrina, the pattern, we can now recall, is remarkably consistent.

Remembrance of Bush's fiascoes does not overshadow the reality that they are not sealed in the past but are continuing catastrophes. As new failures unfold, the old ones appear in their refracted light. Memories of Bush's damage acquire deeper meanings with each new calamity.

Consider: In the New Orleans black community of the Lower 9th Ward, only two hundred of its original 14,400 residents have returned to their blasted homes. Though statistics are unavailable, it is likely that Hezbollah has already rebuilt more homes in southern Lebanon than Bush has a year after Katrina in the Lower 9th Ward.

August 31, 2006

The Enabler

About two weeks after the 2004 presidential election, on November 13, the British Embassy in Washington held a surprise fiftieth birthday party for Condoleezza Rice. Upon her arrival, Ambassador David Manning presented her with a red Oscar de la Renta–designed gown for which the embassy staff had managed to secure the "state secret" of her size. When Rice changed into the dress and emerged like Cinderella she was met by her Prince Charming, dressed in a tuxedo, the man she once called "my husband," President Bush.

At the State Department's senior policy meeting the following Monday, an official remarked about the red dress, "It gives new meaning to 'they have your number.'" The next day Bush announced the appointment of his national security advisor as his new secretary of state.

Bush's relationship with Rice is perhaps the strangest of his many strange relationships. The mysterious attachment involves complex transactions of noblesse oblige and deference, ignorance and adulation, vulnerability and sweet talk. Like his other female enablers, Karen Hughes, his political image-maker and undersecretary of state for public diplomacy, and Harriet Miers, his legal counsel, Rice is ferociously protective. She shields him from worst-case scenarios, telling him to ignore criticism that misunderstands his greatness, and showers him with a constant stream of flattery that he is a world-historical colossus.

Rice so jealously guards her relationship that her former deputy at the State Department, Robert Zoellick, left after only about a year in his post, feeling himself excluded from playing a serious part in foreign policy decision making. Since his resignation in June, there has been no replacement or mention of one. After observing Zoellick's frustration, no serious person wishes to get between Rice and her object of affection, and as a result there is no one in charge of running the State Department on a day-to-day basis.

As national security advisor, before 9/11, Rice protected Bush from counterterrorism chief Richard Clarke's warnings about Al-Qaeda attacks and demoted Clarke. Before the invasion of Iraq she lent her imprimatur to the disinformation about Saddam Hussein's weapons of mass destruction and peddled it to the major media. She did not demand an Iraq postwar stabilization plan. Nor did she object to the Pentagon's seizure of Iraq's civil governance responsibilities from the State Department. Before Israel's attack on Lebanon in July, she did not caution against the possibility of Israeli failure against Hezbollah. She was party to the decision to lend full war materiel and intelligence support to the effort if Israel would undertake it. She requested no potential or actual damage assessment.

In the beginning, the didactic academic lectured her pupil that he stood at a crossroads like 1947, the making of the Cold War policy, "present at the creation," as Truman's secretary of state Dean Acheson described it. After 9/11 she inculcated in Bush the notion that he was a world builder and could imprint his design on a scale to match the Peace of Westphalia of 1648 that established the sovereignty of nation-states.

In July 2005, shortly after Rice became secretary of state, she transported the department's senior professional staff to a West Virginia retreat, where her head of policy planning, Stephen Krasner, delivered a lecture on the Peace of Westphalia followed by a lecture on the Truman Doctrine to explain the magnitude of Rice—and Bush's—ambition for "transformational diplomacy."

This May, as the situation in Iraq drastically worsened, Rice directed the senior staff that she wants no more reporting from U.S. embassies. She announced in the meeting, according to one participant, that people write memos only for each other and that no one else reads them. She said she didn't and wouldn't read them. Instead of writing reports, the diplomats should "sell America," she insisted. "We are salesmen for America!"

On Tuesday, kicking off the midterm elections campaign, Bush delivered a speech that cited Osama bin Laden's screeds, Lenin's "What Is to Be Done?", and Hitler's *Mein Kampf*, and promised "complete victory" in Iraq. Rice contributed her own comparison of the "war on terror" to the American Civil War. "I'm sure there are people who thought it was a mistake to fight the Civil War to its end and to insist that the emancipation of slaves would hold," she said.

But the more delirious the rhetoric, the more hollow the policy. "There is no plan for Iraq," a senior national security official with the highest intelligence clearance and access to the relevant memos told me. "There is no plan. No plan."

September 7, 2006

Dreamland

On the fifth anniversary of the September 11 attacks, President Bush delivered the culmination of yet another series of speeches on Iraq and the war on terror. For more than a year, he has periodically given speeches on military bases and before specially invited audiences who applauded his carefully crafted phrases, slightly altered on each occasion, as though these scenes represented widespread public support for his policies. But this September 11 was different from the other anniversaries, partly because of the passage of half a decade but mostly because of what Bush has done with the years.

Bush hoped with his latest speech to reanimate his early iconic stature in the week after the terrorist attacks, when the whole country and world were unified in sympathy. Even "evil" Syria and Iran offered assistance in tracking down Al-Qaeda. Bush prompted us that, "the wounds of that morning are still fresh." His evocation of emotion was an attempt to filter memory. We were guided to remember the trauma as the primal experience for sustaining Bush's politics. By touching the source of pain he tried to redirect it into an affirmation of every twist and turn he has taken since the fateful day.

He pivoted into a peculiar rationalization for the Iraq war that was defensive and distorted—one that ultimately rested on an appeal to his own waning authority. "I'm often asked why we're in Iraq when Saddam Hussein was not responsible for the 9/11 attacks. The answer is that the regime of Saddam Hussein was a clear threat." But, of course, it was Bush and Dick Cheney and other prominent administration figures who had planted that impression in the public mind in the first place with thorough premeditation. Bush's transparent effort to erase his responsibility was topped by his self-presentation as the truth teller in the matter. Just as quickly as he acknowledged the fiction that was a principal prop in the public support of the invasion, he elided over the absence of weapons of mass destruction, the other principal prop. Bush simply avoided addressing their nonexistence. Instead, he revisited his discredited justification of Saddam's possession of WMD by restating it in the abstract without mentioning the missing WMD.

They had now completely vanished. The assertion that "Saddam Hussein was a clear threat" depended not even on spectral evidence, because no evidence was introduced, only the statement of "a clear threat," based on his insistence that it was so.

Having worked himself through 9/11 and the invasion of Iraq, he turned back to face Osama bin Laden. Bin Laden, said Bush, "calls this fight 'the third world war'—and he says that victory for the terrorists in Iraq will mean America's 'defeat and disgrace forever.'" Bush accepted bin Laden's challenge by accepting his terms. The conflict, Bush declared, was nothing less than "a struggle for civilization." Rather than diminish bin Laden, Bush elevated him. In so doing, he provided the incitement necessary to inflame the imagination of jihadists. Rather than explain to the American people that the ragtag terrorists are a real but not existential threat, that they should not be misconstrued as the central problem in our foreign policy, and that their presence can be coped with through confidence, fortitude, and intelligence, Bush again mounted on a crusade, serving their purposes.

In the end, Bush's speech, the product of his finest speechwriters, was as unreflective and uninformed as his expressed understanding of Albert Camus's *The Stranger*. Bush behaves as though the world is infinitely malleable and can be made over again at his command. He waves aside the consequences of his own policies and imagines them as he wishes. He summons past conflicts—World War II, the Cold War—as though referring to them invests him with the happy ending: "victory." He acts like a man who can speak now of "Iraq" and transform it by the adamant level of his rhetoric. But what he has done eludes his accounting.

Iraq was a dreamland for Bush and the Republicans, a utopian experiment where nearly every Republican panacea, nostrum, and magic potion was applied. This utopia, administered by the Coalition Provisional Authority, employed more than 1,500 people in the Green Zone and lasted from April 2003 through June 2004. But the experiment bore little resemblance to past American utopian efforts, like the benign primitive socialist Brook Farm in Massachusetts, run by Bronson Alcott (father of Louisa May Alcott, who wrote *Little Women*), and memorialized by one of its participants, Nathaniel Hawthorne, in his novel *The Blithedale Romance*. In it, he described a "knot of dreamers" getting close to the soil. In the Green Zone, there were indeed dreamers, but mainly rogues, schemers, and, above all, bunglers.

The true story of this weird American social experiment conducted between the Tigris and the Euphrates is told in a book to be published next week, *Imperial Life in the Emerald City: Inside Iraq's Green Zone*, by Rajiv Chandrasekaran, who was the *Washington Post* reporter in Baghdad. There have been other books on the CPA, written by disillusioned officials, but Chandrasekaran's offers compelling new details. His tale of innocence and pillage is recounted in a journalistic narrative of facts that speak for themselves and cut through the fog of official war rhetoric.

The Green Zone, according to Chandrasekaran, was "Baghdad's Little America," an insular bubble where Americans went to familiar fast-food joints, watched the latest movies, lived in air-conditioned comfort, had their laundry cleaned and pressed promptly, drove GMC Suburbans, and listened to a military FM radio station, "Freedom Radio," that played "classic rock and rah-rah messages." Most Americans in the Green Zone wore suede combat boots. In the office of Dan Senor, the CPA press secretary, only one of his three TVs was turned on—to Fox News.

Jay Garner, a retired lieutenant general, was appointed the head of the Office of Reconstruction and Humanitarian Assistance, the precursor to the CPA. On his way to Iraq, Garner asked the neoconservative Douglas Feith, the undersecretary of defense for policy, for the planning memos and documents for postwar Iraq. Feith told him there were none. Garner was never shown the State Department's seventeen volumes of planning titled "The Future of Iraq" or the CIA's analyses. Feith's former law partner, Michael Mobbs, was appointed head of civil administration. Mobbs had no background in the Middle East or in civil administration. "He just cowered in his room most of the time," one former ambassador recalled. Mobbs lasted two weeks.

Garner was "a deer in the headlights," said Timothy Carney, a former ambassador recruited for ORHA. Feith and the neocons assumed their favorite, Ahmed Chalabi, and his exiles would seamlessly take power and the rest would be a glide path. After Secretary of Defense Donald Rumsfeld allowed the looting of Iraqi ministries—"Freedom's untidy," he said—the U.S. officials supposedly building the new Iraq took weeks to survey the charred ruins. "I never knew what our plans were," Garner said. Rumsfeld personally tried to cut every single State Department officer from Garner's team. Soon, Garner himself fell into disfavor, and a replacement was sought. Moderate Republicans, like William Cohen, a former secretary of defense, were vetoed as being not the "right kind of Republican." L. Paul "Jerry" Bremer III, an experienced rightward-leaning diplomat, was selected. Henry Kissinger told Colin Powell at the time that Bremer, who had worked at Kissinger Associates, was "a control freak."

Bremer claims he argued with Rumsfeld over the failure to commit half a million troops to provide security in the country. But Bremer told Chandrasekaran on the spot, "I think we've got as many soldiers as we need here right now." Feith's office drew up an order banning members of the Baath Party, the only party permitted in Saddam Hussein's Iraq, from holding any responsible position in government or business. Of course, those were just about the only trained personnel in Iraq, and many of them belonged to the party to hold their jobs. "You're going to drive 50,000 Baathists underground before nightfall," warned Garner. "Don't do this." Immediately after receiving Garner's caution, Bremer announced the purge. Then Bremer disbanded the Iraqi military at the suggestion of Feith and Walter Slocombe, a consultant brought in by Feith, who had preceded Feith in his job in the Clinton administration and was now on board. Chandrasekaran asked a former soldier about the disbanded army, "What happened to everyone there? Did they join the new army?" The reply came back: "They're all insurgents now."

Iraq was also without police. The Bush White House sent Bernard Kerik to fix the problem. Kerik had been the New York City police commissioner during the September 11 attacks, Mayor Rudy Giuliani's sidekick. In Iraq, Kerik was uninterested in receiving briefings, according to Chandrasekaran, but gave numerous interviews to the American media proclaiming the situation to be under control and improving. He held precisely two staff meetings during his tenure. His main activity was going on nighttime raids against indeterminate targets accompanied by a shadowy former U.S. colonel and a one-hundred-man Iraqi paramilitary force, and then sleeping most of the day. After accomplishing nothing in three months, training no police forces, he departed. "I was in my own world. I did my own thing," he confessed.

Hiring for the CPA staff was handled by the White House liaison at the Pentagon, James O'Beirne, the husband of right-wing pundit Kate O'Beirne. He requested résumés from Republican congressional offices, activist groups, and think tanks. "They had to have the right political credentials," said Frederick Smith, the CPA's deputy director in Washington. Senior civil servants were systematically denied positions. Applicants were questioned on their ideological loyalty and their positions on issues like abortion. A youthful contingent whose résumés had been stored in the Heritage Foundation's computer files promptly found jobs and ran rampant in the Green Zone as the "Brat Pack."

Bremer declared a flat tax, a constant Republican dream that Congress could never pass at home. He promulgated the wholesale privatization of state-owned industries, which created instant mass unemployment, without acknowledging any consequences. Peter McPherson, a former Reagan administration official close to Dick Cheney, was flown in to run the Iraqi economy. He stated his belief that looting was accelerating the process of privatization—"privatization that occurs sort of naturally."

The CPA's Carney wrote a memo to McPherson warning him that his decisions were being made "without adequate Iraqi participation," by a "small group" in the CPA, and incidentally violated the Geneva Convention against seizing "assets of the Iraqi people." Carney soon left the country, having served ninety days. Bremer, in any case, replaced McPherson with Thomas Foley, President Bush's former classmate at Harvard Business School, a big Republican Party donor, and a banker. Upon his arrival Foley unveiled his plan for total privatization within thirty days, writes Chandrasekaran. "Tom," a contractor told him, "there are a couple of problems with that. The first is an international law that prevents the sale of assets by an occupation government." "I don't care about any of that stuff," Bush's pal replied. "Let's go have a drink." Soon Foley left, and another man with no previous experience in administering transitional economies replaced him. His name was Michael Fleischer, and he was the brother of Ari Fleischer, Bush's press secretary.

Providing private military forces, or mercenaries, became a booming business overnight.

One thirty-three-year-old named Michael Battles, a one-time minor CIA employee and a failed Republican candidate for Congress but with political connections to the White House, partnered with a former Army Ranger named Scott Custer to form a new security firm called Custer Battles. They had no experience in the field at all. "For us the fear and disorder offered real promise," Battles explained. Their contacts won them a lucrative contract to guard the Baghdad airport. Custer Battles became a front for an Enron-like scheme involving shell companies in the Cayman Islands and elsewhere that issued false invoices and engaged in other frauds. Though the Pentagon eventually barred the company from further work for "seriously improper conduct," it had raked in $100 million in federal contracts.

Rumsfeld handed the first effort for political transition in Iraq to Dick Cheney's daughter Liz Cheney, deputy assistant secretary of state for Near Eastern affairs. She had had no experience in the region beforehand. She then handed off the task to someone named Scott Carpenter, the former legislative director to Republican Senator Rick Santorum of Pennsylvania. One disaster followed another as convoluted manipulations of the Iraqis produced frustration, chaos, sectarian friction, and outbursts of violence. The CPA finally chose the leaders of the interim government, writes Chandrasekaran, "in the equivalent of a smoke-filled room."

Bremer assigned the job of dealing with sectarian militias to his director of security, David Gompert, who had served on the elder Bush's National Security Council. Gompert negotiated with the Kurds to demobilize their militia, called the peshmerga. In his agreement with Massoud Barzani, the Kurdish leader, to disband the militia, Gompert allowed that the Kurds would be permitted to have a brigade of "mountain rangers." After Gompert signed the document, he asked Barzani the translation of "mountain rangers" into Kurdish. "We will call them peshmerga," he said. No militias were disbanded.

After the invasion, there was no plan to restore electricity. The United Nations and the World Bank calculated it would cost at least $55 billion over four years for minimal investment in Iraq's infrastructure. By the end of the CPA's existence, only 2 percent of the $18.4 billion authorized by Congress for infrastructure, health care, education, and clean water had been spent. However, $1.6 billion had been paid to Halliburton. One year after that, only one-third of the allocated funds had been spent on Iraq's needs. Unemployment was at least 40 percent, electricity was on only about nine hours a day for the average Iraqi household, and $8.8 billion of Iraqi oil funds was unaccounted for.

A year after the CPA was dissolved, its veterans held a reunion in Washington. As Chandrasekaran writes, most of them had "landed at the Pentagon, the White House, the Heritage Foundation, and elsewhere in the Republican establishment, upon their return from Baghdad." One of them, who worked for Deputy Secretary of Defense Paul Wolfowitz, declared that in that office "the phrase 'drinking the Kool-Aid' was regarded as a badge of loyalty."

To conclude the festivities, Bremer gathered his former employees around the glow of the TV set to watch President Bush deliver one in his series of speeches on Iraq, staunchly declaring that there was "significant progress in Iraq" and that the "mission in Iraq is clear."

John Agresto, the president of St. John's College in Santa Fe, New Mexico, was among the dreamers recruited for the CPA. Rumsfeld's wife was on his board and he had worked closely with Lynne Cheney when she was chairwoman of the National Endowment for the Humanities in the Reagan administration. He came to Iraq to build a whole new university system and left having accomplished almost nothing. "I'm a neoconservative who's been mugged by reality," he said. But he is nearly alone among them in his shock of recognition.

September 14, 2006

A Radical Temperament

Under the duress of whirling sectarian violence in Iraq, President Bush is more determined than ever to "stay the course." Faced with mid-term elections whose outcome will either maintain one-party rule or provide a check on his power, he is entrenching his policies against any changes.

Perhaps another way to approach these questions is to examine how Bush's temperament fuels his radical policies. Oliver Wendell Holmes, Jr., famously remarked about Franklin D. Roosevelt that he had a "second rate intellect but a first rate temperament."

Bush has a radical temperament that is apparent in his willful refusal to assess objective evidence that might upset his ideological preconceptions and harsh rejection of pragmatic adjustments. He has an extraordinarily self-defensive resistance to acknowledge error or responsibility. His inability to accept the notion of accountability, indeed, his denial of it, is profoundly rooted and runs through his policies, permeating to the core of his presidency.

The personal element in presidencies has been well noted by historians and it is certainly strongly influential in Bush's. His radical temperament does not exclude other factors contributing to its makeup: the unprecedented power of Vice President Dick Cheney and the proliferation of networks of Leninist-like ideologues in positions of responsibility, among others. But Bush's temperament is an essential part of the dynamics. His stubbornness, lack of curiosity, shallow reservoir of knowledge, Manichean division of the world, and contempt for "nuance" are parts of a personality that key members of his administration play upon to get their ways. They carefully restrict the flow of information to him and flatter him as a great historical figure misunderstood by the mere mortals of his age. Their constant manipulation of Bush is an important part of the decision-making within the White House, an exercise of cynicism. Or is the exploitation of Bush's foibles by his closest advisers really in the service of higher ideals and principles, or just power and position? These things are not mutually exclusive. Cynical handling of the president does not rule out the radicalism of his policies. The will to absolute power almost always has a radical style. Bush's example is unique, but it also fits the historical pattern.

Bush's temperament was on full display this week in an hour and a half Oval Office meeting with a small, select group of conservative writers, including two who wrote about the experience, David Brooks in *The New York Times* and Richard Lowry in *National Review*. Lowry was impressed with Bush's "easy self-confidence." Brooks wrote, "This is the most inner-directed man on the globe." (Has Brooks interviewed Mahmoud Ahmadinejad?)

Bush presented himself as devout, principled, and unyielding. He declared that he is not about to change his radicalism one iota. "Let me just first tell you that I've never been more convinced that the decisions I made are the right decisions," he said. "I firmly believe—I'm often times asked about, well, you're stubborn and all this. If you believe in a strategy, in Washington, D.C., you've got to stick to that strategy, see." Bush offered himself as a man of the people in his black-and-white view of his "war on terror." "A lot of people in America see this as a confrontation between good and evil, including me," he said.

When questioned about any failures, he retreats into fantasy. "I'm often asked what's the difference between Iran and Iraq," he said. "We tried all diplomatic means in Iraq." But, of course, he forced out the United Nations weapons inspectors before they completed their mission of searching for Saddam Hussein's nonexistent weapons of mass destruction. Bush had announced his intention to topple Saddam long before the inspectors even began their arduous task. He was too impatient to get on with shock and awe to let them find out whether the WMDs were actually there. Now he insists he did allow them to do so. Is this an example of his principles or his cynicism? Is it real or is it Memorex? Does Bush himself know the difference? It should go without saying that he's "never been more convinced . . ."

September 14, 2006

Where Torture Got Him

President Bush's torture policy has provoked perhaps the greatest schism between a president and the military in American history, deeper, broader, and more fundamental than those of previous presidents with individual generals. Seen from the outside, this battle royal over his abrogation of the Geneva Conventions appears as a shadow war. But since the Supreme Court's ruling in *Hamdan v. Rumsfeld* in June deciding that Bush's kangaroo court commissions for detainees "violate both the UCMJ [Uniform Code of Military Justice] and the four Geneva Conventions," especially Article 3 forbidding torture, the struggle has been forced more into the open.

After Hamdan, Bush could have simply allowed the Geneva Conventions to stand. Rather, he sought legislation to reinstate his commissions, permitting hearsay—that is, uncorroborated information gathered by torture—and denying the accused the right to know the charges brought against them, or even that they are being tried or being held for life without trial.

On September 6 he made his case for torture, offering as justification the interrogation under what he called an "alternative set of procedures" of an Al-Qaeda operator named Abu Zubaydah. Bush claimed he was a "senior terrorist leader" who "ran a terrorist camp," had identified a member of the Hamburg cell, Ramzi bin al-Shibh, and provided accurate information about planned terrorist attacks. In fact, Zubaydah was an Al-Qaeda travel agent (literally, a travel agent), who did not finger al-Shibh (already known), and under torture spun wild scenarios of terrorism to gratify interrogators that proved bogus. Zubaydah, it turns out, is a psychotic with multiple personalities and the intelligence of a child. "This guy is insane, certifiable, split personality," said Dan Coleman, an FBI agent assigned to the bureau's Al-Qaeda task force.

Bush's argument for torture is partly based on the unstated premise that the more sadism, the more intelligence. While he referenced Zubaydah, he did not mention Jamal Ahmed al-Fadl, described by the FBI, according to *The New Yorker*, as "arguably the United States' most valuable informant on al Qaeda," and who is wined, dined, and housed by the Federal Witness Protection Program.

On the same day that Bush made this speech, Lieutenant General John F. Kimmons, the U.S. Army's deputy chief of staff for intelligence, presented the army's new field manual on interrogation, which pointedly encoded the Geneva Conventions. Kimmons went out of his way to say, "No good intelligence is going to come from abusive interrogation practices."

On September 15, the Senate Armed Services Committee approved an alternative to Bush's proposal, a bill affirming the Geneva Conventions, sponsored by three Republicans with a military background: John Warner, John McCain, and Lindsey Graham. Former Secretary of State Colin Powell, Bush's "good soldier," released a letter denouncing Bush's version. "The world," he wrote, "is beginning to doubt the moral basis of our fight against terrorism," and Bush's bill "would add to those doubts." That sentiment was underlined in another letter signed by thirty-eight retired generals and admirals and Powell's State Department legal counsel, William Taft IV. Retired Major General John Batiste, former commander of the 1st Infantry Division in Iraq, appeared on CNN to scourge the administration's policy as "unlawful," "wrong," and responsible for Abu Ghraib.

Before the committee vote, the administration had tried to coerce the military's top lawyers, the judge advocates general, into signing a statement of uncritical support, which they refused to do. The Republican senators opposing Bush's torture policy had first learned about the military's profound opposition from the JAGs. For years, the administration has considered the JAGs subversive and tried to eliminate them as a separate corps and substitute neoconservative political appointees.

In the summer of 2004, Major General Thomas J. Fiscus, the top Air Force JAG and one of the most aggressive opponents of the torture policy, privately informed senators that the administration's assertion that the JAGs backed Bush on torture was utterly false. Suspicion instantly fell upon Fiscus as the senators' source. Military investigators were assigned to comb through his e-mails and phone calls, and within weeks he was drummed out under a cloud of anonymous allegations by Pentagon officials of "improper relations" with women. The accusations and his discharge were trumpeted in the press, but his role in the torture debate remained unknown.

Bush had intended to use his post-Hamdan bill to taint Democrats, but instead he has split his own party and further antagonized the military. His standoff on torture threatens to leave no policy whatsoever—and threatens to leave his war on terror in a twilight zone beyond the rule of law.

September 21, 2006

In Denial

President Bush's first response to the report in *The New York Times* was to ridicule it for having "guessed" that the classified National Intelligence Estimate titled "Trends in Global Terrorism: Implications for the United States" stated that the war in Iraq was a major inspiration for jihadist terrorism. His second response, in the ensuing clamor after he declassified the NIE's key judgments confirming the accuracy of the initial *Times* report, was to dismiss those who accepted the NIE's conclusions as "naive." His next reaction was to declare, "I agree with their [the NIE's] conclusion that because of our successes against the leadership of Al-Qaeda, the enemy is becoming more diffuse and independent"—a cause and effect that is nowhere to be found in the NIE.

The collective product of the sixteen U.S. intelligence agencies, the first on Iraq since the invasion in 2003, the NIE was delivered to the White House this April. "The Iraq conflict," it said, "has become the cause célèbre for jihadists, breeding a deep resentment of US involvement in the Muslim world and cultivating supporters for the global jihadist movement." Not only is the Iraq war inspiring terrorism, but the jihadist movement has metastasized into spontaneously generated cells apart from the original Al-Qaeda organization, which itself is vastly reduced. In this struggle U.S. policy is inadequate to the task of containing terrorism's spread. "We assess that the underlying factors fueling the spread of the movement outweigh its vulnerabilities and are likely to do so for the duration of the timeframe of this Estimate."

The disclosure of parts of the NIE by the *Times* prompted Bush's angry denunciation of its public knowledge as little more than a partisan ploy. "And here we are," he railed, "coming down the stretch in an election campaign, and it's on the front page of your newspapers. Isn't that interesting? Somebody has taken it upon themselves to leak classified information for political purposes."

This latest episode indeed illumines the "political purposes" of intelligence, its suppression and distortion, and highlights the administration's intense pressures on the intelligence community, even in this NIE, whose findings on the consequences of the Iraq war have imploded Bush's carefully crafted rhetoric on terror.

Since Bush has possessed the NIE, he has spoken as though he had never received it. Yet, in the light of its revelation, it now seems that he was intent on refuting the report that the public did not know existed. "You know," said Bush at a press conference on August 21, "I've heard this theory about everything was just fine until we arrived, and kind of 'we're going to stir up the hornet's nest' theory. It just doesn't hold water, as far as I'm concerned." Bush did not say where he had "heard this theory." Nor did he present evidence to oppose it. He simply asserted his authority against the phantom critic that unmasked turned out to be the entire intelligence community.

Once the NIE became known, Bush invented a conclusion in order to claim that any difficulties had their source in his success. He advanced a history of the past twenty years based on the tortured logic that because various acts of terror had happened in the absence of an invasion and occupation of Iraq, the invasion and occupation therefore could not be ascribed as a motive for terrorism now. "You know," he said, "to suggest that if we weren't in Iraq, we would see a rosier scenario with fewer extremists joining the radical movement requires us to ignore 20 years of experience. We weren't in Iraq when we got attacked on September the 11th."

Bush's sophistry obscured that he had received many warnings before the invasion that the consequences spelled out in the NIE would come to pass. His father's close associate, Brent Scowcroft, the elder Bush's national security advisor, who was a member of the president's Foreign Intelligence Advisory Board before he was booted out in 2005, told Bush in stark terms that an invasion would lead to sectarian violence within Iraq and stoke terrorism. Scowcroft was not alone. Other former associates of the elder Bush confided in me that they also told President Bush to his face the same things that Scowcroft had.

Those were not the only cautions the Bush administration received at that time. One month before the invasion, in February 2003, the British government's Joint Intelligence Committee reported, "Al Qaeda and associated groups continue to represent by far the greatest threat to western interests, and that threat would be heightened by military action against Iraq." The British circulated the JIC report to U.S. intelligence and the Bush administration, which studiously ignored it.

Within months of the invasion, in August and November, the CIA station chief in Baghdad wrote urgent reports (called "aardwolfs") detailing how U.S. missteps had destabilized Iraq and fueled the insurgency. When Bush was briefed he was furious, not at the blunders or those committing them but at the CIA chief for having the insolence to catalog them. "What is he, some kind of defeatist?" Bush said. Soon, the station chief was replaced. "He had committed the unpardonable sin of telling the truth," writes James Risen, *The New York Times* correspondent, in his book *State of War.*

The selective declassification of the NIE hardly clarifies its full contents and necessarily raises natural suspicion about them. The key judgments cover little more than three pages; the whole document is reportedly more than thirty pages. And the key judgments may be more toned down than parts of the analysis. Caveats, objections, and conflicts may be lodged deep in the text or footnotes, as they were in the flawed October 2002 NIE on Iraqi weapons of mass destruction. The key judgments do not record what the various agencies, the CIA and the Defense Intelligence Agency reported from the field, though that may be reflected elsewhere in the complete document.

Moreover, Representative Jane Harman of California, the ranking Democrat on the House Intelligence Committee, has learned that another, new NIE on Iraq has been produced, and, despite her request for its public release, is being withheld by the administration, even from members of Congress, until January 2007, that is, until after the midterm elections.

Even the key judgments in the April 2006 NIE suggest unacknowledged political compulsions on intelligence by their glaring omissions. Whether these distortions appear as a result of direct pressure of the sort that Vice President Dick Cheney applied to CIA analysts before the invasion or have become assimilated as the modus operandi under Bush cannot be determined. But the static is apparent in the NIE's listing of causes of jihadism. Here are the exclusive reasons given:

"Four underlying factors are fueling the spread of the jihadist movement: (1) Entrenched grievances, such as corruption, injustice, and fear of Western domination, leading to anger, humiliation, and a sense of powerlessness; (2) the Iraq jihad; (3) the slow pace of real and sustained economic, social, and political reforms in many Muslim majority nations; and (4) pervasive anti-US sentiment among most Muslims all of which jihadists exploit."

What are obviously missing are (1) the Israeli-Palestinian conflict and Bush's neglect of the peace process, and (2) the failure of Bush's policy and calls for "democracy" to reduce violence or terrorism—instead contributing to the rise of Hamas and Hezbollah, followed by his refusal to deal with them as political actors.

These fundamental factors must certainly have occurred to the analysts of the sixteen intelligence agencies. Their absence must be attributed to their directors and the political leadership of the administration. These omissions combined with the empty but stentorian rhetoric about "democracy" that pervades the key judgments indicate that the NIE suffers from ideological buffeting, yet another untold story that will perhaps someday surface in a comprehensive history of Bush's abuse of intelligence.

Just before the existence of the NIE was reported, Bush gave an interview in which he offered his historical judgment that the sectarian violence in Iraq will be seen in retrospect as an insignificant passing phase in the glorious march of freedom. "I like to tell people," said Bush, "when the final history is written on Iraq, it will look like just a comma because there is—my point is, there's a strong will for democracy."

Bush's phrase, "just a comma," may just be a signifier to his religious-right base. "Never put a period where God has put a comma" is a common admonition among the faithful. What authority could a National Intelligence Estimate have in comparison with God's will? But Bush's signal to dismiss the disturbances of the external world also points to an underlying premise of his policy. Bush's state of war is a state of denial.

September 28, 2006

The Bob Woodward Version

As soon as President Bush finished the first-year commemoration of Hurricane Katrina he turned to the fifth-year anniversary of the September 11 terrorist attacks in order to restore his faltering popularity and set the themes for the Republican Party in the midterm elections campaign. Through a series of speeches he proclaimed that he would "stay the course" in Iraq, which he conflated with his war on terror. Polls, after all, showed that his standing on Iraq was sliding while his standing on terror was steady. His effort to merge one into the other, as he had done since before the invasion, was an act of political alchemy. Speaking at a Republican fundraiser on September 28, he proclaimed, "The party of FDR and the party of Harry Truman has become the party of cut and run."

But on October 5, an unimpressed Senator John Warner, R-Virginia, chairman of the Armed Services Committee, declared that Iraq was "drifting sideways," and that if Bush's policy was to continue it was time to "change the course." On October 8, James A. Baker III, the former secretary of state, a close associate of the elder Bush and now the chairman of the bipartisan Iraq Study Group that will report its recommendations early next year to the president, declared his support for Senator Warner's call to "change the course." "Yes, absolutely. And we're taking a look at other alternatives."

On Tuesday, a *New York Times*/CBS News poll reported, according to the *Times*, that "83 percent of respondents thought that Mr. Bush was either hiding something or mostly lying when he discussed how the war in Iraq was going." That staggering number is the exact mirror image of the 83 percent of respondents in a *Washington Post*/ABC News poll taken in September 2002 who believed Bush had a clear policy and therefore supported the invasion of Iraq.

Why did this change take so long? Why didn't the public figure out the facts earlier? Was the press an obstacle to information and understanding?

The distance between the two polls has also been marked by the publication of two books written by Bob Woodward, *Bush at War*, in the fall of 2002 as the case for invasion was building, and *State of Denial*, published this fall during the greatest violence in Iraq since the invasion ended. In between, just before the 2004 election, Woodward issued *Plan of Attack*, a transitional volume. Woodward's latest volume has provided further documentary evidence to buttress criticisms of Bush's incompetence in Iraq and has contributed to the collapse of Bush's fall political offensive.

In Woodward's *Bush at War*, Bush, Dick Cheney, and Donald Rumsfeld appeared as decisive, commanding, and resolute. In *State of Denial*, the same characters appear as ignorant, arrogant, and out of control. In one book they are principled and stalwart; in the other they are devious and self-serving. Woodward sees no contrast between these obviously contradictory depictions and says merely that "circumstances" have changed. He judges himself to be the same Bob Woodward today that he was before, the same reporter getting the story, the same collector of facts.

Woodward's self-conviction is that he pursues the story as he always has and as a result gets it straight. He insists he has not altered his method of proof, the sort of evidence he seeks and finds persuasive. Was he looking in the wrong places before? Did he change his mind? He rejects any attempt to reconcile his conflicting portraits. He is Sergeant Friday of *Dragnet*: "Just the facts, ma'am." But his exposés almost always require further explication. His confidence about his power to produce the most revealing story is the basis of his limitations. And the apparent earnestness with which he follows his linear method makes him susceptible to the dangerous liaison.

Woodward doesn't see himself in any political context, but as someone who can be trusted to report what he sees and because of this virtue entrusted by insiders with their true accounts. By secret sharing with insiders he is certified to tell the story, and that certification gives him the aura of truth. As the insiders' insider he becomes the Washington journalists' journalist. He remains assured of the power of his method—matter over mind. In his books, Woodward is the constant narrator and hidden protagonist. Now Woodward becomes Pirandello: *Six Characters in Search of an Author.*

Though Woodward presents himself as antiseptic, wearing a white lab coat and rubber gloves, immune to the political infections he handles, he has made obvious choices to devote himself to certain stories that might have clear consequences rather than others, and these stories have led his readers down a winding road. It is not only the circumstances that have changed; his perception of them has shifted as well, though he does not acknowledge it. Woodward's demurrals obscure his political journey over the past decade.

On one level, the Woodward story is a transparent, easily reported tale of a Washington player who in his own idiosyncratic way represents the drift of chattering class conventional wisdom, from envious contempt for Bill Clinton (and Al Gore) to blind infatuation with Bush the hero to sudden disdain for Bush the failure.

In the 1990s, Woodward hopped aboard the pseudo-scandal bandwagon, hoping to bring down a future president, Gore, by relying once again on a Deep Throat in the FBI. Instead of former Deputy Director Mark Felt, Woodward's Watergate source, he was promoted, befitting his stature, gaining then Director Louis Freeh as his source. Freeh had his own motives. As director of a bureau beset by scandal and mismanagement, threatened with evisceration by the cannibals in the Republican Congress, he threw in his lot with them. Congressional investigations into the FBI screeched to a halt. Freeh assigned more than one thousand agents to a criminal probe of campaign finance corruption in the 1996 Clinton-Gore campaign, the largest FBI investigation in its history until after September 11.

Woodward's drumbeat of stories portended the unmaking of the vice president. His byline appeared on pieces flatly reporting that the Chinese government had siphoned funds into the Clinton-Gore campaign. Here is Woodward on February 13, 1997: "A Justice Department investigation into improper political fund-raising activities has uncovered evidence that representatives of the People's Republic of China sought to direct contributions from foreign sources to the Democratic National Committee before the 1996 presidential campaign, officials familiar with the inquiry said."

On March 2, 1997, as Republicans demanded the appointment of a special prosecutor to investigate Gore, Woodward weighed in with a 2,700-word story on Gore as "solicitor-in-chief." But Woodward's stories came to naught. In the end, no special prosecutor was named, a Republican dominated Senate committee issued a report admitting the charges were baseless, and not a single Clinton administration official was indicted for wrongdoing. Thinking he was a big-game hunter, Woodward had played paintball. But Woodward's splattering of Gore helped set the stage for the Republican smear campaign of 2000. To the degree that Woodward damaged Gore's reputation, he contributed to the narrow vote margin that wound up with the Supreme Court giving the presidency to George W. Bush.

On Bush, Woodward is the storyteller whose self-amazement at the twists and turns of his own stories provides a dramatic element. As he draws back the curtain, he presents his astonishment as the emotion to be mimicked by the audience. It's a manufactured surprise that genuinely surprises him. The reaction to his recent exposés derives impact from his confabulation of the characters in his two previous books. He fails to grasp his complicity in creating the stereotypes he's now debunking. For Woodward, surprise is the lesson—it's the big story. And it's his state of denial.

Woodward's paramount claim of authority is that he has unparalleled access to the inside. But his surprise is the proof he was never an insider. He's not blinkered by being too much the insider, as some critics assert, but by the illusion of being an insider.

The Bush administration critique of Woodward's latest book is that he has provided an outlet for losers. Rather than being the story of the insiders and the winners, like *Bush at War*, this is the tale of the defeated. "In a book like this," White House press secretary Tony Snow briefed on September 29, "you're going to see people who are on the losing side of arguments being especially outspoken about their opinions and nobody will listen to them."

The things Woodward discovered were not what the Bush administration was prepared for him to find. In *Bush at War*, he was leaked National Security Council documents with official approval and given unexampled access to top officials, including hours of valuable face time with the president himself. Woodward, in fact, had never had much access to a president before. He confused the interviews with access to truth and perhaps intimacy.

Woodward was even more expansive in his laudatory description of Bush during his TV interviews than in the book itself. On CNN's *Larry King Live*, on November 18, 2002, Woodward explained that Bush was "very reflective about how he digested the presidency, what he had learned, what he had learned from his father, some of the convictions he had." (In *State of Denial*, we learn some of what Bush ignored from his father.) "Bush is in control," Woodward continued. (In *State of Denial*, we learn some of what the president didn't know and when he didn't know it.) Woodward also rebutted the notion that Vice President Cheney had amassed unusual power in his office. "There is this idea out in the land that Cheney is really secretly running things, or somebody else is running things," Woodward explained. "Cheney is the first adviser in many ways, but the president makes the decisions. He's the one who makes the calls." (In *State of Denial*, we learn about Cheney's unbound power.)

A month later, on December 11, 2002, as Bush began ratcheting up the campaign for an invasion of Iraq, Woodward appeared again on *Larry King Live*, to lend his credibility to Bush's motives. "He is very, being very practical about this," said Woodward. In *Bush at War* Woodward did what the administration could not do for itself. The renowned journalist lent his reputation to the image of Bush as Karl Rove wished him to be portrayed—as a master of men. Bush's political strategist and others in the administration had figured out Woodward's method and timeworn plot structure and filled it up. They calculated that he would report without context and promote the carefully arranged access as the ultimate truth. The still glistening veneer of Watergate made the sheen Woodward put on Bush that much more believable. But in the run-up to the Iraq war, Woodward's informative method had the effect of helping to cover up the disinformation campaign. Woodward's objectivity was the most convincing mode for spin.

Given Woodward's past close cooperation, the Bush administration is now suffering a profound sense of betrayal. In *State of Denial* Woodward has relied upon malcontents, which is what makes this book his most valuable and telling since *All the President's Men*, also, one remembers, based on sources who were outside the charmed circle of power. The anecdotes that cut to the bone in *State of Denial* come from those shunted to the periphery.

For all the nuggets of gold he has unearthed, Woodward's mining of sources has characteristically missed potentially rich veins. Once again, he is omniscient without discernment. The jagged pieces of information he has dug up are smoothed over by his authorial authority. He often doesn't follow up on his best material because he is chained to his one-dimensional objectivity.

State of Denial begins in 2000, with George H. W. Bush fretful about George W. Bush's utter ignorance of foreign policy, and the elder Bush's securing Prince Bandar bin Sultan, the Saudi ambassador to the United States, a longtime friend and ally of the former president's, as tutor. "Bandar," Woodward reports George W. Bush saying at an early encounter, "I guess you're the best asshole who knows about the world. Explain to me one thing . . . Why should I care about North Korea?" Woodward quotes the former president speaking to Bandar in the immediate aftermath of September 11 about the current one: "He's having a bad time. Help him out." However delicious these and the other Bandar stories, Woodward never ponders the House of Saud/House of Bush family ties or the appropriateness of the father entrusting his son's education to a Saudi prince and its implications for U.S. policy.

Similarly, in describing the blackballing of State Department experts from the civil reconstruction team in post-invasion Iraq by Cheney and a "cabal" in his office, Woodward never defines who or what this "cabal" might be. Woodward also mentions that Iraqi exile leader Ahmed Chalabi had influential "patrons" within the administration, but doesn't say who they were. The words "neoconservative" and "neoconservatism" do not appear in *State of Denial.*

The contradictions among his various books on Bush don't concern Woodward. They might bother him if he demonstrated an interest in the motives of the individuals he writes about, and their politics, histories, and ideas. But these are beyond his ken. Woodward's *State of Denial,* in its implicit repudiation of his previous work, stands at the far end in the recent literature of political disillusionment from Francis Fukuyama's *America at the Crossroads: Democracy, Power and the Legacy of Neoconservatism.* In it, one of the progenitors of neoconservatism agonizingly comes to terms with its unintended consequences. "I have concluded," Fukuyama writes, "that neoconservatism, as both a political symbol and a body of thought, has evolved into something that I can no longer support."

That sort of self-conscious reappraisal is alien to Woodward, who clings to the fallacy of objectivity. He continues his adamant claim that he is consistent, operating as usual with the same tools and same approach. Because he accumulates stories in the same way, he cannot see or admit that some of them make others false. All the stories, as he understands it, are factual, so how can they be at odds?

By his inability to acknowledge that he has changed, Woodward sells himself short. In *State of Denial,* chronicling the "losing side," the opponents of the prevailing insiders, his vitality as a reporter has been restored. But Tony Snow is more cogent on Woodward than Woodward. The Bush administration, from the start, for good or ill, has had him dead to rights.

October 11, 2006

Instant Messages

Maf54 (7:37:27 PM): how my favorite young stud doing

"Maf54" is Mark A. Foley, the congressman who represented the wealthy district of Palm Beach, Florida, and chaired the Missing and Exploited Children's Caucus of the House of Representatives, writing an e-mail in 2003 to a teenage former House page, one of the young interns who run errands for members of Congress. When several of his instant message chats and e-mails to pages were exposed last week, Foley resigned. One page, who had forwarded Foley's e-mail messages to a congressional staffer with the description "sick sick sick sick," told his parents, who in turn told their Republican congressman, who told the House Republican leaders, who kept the sexual predator in their midst a secret.

Maf54 (7:39:32 PM): you need a massage

As Republican control of Congress in the midterm elections teeters on the precipice, the party leaders suddenly find themselves rediscovering the harsh reality of Richard Nixon's commentary on the Watergate scandal, that it's not the crime that kills you but the coverup.

Maf54 (7:47:11 PM): good so your getting horny

Mark Foley was elected in the so-called Republican revolution of 1994. He was a voluble, excitable, and genial member, involved in various plots against Speaker Newt Gingrich, a shrill right-winger, for not being hard-line enough, and yet at the same time adopting the stance of a social moderate. Foley's particular interest was in legislation protecting children; he most recently sponsored a bill to protect them from online sex predators.

Maf54 (7:55:02 PM): completely naked?

From the moment he arrived on the scene, many people in the press and politics knew that Foley was gay, among several gays in the Republican Party. As the Republicans demonized gays for partisan advantage, the party became the largest walk-in closet in Washington. After the scandal broke, one gay Republican described Foley to me as incredibly indiscreet, groping young men in public places. Almost everyone on Capitol Hill knew that Foley spent an inordinate amount of time hanging out with pages.

Maf54 (7:55:51 PM): cute butt bouncing in the air

Foley's obvious vulnerability did not inhibit him from holding forth during the impeachment trial of President Clinton: "It's vile. It's more sad than anything else, to see someone with such potential throw it all down the drain because of a sexual addiction."

Maf54 (8:00:53 PM): i like steamroom

Republican leaders have known about Foley's preying on pages since at least 2001. As soon as hints of their coverup were revealed, they began falling over each other offering shifting and conflicting stories. The congressman first contacted by the parents of one page, Representative Rodney Alexander, said he first informed Thomas Reynolds, chairman of the National Republican Congressional Committee. Shortly after Reynolds learned about Foley, Foley gave the Republican committee $100,000. Speaker Dennis Hastert at first claimed he had learned about Foley only last week, but then admitted he had known for almost a year. Majority

Leader John Boehner said he learned nearly a year ago and had passed on the information to the speaker, who told him, "We're taking care of it." In 2005, Foley said, "We track library books better than we do sexual predators."

Maf54 (8:01:21 PM): i am hard as a rock ... so tell me when your reaches rock

This week, Foley announced he was an alcoholic, entered a rehabilitation clinic, and said a Catholic priest had molested him as a child. The FBI began an investigation. Hastert, who had tried to downplay the scandal as about "overly friendly" e-mails, referred the matter to the Bush Justice Department to try to limit any probe into the coverup. White House press secretary Tony Snow pooh-poohed the scandal as "simply naughty e-mails." One Republican congressman declared that anyone in the leadership who knew should resign. Another returned contributions from the NRCC as tainted. The conservative *Washington Times* editorialized, "Resign, Mr. Speaker."

Maf54 (8:08:31 PM): get a ruler and measure it for me

In 2004, Republicans galvanized the turnout of their base voters through referendums against gay marriage in sixteen swing states. This June, Hastert unveiled the Republican platform for the 2006 campaign, the "American Values Agenda." Atop his Web site he posted: "Hastert Drives Effort to 'Keep Kids Safe in Cyberspace.'" Now, the Republican leaders' blame casting resembles the last scene of *The Treasure of the Sierra Madre*, in which the varmints battle each other as their gold dust blows away.

Maf54 (8:10:40 PM): take it out

Xxxxxxxxx (8:10:54 PM): ... my mom is yelling

Maf54 (8:11:06 PM): ok

Xxxxxxxxx (8:14:02 PM): back

Maf54 (8:14:37 PM): cool hope se didnt see any thing

October 5, 2006

Queer and Loathing on Capitol Hill

The spectacle of hypocrisy, impunity, and corruption engulfing the Republican Congress has its origins in its rise in 1994, extolled as its "revolution." At first came the Republican Lenin, Speaker Newt Gingrich, determined to annihilate his enemies and extirpate the "counterculture." But after he shut down the federal government twice and was cited for ethics violations, Republicans on the eve of the impeachment trial of President Clinton forced Gingrich's resignation. (They had private knowledge: Gingrich promptly abandoned his second wife for the mistress he had maintained on the House payroll for years.)

The next designated speaker, Bob Livingston, resigned almost at once when pornographer Larry Flynt threatened to release tape recordings of Livingston's moaning with a mistress, which Flynt had purchased from the scorned woman. In that vacuum, the most powerful figure in the House, then whip and later Majority Leader Tom DeLay, the former exterminator from Sugar Land, Texas, inserted a dull, reliable frontman as speaker— Dennis Hastert, known as "Coach," for having coached high school wrestling in small-town Illinois, his greatest previous distinction.

DeLay was the Republican Stalin, the ruthless consolidator and centralizer. His "K Street Project" forged an iron triangle of lobbyists, special interests, and Republicans whom he believed would rule forever. But DeLay overreached and was indicted for corruption. His master gone, Hastert was left to fend for himself.

When the story broke about the happy-go-lucky sexual predator, Mark Foley, the Republican congressman from Palm Beach, Florida, who had been luring teenage congressional pages to his townhouse of iniquity, Hastert lumbered forth like an agitated but dazed bear. "The people who want to see this thing blow up," he said, "are ABC News"—the network that first broadcast the story—"and a lot of Democratic operatives, people funded by George Soros," a Jewish Hungarian-born international financier who funds liberal causes.

Despite his demonizing of the rootless cosmopolitan, GOP staff aides have trooped day after day before the suddenly reassembled House Ethics Committee to offer testimony that Hastert and other leaders were well informed for years of Foley's preying. And these and other aides have been exposed as a network of mostly closeted gays who advanced and protected one another while working for politicians whose careers were propelled by gay bashing. The unmasking of Republican Capitol Hill as an unreconstructed bastion of self-loathing "Boys in the Band" has excited leaders of the religious right to demand a witch hunt.

As Christians battle Sodomites under the crashing Republican "big tent," several high-wire acts have fallen to earth. Last week, Representative Bob Ney of Ohio pleaded guilty to bribery, caught in the tangled web of Republican super-lobbyist Jack Abramoff. Despite his plea, Ney refused to quit his seat. This week, another Republican congressman, the wacky Curt Weldon of Pennsylvania, renowned for his conspiracy theories and personal hunt for WMD in Iraq, came under investigation for corrupt practices. His daughter, whose lobbying firm, Solutions North America Inc., worked on behalf of friends of Slobodan Milosevic and a Russian gas company out of her father's congressional office, was raided by the FBI. (True to form, Weldon charged that the FBI was operating as a tool of former President Clinton.)

The beset Hastert rushed to be embraced by President Bush as though the White House were a sanctuary. There, Karl Rove's assistant Susan Ralston (formerly Abramoff's assistant) had resigned for facilitating Abramoff's access to and favors for and from Rove and others, including Ken Mehlman, Republican National Committee chairman and former White House political director. This week another Republican congressman, John Doolittle of California, announced he was turning cooperative witness in the continuing federal investigation.

Out in the countryside of red-state America, the Republican Party has turned into a force field of negative attraction. Hastert's offer to help his members' campaigns is being met with nearly universal rejection. Even Representative Don Sherwood of Pennsylvania, a "traditional values" Republican who settled out of court in a $5.5 million suit filed by his mistress for attempting to strangle her, has refused Hastert's blighting presence. Sherwood, for his part, is flooding his district with a TV ad: "I made a mistake that nearly cost me the love of my wife."

Sidney Blumenthal

The concatenation of scandals is shattering the remaining shards of the "revolution." "Reform" has metastasized into the Abramoff scandal. The "culture war" has degenerated into the Foley coverup. And Dennis Hastert has transmuted from omnipotent Leonid Brezhnev into ghostly Konstantin Chernenko, presiding over the final decrepit stage.

October 19, 2006

The Intervention

The post-midterm-elections politics over Iraq have already begun. Many serious factors weigh on President Bush's mind as he speaks about his quagmire. Besides the state of the war and the stability of the Iraqi government, the one that he stresses repeatedly and spontaneously is the commission on Iraq policy chaired by former Democratic Representative Lee Hamilton and, most important, James A. Baker III, the elder Bush's close associate and his secretary of state, who is scheduled to report to Congress and the president after the elections, when, presumably, one or both houses of Congress will fall to the Democrats. A new Democratic House (and perhaps Senate) will be receptive to Baker's proposals. But will Bush?

Baker, the ultimate cold-eyed realist and authority figure who field-marshaled the strategy in Florida that secured the presidency for Bush, has publicly suggested in the past three weeks that he will offer policy changes. Since then, Bush has plunged into rhetorical contortions to explain that he is "staying the course," that he is altering his "tactics," and, finally, that he never said "stay the course." He has adopted the Groucho Marx doctrine: Who are you going to believe, me or your lying eyes, or, in this case, ears?

Bush is engaged in a shadow politics of fending off Baker that he can't admit and that require new disingenuous explanations for rejection even before receiving Baker's report. But will consummate political player Baker permit a dynamic in which he is humiliated and join the ranks of the dismissed and discarded, like "good soldier" Colin Powell? If Baker, taking his cue from Bush's rebuke, simply closes ranks, what would have been his

113

point, except to highlight his failure at an attempted rescue? By undermining Baker, especially beforehand, Bush sends a signal that he is determined to maintain his counterproductive strategies in Iraq and the Middle East. Yet his tightening coil will trigger further attempts among U.S. allies and Arab governments to disentangle themselves.

In a small office of the U.S. Institute of Peace in downtown Washington, the Baker-Hamilton Commission (aka Iraq Study Group) has been listening to the unvarnished assessments of Middle East experts, former intelligence officers and other government officials, and a host of journalists with experience in the region. Though its report is yet unwritten and none of the witnesses have divulged their testimony, the commission's recommendations are apparent from Baker's statements and those close to him. Baker has made clear that stabilizing Iraq demands a new strategy for the whole Middle East. He favors restarting the peace process between Israel and the Palestinian territories with a strong U.S. hand. And he urges direct diplomatic negotiations with Syria and Iran. "I personally believe in talking to your enemies. Neither the Syrians nor the Iranians want a chaotic Iraq," Baker has said.

"The Iraq situation is not winnable in any real sense of the word 'winnable,'" said Richard N. Haass, the president of the Council on Foreign Relations, who was chief of the Middle East desk of the National Security Council for the elder Bush and director of policy planning in the State Department during President Bush's first term, last week. Haass's views are a surrogate for Baker's, as well as those of Brent Scowcroft, who was the former President Bush's national security advisor and who remains close to both him and Baker.

In "A New Middle East," an article in *Foreign Affairs*, the journal of the Council on Foreign Relations, and a shorter version of that article in the *Financial Times*, Haass lays out the outline of the Baker plan that will be presented to Bush. His analysis ruthlessly casts aside Bush's high-flown rhetoric and attributes its emptiness to Bush's failures. He writes:

> Visions of a new Europe-like Middle East that is peaceful, prosperous and democratic will not be realized. Much more likely is the emergence of a new Middle East that will cause great harm to itself and the world.

The American era was one in which, after the Soviet Union's demise, the US enjoyed unprecedented influence and freedom to act. What brought it to an end after less than two decades? Topping the list is the Bush administration's decision to attack Iraq and its conduct of the operation and resulting occupation.

On Wednesday, Bush held a press conference that can only be interpreted as a preemptive repudiation of Baker. Of course, other motives underlay the press conference as well. It was an effort to repackage Bush's unpopular Iraq policy on the eve of the elections and to demonstrate that he is in charge of circumstances that have careened out of control.

In his remarks, Bush digressed at length to give rote explanations that were elementary, irrelevant, or misleading. His supposed admissions of error were attempts at deflecting responsibility. Rather than stating the facts that his Coalition Provisional Authority in Iraq had forced the disbanding of the Iraqi army and the civil service (by banning those with Baathist Party membership, which included nearly every bureaucrat), he passively said, "We overestimated the capability of the civil service in Iraq to continue to provide essential services to the Iraqi people." And: "We did not expect the Iraqi army, including the Republican Guard, to melt away in the way that it did in the face of advancing coalition forces."

Sticking to his Karl Rove-inspired script before the elections, Bush said the word "victory" as often as possible and even explained that if he didn't do that, public opinion would falter: "I fully understand that if the people think we don't have a plan for victory, that they're not going to support the effort." Having given "victory" a cynical signature, he brought up the Baker commission, setting terms for his acceptance of its proposals. "My administration will carefully consider any proposal that will help us achieve victory." As far as can be determined, this "victory" consists of yet to be determined "benchmarks" to be negotiated with the Iraqi government, whose prime minister, Nouri al-Maliki, hours before Bush's press conference, denounced the idea of benchmarks or "timetables."

When Bush was asked if he supported Baker's suggestion of negotiations with Iran, he knocked it down, putting the onus entirely on the Iranians and making any negotiations dependent on their acceptance of U.S.–European demands not to develop nuclear weapons. Baker's idea is not tied to those conditions. On Syria, Bush reiterated his old position and said, "They know our position, as well." Since they already know it, there is no need for the diplomatic initiative Baker proposes.

While giving the back of his hand to Baker, Bush went out of his way to lavish praise on his secretary of defense, Donald Rumsfeld. "And I'm satisfied of how he's done all his jobs," said Bush. "He is a smart, tough, capable administrator." Once again, Bush was deciding in favor of Rumsfeld.

On Tuesday, the day before the press conference, Rumsfeld acted as the blunt truth teller. On Sunday, Bush had said, "We've never been 'stay the course.'" But Rumsfeld called reports about any Bush plan to reverse course "nonsense," adding that "of course" Bush was "not backing away from 'stay the course.'"

Now it's Baker's move.

October 26, 2006

Rove's Last Campaign

Karl Rove remains supremely confident, assuring fretful party leaders that Congress will continue to be under their control despite the stream of new polls revealing previously impregnable Republican incumbents suddenly vulnerable. "I believe Karl Rove," President Bush's chief of staff, Joshua Bolten, proclaimed in a faith-based confessional. While hardly any Republican candidates are running on the Bush record, many are airing TV commercials separating themselves from Bush, and few will even appear on a public platform with him, Republicans cling to Rove's Svengali-like reputation like a life raft. Only Rove stands between the president and the deep blue sea.

Now, however, it is apparent that Rove's short-term ploys have undermined long-term Republican possibilities. His tactical successes have laid the groundwork for strategic failure. His polarizing and paranoid politics have been an intrinsic aspect of Bush's consistently radical presidency, which may be checked and balanced for the first time with the election of the 110th Congress. Rove's legacy may be to leave Republicans with a regional Southern party whose constrictive conservatism fosters a solid Democratic North.

Rove's dismissal of the very notion of a political center was enabled by September 11, which provided him with dramatic material to stigmatize the opposition as dangerously soft and to turbo-charge inflammatory social issues such as gay marriage. By defending hearth and home from enemies at the door and behind closed doors, Rove maximized turnout of the galvanized hardcore.

Yet Rove did not achieve his ambition of a grand realignment of American politics. In Bush's second term, Rove attempted to force privatization of Social Security, but Bush's plan never received even a single committee hearing in Congress. Hurricane Katrina exposed the corrupt political swamp of his government. And Iraq corroded the thin mandate Bush had left.

After having set the theme of the midterm elections campaign as "staying the course" in Iraq, Bush declared a week ago that he had never uttered the phrase he had used dozens of times. Nonetheless, on the stump, he follows the Rove script of politicizing terror, claiming that the opposition is unwilling to defend the country and is un-American. Speaking in the heavily Republican small towns where he is welcome to campaign, Bush turns torture and warrantless domestic surveillance into rhetorical points proving the Democrats' betrayal, whipping up crowds to shout, "Just say no." Bush: "When it comes to questioning terrorists, what's the Democrat answer?" "Just say no!" Bush: "Their approach comes down to this: The terrorists win and America loses!"

Though Bush has abandoned his "staying the course" slogan, Rove explains that the administration's Iraq war policy is clear and simple: "The real plan is this: Fight, beat 'em, win." His formulation, in the spirit of the cheerleading squad at the University of Utah, which he attended, is aimed less at the Shiite-dominated government of Iraq, recalcitrant about disbanding murderous militias, than at the disillusioned Republican base, especially white evangelicals, whose support in recent polls has fallen one-third from what it was in 2004.

Frantic Republicans are reduced to raising the specters of racial and sexual panic. In Tennessee, where Harold Ford, Jr., an African American, is running even with the Republican candidate, a Republican National

Committee TV ad produced by a Rove protégé features a blond vixen beckoning in a sultry voice, "Call me, Harold." In Virginia, former Reagan Secretary of the Navy turned Democratic candidate James Webb, who is also an acclaimed novelist, is being attacked for sexually explicit passages in his books written decades ago based on his experiences as a soldier in Vietnam. On these time-honored tactics in the South that inevitably alienate the North, the balance of power in the Senate rests.

It is conjectural but conceivable that had Bush governed after September 11 as he had campaigned in 2000, as a "uniter, not a divider," he might have been able to forge a durable center-right consensus. That would have required appointing prominent Democrats to his Cabinet, reining in his power-mad vice president and secretary of defense, making moderate court nominations, and listening to the voices of skeptical realism on invading Iraq. Imagining this parallel universe underscores how Rove's victories helped pave the way to losing the potential for a lasting majority.

Few people foresaw the consequences of Bush's radicalism, perhaps least of all Bush himself. Last week, I was in Austin for the Texas Book Festival, where I met a woman who had encountered then Governor Bush immediately after the Supreme Court handed down its decision in *Bush v. Gore*. "Can you believe I'm going to be the fucking president?" he said.

November 1, 2006

PART TWO

Repudiation: From the
2006 Elections to the
Baker-Hamilton Report

Downfall of the Culture War

The cultural crackup of conservatism preceded the final political result. For weeks before Election Day, prominent figures on the right threw themselves into their culture war only to be left in the trenches battered, scorned, and disoriented. They were unable to shield themselves through their usual practices. Their prevarications were easily penetrated; derision hurled at their targets backfired; hypocrisy was fully exposed. These self-destructive performances were hardly peripheral to the campaign but instead at the heart of it.

The Bush administration and the Republican Congress could not defend themselves on their public record and urgently needed to change the subject. They required new fields of combat—not the Iraq War, certainly not convicted lobbyist Jack Abramoff, convicted Representative "Duke" Cunningham, investigated Representative Mark Foley, or indicted House Majority Leader Tom DeLay. So they launched offensives on Michael J. Fox's Parkinson's disease, Jim Webb's novels, and gay marriage. Yet battle-hardened cultural warriors—Rush Limbaugh, Lynne Cheney, and the Reverend Ted Haggard, among others—did not find themselves triumphant as in the 2004 campaign, but unexpectedly wounded at their own hands.

The president, vice president, and secretary of defense, meanwhile, marched to their Maginot line to defend the fortifications of the "war president" and his war paradigm ("alternative interrogation techniques" . . . "terrorist surveillance program" . . . "terrorists win, America loses"). Bush, Dick Cheney, and Donald Rumsfeld behaved as though they were the latest in a straight line of descent from heroes past, inheritors of Franklin Roosevelt, Harry Truman, and Winston Churchill. Mythologizing themselves as they struggled to gain support for "victory," they sought to distract from catastrophe by casting deepening failure as inevitable success. Envious of the "Greatest Generation," they claimed its mantle. But elevating themselves into the latter-day versions of the leaders from World War II was delusional imitation as the highest form of self-flattery.

And now the first of the Bush "warrior-heroes" has fallen. Although President Bush had said he would keep Rumsfeld in his job until the end of his term, on Wednesday Bush announced Rumsfeld's resignation, naming former CIA director (under the elder Bush) Robert Gates as his replacement. Currently serving on the Iraq Study Group led by James Baker, secretary of state under the elder Bush, Gates remains close to the realist foreign policy circle that has been excluded and dismissed for six years. With Gates' appointment, it appears that the son is at last acknowledging the father.

The cultural style of the Bush warriors is the latest wrinkle in one of the most enduring modes of antimodern aesthetic expression. "Kitsch is mechanical and operates by formulas," wrote art critic Clement Greenberg in his seminal essay, "Avant-Garde and Kitsch," in 1939. "Kitsch is vicarious experience and faked sensations. Kitsch changes according to style, but remains always the same. Kitsch is the epitome of all that is spurious in the life of our times."

Kitsch is imitative, cheap, sentimental, mawkish, and incoherent, and derives its appeal by demeaning and degrading genuine standards and values, especially those of modernity. While the proponents of the faux retro style claim to uphold tradition, they are inherently reactive and parasitic, their words and products a tawdry patchwork, hastily assembled as declarations against authentic complexity and ambiguity, which they stigmatize as threats to the sanctity of an imaginary harmonious order of the past that they insist they and their works represent. Kitsch presumes to be based on old rules, but constantly traduces them.

The Bush kitsch warriors have created a cultural iconography that attempts to inspire deference to the radical making of an authoritarian presidency. These warriors pose as populists, fighting a condescending liberal elite. Wealthy, celebrated, and influential, their faux populism demands that they be seen however as victims.

Having risen solely by association with sheer political power and economic force (News Corp., etc.), the cultural charlatans become the arbiters of social standing (especially in a capital lacking a secure and enduring establishment). In Washington, the more status-conscious elements of the press corps, aspiring to the shabby fringes of the talk-show media (the low end of the entertainment state), often serve as publicity agents in the guise of political experts, and it is from this platform that they then derive greater status. Indeed, the conservative kitsch cultural industry is centered in Washington, where Republican political power has protected philistinism from the ravages of cosmopolitanism, unlike in New York, Los Angeles, or Chicago.

Under Ronald Reagan, conservative kitsch was the last nostalgic evocation for a glowing small-town America before the New Deal, with its raucous city dwellers, brain-trusters, and an aristocratic president gleefully swatting "economic royalists." Reagan drew his raw material for "morning again in America" from an idealized view of his boyhood in Dixon, Illinois, where his father was the town Catholic drunk, rescued at last only by a federal government job. Reagan also had a well of experience acting in movies romanticizing small-town life, produced by the Jewish immigrant moguls of Hollywood for whom these gauzy pictures enabled them to assimilate into a country that had richly rewarded them but in which they remained outsiders.

Bush's America contains no nostalgic evocation of small-town life. The scion of the political dynasty, raised in the oil-patch outpost of Midland, Texas, where the streets are named for Ivy League universities, and whose family retained its summer home in its New England base of Kennebunkport, Maine, attended all the right schools as a legacy, one of the last of his kind before more meritocratic standards were imposed and religious and racial quotas abolished. George W. Bush's inchoate resentment at the alteration of the world of his fathers impelled the son of privilege to align with the cultural warriors of faux populism.

The pathology of Bush's kitsch is the endless reproduction of vicarious hatred of the "other" that is the threat to the sanctity of what kitsch represents. The "other" lies beyond the image of the lurking terrorist to the lurking Democrat—"America loses." "You're either with us or with the terrorists," Bush said famously. You either have a "pre-9/11" mind-set or a "post-9/11" one, according to his strategist Karl Rove, who carefully set the terms of demonization. In the great act of kitsch, Bush et al. apotheosized their fiasco in Iraq into a battle against Hitler—"appeasers" . . . "Islamofascism." By impersonating a historical context, they projected themselves into it.

Unlike the kitsch before and during the Reagan era, the Bush warriors' kitsch lies beyond unintentional camp. Their kitsch lacks more than irony or self-consciousness. It is deliberately sarcastic, mean-spirited, fearsome, and fearful. Their unbridled bullying reveals their deep fears within. Their personal disintegrations expose what they fear most about themselves. Whether it is accused sexual harasser Bill O'Reilly (the biggest right-wing TV star), thrice-divorced drug addict Rush Limbaugh (the biggest radio star), or closeted gay drug abuser Ted Haggard, their self-destructive patterns invariably emerge.

The results of exit polls on election night 2006 showed that the voters were most outraged by "corruption" as well as the predictable issue of Iraq. This revulsion at "corruption" was more than the sordid wheeling and dealing of the Republican congressional barons. It was disgust at the moral hypocrisy and false sanctimony of the cultural warriors and the transparent fakery of Bush's imagery. The fate of the Senate turned on many contests, including crucial ones in Missouri and Virginia. In Missouri, an initiative that would authorize embryonic stem cell research that could lead to cures of many diseases divided the candidates. Actor Michael J. Fox made a TV commercial for the Democrat, Claire McCaskill. Looking straight into the camera, with no imagery other than his constantly swaying body, racked with the effects of his medication for Parkinson's disease, Fox made a simple appeal wholly on the basis of the stem cell research issue. Fox was a promising young actor whose career came to a halt when his disease seized control of him. Now he plays only himself.

Immediately, Rush Limbaugh threw himself into the breach against the new enemy. Earlier this year, he had declared, "What's good for Al-Qaeda is good for the Democratic Party in this country today." Mocking Fox by spastically wriggling in his chair as he spoke on his syndicated radio show, Limbaugh told listeners that Fox's jerky movements were "purely an act" and that he'd whack him "if you'd just quit bobbing your head." In the ensuing uproar, Limbaugh steadfastly refused to apologize. He depicted his mockery and physical threats as expressions of conservative conviction: "I stand by what I said. I take back none of what I said. I wouldn't rephrase it any differently. It is what I believe. It is what I think. It is what I have found to be true." As the criticism built, he acknowledged: "So I will bigly, hugely admit that I was wrong and *I will* apologize to Michael J. Fox, *if I am wrong* in characterizing his behavior on this commercial as an act."

Limbaugh's act as an embattled profile in courage continued to influence his followers. In Wyoming, the hard-pressed Republican incumbent,

124

Representative Barbara Cubin, after a televised debate, vented her frustrations by turning on her Libertarian opponent, Thomas Rankin, who has multiple sclerosis and uses a wheelchair. "If you weren't sitting in that chair, I'd slap you across the face," she said. After apologizing, she explained that she had been inspired by Limbaugh's example in his attack on Fox. Cubin narrowly survived on Election Day. But, in Missouri, McCaskill ousted the Republican, Senator James Talent, in an indispensable victory in turning the Senate Democratic.

In Virginia, Senator George Allen had planned for this race to serve as the trampoline for a presidential campaign in 2008, where he expected to become the consensus conservative candidate and thus the Republican nominee. His opponent, James Webb, had a résumé that not only included winning the Navy Cross in combat in the Vietnam War, and serving as Reagan's Navy secretary, but a career as an acclaimed novelist. His novels, based on his experience in Vietnam, are realistic, harsh, and disturbing. For the beleaguered Allen and his Republican supporters, Webb's writings provided a source for out-of-context negative attacks. Scenes depicting unsettling sexual behavior were lifted to taint Webb as a pervert. Allen ran TV spots with Webb's words obliterated by huge red letters: "Censored." On October 27, Lynne Cheney, wife of the vice president, who bills herself "Grandmother of the United States," but who is also an ardent conservative, resident scholar at the American Enterprise Institute, and ferocious former chairman of the National Endowment for the Humanities during the Reagan period (during which she established her bona fides as a cultural warrior), appeared on CNN to discuss her new children's book, *Our 50 States: A Family Adventure Across America,* and to attack Webb's novels. "His novels are full of sexual explicit references to incest, sexually explicit references—well, you know, I just don't want my grandchildren to turn on the television set," she told interviewer Wolf Blitzer. In fact, in 1981, she had published a novel, written in the kitsch soft-core pornographic style of a Harlequin romance, featuring a bisexual heroine in the Old West. To wit: "The women who embraced in the wagon were Adam and Eve crossing a dark cathedral stage—no, Eve and Eve, loving one another as they would not be able to once they ate of the fruit and knew themselves as they truly were." The attack on Webb as a novelist failed; he narrowly defeated Allen. On Amazon.com, used copies of Cheney's novel are selling for $495.

In Colorado, as Republicans tried to muster support for their candidates through a statewide initiative against gay marriage, a homosexual prostitute named Mike Jones disclosed that the Reverend Ted Haggard, president of the National Association of Evangelicals, confidant and one of the most influential backers of President Bush, a participant in a weekly White House telephone conference call with evangelical leaders, was one of his regular clients for three years and also a purchaser of methamphetamine. After initially denying the accusations, Haggard resigned from his New Life Church in Colorado Springs and issued an apology. "I am a deceiver and a liar," he said. "There is a part of my life that is so repulsive and dark that I've been warring against it all of my adult life." Haggard's self-loathing confession continued his projective campaign against homosexuality as satanic, even within himself. However personal his drama, the fallout had a political effect. In Colorado, Democrats took the governorship and a congressional seat.

At the White House, on October 25, Bush summoned a gaggle of conservative columnists to the Oval Office. He confided in them his self-comparison to presidents past. "That's what makes this more difficult—I don't know what Harry Truman was feeling like, or Franklin Roosevelt."

The day before, the White House had summoned dozens of right-wing radio talk-show hosts to conduct interviews with officials to rally the Republican faithful before the election. Vice President Cheney, interviewed by Scott Hennen of WDAY in Fargo, North Dakota, posed as the virile tough guy. Hennen asked Cheney if he was in favor of waterboarding detainees, an interrogation technique that is a form of torture. "Would you agree a dunk in water is a no-brainer if it can save lives?" "Well," said Cheney, "it's a no-brainer to me, but I—for a while there, I was criticized as being the vice president for torture. We don't torture. That's not what we're involved in." For the next week, the White House issued a series of denials that Cheney had said anything about waterboarding or torture.

Rumsfeld, who had been holding forth for years about his fascination and identification with Churchill, on October 26 held a peevish press conference at the Pentagon in which he said simply, "Back off." His analogies had run their course—but by Wednesday he no longer needed them.

With their fabrication of faux identities, Bush, Cheney, and Rumsfeld were of a piece with the other cultural warriors. Fashioning themselves in the image of historical characters was ultimately fashion. Rather than the real things, they were impersonating the genuine articles. And after the judgment of Election Day, they were revealed as historical reenactors without the costumes.

November 8, 2006

Realignments

The concession by George Allen that confirms that James Webb has won in Virginia, a victory that gives the Democrats a majority in the Senate, completes the party's sweep of both houses of the Congress and ratifies the repudiation of President Bush and his policies, especially in the Iraq war.

Bush's radical presidency was the number one issue in the midterm elections. Republican candidates lived in fear that they would receive calls from the White House suggesting that the president wanted to campaign for them. His last-minute blitz in Montana on behalf of Senator Conrad Burns seemed momentarily to lift the beleaguered incumbent, but virtually the moment Air Force One departed the Republican sank once again, this time for good. In Florida, the Republican candidate for governor, Charles Crist, fled upon the president's arrival at a rally on his behalf in the state capital of Tallahassee. Crist's disloyalty and rudeness, leaving Bush in the lurch, was the better part of wisdom. Crist, like other Republicans caught in the storm, managed to survive only by avoiding him. The once eagerly sought presidential photo-op had become the kiss of death.

Before the spotlight turns to the repositioning of the president, the appointment of a new secretary of defense, and the machinations of the new 110th Democratic Congress, it is worthwhile to sift through the extraordinary election returns, which contain the makings of a further realignment of American politics in the presidential election of 2008 and beyond.

Bush's radical presidency consolidated the grip of Southern conservatism over the Republican Party. He completed the "Southern Strategy" launched by Richard Nixon in 1968 in the aftermath of the civil rights movement, a strategy that assimilated the Dixiecrat George Wallace third party into the Republican ranks. Over time, the strategy that was supposed to be an add-on to the traditional GOP engulfed it. Bush finished the project that Nixon began. Karl Rove, his chief political aide, hypothesized a permanent national majority rooted in a Southern Strategy in which the rest of the country was an add-on. But in his quest for realignment Rove has left a rump regional party mired in the swamps of Dixie. What purpose does Rove with his scenarios of polarization now serve Bush?

After the midterm elections, the GOP has become a regional party of the South. And, in the future, Republicans can only hold their base by asserting their conservatism, which alienates the rest of the country. More than ever, the Republicans are dependent upon white evangelical voters in the South and sparsely populated Rocky Mountain states. The Republican coalition, its much-touted "big tent," has nearly collapsed.

Republicans under Bush are beginning a downward spiral that parallels the decline of the Democrats. From 1968 through 1988, the story of the Democratic Party had been its internal disintegration and reduction to its base. Clinton's presidency served as an interregnum, which might have broken the Republicans had his vice president Al Gore been permitted to assume the office he won by a popular majority but was thwarted by the conservative bloc on the Supreme Court.

The 2006 elections have started to hollow out the Republican Party outside the South. Of the Democratic gains reported thus far (there are still races too close to call), eleven of thirty-six House seats held by Republicans in the Northeast were captured; that is, nearly one-third of the Republicans there were wiped out. In the Midwest, nine of sixty flipped, that is, 15 percent. These Republicans are not the more conservative members, but the most liberal and prominent moderates in their party. According to an unpublished post-election study by Thomas Schaller, a University of Maryland political scientist, fourteen of forty-eight of the most "liberal" Republicans were defeated.

The Democrats who defeated them can be expected to hold these seats indefinitely. Historically Republican districts going back to the founding of the GOP in the Civil War are turning into Democratic bastions. After the failure of Reconstruction, the South became wholly Democratic, the Solid South, and the basis of a Democratic Party that was mostly out of power, unless the Republicans split, until the rise of Franklin D. Roosevelt and the New Deal during the Great Depression. The pre–FDR Republicans, after

Reconstruction, gave up on ever building a two-party system in the South. Instead, in reaction to the Solid South, the Republicans consolidated national power in the Solid North.

This post–Civil War/pre–New Deal pattern is now turned on its head. Voting patterns today almost exactly resemble voting patterns of the late nineteenth and early twentieth centuries, but with the parties in reverse positions.

The Democratic Party that has advanced from the 2006 elections reasserts the Solid North, with inroads in the metropolitan states of the West, and, like the GOP of the past, challenges in the states of the peripheral South such as Arkansas, Tennessee, and Virginia. This Democratic Party has never existed before. It is a center-left party with wings that can flap together. The party's opposition to the Republicans on economic equity and social tolerance are its defining characteristics.

The pace of this realignment is uncertain, but the underlying dynamics are not. That the Senate fell to the Democrats in Virginia is telling about the weakness of the Republicans and suggestive about the future. Senator George Allen represented the fulfillment of the Republican Southern Strategy. He intended to use his win in this contest as a platform for his presidential campaign in 2008. He had already assembled around him throngs of experienced and expensive Republican political consultants. James Webb, who had originally been a Democrat, but became a Republican long ago and rose to be Reagan's secretary of the navy, returned to his roots in response to Bush. His victory represents the emergence of a Democratic Party that even has a new appeal in the upper South.

November 9, 2006

Deep Currents

The midterm elections of 2006 may be among the most momentous in two generations—if their trends carry through the 2008 presidential election and beyond. These changes include a Democratic Congress that reflects a more politically cohesive national majority than any previous one; shifts of crucial constituencies that may represent a decisive repudiation of the Republican Party in its current incarnation; and the emergence of a younger generation that is overwhelmingly Democratic. In retrospect, it is conceivable that the 2006 results will be revealed to be just one movement of a rapidly swinging pendulum whose internal mechanism is a fickle electorate of no discernible loyalties or commitments but propelled by constant and uncontrollable moods of discontent. Or it may be that the long conservative ascendancy has merely encountered a slight stumbling block that will soon be overcome once the difficulties associated with Iraq are neatly squared away. Or it may be that the Democrats are as incorrigibly self-destructive as they were when the Republican era began. Or it may that the newly elected Democrats are really conservative Republicans operating under another party label. But these possibilities are not foretold by the 2006 results.

As in elections past, President Bush's chief strategist, Karl Rove, predicted that his fabled seventy-two-hour get-out-the-vote mobilization would churn the Republicans to victory. In the end, he was not proved wrong that this effort managed to produce a large Republican turnout at the polls, as big as in the midterm elections of 2002, when the Republicans made stunning gains. White evangelicals, who constitute 35 percent of all Republican voters, massed for Republican candidates at levels close to those in 2004—this year's 72 percent was just three points off the prior 75 percent. Once again, evangelicals, by a share of 59 percent, insisted that social issues such as gay marriage were "extremely important." Rove's problem was that only 29 percent of other voters shared that view and that the other side turned out in greater numbers. What he did was his unmaking.

The numbers are both conclusive and suggestive. Exit polls showed that the Democrats won the popular vote by 52 to 46 percent. Given that Bush won the popular vote by three points in 2004, this was a reversal of not six but nine points. An analysis of the actual popular vote for the Senate, however, reveals an even greater Democratic margin of 55 to 42.4 percent. That number also coincidentally corresponds to the margin by which Democrats won women, the greatest margin since 1988. Yet Democrats won independents by an even bigger margin, eighteen points, the greatest spread in House races in twenty-five years. The profile of independents on issue after issue now mostly resembles the profile of Democrats.

One of the largest shifts appeared among Hispanics, the group that Rove targeted most intensively for six years. In 2006, Hispanics went for the Democrats 69 to 30 percent, a ten-point increase in the spread from two years ago. Unpopular as Bush may be today, he has been the most accessible Republican to Hispanics ever, a Spanish speaker from a state with a large Hispanic population. Next time, in 2008, the Republicans do not have a potential candidate who can remotely approach Bush's appeal.

Democrats' gains among Hispanics paralleled and overlapped their gains among Roman Catholics, whom they carried by 55 percent, a ten-point increase over 2004, when Bush defeated liberal Catholic Senator John Kerry in a campaign that enlisted conservative Catholic bishops as allies. Winning back Catholics was a feat exceeded by the gains among white Protestants, where Democrats captured 47 percent, a fourteen-point increase over 2004 and their greatest share since Bill Clinton won in 1992, achieving nearly a draw with Republicans. But the composition of the white Protestant vote this time is different. Clinton, a Southern Baptist, won a sizable percentage of evangelicals, though not a majority, in 1992 and 31 percent in 1996. The white Protestant vote that went Democratic in 2006 was largely mainline non-evangelical Protestant, previously aligned as traditional Republican. White Protestants' break with the GOP came in great part as a recoil from the overbearing evangelical influence.

While voters under thirty were the most favorable age group in 2004 for Kerry, casting 54 percent of their votes for him, Democratic House candidates in 2006 received 60 percent of their votes, compared with 38 percent for Republicans. Nationally, partisan identification breaks 38 percent Democratic to 35 percent Republican, but among those under age thirty the percentages are forty-three to thirty-one in favor of Democrats. This pattern runs as strongly in the West as in the East, the Midwest, and the Pacific states, a clear indication that the Western states are heading out of the Republican camp—out of alliance with the deep South's Republican states and into coalition with the broad majority. In Wyoming and Arizona, where Republicans won elections for the House and Senate, the Democrats would have won by sixteen and fifteen points, respectively, if the elections had been conducted only among under-thirties. In Montana, where Democrat Jon Tester won by 1 percentage point, fewer than three thousand votes, his margin among under-thirties, who were 17 percent of the electorate, was twelve points.

Bush has been the formative political experience for the youngest generation of voters, those eighteen to thirty. Studies of voting preferences show that the experience imprinted on a generation in its twenties largely determines its future political complexion. This generation is the most Democratic generation ever—more Democratic than the youngest voting generations of the New Deal and the 1960s. In generational terms, their political alignment is also logical. As the children of the 1960s generation and the grandchildren of the New Deal generation, they have inherited those generations' political genes. The in-between, more conservative generations—the so-called Silent Generation of the 1950s and their children— are smaller in numbers and weaker in cultural and political influence.

The dramatic turnover of both the House and the Senate should not obscure the profound transformations going on in the states, where ten state legislative chambers switched to the Democrats, and, as political analyst Charlie Cook points out in the *National Journal*, "the Democratic advantage over Republicans in state legislatures went from fifteen seats (3,650 versus 3,635) to 662 seats (3,985 versus 3,323), with gains in every region." Democrats control both chambers in twenty-four states, compared with sixteen for Republicans. Democrats also gained six governorships, giving them a majority of twenty-eight. These political conditions, assuming they are stable or augmented through 2008, set up the Democrats to dominate the redistricting that will follow the 2010 census—and thus potentially the patterns of power in the House for the next decade.

The Southern strategy of the Republican Party, accelerated and radicalized under Bush, has finally created a more than equal reaction in the North. Ten years ago, ten moderate Republican senators, all from the Northeast, met weekly for lunch. After the 2006 election, only three remain, in Pennsylvania and Maine. When they retire they are likely to be replaced by Democrats.

New England was once the bastion of rock-ribbed Republicanism, personified by Senator Prescott Bush of Connecticut, grandfather of the current president. But now, from six New England states, there is only one Republican left standing in the entire House, Christopher Shays, who barely scraped by in a previously safe Republican district. (Republicans won eight other House seats across the country by less than one point, and thirty-four by less than five points. Many of these may be at risk in two years.)

The fatal environment for Republicans in New England is exemplified by New Hampshire, by far the most conservative of the New England states. There, Democratic Governor John Lynch won reelection with 74 percent. As *Washington Post* columnist David Broder wrote: "The Executive Council, which has the power to confirm appointees and approve state contracts, switched from 4-1 Republican to 3-2 Democratic. The state Senate, which Republicans controlled 16-8, is now Democratic by a 14-10 margin. The state House of Representatives, which is dwarfed in size only by the British House of Commons and the U.S. House of Representatives, went from 242-150 Republican, with eight vacancies, to 239-161 Democratic." Both U.S. House seats in New Hampshire fell to the Democrats. In 2008, the Senate seat held by a Republican is suddenly exposed.

In Rhode Island, which has a long history of working-class deference to patrician politicians, Senator Lincoln Chafee, a moderate, even liberal figure, whose father had been a popular U.S. senator and whose own popularity was above 60 percent on Election Day, was defeated by six points. His Republican label alone condemned him.

In states that will be crucial in the 2008 presidential race, Democrats made extraordinary gains. Bush won Iowa by 0.67 percentage points in 2004. This year the Democratic candidate for governor, Chet Culver, swept the race by a ten-point margin, both houses of the Iowa Legislature flipped Democratic, and respected, longtime moderate Republican Representative Jim Leach was ousted. In Colorado, which Bush won by less than five points, the Democrat, Bill Ritter, won by fifteen points, and a House seat previously held by a Republican went Democratic by thirteen points. In Arkansas, which Bush won by ten points, the Democratic candidate for governor, Mike Beebe, won by fifteen. Of all the Southern states, Arkansas is the most progressive and Democratic—the only Confederate Southern state with two Democratic senators. Were a Democratic candidate for president in 2008 to win these states, along with the rest of the states won by Kerry, he or she would comfortably win the White House. This equation does not include Ohio, which Bush won by two points, but which saw a Democratic sweep this year of every statewide office, the governorship, and a Senate seat.

African Americans, meanwhile, were unmoved by any and all Republican overtures. Though the Republicans slated African Americans as candidates for the governorships of Pennsylvania and Ohio, as well as for the Senate in Maryland, not one of the Democrats running against them received less than 75 percent of the African-American vote. The campaign speeches of Secretary of State Condoleezza Rice made not the slightest impression. African Americans remained the most discerning voters.

The strongest race run by any Republican did more than prove the rule of 2006. Arnold Schwarzenegger won reelection as governor of California by 17 percentage points by openly attacking President Bush, firing his Republican chief of staff and hiring a lesbian activist who had worked for his Democratic predecessor as a replacement, and adopting liberal positions across the board. As major figures from California often demonstrate, Schwarzenegger may represent the future of American politics but not the future of the Republican Party. Any Republican attempting this trick in another state would almost certainly be destroyed by the party's right wing. The sui generis character of an overwhelmingly popular Republican governor of California suggests how deviant the national party has become, even since Ronald Reagan.

The modern Republican rise was first apparent in the midterm elections of 1966, in the wake of early frustrations over Vietnam and racial turmoil after the passage of civil rights legislation. The closely fought presidential contest of 1968, whose outcome was hardly inevitable, in which Richard Nixon was elected, was ratified four years later in his forty-nine-state landslide. Nixon's strategy was to revitalize the Republicans as a party by assimilating Southern Democrats and ethnic suburban white-flight Catholics in reaction to a post–New Deal Democratic Party tainted by antiwar dissent, minority protest, and countercultural experimentation—"amnesty, acid and abortion," as Vice President Spiro Agnew captiously put it.

Nixon's Republican majority was the template for Reagan's consolidation. Reagan's grin replaced Nixon's scowl, but the strategy was basically unaltered. Watergate had only temporarily derailed the project. Reagan's chief innovation was to acknowledge and encourage the nascent religious right as an evolved form of Southern Democrats metamorphosing into Southern Republicans.

Unlike Nixon and Reagan, the native and transplanted Californians, or George H. W. Bush, the Connecticut Yankee with shallow roots in the Texas political soil, George W. Bush was the first elected Southern conservative in American history. (The two previous Southern conservatives, John Tyler and Andrew Johnson, acceded to the presidency by the deaths of presidents and never won election in their own right.) By 2000, California had been lost to the Republican coalition through the party's social conservatism and hostility to Hispanic immigrants. Without California, the Republicans became ever more dependent on their Southern base. As the Southern influence grew, traditional moderates from other parts of the country were assailed as "Republicans in name only," though they were the original Republicans.

George W. Bush became the first Republican ever to become president without winning California. Since Herbert Hoover's election in 1928, every elected Republican had either been a Californian (like Hoover, Nixon, and Reagan) or had run with one as vice president (as Dwight Eisenhower did with Nixon). The only Republican in that line to win the presidency on a ticket without a Californian was the elder Bush (with the Indianan Dan Quayle, an ersatz version of one of the Bush sons).

Without California, Bush's coalition was invariably narrow and his conservatism a product of his constricted Southern orbit. While Bush presented himself as the true fulfillment of Reagan, resolving the political tensions of his half-breed father, the idea of Reaganism without California was utterly novel. Bush's conservatism was a far more intensified strain than Reagan's, drawing inspiration from the radical Southern Republican-led Congress of the late 1990s that Bush pretended to disavow in the 2000 campaign in order to present himself as "a uniter, not a divider." The absence of California in the Republican coalition was hardly the main factor in fostering Bush's radicalism, but the changed composition of the party contributed to his insularity.

The strategies of Rove were dictated by the felt necessity of operating within cramped political boundaries as much as by arrogance fed by a craven press corps. Bush's loss of the popular vote in 2000 had had a traumatic impact. The revelation of his covered-up drunken-driving arrest near the end of the campaign that cost him some votes on the religious right was taken as a cautionary lesson to pay special heed to get those voters. Never again would Bush run as anything other than a conservative. But without the intervention of the terrorist attacks of September 11, there can be little doubt that he would have followed in the footsteps of all his predecessors who had lost the popular vote by becoming a one-term president. To the extent that he averted that fate, the politics of fear that has sustained him has been unnatural. Barring further terrorist attacks this hysteria was doomed to exhaustion. Rove's frantic effort to revive it in the closing days of the 2006 elections through sheer name-calling was as essential as it was artificial.

In 2006, as in 2004, Bush and Rove subjected Northern states to their Southern strategies. The border state of Missouri and the split-personality state of Ohio were relentlessly treated as one-dimensionally Southern. But the ploys on gay marriage and stem cell research that had worked in 2004 had lost their magic, and Democrats took Senate seats in both states.

In January, when the 110th Congress is sworn in, it will be the first Congress since the 83rd Republican Congress (swept into office on Eisenhower's coattails) in which the majority party in both chambers is a minority party in the South. While there will be Southerners in the Democratic Congress, their presence is not that of a unitary bloc threatening progressive legislation. In the past, Southerners rose through a one-party system (which denied African Americans voting rights) and, once elected, went unchallenged. The region's political power rested on the seniority of the congressional barons who controlled the chairmanships of the committees. But that Democratic Party is gone with the wind. Now, as the political scientist Thomas Schaller has calculated, the House Republican Conference is 43 percent Southern, more disproportionate than when Dixie ruled the Democrats. As the Democratic majority has become more national than ever, the Republicans are more dominated by their conservative base. Their Southern strategy, perfected by Bush and Rove, has become a downward spiral.

The overriding strategic imperatives for the Democratic Congress, besides restoring the constitutional obligation of oversight of the executive branch, are several-fold. The leaders of the new Congress plan to pass legislation that addresses working- and middle-class economic insecurity. If Bush vetoes it, he will be defined as their antagonist. On domestic policy, therefore, casting Bush as rejectionist works to the Democrats' advantage. On foreign policy, it's more complicated, even treacherous.

In their enthusiasm at finally attaining a measure of power, Democrats have not yet clarified that congressional power is inherently limited in foreign policy. By offering alternative tactics for Iraq that are overly precise, the Democrats may assume a share of the blame for a debacle that properly and solely belongs to Bush. Nonetheless, they can use their powers to illustrate the heedlessness of the president.

Winning Congress does not inevitably lead to winning the White House. Still, it is hard to foresee any single issue deeply dividing the prospective Democratic presidential candidates in 2008, as Vietnam did in the past or even the Iraq war briefly did in 2004 through Howard Dean's campaign. Bush remains president and unrepentant. The impulse for reflection and reform within the Republican Party is nil. From 2004 to 2006, Bush turned victory into dust. What will two more years of Bush bring?

November 30, 2006

All the Father's Men

Even before the electoral repudiation of President Bush, or "Sonny," as Colin Powell refers to him, the guardians of the Bush family trust surfaced as the presumptive executive committee of the executive branch. For years, Bush's father and his former national security team have attempted to rescue the president from himself—and the clutches of Dick Cheney, Donald Rumsfeld, and their neoconservative centurions. Earlier this year the elder Bush quietly approached a retired four-star general to inquire whether he would be willing to replace Rumsfeld, but that premature coup came to naught.

Several of the father's associates personally warned President Bush before the Iraq war that it would lead to sectarian civil war, only to be dismissed with disdain. Immediately after the invasion, James Baker said, "I told him not to do that," a friend of Baker's told me.

The elder Bush's former tennis doubles partner at Houston's exclusive Bayou Club and subsequently his campaign manager and secretary of state, charged for decades with cleaning up family messes, Baker is now chairman of the Iraq Study Group and has assumed the aura of a regent. He is burdened with more tasks than those specified in his commission's brief about Iraq. Not only is he developing a whole new U.S. foreign policy, he is trying to salvage whatever can be retrieved from the wreckage of Bush's presidency for its last two years—and to prevent the Republican Party,

137

already having lost the crown jewel of the Congress, from being permanently tainted.

It is as though a merciless, omniscient narrator has inserted him to undo and rectify everything at the end of a tragedy. F. Scott Fitzgerald, near the conclusion of *The Great Gatsby*, described the reckless scions of privilege: "They were careless people . . . They smashed up things and creatures and then retreated back into their money or their vast carelessness, or whatever it was that kept them together, and let other people clean up the mess they had made."

There are complications. The discrediting and disloyalty of the neoconservatives have not removed them from the play. Just before the impending electoral doom, they scurried off the sinking ship. Richard Perle, former chairman of the Defense Policy Board, put the onus on Bush in an interview in *Vanity Fair*: "At the end of the day, you have to hold the president responsible." Kenneth Adelman, another neocon DPB member, who famously predicted the invasion of Iraq would be a "cakewalk," said of the Bush administration policymakers: "Not only did each of them, individually, have enormous flaws, but together they were deadly, dysfunctional."

Yet the neocons are still plotting to confound Baker. Clifford May, president of the neoconservative Foundation for the Defense of Democracies, and a member of the Iraq Study Group advisory panel, told me that ISG member Edwin Meese, Ronald Reagan's former attorney general, will thwart consensus by opposing the ISG's recommendations.

The neocon logic in favor of the Iraq war was that the road to Jerusalem led through Baghdad. In other words, an invasion would install an Iraqi democracy that would inevitably force the Palestinians to meekly submit to the Israelis. Now near unanimity exists on Baker's commission to reverse that formula, advisory panel members have told me. The central part of a new policy must be, they believe, that the road to Baghdad leads through Jerusalem.

Brent Scowcroft, the elder Bush's former national security adviser, who is very close to Baker, spelled out the notion that security and stability in the region, including Iraq, can only be achieved by reestablishing the Middle East peace process in an article published in the *Washington Post* on July 30. Scowcroft's piece is a précis of Baker's views as well. On September 15, Philip Zelikow, Secretary of State Condoleezza Rice's counselor and a former Scowcroft protégé, echoed Scowcroft's ideas in a speech at

Washington's Middle East Institute. Afterward, Cheney pressured Rice and she rebuked her closest deputy, underlining her own weakness.

Since then the electoral catastrophe has intervened, giving Baker leeway (and sidelining the feeble Rice). Baker even summoned Tony Blair to testify on Tuesday in support of a restart of the Middle East peace process. If Baker were to propose that, he would not explicitly state, though he well knows, that its enactment would require firings of strategically placed neoconservatives on the National Security Council and Cheney's staff, in particular Elliott Abrams, deputy national security advisor for global democracy strategy, who also handles Near Eastern affairs.

In the event that Baker actually advocates what he thinks, Bush's options will be to admit the errors of his ways and the wisdom of his father and father's men or to cast them and caution aside once again. His choice is either Shakespearean or Wagnerian.

November 16, 2006

"This business about a graceful exit"

The Iraq Study Group's report, released Wednesday, calling the situation in that country "grave and deteriorating," is hardly the first caution that President Bush has received. Two years ago, in December 2004, two frank face-to-face briefings were delivered to him from the field. In the first, the CIA station chief in Baghdad, who had filed an urgent memo the month before titled "The Expanding Insurgency in Iraq," was invited to the White House. The CIA officer had written that the insurgency was becoming more "self-confident" and in Sunni provinces "largely unchallenged." His report concluded: "The ease with which the insurgents move and exist in Baghdad and the Sunni heartland is bolstering their self-confidence further." He predicted that the United States would suffer more than two thousand dead. Bush's reaction was to remark about the station chief, "What is he, some kind of defeatist?" Less than a week after the briefing, the officer was informed he was being reassigned from his post in Baghdad.

A few days after that briefing, on December 17, 2004, Colonel Derek Harvey, the Defense Intelligence Agency's senior intelligence officer for Iraq, was ushered into the Oval Office. Harvey, who had "conversed repeatedly with insurgents, and had developed the belief that the U.S. intelligence effort there was deeply flawed," according to Thomas Ricks in *Fiasco*, briefed the president about the insurgency: "It's robust, it's well led, it's diverse. Absent some sort of reconciliation it's going to go on, and that risks a civil war. They have the means to fight this for a long time, and they have a different sense of time than we do, and are willing to fight. They have better intelligence than we do." Harvey also explained that foreign fighters, jihadists, and Al-Qaeda were marginal elements. Ricks reported that after the briefing, Bush in his speeches still "would refer to setbacks only in vague terms."

But there is more to the story. A former high-ranking intelligence officer and close associate of Harvey's told me that during Harvey's briefing the president interrupted, turning to his aides to inquire, "Is this guy a Democrat?" Harvey's warnings, of course, were as thoroughly ignored as those of the CIA station chief.

In the weeks before the delivery of the Iraq Study Group (aka Baker-Hamilton Commission) report, Bush repeatedly insisted that Al-Qaeda was the principal foe in Iraq. Harvey, meanwhile, served as an advisor to the commission. After two years of Bush's contemptuous disdain for accurate intelligence reports, the commission dryly noted as a basic assumption: "No one can guarantee that any course of action in Iraq at this point will stop sectarian warfare, growing violence or a slide toward chaos. There is no magic formula to solve the problems of Iraq." Upon receipt of the report, Bush responded with perfunctory and dismissive courtesy, "We probably won't agree with every proposal . . . We'll act on it in a timely fashion. Thank you very much." Good night, and good luck.

The commission's report, a bipartisan consensus, is a surprisingly tough-minded document, clear in its proposals and cold-eyed about the prospects in Iraq. Bush's disinclination to immediately implement the commission's recommendations reflects his persistent delusion in military victory. It also marks his ultimate rejection of his father's and father's men's efforts to salvage him from his wreckage.

Ever since the commission was announced, Bush's energy has been devoted to beating off the rescue party. "This business about a graceful exit just simply has no realism to it whatsoever," he said last week in anticipation of the commission's report, mocking the "realism" universally attributed to former Secretary of State James Baker. Then, on Monday, in an interview with Fox News, he held forth on his superior knowledge over his father's. "I love to talk to my dad about things between a father and a son, not policy," he said. "No," he replied, when asked if he consults his father for advice. "He understands what I know, that the level of information I have relative to the level of information most other people have, including himself, is significant and that he trusts me to make decisions . . . I am the commander in chief." He is the "Decider" and the Decider decides that Father does not know best.

Since the midterm elections loss, Bush has conducted a foreign policy intended to counter the Baker-Hamilton Commission. In a sense, his entire foreign policy is a case study in reaction formation. From the start, he was determined to do everything opposite from what President Clinton had done. Bush abandoned the Middle East peace process, cast aside the negotiations with North Korea over its development of nuclear weapons, withdrew from the secret diplomacy with reform-minded Iranian President Mohammad Khatami, and brushed aside concerns about terrorism. Even before September 11, Bush entertained scenarios about invading Iraq. In this he was operating in the shadow of his father, who refused to march to Baghdad in the Gulf War to topple Saddam Hussein. Bush envisioned himself succeeding where he believed his father had failed, thereby exceeding him.

As soon as Baker declared that staying the course was an unacceptable option, Bush furiously initiated rounds of diplomacy guaranteed to disqualify Baker's proposals before they were formally presented. He rejected talks with Iran. He suggested that Syria comply with his demands, which Baker would propose as the proper subject of negotiations, before there could be any direct relations. Israeli Prime Minister Ehud Olmert was prompted to repackage long-rejected proposals to the Palestinians as the basis for peace talks there. Secretary of State Condoleezza Rice was sent to the region to engage in predetermined fruitless nondiplomacy in order to suggest the appearance of diplomacy. Thus Bush created a series of false events so that he might claim he had tried Baker's approach but that it had failed.

The leaking of a memo by National Security Advisor Stephen Hadley on the weakness of Iraqi Prime Minister Nouri al-Maliki to *The New York Times* by an unnamed administration official on the eve of President Bush's meeting with Maliki in Amman, Jordan, dramatized the fragility of the Iraqi situation. Hadley described a leader who gave lip service to national aspirations but was really a sectarian. "He impressed me as a leader who wanted to be strong but was having difficulty figuring out how to do so," Hadley wrote. "The information he receives is undoubtedly skewed by his small circle of [Islamic] Dawa [Party] advisers, coloring his actions and interpretation of reality. His intentions seem good when he talks with Americans, and sensitive reporting suggests he is trying to stand up to the Shia hierarchy and force positive change. But the reality on the streets of Baghdad suggests Maliki is either ignorant of what is going on, misrepresenting his intentions, or that his capabilities are not yet sufficient to turn his good intentions into action."

Hadley added, "Maliki and those around him are naturally inclined to distrust new actors." The solution, Hadley suggested, was to construct "an alternative political base" for him of "moderate" groups that would enable him to cease being sectarian.

On the most obvious level, Hadley revealed the dearth of progress within Iraq, the dominance of sectarian forces that the United States had installed, and the absence of solutions arising within its own system, requiring the national security advisor to engage in an exercise of sheer fantasy.

On an ironic level, Hadley apparently did not recognize that the leader he was describing—sectarian, bluff but essentially weak, surrounded by fawning advisors who reinforced his skewed sense of reality, ignorant of the facts on the ground, and incapable of reaching out to forge a political center—was a sharply drawn if unintentional portrait of his own president.

After Maliki postponed his meeting with Bush, perhaps to inflict a little humiliation for the embarrassing leak of the Hadley memo, he and Bush conferred. Bush praised him as "the right guy," identified the primary enemy in Iraq as Al-Qaeda, declared there would be no drawdown of U.S. forces, rebuffed the idea of direct talks with Iran, and said the United States would stay in Iraq indefinitely. "We're going to stay in Iraq to get the job done, so long as the government wants us there." He had touched nearly all the bases in his rejection of Baker's coming proposals while undermining his own leverage vis-à-vis the Iraqis.

Bush followed this performance by diving deep into the dark pool of sectarian Iraqi politics, meeting at the White House on Monday with Abdul

Aziz al-Hakim, a Shiite cleric and leader of the Supreme Council for Islamic Revolution in Iraq, who has his own militia, the Badr Brigade, long linked to and subsidized by the Iranians (al-Hakim spent twenty years in exile there), and a rival of Maliki's chief political sponsor, Shiite cleric Muqtada al-Sadr. Perhaps this was the "moderate" new base Hadley imagined the United States might fabricate for Maliki. Hakim used the meeting to elevate his legitimacy and to call for increased attacks on the Sunnis. Thus, while opposing direct diplomacy with Iran and cultivating military options against it, Bush lent his support to those most closely aligned with Iranian influence in Iraq.

Two days before, a memo written by outgoing Secretary of Defense Donald Rumsfeld was leaked to *The New York Times*. Once again, an administration that had launched federal investigations of national security leaks to the *Times* and the *Washington Post* was remarkably taciturn about the source of the leak, undoubtedly Rumsfeld himself. The memo was a slapdash series of bullet points, calling for "a major adjustment." Rumsfeld urged: "Recast the U.S. military mission and the U.S. goals (how we talk about them)—go minimalist." As the first of "less attractive options" he listed: "Continue on the current path." The second: "Move a large fraction of all U.S. Forces into Baghdad to attempt to control it." Thus, in a last gasp to recast his image on the eve of the release of the Baker-Hamilton Commission report Rumsfeld instead repudiated his entire policy with a self-serving memo.

The day before the report was made public, Robert Gates, a former member of the commission, and the former director of the CIA under the elder Bush, appeared at his confirmation hearings before the Senate Armed Services Committee. "Do you believe that we are currently winning in Iraq?" Senator Carl Levin, D-Michigan, asked him. "No, sir," Gates replied. He added, "It's my impression that frankly there are no new ideas on Iraq." For this show of candor, establishing the image of an anti-Rumsfeld, the committee instantly and unanimously voted for his confirmation, a leap of faith. Will Gates, who has a reputation for compliance with superiors, resist the regime of delusion?

For James Baker, the consummate Republican political player of the Reagan-Bush era, the cool Texas patrician, summoned by his old friend George H. W. Bush whenever the family political fortunes are threatened, the rejection of his commission's report is the final act of ingratitude. He had managed the elder Bush's faltering campaign in 1988 and righted it; he had had to resign from the job he loved the most, secretary of state, to return as last-minute political handler to attempt to save the elder Bush from defeat in 1992; blamed by Barbara Bush for his efforts, because she claimed he had not come over as campaign manager early enough, the family still called him back to save George W. Bush in the 2000 Florida contest; then, his advice to the new president not to invade Iraq was ignored; but, once again, as Bush sank in the Iraqi quagmire, the family demanded his services; and now, his intervention has failed, and his diligence has been dismissed.

In preparation for his rejection of the Baker-Hamilton Commission report, Bush created two other study groups within his administration, one led by General Peter Pace, chairman of the Joint Chiefs of Staff. The effect was to diminish the commission as merely one among several groups offering advice. For all intents and purposes Pace's group is a counter-commission. In opposition to the Baker-Hamilton Commission proposals for the strategic withdrawal of troops by 2008 and diplomatic openings to Syria and Iran, as well as a regional conference on Iraq and a renewal of the Middle East peace process, Pace will suggest a new military offensive— twenty thousand more U.S. troops to secure Baghdad (exactly the idea Rumsfeld cautioned against in his memo), ten thousand more U.S. advisors for the Iraq army, and hundreds of billions more in appropriations to sustain a commitment stretching indefinitely.

Pace's plan reflects the notion that with one more concerted offensive, one more application of overwhelming might, the United States can at last gain the upper hand and prevail. Even though commanders in Iraq, along with Pace, have stressed that only a political solution can pacify Iraq, some, along with Pace, are still in thrall to the chimera of military victory. So long as someone with stars on his shoulder promises victory to Bush, he will cling to it. So long as he dreams of victory, he will find someone with stars to tell him he can have it. The alternative to wishful thinking would be acknowledgment of his error and acceptance of his fate.

December 7, 2006

The Prime of Ms. Jeane Kirkpatrick

The death last week of Jeane Kirkpatrick—ambassador to the United Nations during Ronald Reagan's first term and the highest-ranking neoconservative in his administration—coincided with President Bush's rejection of the Baker-Hamilton Commission report on Iraq and his subsequent consultations with neoconservatives to entrench his belief in "victory." But rather than providing a sobering but inspirational backdrop for Bush's heroic stand against the foreign-policy establishment, Kirkpatrick's passing illuminates the conflicting legacies of the ideological movement of which she was once an icon and the confusion that surrounds a president who demands certitudes.

In its obituary, *The New York Times* buried a surprising scoop about her last act of diplomacy, when she was sent by President Bush on a secret mission to Geneva in March 2003 to justify the invasion of Iraq to Arab foreign ministers. "The marching orders we received were to argue that preemptive war is legitimate," Alan Gerson, her former general counsel, recalled. "She said: 'No one will buy it. If that's the position, count me out.'" Instead, she argued that Saddam Hussein was in violation of United Nations resolutions. Her hitherto unknown rejection of Bush's unilateralism and extolling of international order apparently was her final commentary on neoconservatism.

"A neoconservative is a liberal who has been mugged by reality," neoconservative godfather Irving Kristol remarked in a famously cynical line. At the time of her death, Kirkpatrick was a neoconservative mugged by reality and a shadow of her former ferocious self. Once the warrior queen of neoconservatism, she ended as an unexplained skeptic, less the Valkyrie than the world-weary doubter, akin to the disillusioned Francis Fukuyama but without the tears of an apologetic manifesto. She checked out silently, leaving no equivalent of a political testament.

Norman Podhoretz, who had been her editor at *Commentary*, disclosed near the end of an obituary he published in *The Weekly Standard* that she

145

had grown disenchanted. "She had serious reservations about the prudence of the Bush Doctrine, which she evidently saw neither as an analogue of the Truman Doctrine nor as a revival of the Reaganite spirit in foreign policy," he wrote. "Even so, she was clearly reluctant to join in the clamor against it, which for all practical purposes meant relegating herself to the sidelines." But Podhoretz declined to reveal more details of her disapproval. Abruptly, he assumed the pose of a commissar, praising her "brilliant service on the ideological front" and awarded her "laurels" for what she "earned in World War III," though "what I persist in calling World War IV" failed to "tempt her back into battle." Comrade Podhoretz's oblique admission of her absence "on the ideological front" and the posthumous anecdote in the *Times* obituary are the runes of her alienation.

Jeane Kirkpatrick first came to public attention when her article "Dictatorships and Double Standards" was published in *Commentary* in November 1979. The Georgetown University professor's slashing attack on the Carter administration, appearing just as the Soviet Union invaded Afghanistan and the Iranian hostage crisis began, became one of the principal theoretical documents of neoconservatism and platforms for the Reagan campaign. In this seminal piece, which immediately vaulted her to prominence, Kirkpatrick argued that Carter's adherence to human rights undermined traditional authoritarian regimes allied with the United States in the Cold War. "Authoritarian" states, she posited, could slowly change into democratic ones, unlike "totalitarian" ones. "The history of this century provides no grounds for expecting that radical totalitarian regimes will transform themselves," she wrote.

History has not been kind to most of her ideas. The opening sentence of her essay betrays it as a howling anachronism. "The failure of the Carter administration's foreign policy is now clear to everyone," Kirkpatrick began. But where was she going? Her devastating punch line was that Carter's "crowning achievement has been to lay the groundwork for a transfer of the Panama Canal from the United States to a swaggering Latin dictator of Castroite bent." It may be hard to remember that Carter's Panama Canal Treaty was then a red-hot right-wing cause, especially seized upon by Reagan as a surrender of America's Manifest Destiny, and that the supposed "Latin dictator" is long gone.

Kirkpatrick's central idea that Communism was implacably resistant to change was, of course, belied by the collapse of the Soviet Union. And

Carter's advancement of human rights is generally acknowledged as a contributing factor in its downfall. Kirkpatrick's awestruck description of gathering Soviet strength, universally shared on the right, was a fundamental misreading of the symptoms of a rapidly decaying system entering its terminal crisis. But in its time her view about the perpetual survival of Communism was accepted as an eternal verity.

It may also be little recalled that alongside her mocking of human rights and "moralism" as "continuous self-abasement," Kirkpatrick ridiculed Carter for not invading Iran, even before the hostage taking. "Where once upon a time an American President might have sent Marines to assure the protection of American strategic interests, there is no room for force in this world of progress and self-determination," she wrote.

Kirkpatrick's record in office was as callous as her rhetoric was caustic. The barbarity of Reagan's policies in Latin America is largely forgotten, while the sordid assault on constitutional government in the Iran-contra scandal that flowed from it is rarely discussed. Kirkpatrick was obsessively fixed on Central America as a decisive cockpit of the Cold War and helped direct the administration's focus there. In the name of ideological struggle, she rallied support for authoritarian juntas throughout the Western Hemisphere.

On December 2, 1980, a month after Reagan's election, four Roman Catholic Maryknoll nuns, dedicated to assisting peasants in El Salvador, then ruled by a junta that had provoked a guerrilla insurgency, were murdered; independent investigations and a trial later proved that Salvadoran National Guardsmen killed them on orders from above. Two weeks after these targeted assassinations, Kirkpatrick, just named to the U.N. post, leaped to the defense of the junta. "I don't think the government of El Salvador was responsible," she declared. "The nuns were not just nuns; the nuns were political activists."

Kirkpatrick was an ardent protector of the El Salvador junta, among other juntas from Guatemala (where the regime waged a genocidal war against Indian peasants) to Honduras, and from Chile to Argentina. (After the National Guard massacred more than nine hundred men, women, and children in the Salvadoran village of El Mozote on December 11, 1981, the Reagan administration sent Kirkpatrick's closest neoconservative ally within the administration, Elliott Abrams, then assistant secretary of state for human rights, before a Senate committee to testify that the reports of slaughter at El Mozote, later proved conclusively, "were not credible." (After pleading guilty to lying to Congress in the Iran-contra scandal, Abrams was pardoned; he is currently deputy national security advisor in charge of Middle East affairs.)

In August 1981, Kirkpatrick flew to Chile to meet with General Augusto Pinochet, who had overthrown the democracy there eight years earlier. "Most pleasant," said Kirkpatrick about their conversation. She announced that the Reagan administration's intention was to "normalize completely its relations with Chile," including reinstating arms sales. Two days after her visit, Pinochet used Kirkpatrick's bestowal of legitimacy to expel the chairman of the Chilean Human Rights Commission and other prominent opposition leaders. One month later, Amnesty International issued a report noting that "torture still appears to be a systematic part of official policy."

Kirkpatrick considered herself a special friend of the Argentine junta. On April 2, 1982, she attended a dinner at the Argentine Embassy in Washington. While she was there, the regime launched an invasion of the British-governed Falkland Islands off the Argentine coast. The Argentines took Kirkpatrick's presence as evidence of tacit official approval. The Falklands war that followed between an authoritarian regime and a democracy, between countries led by a military strongman and a conservative prime minister, Margaret Thatcher, to whom Kirkpatrick was occasionally compared, had not been foreshadowed in Kirkpatrick's theories. Nor did she imagine the overthrow of the Argentine junta when it lost the war.

Another war between two authoritarian regimes required the United States to choose sides. In the Iran-Iraq War, Kirkpatrick played a key part in preventing international condemnation of Saddam Hussein's use of weapons of mass destruction. By 1983, Iraq was reeling from Iran's human wave attacks and in danger of losing, prompting a U.S. tilt. In December, President Reagan sent a special envoy, Donald Rumsfeld, to meet with Saddam, a dictator with whom it was decided we could do business. Loans and trade deals were soon arranged. And Iraq unleashed chemical-weapons attacks against Iranian troops, contrary to international law. After both the State Department and the United Nations reported that Iraq was using WMD, Iran submitted a resolution demanding U.N. condemnation of Iraq's violations. But U.S. ambassador Kirkpatrick lobbied against its approval, urging "restraint" in denouncing Iraqi chemical warfare. Her action succeeded in thwarting any specific censure of Iraq, leading on March 30, 1984, to a U.N. Security Council statement against the use of WMD only in general terms. Saddam Hussein was spared.

By this time, the campaign of the right to install Kirkpatrick as national security advisor had failed. Her support within came from CIA director William J. Casey and Secretary of Defense Caspar Weinberger, but Secretary of State George Shultz viewed her temperament as "not well suited to the job," and she reached her ceiling.

From the beginning of the Reagan administration she had championed the contras as a force to overthrow the Sandinista government in Nicaragua. She construed this battle as the flashpoint of the Reagan Doctrine that justified financing anti-Communist guerrilla movements from Afghanistan to Central America. (Her theories did not anticipate that the funding of the mujahedin in Afghanistan would help foster the Taliban and Al-Qaeda.) In March 1981, she participated in the White House meeting that authorized the $19 million in covert funding that created the contras. Congress, however, passed legislation forbidding such subsidies. The Iran-contra scandal began in the illegal effort by elements of the Reagan administration to evade the ban by tapping foreign sources of money. Eventually, missiles were sold to Iran in order to finance the contra war. In June 1984, Kirkpatrick attended the secret meeting where Casey argued for going around the law. "It is an impeachable offense," Shultz warned. But Kirkpatrick, undeterred, argued, "We should make the maximum effort to find the money." Her good luck was not to be appointed to any position in Reagan's second term; if she had been, she would undoubtedly have been found in the thick of the scandal.

At the 1984 Republican Convention she appeared as the keynote speaker, delivering a speech in which she railed against "the San Francisco Democrats" for "always blaming America first." Using her identification as a nominal Democrat, her emblem as a neoconservative, she lent credence to the atavistic Cold War fear of homosexual subversion. Thus her most memorable performance was less as foreign policy mandarin than as J. Edgar Hoover in drag.

Despite the rapturous reception for her speech, it was her swan song. Conservative columnists lamented her leaving. George Will wrote, "She unites thought and action, theory and practice, better than anyone in government in this generation," and called her "the one indispensable person in government." William Safire extolled her as, "the only woman who could today be considered as a serious possibility for President of the United States." But she received no further appointments and returned to academic life. And after the Iran-contra scandal, Reagan purged his administration of ideologues and swiftly entered negotiations with Soviet leader Mikhail Gorbachev to end the Cold War, the happy ending that Kirkpatrick had argued was an impossibility, the ultimate refutation. In 1987, spurred by her pundit fans and anxious about the dangers of Vice President George H. W. Bush's moderate tendencies, she considered running for the Republican nomination for president, but upon receiving no support within the party, she abandoned the quixotic campaign.

Without Communism, neoconservatism was an ideology lacking a political context. A peculiar variant of anti-Communism, neoconservatism had its origins as a strain of Trotskyism; it was composed of cadres imbued with a Leninist mentality; it had few adherents who had participated in Democratic electoral politics (Kirkpatrick was a glaring exception); and it was dependent on the patronage of a Republican White House for its influence.

In light of the fall of Communism, Kirkpatrick's seamless dialectics were proved wrong in nearly every important respect. Her principles appeared as instruments of expedience, her strategies as polemics, and supposed evidence as sheer assertions. More than her substance, her style remained. Neoconservatives after Kirkpatrick carried on her stridency, denunciatory bullying, inflation and conflation of putative threats, fear-mongering, and abuse of history, especially of the Munich analogy in which Democrats are accused of being appeasers and neoconservatives posture as contemporary Churchillians. During their post-Reagan, post-Communism wilderness years, the neoconservatives tried to reorganize themselves as a movement initially in opposition to the elder Bush's foreign policy realism and then against Clinton's pragmatic internationalism. They considered Clinton's emphasis on nation building, the social problems of globalization, and the threat of terrorism hopelessly soft. All along they sought a new enemy on the scale of Communism that would recommend their own indispensable relevance to a Republican president.

Under Bush, Dick Cheney and Donald Rumsfeld brought them back into power, and after the jolt of September 11, fixated on an invasion of Iraq, they seemed to surpass their former glory. But the post-Communist version of neoconservatism was Kirkpatrickism turned on its head. Neoconservative theorists equated Saddam with totalitarians past and bundled him up with Al-Qaeda terrorism, cast as totalitarian as well, a rhetorical approach that evoked but twisted Kirkpatrick's earlier work. Neoconservatism had become more an attitude than a policy, much less a doctrine. Quietly, the original godmother of neoconservatism dissented.

In their crusade to remake the Middle East in the American image, the neoconservatives mangled beyond recognition Kirkpatrick's ideas, once the holy writ of Reaganism, and embraced the "moralism" she deplored. While her theories did not stand the test of time as applied to Communism, they provide a stinging if unintended critique of latter-day neoconservatism.

In her 1979 essay, she cautioned against simplistic thinking about transforming long-settled authoritarian regimes into democracies. "Although most governments in the world are, as they always have been, autocracies of one kind or another, no idea holds greater sway in the mind of educated Americans than the belief that it is possible to democratize governments, anytime, anywhere, under any circumstances," she wrote. "This notion is belied by an enormous body of evidence based on the experience of dozens of countries which have attempted with more or less (usually less) success to move from autocratic to democratic government."

Even more pointedly, she predicted the chaos that could envelop a country long ruled by a dictator upon his overthrow. Her description prophesies almost precisely the blunders of the Bush occupation of Iraq and reveals the omniscience of the neoconservatives as mere naiveté. "The fabric of authority unravels quickly when the power and status of the man at the top are undermined or eliminated," she wrote. "The longer the autocrat has held power, and the more pervasive his personal influence, the more dependent a nation's institutions will be on him. Without him, the organized life of the society will collapse, like an arch from which the keystone has been removed . . . The speed with which armies collapse, bureaucracies abdicate, and social structures dissolve once the autocrat is removed frequently surprises American policymakers and journalists accustomed to public institutions based on universalistic norms rather than particularistic relations."

This passage reads like a recent report on the blind arrogance of the neoconservatives and errors of the Coalition Provisional Authority. But the neoconservatives did not bother to reread her yellowing article, and her qualms gave them no pause as they distorted her arguments and plunged headlong toward Baghdad. In the final irony, it turns out that the regime that cannot change is Bush's.

December 14, 2006

The Escalation of Delusion

"We're going to win," President Bush told a guest at a White House Christmas party. Another guest, ingratiating himself with his host, urged him to ignore the report of the bipartisan Iraq Study Group, cochaired by James Baker, the former secretary of state and his father's close associate, which described the crisis in Iraq as "grave and deteriorating," and offered seventy-nine recommendations for diplomacy, transferring responsibility to the Iraqi government, and withdrawing nearly all U.S. troops by 2008. "The president chuckled," according to an account in the neoconservative *Weekly Standard*, "and said he'd made his position clear when he appeared with British Prime Minister Tony Blair. The report had never mentioned the possibility of American victory. Bush's goal in Iraq, he said at the photo op with Blair, is 'victory.'" Bush reasserted his belief that "victory in Iraq is achievable" at his Wednesday press conference.

Two members of the ISG were responsible for George W. Bush's becoming president. Baker had maneuvered through the thicket of the 2000 Florida contest, finally bringing *Bush v. Gore* before the Supreme Court, where Sandra Day O'Connor was the deciding vote. (Jeffrey Toobin of *The New Yorker* reported that she had complained before hearing the case that she wanted to retire but did not want a Democrat to appoint her replacement.) Through the Iraq Study Group Baker and O'Connor were attempting to salvage what they had made possible in *Bush v. Gore*. Upon Bush's receipt of the report, a White House spokesman told the press, "Jim Baker can go back to his day job."

The day after the report was submitted, on December 8, Tony Blair appeared at the White House. He had testified before the Baker-Hamilton Commission, and supported its main proposals, but now stood beside Bush as the president tossed them aside, talking instead of "victory." "The president isn't standing alone," explained White House press secretary Tony Snow. Blair left to pursue a vain mission for Middle East peace, emphasizing by his presence the U.S. absence. His predetermined failure outlined the dimensions of the vacuum that only the U.S. could fill. On December 18, Chatham House, the former Royal Institute of International Affairs, issued a report on Blair's foreign policy: "The root failure of Tony Blair's foreign policy has been its inability to influence the Bush administration in any significant way despite the sacrifice—military, political, and financial—that the United Kingdom has made."

The day before the Chatham House report was released former Secretary of State Colin Powell appeared on CBS News's *Face the Nation* to announce his support for the rejected Iraq Study Group and declare, "We are not winning, we are losing." He made plain his opposition to any new "surge" of troops in Baghdad, a tactic he said had already been tried and failed. Powell added that Bush had not explained "the mission" and that "we are a little less safe."

The Chatham House report describes Blair and Powell as partners before the invasion of Iraq who had concluded that Bush was set on war and decided to lend their voices to its defense. "The British role was therefore to provide diplomatic cover," the report states. Powell, of course, delivered the most important speech of his career justifying the invasion before the United Nations Security Council on February 5, 2003, which was later disclosed to have been a tissue of falsehoods and which he called a "blot" on his record. Since the time of the Reagan administration, when he was national security advisor, Powell had been aligned with Baker, the elder Bush and other foreign policy realists. But during his tenure as secretary of state he had suppressed his skepticism and obligations as a constitutional officer in favor of his loyalty as a "good soldier" to his commander in chief. Now, his reputation in tatters, he is trying to restore himself as a member of his original team and speaking for the unanimous opposition to Bush's new plans from the Joint Chiefs of Staff of which he was once chairman.

Bush's touted but unexplained "new way forward" (his version of the ISG's "the way forward") may be the first order of battle, complete with details of units, maps, and timetables, even posted on the Web site of a think tank. "I will not be rushed," said Bush. But apparently he has already accepted the latest neoconservative program, artfully titled with catch-phrases appealing to his desperation—"Choosing Victory: A Plan for Success in Iraq"—and available for reading on the site of the American Enterprise Institute.

The author of this plan is Frederick W. Kagan, a neoconservative at the AEI and the author of a new book, *Finding the Target: The Transformation of American Military Policy*, replete with up-to-date neocon scorn of Bush as "simplistic," Donald Rumsfeld as "fatuous," and even erstwhile neocon icon Paul Wolfowitz, former deputy secretary of defense and currently president of the World Bank, as "self-serving." Among the others listed as "participants" in drawing up the plan are various marginal and obscure figures including, notably, Danielle Pletka, a former aide to Senator Jesse Helms; Michael Rubin, an aide to the catastrophic Coalition Provisional Authority; and retired Major General Jack Keane, the former deputy army chief of staff.

This rump group of neocons is the battered remnant left of the phalanx that once conjured up grandiose visions of conquest and blowtorched ideological ground for Bush. Although neocons are still entrenched in the vice president's office and on the National Security Council, they mostly feel that their perfect ideas have been the victims of imperfect execution. Rather than accepting any responsibility for the ideas themselves, they blame Rumsfeld and Bush. Meyrav Wurmser, a research fellow at the neo-conservative Hudson Institute, whose husband, David Wurmser, is a Middle East advisor on Dick Cheney's staff, recently vented the neocons' despair to an Israeli news outlet: "This administration is in its twilight days. Everyone is now looking for work, looking to make money . . . We all feel beaten after the past five years." But they are not so crushed that they cannot summon one last ragged Team B to provide a manifesto for a cornered president.

"Choosing Victory" is a prophetic document, a bugle call for an additional thirty thousand troops to fight a decisive Napoleonic battle for Baghdad. (Its author, Kagan, has written a book on Napoleon.) It assumes that through this turning point the Shiite militias will melt away, the Sunni insurgents will suffer defeat and from the solid base of Baghdad security will radiate throughout the country. The plan also assumes that additional combat teams that actually take considerable time to assemble and train are instantly available for deployment. And it dismisses every diplomatic initiative proposed by the Iraq Study Group as dangerously softheaded. Foremost among the plan's assertions is that there is still a military solution in Iraq—"victory."

The strategic premise of the entire document rests on the incredulous disbelief that the U.S. cannot enforce its will through force. "Victory is still an option in Iraq," it states. "America, a country of 300 million people with a GDP of $12 trillion, and more than 1 million soldiers and marines can regain control of Iraq, a state the size of California with a population of 25 million and a GDP under $100 billion." By these gross metrics, France should never have lost in Algeria and Vietnam. The U.S. experience in Vietnam goes unmentioned.

Bush's rejection of the Iraq Study Group report was presaged by a post-election speech delivered on December 4 by Karl Rove at the Churchill dinner held by Hillsdale College, a citadel of conservative crankdom. Here Rove conflated Winston Churchill and George W. Bush, Neville Chamberlain and James Baker, and the Battle of Britain and the Iraq War. "Why would we want to pursue a policy that our enemies want?" demanded Rove. "We will either win or we will lose . . . Winston Churchill showed us the way. And like Great Britain under its greatest leader, we in the United States will not waver, we will not tire, we will not falter, and we will not fail."

A week later, on December 11, Bush met at the White House with Jack Keane, from the latest neocon Team B, and four other critics of the ISG. But even before, on December 8, in a meeting with senators, he compared himself to an embattled Harry Truman, unpopular as he forged the early policies of the Cold War. When Senator Dick Durbin, D-Illinois, offered that Truman had created the NATO alliance, worked through the U.N. and conducted diplomacy with enemies, and that Bush could follow his example by endorsing the recommendations of the ISG, Bush rejected Durbin's fine-tuning of the historical analogy and replied that he was "the commander in chief."

The opening section of the ISG report is a lengthy analysis of the dire situation in Iraq. But Bush has frantically brushed that analysis away just as he has rejected every objective assessment that had reached him before. He has assimilated no analysis whatsoever of what's gone wrong. For him, there's no past, especially his own. There's only the present. The war is detached from strategic purposes, the history of Iraq and the region, and political and social dynamics, and instead is grasped as a test of character. Ultimately, what's at stake is his willpower.

Repudiated in the midterm elections, Bush has elevated himself above politics, and repeatedly says, "I am the commander in chief." With the crash of Rove's game plan for using his presidency as an instrument to leverage a permanent Republican majority, Bush is abandoning the role of political leader. He can't disengage militarily from Iraq because that would abolish his identity as a military leader, his default identity and now his only one.

Unlike the political leader, the commander in chief doesn't require persuasion; he rules through orders, deference, and the obedience of those beneath him. By discarding the ISG report, Bush has rejected doubt, introspection, ambivalence, and responsibility. By embracing the AEI manifesto, he asserts the warrior virtues of will, perseverance, and resolve. The contest in Iraq is a struggle between will and doubt. Every day his defiance proves his superiority over lesser mortals. Even the Joint Chiefs have betrayed the martial virtues that he presumes to embody. He views those lacking his will with rising disdain. The more he stands up against those who tell him to change, the more virtuous he becomes. His ability to realize those qualities surpasses anyone else's and passes the character test.

The mere suggestion of doubt is fatally compromising. Any admission of doubt means complete loss, impotence, and disgrace. Bush cannot entertain doubt and still function. He cannot keep two ideas in his head at the same time. Powell misunderstood when he said that the current war strategy lacks a clear mission. The war *is* Bush's mission.

No matter the setback it's always temporary, and the campaign can always be started from scratch in an endless series of new beginnings and offensives—"the new way forward"—just as in his earlier life no failure was irredeemable through his father's intervention. Now he has rejected his father's intervention in preference for the clean slate of a new scenario that depends only on his willpower.

"We're not winning, we're not losing," Bush told the *Washington Post* on Tuesday, a direct rebuke of Powell's formulation, saying he was citing General Peter Pace, chairman of the Joint Chiefs, and adding, "We're going to win." Winning means not ending the war while he is president. Losing would mean coming to the end of the rope while he was still in office. In his mind, so long as the war goes on and he maintains his will, he can win. Then, only his successor can be a loser.

Bush's idea of himself as personifying martial virtues, however, is based on a vision that would be unrecognizable to all modern theorists of warfare. According to Carl von Clausewitz, war is the most uncertain of human enterprises, difficult to understand, hardest to control, and demanding the highest degree of adaptability. It was Clausewitz who first applied the metaphor of "fog" to war. In his classic work, "On War," he warned, "We only wish to represent things as they are, and to expose the error of believing that a mere bravo without intellect can make himself distinguished in war."

December 20, 2006

No Time to Heal

During the holiday interregnum between the election of the new Congress and its swearing in, the death of former President Gerald R. Ford at the age of ninety-three evoked nostalgia for his interim "time to heal" (the title of his memoir) after the resignation of President Nixon. Like all nostalgia, it was distorting and disabling. Surprisingly, the one shattering the false mood was none other than Ford himself, speaking from the grave. Beyond the River Styx he could hardly silence the broadcasters attempting to outdo one another in reaching for high notes of banality. But he left behind words cautioning against the abuse of history, especially by those who served as his aides, Dick Cheney and Donald Rumsfeld, who twisted the lessons of his presidency to provide the underpinnings of George W. Bush's policies. Ford's condemnation demonstrated the continued relevance of the contentious politics that enveloped his administration and revealed just how little healing has occurred among the divided Republican elites since Richard Nixon's fall.

His last testament was a final act of political finesse. Obeying the unwritten protocol of former presidents not to criticize a sitting one (a sketchy rule never upheld by Herbert Hoover or Jimmy Carter), he vouchsafed his commentary to a reporter guaranteed to publish it for maximum exposure and thus, Ford must have known, damage. Having suffered a stroke in

2000, Ford must also have known that his remarks on Bush and the others would appear while Bush was still in office and therefore of more than historical interest.

"I don't think I would have gone to war," Ford told Bob Woodward in an interview conducted two and a half years ago. "Rumsfeld and Cheney and the president made a big mistake in justifying going into the war in Iraq. They put the emphasis on weapons of mass destruction," Ford said. "And now, I've never publicly said I thought they made a mistake, but I felt very strongly it was an error in how they should justify what they were going to do . . . I don't think, if I had been president, on the basis of the facts as I saw them publicly, I don't think I would have ordered the Iraq war."

Ford also agreed with Colin Powell's assessment of Cheney as having a "fever" about invading Iraq. "I think that's probably true," he said, adding that Cheney had become "more pugnacious."

Ford's judgments are best understood as reflections on his own presidency. He describes Bush with a disdain he reserved previously only for one other man he believed had contempt for facts—Ronald Reagan. If he was anything, Ford was consistent, and he was consistently hostile to Reagan's right-wing politics, which he grasped had metastasized into Bush's radicalism. Even worse, two of his formerly close staff members were chiefly responsible for the "justifying" of a disastrous policy, "a big mistake," contrary to "the facts."

Nixon chose Ford as his vice president after Spiro Agnew pleaded nolo contendere to bribery charges and resigned. Nixon still had faith in his own obstruction of justice. He never anticipated that he himself would be compelled to resign rather than face certain removal from office in the Watergate scandal. When he did, the pins of his political act collapsed onto Ford. Nixon's style had been to play both ends of the Republican Party against the middle, which he could then claim to occupy. He convinced conservatives and moderates that he was really one of them even as they rightly suspected him of cynical manipulation. When he imploded, the Republican center that he had come to personify was incinerated too. Ford was left to stir the ashes.

As the first unelected vice president, he was the first person to accede to the presidency as the result of a Senate confirmation, not the people's vote. Throughout his brief term he struggled for legitimacy. His pardon of Nixon a month after assuming office heightened his crisis. Saving the country from a drawn-out criminal trial of the disgraced Nixon, he thought he would be relieved of the burden of the past—"I had to get the monkey off my back," he wrote in his memoir—but instead he sacrificed himself. His popularity plummeted, never to rise above 50 percent again. The absence of legitimacy impinged on his ability to fend off the Republican right.

Upon becoming president Ford had called for "recovery, not revenge." But revenge was already in the air. Governor Reagan of California refused to call on the new president when he traveled to Washington, a calculated snub. Ford's selection of Nelson Rockefeller as vice president triggered Reagan's decision to run against him for the Republican nomination. Within the Republican Party, Ford's nomination of Rockefeller received far more disapproval than his pardon of Nixon. The governor of New York was the symbol of moderate Republicanism, a hate object for decades. Reagan's motive, however, was ultimately personal pique—he was "disappointed that he had been passed over himself," according to his biographer Lou Cannon. Reagan thought of himself as the rightful heir apparent and Ford as nothing but a "caretaker."

Ford had a dismally low regard for Reagan, dismissing the threat of his potential challenge. "I hadn't taken those warnings seriously because I didn't take Reagan seriously." Ford considered Reagan "simplistic," dogmatic, and lazy. Reagan, for his part, argued that Nixon's 1972 mandate was not a Republican victory but an ideological one for junking the old Republicanism and that Ford was betraying it. "The tragedy of Watergate," Reagan said, was that it "obscured the meaning of that '72 election."

Reagan accused Ford of fatally weakening national security. He opposed Ford's pursuit of détente with the Soviet Union through Strategic Arms Limitation Talks that led to treaties reducing the production of nuclear weapons and Ford's signing of the Helsinki Accords in August 1975, which held the Soviet Union for the first time to standards of human rights. Reagan's critique appeared against the backdrop of the collapse of South Vietnam and the scene on April 30, 1975, of helicopters evacuating U.S. personnel from the roof of the U.S. embassy.

Ford's battles with the Democratic Congress made him seem impotent. He issued sixty-five vetoes of major pieces of legislation, including appropriations bills intended to ameliorate the harsh effects of a recession.

In April 1975, the Senate Operations Committee under the chairmanship of Senator Frank Church, D-Idaho, released fourteen reports on the abuse of intelligence. It chronicled "excessive executive power," "excessive secrecy," "avoidance of the rule of law," "rogue" operations, and even spying on domestic politics. "Whatever the theory," the report concluded, "the fact was that intelligence activities were essentially exempted from the normal system of checks and balances. Such executive power, not founded in law or checked by Congress or the courts, contained the seeds of abuse and its growth was to be expected."

Meanwhile, Donald Rumsfeld—moved from White House chief of staff to secretary of defense as his deputy, Dick Cheney, was promoted to the chief of staff job—created a Team B of hawks within the Pentagon who attacked the CIA's National Intelligence Estimate for supposedly underestimating the Soviet Union's military strength. Rumsfeld began making speeches assailing détente claiming that the Soviets were flagrantly violating treaties negotiated by Secretary of State Henry Kissinger, another hate object of the right who was long associated with Vice President Rockefeller. The CIA officially responded by calling the Team B report "complete fiction." And CIA Director George H. W. Bush said that Team B set "in motion a process that lends itself to manipulation for purposes other than estimative accuracy." Nonetheless, Rumsfeld's inflation of the Red menace, based on faulty data, turned up the flame under Ford. Rumsfeld had his own motive: He wanted to be named vice president, a nomination that in the end went to Senator Bob Dole, considered acceptable to Reagan.

In anticipation of the contest with Reagan, in December 1975, Ford pressured Rockefeller to announce he did not want to run as his vice president. Ford later confessed that dumping Rockefeller was the "most cowardly thing I've ever done," Barry Werth reports in his recent book on Ford's presidency, *31 Days: The Crisis That Gave Us the Government We Have Today*. "I was angry at myself for showing cowardice in not saying to the ultraconservatives: it's going to be Ford and Rockefeller, whatever the consequences."

Rockefeller advised Ford: "I'm now going to say it frankly . . . Rumsfeld wants to be President of the United States. He has given George Bush [another potential vice-presidential choice] the deep six by putting him in the CIA, he has gotten me out . . . He was third on your list and now he has gotten rid of two of us . . .You are not going to be able to put him on the [ticket] because he is defense secretary, but he is not going to want anybody who can possibly be elected with you on that ticket . . . I have to say I have a serious question about his loyalty to you."

Had Ford run with Rockefeller it's possible he would have lost the GOP nomination to Reagan. Reagan would likely have been buried in a landslide—and perhaps the right wing along with him. If Ford had been the nominee, it's very possible he would have won the election because having Rockefeller on the ticket would probably have helped him carry New York.

In the Republican primaries, after faltering initially, Reagan seized on Ford's agreement to turn over the Panama Canal to Panamanian administration as a "giveaway." "We bought it, we paid for it, it's ours, and we're going to keep it!" He won the primary in North Carolina, revived his chances, and marched into the convention just short of the delegate votes he needed. There he proposed a series of platform challenges to détente, including a denunciation of the Helsinki Accords as "taking from those who do not have freedom the hope of one day getting it." The Ford camp at the convention, led by Cheney, accepted all of these planks.

When Ford barely gained the nomination (James A. Baker, a friend of George H. W. Bush's, served as his delegate counter), Reagan gave the most grudging acknowledgment. At the convention, on the final night, only when Ford persistently pleaded with Reagan, who was sitting in a skybox, to address the convention did he do so. Reagan delivered a speech that ended with an unreferenced quotation from the hero past of the Republican right, General Douglas MacArthur: "There is no substitute for victory." It could not have been a more stinging ideological rebuke of Ford. Afterward, Reagan gingerly campaigned for the Republican ticket, declining Ford's request to join him on the stump in California. After his narrow loss, Ford told interviewers that Reagan's "divisive" candidacy and subsequent behavior had cost him the election. Thus the "time to heal" ended.

Ford was the last regular Republican to serve as president. Reagan became president campaigning against Jimmy Carter on almost exactly the same charges of weakness and appeasement that he had leveled against Ford, down to the Panama Canal Treaty, which Carter signed. Reagan's running mate, George H. W. Bush, had already made compromises, as a failed U.S. Senate candidate opposing the Civil Rights Act of 1964, for example, to lend him the coloration of a Texas Republican. Swallowing Reagan's program, including what Bush had earlier called "voodoo economics," was essential to his rise. Yet his son traced the causes of his father's defeat in 1992 to his remaining moderation. George W. Bush's running mate agreed. That Cheney, Ford's chief of staff and the elder Bush's secretary of defense, bolstered and encouraged these impulses provided Bush with conclusive proof of their correctness.

Cheney and Rumsfeld, since their days in the Nixon White House, had observed the imperial presidency besieged. Under Ford, they saw it reach its low ebb, and they were determined to restore the presidency as they imagined it should be—unchecked by an intrusive Congress, shielded from the press, and unobstructed by staff professionals in the intelligence community who did not clearly understand the present dangers that required just such an executive.

After the 2000 election, Vice President-elect Cheney held a dinner at his house where he held forth that the new administration would finish off Saddam Hussein, a job that the elder Bush had left undone, opening him to charges of softness. Rumsfeld, appointed by the new president as secretary of defense at the suggestion of Cheney, named one of the key members of the Ford-era Team B, Paul Wolfowitz, as deputy secretary. At the first meeting of the National Security Council with Bush, Wolfowitz raised the question of invading Iraq.

Ford's posthumous dissent on Iraq has carried no more weight with President Bush than those of Ford's (and the elder Bush's) national security advisor, Brent Scowcroft, and James Baker, or even the quiet repudiation of the late Jeane Kirkpatrick, theoretician of the Reagan doctrine. Ford stands for the side of his father that Bush associates with defeat.

But as Bush prepares to announce his escalation of the Iraq war he and Cheney made a final use of Ford, eulogizing him for his pardon of Nixon, which they turned into a metaphor for their own will in the face of crumbling support. "The criticism was fierce," said Cheney. "But President Ford had larger concerns at heart." Bush hailed him for his "firm resolve" and "character." "In politics," Cheney said, "it can take a generation or more for a matter to settle, for tempers to cool." This is no time to heal. Let history sort it out.

January 3, 2007

Washington's Political Cleansing

James Baker, the consummate Republican political operator over the past thirty years, did not expect that President Bush would accept the recommendations of the Iraq Study Group he cochaired simply on its merits. Baker's hidden political hand was unrevealed in the report's dire analysis or in its urgent suggestions for diplomacy or force redeployment. Baker summoned as witnesses the Joint Chiefs of Staff, the military commanders in Iraq past and present (including the recently named commander there, General David Petraeus), and even British Prime Minister Tony Blair. But he understood that enlisting all of these formidable figures was insufficient. Baker privately negotiated with Bush, but he did not rest solely on his own powers of persuasion to convince the president, as the report put it, that the "situation is grave and deteriorating" and his policies are "not working."

Ultimately, Baker's political strategy counted on the decisive intervention of one person in the president's closed inner circle—who sees him alone and could not be kept from him, and on whom he has become dependent for support and trusts implicitly—to deliver the bad news that continuing those policies would only deepen the disaster and explain that he had no way out except to change course.

After the debacle of the Israeli invasion of southern Lebanon, which Secretary of State Condoleezza Rice called "the birth pangs of a new Middle East," her former mentor, Brent Scowcroft, the elder Bush's national security advisor and still his public voice, published an article on July 30, 2006, in the *Washington Post* titled "Beyond Lebanon: This Is the Time for a U.S.-Led Comprehensive Settlement." In it, he argued that the peace process the Bush administration had abandoned was essential in stabilizing the whole region, not least Iraq, and in reducing the influence of Iran.

With the knowledge of the elder Bush and Baker, Scowcroft traveled to Egypt and Saudi Arabia, broaching his ideas to President Hosni Mubarak and King Abdullah. They told him they were fully supportive and prepared to step forward, but were skeptical that Rice or Bush would embrace Scowcroft's program. Meanwhile, Scowcroft and Baker began reassembling the elder Bush's national security team, using the Iraq Study Group as a mobilizing tool. They saw this as a last chance to save the Bush presidency, which was indelibly tainting the father's legacy, and replace neoconservatism with foreign policy realism.

At the end of August 2006, Scowcroft briefed Rice, according to a national security official close to Scowcroft. She seemed to concur with his views and asked him, "How are we going to present this to the president?" "Not we," replied Scowcroft. "You." She appeared taken aback, but he emphasized that she was the only one who could induce Bush to change his policies. Thus Rice became the linchpin for Scowcroft's and Baker's plans.

Rice now confronted the biggest quandary of her career. On one side were the authorities that had shaped her foreign policy experience, not only Scowcroft and Baker but also, as she well knew, the looming shadow of Bush's father. On the other was the president, who had raised her into Baker's seventh-floor office in Foggy Bottom, whom she had flattered as the equal of Lincoln and Churchill, and whom, in a telling Freudian slip, she had referred to as "my husband" before a roomful of reporters and editors of *The New York Times*. Throughout the run-up to the invasion of Iraq and afterward Rice had been Bush's enabler. It was because Scowcroft understood her special relationship that he sought to win her over.

Rice's turn appeared to be reflected in a speech delivered at the Middle East Institute in Washington on September 15 by Philip Zelikow, her counselor, closest aide and friend, who had served with her under Scowcroft on the elder Bush's National Security Council. Well publicized in advance, he asserted that "some sense of progress and momentum on the Arab-Israeli dispute is just a sine qua non for their ability to cooperate actively with the United States on a lot of things that we care about." Immediately, Zelikow came under fierce criticism from Vice President Cheney's office and Rice publicly rebuked him, which provoked his abrupt resignation. In a November 27 letter to her, he wrote that he had "some truly riveting obligations to college bursars" for his children's tuition and instantly had to return to his professorship at the University of Virginia (not exactly Goldman Sachs).

Nine days after Zelikow's resignation the Iraq Study Group report was released. Informed correspondents of the *Washington Post* and *The New York*

Times related in conversation that Bush furiously called the report "a flaming turd," but his colorful remark was not published. Perhaps it was apocryphal. Nonetheless, it conveyed the intensity of his hostile rejection. Still, Scowcroft and Baker, like Vladimir and Estragon in *Waiting for Godot*, waited for Rice.

Just as they used the Iraq Study Group as their instrument, Cheney galvanized his neoconservative allies inside and outside the administration to counter it. In order to have their own proposal they put Jack Keane, a former Army vice chief of staff and longtime neocon fellow traveler, in touch with Frederick Kagan, an analyst at the neocon American Enterprise Institute, who urged a massive "surge" of troops into Iraq. Keane's presence lent a patina of military credibility. Encouraged by Cheney's office, Kagan and Keane and a team of neocons at AEI whipped up a PowerPoint presentation, and one week after the ISG report release, on December 11, they were ushered into Bush's presence.

The president had become enraged at the presumption of the Baker-Hamilton Commission even before its members gave him their report. "Although the president was publicly polite," the *Washington Post* reported, "few of the key Baker-Hamilton recommendations appealed to the administration, which intensified its own deliberations over a new 'way forward' in Iraq. How to look distinctive from the study group became a recurring theme. As described by participants in the administration review, some staff members on the National Security Council became enamored of the idea of sending more troops to Iraq in part because it was not a key feature of Baker-Hamilton."

Donald Rumsfeld had been sacrificed as the secretary of defense, but his replacement, Robert Gates, a former director of the CIA and member of the ISG, turned from skeptic into team player. The Joint Chiefs of Staff, General John Abizaid, head of Central Command, and General George Casey, commander in Iraq, all opposed the "surge" as an answer. Cheney and the neocons saw their opposition as the opening for purging and blaming them. The Joint Chiefs were ignored and sidelined, Abizaid was forced into retirement, and Casey was removed (sent into internal exile as Army chief of staff). Their dissent, leaked to the *Washington Post* for appearance in the paper on the day of Bush's "surge" speech, was an extraordinary gesture by the senior military leaders to distance themselves from impending failure.

Rice, who had fallen into radio silence, canceling a scheduled speech on "transformational diplomacy," finally intervened. When the U.S. military commanders in Iraq and U.S. ambassador Zalmay Khalilzad protested against a rush by the Iraqi government to hang Saddam Hussein, Rice overrode their objections and gave the signal to Iraqi Prime Minister Nouri al-Maliki to proceed.

Maliki's management and subsequent defense of the gruesome circus surrounding Saddam's execution disabused any illusion that he could act in the larger Iraqi national interest rather than as a political representative of Shiite sectarianism. He is to his marrow a creature of the Dawa Party, founded by Muqtada al-Sadr's father, and his alliance with al-Sadr. While the intent of the surge is to revitalize the Maliki government, that government cannot and does not wish to be reformed. The problem is not merely that Maliki is a weak political leader, or that his political coalition wouldn't permit it, or that his Iranian sponsors wouldn't allow repudiation—all of which are indisputably true. The irreducible reason is that Maliki exists only to achieve Shiite control, and if he did not he would not exist. There is no other Maliki. Nor can Bush invent one.

Bush's "surge," therefore, is a military plan that cannot produce its stated political outcome and will instead further unleash the forces he claims will be controlled. His offensive to subdue the Sunni insurgents, for example, is already accelerating the ethnic cleansing of Baghdad by the Shiite militias, which, rather than being contained, are further empowered.

Bush's rhetoric about "democracy" underlines his studied error in ignoring the lessons of nation building deeply ingrained in the experience of the U.S. Foreign Service and U.S. military in Bosnia and Kosovo. From the start, in the 2000 campaign, Bush disdained "nation building" as Bill Clinton's project. During and after the Iraq invasion, his ideological preconceptions and hostility to the State Department precluded him from adopting its successes.

In Bosnia and Kosovo, full sovereignty was not granted through an election—to this day—which would have turned over the country to one of the three contending religio-ethnic groups and fomented opposition insurgencies. Instead, the U.S. led in organizing a broad range of international partners and institutions in creating a structure of stability that is a basis for gradual democratic development. By contrast, the election Bush promoted in Iraq was political grandstanding in the name of "democracy" that incited the exclusion of Sunnis and aggravated civil warfare. Almost everything in place in Bosnia and Kosovo is absent in Iraq. The former is an example of U.S. leadership, the latter a case study in amateurish blundering. Moreover, Bush has turned "democracy" into a synonym for failure.

The State Department has been completely sidelined in the making of Bush's latest and last policy on Iraq. Its experience in the Balkans remains thoroughly ignored. And Rice does nothing to call it to Bush's attention, for that would require her to point out his shortcomings. The State Department founders like a ghost ship. Rice meanders back and forth to and from the Middle East, the shuttle without the diplomacy.

After twice rejecting the job of deputy secretary of state, John Negroponte, the director of national intelligence, was implored to accept it. In exchanging a Cabinet post for a sub-Cabinet one, a position of policymaking for an administrative post, Negroponte excited rumors that he would only have decided to make the switch if he believed that Rice would eventually leave and he would ascend to her job. But, once again, the logic of that Washington gossip is merely rational. Rice the irrelevancy remains.

January 11, 2007

PART THREE

Delusion: From the Trial of I. Lewis Libby to the Testimony of General David Petraeus

Contortions of Power

Few issues more agitated and preoccupied Vice President Dick Cheney in the early months after the declaration of "Mission Accomplished" in Iraq than former ambassador Joseph Wilson's disclosure that the intelligence underlying the administration's central justification for the invasion was bogus. So far as the occupation of Iraq was concerned, Cheney was in a triumphal mood. In a speech before a conservative group in Washington on July 30, 2003, he repeated his rationales for the war with a sense of finality: "In Iraq, a dictator with a deep and bitter hatred of the United States, who built, possessed and used weapons of mass destruction and cultivated ties to terrorists, is no more." Behind his serene public face a distressed vice president frantically micromanaged a campaign of press leaks to discredit Wilson. Cheney even scripted talking points to aides about what to tell reporters. And he fretted about what was said on cable TV talk shows like MSNBC's *Hardball*. His chief agent in this intense effort to discredit Wilson was his chief of staff, I. Lewis "Scooter" Libby, finely attuned to his principal's wishes.

Cheney was distraught over Wilson's revelation that on his mission to Niger he had discovered that Saddam Hussein was not purchasing yellow cake uranium to develop nuclear weapons and that the documents that allegedly proved it were forgeries. He could have ignored Wilson, whose complaint might have faded into the woodwork. But Cheney was not trying to correct the record, but to suppress it. He knew that what Wilson had written in his *New York Times* op-ed of July 6, 2003, and what Wilson had said earlier about it at a public forum, obliquely reported, were accurate. Wilson posed a potential menace not only to the legitimacy of the Iraq invasion but also to the reelection of Bush-Cheney.

Cheney knew that the intelligence for the war had been cooked. He was not obsessed with Wilson because he was angry that Wilson was allegedly falsifying information. Cheney was not seized with a feeling of injustice or a need to inform the public of the truth. Cheney is not a fool. "Cheney knows how to read intelligence reports. He knows how to read classified information," Richard Clarke, former director of counterterrorism on the National Security Council, told me. Of course, Clarke said, "Cheney had read the reports" that disproved the administration's line. "Cheney knew it was false," said Clarke. What worried Cheney was that he was keenly aware that the so-called intelligence the administration propagated was phony, shabby, and shaky. What also peeved him was that Wilson had said that his mission had been triggered by a request from the Office of the Vice President.

In the aftermath of the invasion, as President Bush swaggered in a fighter pilot's flight suit on the deck of the USS *Abraham Lincoln,* the administration's sway in Washington was at its zenith. The president's poll ratings were sky-high, the Republican control of the Congress airtight, and the press corps embedded. Wilson was targeted as an enemy of the state. The same methods that had been used to whip up support for the war were now deployed against the straggler. Cheney's overbearing intensity was transmitted through his chief of staff. Once again, a compliant press would be exploited to do their bidding.

Libby's obedience produced a comedy of errors wrapped inside a conspiracy. Time and again, the efficient, experienced, and loyal aide told the grand jury that it was not he who told selected journalists that Wilson's wife, Valerie Plame, an undercover CIA operative, was responsible for sending him to Niger, but the journalists who, one after another, had told him about her. None of the favored reporters to whom Libby retailed the story published or broadcast it, neither Judith Miller of *The New York Times* nor Tim Russert of NBC's *Meet the Press.* Nor did Ari Fleischer, the White House press secretary, propelled into action, manage to sell it to NBC's David Gregory or *Time* magazine's John Dickerson. (The Fleischer incident contains several layers of sociology. Libby had never deigned before to have lunch with Fleischer. In the Bush White House pecking order, the press secretary ranked far beneath the vice president's chief of staff. Libby, who had written a novel and prided himself on his cultural acumen, began his conversation by saying to Fleischer that what he was telling him was "hush-hush" and "on the q.t."—a line whose provenance was apparently lost on the press secretary—quoted from the gossipmonger played by Danny DeVito in the film *L.A. Confidential.*) Libby told the grand jury lies within a lie (about being the source for reporters who wrote no stories) to sustain another lie—that the Office of the Vice President hadn't set in motion Wilson's report—and he was subsequently indicted on five counts of perjury and obstruction of justice.

On February 21, 2002, Wilson left for his mission to Niger, where he found no evidence of Saddam seeking uranium. Before he returned, on March 1, the State Department's Intelligence and Research Bureau (INR) circulated its analysis, "Niger: Sale of Uranium to Iraq Is Unlikely." About a week later, the CIA produced its own report, based on Wilson's and other assessments, but that did not deter Cheney from declaring on three Sunday TV interviews on March 24 that Saddam was indeed trying to make nuclear weapons. Cheney was briefed on the CIA report immediately before or after his portentous remarks on television. (The CIA briefer, Craig Schmall, testified in the Libby trial that Cheney "did ask" for and "received" the report in "early 2002.")

In early September 2002, senior administration officials—Cheney, Donald Rumsfeld, and National Security Advisor Condoleezza Rice, launched an intensive campaign to persuade public opinion of Saddam's nuclear threat. "We don't want the smoking gun to be a mushroom cloud," said Rice. When the White House speechwriters and NSC staff sought to insert the Niger claim into a speech Bush was to deliver at the United Nations on September 11, the CIA told them it was unproved and the charge was stricken from the text.

The White House tried again, this time to get the accusation included in a Bush speech on October 7 delivered in Cincinnati on the eve of the congressional vote on the "Authorization for Use of Military Force Against Iraq." Before the speech, on October 5 and October 6, the CIA sent two memos warning the White House to delete the reference, and it was removed from the speech.

On October 11, the AUMF passed overwhelmingly on the administration's assurances that Saddam possessed weapons of mass destruction and was pursuing nuclear weapons. The casus belli for preemptive war was at the heart of the resolution. It read: "Iraq had an advanced nuclear weapons development program that was much closer to producing a nuclear weapon than intelligence reporting had previously indicated." This incendiary line, more than any other, had galvanized the public in support of an invasion, and Congress to pass the resolution, and was based on sheer disinformation the White House had repeatedly been warned against using—and had dropped twice. Yet it was advanced as the central premise of congressional approval, though the White House, Cheney perhaps above all, knew that it was false.

In December, Mohamed ElBaradei, director of the U.N.'s International Atomic Energy Agency, sent the White House and the NSC a letter informing them that the Niger documents were forgeries and should not be used as evidence. Feeling a sense of urgency, he made a series of calls to the White House but received no reply of any kind.

On January 12, 2003, the State Department's INR sent a memo to the CIA "that the documents pertaining to the Iraq-Niger deal were forgeries." The next day, the chief INR Iraq nuclear analyst circulated a memo warning that "the uranium purchase agreement probably is a hoax."

That month, the senior African analyst for the National Intelligence Council wrote an authoritative memo that the *Washington Post* reported "was unequivocal: The Niger story was baseless and should be laid to rest. Four U.S. officials with firsthand knowledge said in interviews that the memo, which has not been reported before, arrived at the White House as Bush and his highest-ranking advisers made the uranium story a centerpiece of their case for the rapidly approaching war against Iraq."

Despite these numerous red flags, President Bush uttered his infamous sixteen words in his January 28, 2003, State of the Union address: "The British government has learned that Saddam Hussein recently sought significant quantities of uranium from Africa." A neoconservative member of the NSC, Robert Joseph, had contrived to sneak the falsehood into the speech by attributing it to British intelligence.

On February 5, Secretary of State Colin Powell made the case for war before the United Nations. In preparing for his speech he discarded a lengthy memo from Libby because Powell and his people believed it was filled with unproven charges. Ultimately, however, Powell's speech still contained more than two dozen falsehoods and was exposed as based on disinformation.

In fact, CIA officers believed they had cautioned Powell against using material they had already disproved. Tyler Drumheller, CIA station chief in Europe, in an interview published this week in *Der Spiegel*, said, "So the first thing I thought, having worked in the government all my life, was that we probably gave Powell the wrong speech. We checked our files and found out that they had just ignored it. The policy was set. The war in Iraq was coming and they were looking for intelligence to fit into the policy."

On March 16, Cheney appeared on *Meet the Press*, where he attacked ElBaradei's credibility and insisted that Saddam had nuclear weapons. "And we believe he has, in fact, reconstituted nuclear weapons. I think Mr. ElBaradei frankly is wrong." Three days later, the invasion of Iraq was launched.

Upon the publication of Nicholas Kristof's column in *The New York Times* on May 6 that described the Wilson mission but did not identify him, Cheney went into a fury. Libby was dispatched to unearth material about Wilson. He called Robert Grenier, chief of the CIA's counterterrorism unit, on June 11 and learned from him the identity of Valerie Plame, according to Grenier's testimony this week in the Libby trial. From that moment, Libby began his disinformation campaign that she was responsible for sending her husband on the mission, which was authorized by higher CIA officials. Under oath to Patrick Fitzgerald's grand jury, Libby claimed that he first learned about her identity from Tim Russert on July 10. (Grenier, for his part, was forced out of the CIA in early 2006 for opposing the administration's torture policy.)

The INR memo on Wilson, released as a trial exhibit, disproved the additional falsehood peddled by the Republican report of the Senate Intelligence Committee of 2004, which claimed Wilson had in fact bolstered the case that Saddam was seeking uranium in Niger—a report cited by the *Washington Post* editorial page to label Wilson as untruthful, a crucial element in the smear campaign.

In his meeting with Judith Miller, according to her testimony on the witness stand, Libby confided that the CIA "was beginning to backpedal from the unequivocal intelligence" it had provided prewar about Saddam's nuclear program. Of course, that was a complete lie. Libby was deliberately misleading the reporter, covering up the CIA's many warnings and reports to the contrary, as he tried to get her to publish falsehoods about Wilson and reveal Plame's identity. Libby appealed to Miller's sense of justice. The CIA, he told her, was engaged in "a perverted war of leaks" against the wholly innocent administration.

In October 2003, neoconservative Undersecretary of Defense Douglas Feith sent the Senate Intelligence Committee a classified report, "Summary of Body of Intelligence on Iraq-al Qaeda Contacts," a farrago of disinformation that had been the basis of the Libby memo given to Powell. Feith had been in charge of the Pentagon's Office of Special Plans, a parallel intelligence unit that stovepiped disinformation from Iraqi exiles to the Office of the Vice President and the NSC with a stamp of approval that evaded the normal channels of verifying intelligence. Within weeks, Feith's report was leaked to the neoconservative *Weekly Standard* and published under the headline "Case Closed: The U.S. Government's Secret Memo Detailing Cooperation Between Saddam Hussein and Osama bin Laden." On January 9, 2004, Cheney took it upon himself, in an interview with the *Rocky Mountain News*, to promote *The Weekly Standard*'s story as "the best source of information." Cheney's support for the disinformation continued through the 2004 campaign and beyond. Then Cheney named the writer of *The Weekly Standard*'s article, Stephen Hayes, as his official biographer.

Cheney is scheduled to testify soon at the federal courthouse as a defense witness, where he will be questioned about his direction of the operation in which Libby acted as his pawn. Meanwhile, a few blocks down Pennsylvania Avenue, Congress debates resolutions against Bush's escalation of the war, haunted by the original "Authorization for Use of Military Force," which was approved with a naive trust that on a matter of war the president and the vice president would tell the truth.

February 1, 2007

Preparing for Failure

Deep within the bowels of the Pentagon, policy planners are conducting secret meetings to discuss what to do in the worst-case scenario in Iraq about a year from today if and when President Bush's escalation of more than twenty thousand troops fails, a participant in those discussions told me. None of those who are taking part in these exercises, shielded from the public view and the immediate scrutiny of the White House, believes that the so-called surge will succeed. On the contrary, everyone thinks it will not only fail to achieve its aims but also accelerate instability by providing a glaring example of U.S. incapacity and incompetence.

The profoundly pessimistic thinking that permeates the senior military and the intelligence community, however, is forbidden in the sanitized atmosphere of mind-cure boosterism that surrounds Bush. "He's tried this two times—it's failed twice," Speaker of the House Nancy Pelosi said on January 24 about the "surge" tactic. "I asked him at the White House, 'Mr. President, why do you think this time it's going to work?' And he said, 'Because I told them it had to.'" She repeated his words: "'I told them that they had to.' That was the end of it. That's the way it is."

On February 2, the National Intelligence Council, representing all intelligence agencies, issued a new National Intelligence Estimate on Iraq, as harsh an antidote to wishful thinking as could be imagined. "The Intelligence Community judges that the term 'civil war' does not adequately capture the complexity of the conflict in Iraq, which includes extensive Shia-on-Shia violence, Al-Qaeda and Sunni insurgent attacks on Coalition forces, and widespread criminally motivated violence. Nonetheless, the term 'civil war' accurately describes key elements of the Iraqi conflict, including the hardening of ethno-sectarian identities, a sea change in the character of the violence, ethno-sectarian mobilization, and population displacements."

The report described an Iraqi government, army, and police force that cannot meet these challenges in any foreseeable time frame and a reversal of "the negative trends driving Iraq's current trajectory" occurring only through a dream sequence in which all the warring sects and factions, in some unexplained way, suddenly make peace with one another. Nor does the NIE suggest that this imaginary scenario might ever come to pass. Instead, it proceeds to describe the potential for "an abrupt increase in communal and insurgent violence and a shift in Iraq's trajectory from gradual decline to rapid deterioration with grave humanitarian, political, and security consequences."

Bush justified his invasion on the basis of false intelligence in the now notorious NIE of October 2002 that claimed Saddam Hussein possessed weapons of mass destruction. Now, as the latest NIE forecasts nightmares, he is escalating the war. But almost everything has changed in the nearly four years since the invasion.

A newly elected Congress has been galvanized to debate a bipartisan resolution disapproving of Bush's escalation. Yet in the Senate, where sixty votes are necessary to establish cloture on a filibuster, the Republican minority has blocked a vote. Though many Republicans are keenly aware that continued support for Bush's policy amounts to political suicide in 2008, all but two of them have joined a phalanx to shut down the vote. By mustering behind him, they tie their fate to his policy. Bush, however, will be gone, while they remain exposed to the political elements.

Even Senator John Warner of Virginia, the Republican cosponsor of the resolution against the escalation along with Senator Carl Levin, D-Michigan, cast his lot with the Republican martyr brigade, voting to suppress his own measure. In 2002, the Republican right mounted a primary campaign against Warner in retribution for his deviation from their ideological line, but failed feebly. Warner could not fear a repetition of the right's vengeance. Could he have been undermining himself out of deference to the authority of a commander in chief whose course he believes is reckless? The next day, Warner and six other Republican senators issued a letter calling for a "full and open debate" on the resolution they had already voted against voting on.

The Republican prevention of a vote on the Warner-Levin resolution reflects an effort to close debate on the war itself. It amounts in effect to a gag rule on Bush's Iraq policy. During the Vietnam War, under President Johnson, neither party attempted to shut down debate. After 1969, President Nixon's Vietnam policy consisted of misdirection, deception, covert action, and fait accompli, such as the counterproductive and ultimately catastrophic invasion of Cambodia. The Bush administration's methods can be traced to the Nixon administration, with Dick Cheney as the connecting thread.

The reception of the latest NIE, even more than the NIE itself, indicates again Bush's and Republicans' denial of objective analysis from the professional intelligence community. The October 2002 NIE was produced under intense pressure from the White House, especially Vice President Cheney, to validate its preconceived views. "The administration used intelligence not to inform decision-making, but to justify a decision already made," Paul Pillar, the national intelligence officer for the Middle East who oversaw the assembling of that NIE, wrote a year ago. In the shadow of this travesty, the new NIE was written with great care; its frightening descriptions, therefore, should be considered to be deliberately guarded and reserved in tone.

Just as Bush and the Republicans rejected the bipartisan wise men of the Baker-Hamilton Commission, they have now rejected the objective assessment of the professionals. By thwarting the bipartisan Warner-Levin resolution, they have declared that they will operate on their own fanciful criteria, even against their own political interests.

As the Senate curdles in frustration over Republican tactics, the trial of Scooter Libby continues to clarify the degree to which the administration covered up its disinformation campaign that led the country into war with another disinformation campaign to cover up the role of the vice president as the prime mover of the smear campaign against former ambassador Joseph Wilson for committing the unforgivable act of revealing the truth. For the Senate Republicans, Scooter Libby is not an object lesson. The lesson they take away, if any, is not the necessity of open government but once again the need to burn the tapes.

Libby's effort to prevent his grand jury tapes from being entered into evidence in his trial resembled nothing so much as Nixon trying to suppress his tapes. Both in the end revealed their respective coverups. Cheney learned from Nixon to burn the tapes at least figuratively; now, his chief of staff, Cheney's Cheney, has tried to protect Cheney by literally and futilely suppressing the tapes. Cheney finds himself back at the beginning. For him, life has come full circle. From the entire history of deception, from the Nixon to the Libby tapes, the Republicans have learned nothing.

The new NIE offers more than "key judgments" on "the Prospects for Iraq's Stability." It is also a template for the short-term future of American politics. The ruthlessly cruel events projected for Iraq will blow back to the United States. The more Bush fights there, the more the embattled Republicans must fight here.

The Senate Republicans' vote to suppress the resolution on the war was the moment when they irrevocably aligned themselves completely with a president who rejects objective analysis. Unable to shield him or themselves from the inevitable consequences, they have made a conscious decision to place the president's delusions above the welfare not only of the Republican Party but also of the troops sent into the deadly labyrinth of Baghdad. Quietly and calmly, as the Republicans hype the "surge," the war planners prepare for the worst.

February 8, 2007

United States v. I. Lewis Libby:
Washington Anthropology

Throughout the anxious months before the trial of *United States v. I. Lewis Libby*, one of Scooter Libby's old mentors, a prominent Washington attorney and Republican with experience going back to the Watergate scandal and with intimate ties to neoconservatives, implored him repeatedly to stop covering up for Vice President Cheney and to cut a deal with the special prosecutor. Yet another distinguished Washington lawyer and personal friend of Libby's, privy to the mentor's counsel, reinforced his urgent advice and offered to provide Libby with introductions to former prosecutors who might help guide him. But Libby rebuffed them. He refused to listen. He insisted on the trial.

This Tuesday, Theodore Wells, Libby's chief defense lawyer, abruptly announced that neither Cheney nor Libby would testify on his behalf. In effect, the defense was resting. Did his own lawyers mistrust Libby on the stand? Would he lie and prompt another count of indictment? Would Cheney, indisputably the director of the campaign against former ambassador Joseph Wilson, be stepping into a perjury trap or open the door to conspiracy charges implicit from the beginning? Those questions, along with their testimony, remain moot.

According to prosecutor Patrick Fitzgerald, Libby's case amounts to an attempt at "jury nullification." Libby is charged with five counts of perjury and obstruction of justice for lying about where he learned the identity of CIA undercover operative Valerie Plame (Wilson's wife) and to whom he spread that information. Fitzgerald presented two government officials, former CIA officer Robert Grenier and State Department official Marc Grossman, who swore they were the first to inform Libby. Libby was in pursuit of that information, Fitzgerald further revealed through testimony from past and present Bush administration officials, because the vice president had tasked him to find and spread it. And Libby also passed on the information to Ari Fleischer, the White House press secretary, to get him to pass it on to the press. Two reporters, Matt Cooper (then at *Time* magazine) and Judith Miller (then at *The New York Times*) testified that Libby had conveyed to them the information about Plame and NBC's Tim Russert testified that he did not first inform Libby about her as Libby told the grand jury. Fitzgerald's prosecution was well honed, unadorned, and a straight arrow.

Libby's defense was the legal equivalent of the fog of war. He sought to obfuscate the clarity of the prosecution's case by raising irrelevant issues, turning the jury's attention away from the charges themselves, and creating doubt by getting witnesses to admit small lapses of memory, thereby underlining Libby's memory defense. So Libby's lawyers highlighted Cooper's incomplete note taking, whether Miller raised the issue of writing a piece based on Libby's information, and whether Russert followed strict journalistic protocol when he spoke freely to the FBI. Libby's team also summoned a parade of reporters to relate that Libby had not dropped Plame's name with them. By demonstrating a negative, Libby sought to dispute a positive. The intent to sow confusion among the jurors in order to raise a shadow of a doubt and produce an acquittal partly depended on their ignorance of Washington anthropology.

Fitzgerald's case elicited significant evidence of the planned and concerted attack on Wilson. Libby, along with a host of other White House aides, leaked Plame's secret identity to reporters. The methods of communications strategy were disclosed in the testimony of Cathie Martin, Cheney's deputy P.R. aide, who explained the art of talking points, and of Fleischer, among others. "It was decided that Scooter would call [reporters] to try to get into the story and correct the false information," Martin said. "That was [Cheney's] decision." Trial exhibits included the notes of Cheney's former communications advisor, Mary Matalin, who suggested that Libby call Russert to complain about MSNBC *Hardball* host Chris Matthews: "Tim hates Chris." Martin expressed awe of Matalin's skills, but Matalin's Heather-like remarks illuminated Republican Washington as *High School Confidential.*

On Monday, I sat in the courtroom as the dapper, slightly built Libby took his place at the defense table, half smiling at his half-dozen attorneys while occasionally flicking his head to the side, betraying a wary glance. In the bench behind him sat his wife, Harriet Grant (herself a lawyer), and

Barbara Comstock, a conservative operative hired as a P.R. specialist, playing with her BlackBerry during the testimony and chewing gum. The jurors marching to their seats were impassive; it was impossible to read anything from their immobile faces.

On that day, the busiest for the defense, the witnesses flew through the courtroom with speed. Every one called by the defense was a reporter whose presence was intended to contribute to the confusion of the jury and direct their gaze away from the actual charges. Walter Pincus of the *Washington Post* was the first one in the stand. He revealed that he had spoken with Libby but that it was Fleischer who disclosed to him Plame's name, as though that somehow proved exculpatory. Of course, it was Libby who told Fleischer about Plame—"hush-hush" and "on the q.t." Pincus is the reporter in the run-up to the invasion of Iraq who persistently wrote skeptical stories on administration claims about Saddam Hussein's possession of weapons of mass destruction. Those stories were typically buried, earning Pincus the sobriquet among his friends of Walter "A-14" Pincus.

Fleischer told Pincus about Plame as a consequence of Pincus's diligence as he sought to get to the bottom of the Wilson smear. It was Pincus who called Fleischer. Pincus was not necessarily the person whom Libby would trust to leak to himself. Pincus was known within the White House as a skeptic of its disinformation and as a reporter with many independent sources in the intelligence community, which the neoconservatives regarded as an adversary. Pincus was not the sort of reporter whom Libby would provide with this "hush-hush" information. But if Fleischer did so, it was a different matter. In any case, Pincus did not publish Plame's name. Unlike Bob Novak, he had compunctions about the sensitivity of exposing a CIA operative.

Next up was Pincus's colleague Bob Woodward, who explained that then Deputy Secretary of State Richard Armitage had told him about Plame. A snippet of audiotape of their conversation, recorded by Woodward as part of his research for his book *Plan of Attack*, was played. This was another attempt at exculpation by showing that it was not Libby who was the source, once again trying to cloud the accusations of perjury and obstruction. Armitage, Colin Powell's best friend, had been a source for Woodward for decades. Libby would know that however useful Woodward might be as an outlet for leaks, as he demonstrated in *Bush at War*, depicting President Bush and his team as decisive, prudent, and courageous, he would ultimately tilt in

Powell's direction. But there was another reason for Libby not to leak Plame's identity to Woodward that was even more basic. Woodward husbanded material for his bestselling books and did not dribble out his exclusives in the daily newspaper. Leaking to Woodward was pointless if one wanted to get a story published immediately.

Armitage's leak was at best mindless, at worst the trading of national security secrets to ingratiate himself with a star reporter. On the tape, Armitage's tough-guy, obscenity-spewing persona is coached along by an eager, laughing Woodward. The more Woodward laps it up, the more Armitage spills the beans. Woodward: "But why would they send him?" Armitage: "Because his wife's a fucking analyst at the agency." Woodward: "It's still weird." Armitage: "It, it's perfect. This is what she does, she is a WMD analyst out there." Woodward: "Oh she is." Armitage: "Yeah." Woodward: "Oh, I see."

Armitage had learned of Plame from reading a State Department memo that conspicuously marked an "S" next to her name, indicating that her identity was top secret. Armitage, who had years of experience at high levels of government, was more intent on impressing Woodward than on keeping the secret. The tape ends with Armitage repeating with emphasis: "But his wife is in the agency and is a WMD analyst. How about that shit?" Armitage's buffoonery about "that shit" had no bearing on the charges against Libby, but Libby's lawyers hoped it would provide a tawdry distraction, as it has for numerous Washington columnists and pundits.

Novak was the next witness. He spelled his last name and then his first: "B-O-B." He explained that his sources were Armitage and Karl Rove. "I wouldn't call him a good friend. I would call him a very good source," Novak said about Rove. "I talked to him two or three times a week at that point." Unlike Rove, Libby was not a regular source. "I had no help and no confirmation from Mr. Libby on that issue," Novak said about the Plame story. Just when it appeared that Novak was done, a juror asked a question, read by Judge Reggie Walton, about whether Novak had spoken to anyone else about the information in his notorious column exposing Plame besides the two "senior administration officials" cited in it before its publication. Novak said that he had spoken with Bill Harlow, the public affairs officer at the CIA.

The judge prodded him on whether there was anyone else. Novak revealed that he gave a copy of his column to Richard Hohlt, whom he described as one of his "closest friends," and to whom he said he spoke daily. Hohlt, Novak went on, is a "lobbyist about town." (In fact, he's a little known but influential Republican lobbyist.) And, the judge wondered, did Mr. Hohlt share the column with anyone? Novak further revealed that Hohlt showed it to people at the White House. Thus, through Novak's cutout, or go-between, the White House was informed that Novak would publish Plame's identity. None of this had any bearing on Libby's guilt or innocence, but it was a fascinating glimpse at Novak's methods.

David Sanger, the chief Washington correspondent for *The New York Times*, followed Novak in the witness chair. What Sanger had to offer is that he had spoken with Libby but that Libby had not told him about Plame. Sanger was another bit player in the Libby defense of distraction. Indeed, there was no cause to leak to Sanger. He was not the type of reporter with whom that sort of delicate political information would be shared. Indeed, Libby was working *The New York Times* through Judith Miller, the past reliable outlet for disinformation on WMD stories. Libby could not know that Miller would be thwarted in getting permission to write a Plame story. Going to someone like Sanger would only have undermined his attempt to use the *Times*. But none of that was drawn from the witness.

The next day, instead of calling Cheney, Libby's team put John Hannah, a neoconservative Middle East policy analyst on the vice president's staff, on the stand. For two hours, Hannah held forth on Libby's forgetfulness and the overwhelming crush of his job. Hannah was Cheney's stand-in, but without Cheney's enormous potential liabilities that might be explored through cross-examination. Hannah's role was to be the first-person witness to buttress Libby's memory defense.

Yet, under cross-examination by Fitzgerald, Hannah was cracked apart in a matter of minutes. Fitzgerald asked him whether defending Cheney in the media was an important part of Libby's job. "It would be important to push back on those issues, yes," Hannah said. Fitzgerald then got Hannah to acknowledge that getting Libby to give up an hour's worth of his time, given his heavy load of work, would be difficult. Fitzgerald zeroed in on Libby's two long meetings in the St. Regis Hotel's dining room on June 23 and July 8, 2003. "So, during the time of all these threats if he gave someone an hour or two of his time . . . it was something Mr. Libby would think was important, correct?" Fitzgerald asked. Hannah answered that it was. "Is it fair to say that what was important to the vice president was important to Mr. Libby?" Fitzgerald asked. "Yes, that's correct," Hannah replied.

But the demolition of Hannah was not done. A juror had a question, posed to the witness by the judge: Aside from Libby's difficulty with memory, did it lead him to have concerns about his effectiveness? "Never," said Hannah. The barbed question was a sharp indication of at least one juror's cynicism about Libby's defense.

On Wednesday, the next day, Judge Walton ruled that Libby's lawyers had misled the court into believing that Libby would testify on his own behalf. Walton, therefore, disallowed admission into court of questioning of Libby's CIA briefers, who would supposedly show how busy Libby was, another element of his effort to confuse the jury. Undoubtedly, Walton's displeasure at Libby's refusal to testify will shape the instructions he gives to the jurors.

Closing statements will occur on February 20. Judge Walton will charge the jury, and they will decide Libby's fate. Libby must hope that the testimony presented by Fitzgerald has been obscured enough to prevent his conviction. Then the advice he rejected from his concerned mentor and other friends will have been proved to be a gamble he never needed to accept. If declared not guilty, Libby can return to his White House office, where he can resume the vice president's campaigns of disinformation.

February 15, 2007

United States v. I. Lewis Libby: Closing Arguments

On Tuesday, I observed the closing arguments at the federal courthouse in Washington in the case of *United States v. I. Lewis Libby*. The prosecution's systematic presentation of the evidence supporting the five-count indictment of perjury and obstruction of justice did not foreshadow the dramatic accusation about Vice President Dick Cheney that was to come at the day's end. "This case is about lying," deputy prosecutor Peter Zeidenberg dryly began. It was, he explained, about how Scooter Libby learned that former ambassador Joseph Wilson's wife, Valerie Plame, was a covert CIA operative, and about whom Libby spoke with about the revelation and what he said.

The defense, for its part, appealed to the jurors' empathy for what it characterized as Libby's bad memory, called the prosecutors "mad," conjured up the defendant's two young children for sympathy, and described him as a decent man diligently doing his job despite being surrounded by the chaos of an administration in which he was indispensable but for whose actions he apparently bore no responsibility.

Finally, hour after hour, the defense attacked not only the credibility of the journalists who had been witnesses but also the very notion that journalism itself has to do with representing the truth. After journalists, one after another, were held up to derision as clownish boobs and blamed for Libby's predicament, the defense appealed to the jury's common sense to dismiss the craft of journalism as false by nature, always to be discredited, and on that basis to find Libby not guilty. On one level, the final argument on behalf of Scooter Libby was Libby's last disinformation campaign. On another, it was a summation of the Republican hostility toward the press, as official an imprimatur as Richard Nixon's malevolent enemies list or George H.W. Bush's sophomoric 1992 campaign slogan: "Annoy the Liberal Media."

The prosecution and the defense appeared before the jury with more than two contending accounts of the Libby story. Indeed, the defense did little if anything to counter the prosecution. Poor Libby's errors were just attributable to his bad memory. While the prosecution operated on the plane of reason, the defense retreated to high emotion. Libby's case began with accusations of a dark plot within the White House to feed Libby to the wolves to save the skin of Karl Rove—a conspiracy that was never mentioned during the trial—and ended in tears with the sudden and choked sobbing of defense attorney Theodore Wells.

"Did you ever hear any evidence about a conspiracy to scapegoat Mr. Libby? It's not a problem with your memory," Zeidenberg said. The case, he went on, is not about "scapegoating, conspiracies or bad memory." With businesslike swiftness, he detailed how Libby conveniently forgot nine conversations with eight individuals about Plame and fabricated out of whole cloth two conversations with two reporters. Names, dates, and places were cited, all supported by the evidence. Libby's memory failed him on what had happened, but worked on what hadn't.

Zeidenberg ran through the narrative of the loyal Libby, doing the bidding of his principal, Vice President Dick Cheney, who was angered at Wilson's public revelations concerning the falsehoods about the justification for the invasion of Iraq, a CIA mission set in motion by Cheney's own inquiries, which particularly enraged him. Cheney tasked Libby to learn about Wilson's wife, the CIA operative, so that Wilson's trip to Niger could be traced to her and not to Cheney's initial request to dig up information about Saddam Hussein's seeking yellow cake uranium for nuclear weapons.

Libby tapped government official after official, Marc Grossman at the State Department and Robert Grenier at the CIA, from whom he demanded information on Plame. The officials each testified at the trial, vividly recalling his unusual questioning; but Libby remembered nothing about them in his grand jury testimony. Nor did Libby remember his conversations about Plame with Cheney's communications aide, Cathie Martin, or his CIA briefer, Craig Schmall, who also remembered the conversations well. Nor did Libby remember his conversations with Judith Miller, *The New York Times* correspondent, to whom he leaked Plame's name and an exclusive story about the contents of the National Intelligence Estimate on Iraq. President Bush had declassified the NIE at the insistence of Cheney; the only other person aware of the declassification was Libby—not then National Security Advisor Condoleezza Rice or her deputy, Stephen Hadley. But Libby did not remember it. Libby did not remember his conversation with White House press secretary Ari Fleischer, which was "hush-hush" and "on the q.t.," he said, divulging Plame's identity to him. Nor did he remember his conversation with David Addington, Cheney's counsel, Libby's Libby, telling Addington to keep his voice down behind a closed door as Libby asked him about Wilson's spouse sending him on his mission.

But Libby remembered conversations with Tim Russert, the host of NBC's *Meet the Press*, and Matthew Cooper, former correspondent for *Time* magazine. Zeidenberg played tape recordings of Libby's grand jury testimony in which Libby recalls precisely all the words that Russert and Cooper say were never uttered. On the tapes, Libby blames the reporters. "All I had was information coming from reporters . . . all I had was reporters telling us that . . . I didn't know he had a wife . . . I told a couple of reporters what reporters told us."

Libby's invented conversations, putting the onus of revealing Plame's identity on reporters, disclosed the broad attitude of the Bush White

House toward the press. Having used reporters to plant false stories in the run-up to the war, Libby believed he could hide behind them. They tell so many stories, their habits are not always perfect, they get things wrong as they labor to get them right, they inhabit an inferno of petty envies about their fellow reporters, and they might never tell. They would not tell and if they did, ultimately, who would believe them? Who would find his way through the wilderness of the Washington press corps?

But Libby knew what he did, Zeidenberg explained. He feared he might be found out. The FBI came to his door. If he told the truth he would implicate the vice president in a smear campaign against a critic and give credence to Wilson's statements that the administration had led the country into war on a falsehood. But if Libby blamed the reporters, Libby's—and Cheney's—actions would seem "innocuous," said Zeidenberg. "He decided to lie." With that, the first part of the prosecution summation concluded.

Libby's attorney, Wells, strode before the jury and used his precious opening minutes to denounce Zeidenberg for a "personal attack," namely, Zeidenberg's reference to Wells' failure to develop the White House conspiracy he claimed at the start of the trial was the center of his defense. "Maybe I was drunk when I made my opening," said Wells. He described Libby as a sheer victim, using language that evoked the image of an abused prisoner: "They get Mr. Libby in the grand jury and start beating on him." Who can blame a beaten man for what he might blurt out? The prosecution, said Wells, was "madness."

Wells concocted a fantasy of how Russert, who testified that he did not tell Libby about Plame, might have done so even though there was no evidence whatsoever to prove it. Wells spun a tale about Robert Novak's infamous column of July 14, 2003, revealing Plame's identity, observing that it was distributed to various news outlets that subscribe to Novak's column through the Associated Press wire on July 11. "Maybe," said Wells, Russert read the column on the AP wire, misremembered the date, and misremembered the entire conversation. "Maybe all that happened . . . Maybe he's confused." Maybe Wells was trying to sow confusion.

How could Libby be expected to remember? "He didn't get to lay [sic] on a beach. He didn't get to see his wife and family. He was working on important issues." Wells looked up. "How much time do I have?" He had squandered too much of it defending his nonexistent conspiracy-mongering. Quickly, he shifted back to Russert. Russert isn't necessarily a liar, but what he says is "impossible." The jury "can't rely on him." Russert has "memory problems." He ridiculed Russert: "I don't recall! I don't recall! I don't recall!" He called NBC "not a friendly network . . . It was Wilson's home spot!"

Wells tried new fantasies. He admitted that Libby "got things wrong in the grand jury." He was "confused." So: "Maybe Libby did nothing more than confuse Novak with Russert." And: "Maybe he got Cooper confused with Russert." It's "impossible" to show that Libby engaged in "intentional lies."

After a lunch break, Wells's cocounsel, William Jeffress, less bombastic and more conversational but no less conjectural, took over. After making conventional defenses about memory, he launched into an assault on journalists and journalism. "You can't take anything in these newspaper articles as true," he said. "Maybe some journalists wish you could. But you can't." This extraordinary defense—that nothing in any newspaper can be considered true—was the reductio ad absurdum of the Bush administration's use and abuse of the press corps. Having manipulated it to plant stories on weapons of mass destruction to legitimize the Iraq war, Libby, who was centrally involved in those disinformation efforts, was reduced to defending himself on the basis that newspapers cannot be trusted to publish the truth.

On the screen mounted inside the courtroom, Jeffress introduced Libby's Exhibit A for mistrusting the press: Miller, the reporter who was the chief repository of the administration's leaks on WMD and to whom Libby leaked Plame's identity. Videotapes unreeled of Miller recollecting that she could not remember certain things, speaking nervously, disjointedly and carelessly, and contradicting herself. "It's really easy to forget about a story you're not writing," she said. "She's got a bit of a memory problem," Jeffress said, stifling a snicker. "Judith Miller is not a reliable witness." If Miller is flaky, Libby must be innocent.

Like Wells, Jeffress leaped into the unknown, inventing scenarios and testimony and inviting the jury to suspend their disbelief. He projected a completely garbled line from Cooper's reporter's notebook and filled in phrases to make it appear almost word for word to be congruent with Libby's testimony that he supposedly told Cooper he had heard about Plame from reporters and didn't know if it was true, even though Cooper testified that Libby had said no such thing. "Libby got it right!" proclaimed Jeffress triumphantly about his fictionalization. He turned to the jury and urged its members to acquit: "You're not journalists!"

Wells had less than an hour to finish for the defense. Libby, he said, "didn't leak to anybody." Miller is not "anybody." "The only person," said Wells, "is Miller, and I don't think it happened . . . Judith Miller has bad information . . . He didn't leak to anybody." Moreover, Wilson's "wife was not important to Scooter Libby." Libby received briefings on terrorism "that make your toes curl . . . Give him the benefit of the doubt." Though he "got things wrong in the grand jury . . . it's unfair to expect him to remember exact words."

Wells, a six-foot-two-inch African American, approached the jury members, standing directly in front of them, and urged them to help each other avoid prejudice. "If someone says, 'He's a Republican, he worked for Cheney, let's just do him,' help that person. Don't sacrifice Scooter Libby for how you may feel about the war in Iraq or Bush administration. Treat him the way he deserves to be treated . . . Fight any temptation for your views if you're a Democrat, whatever party. This is a man who has a wife and kids. He's been under my protection for the last month. Just give him back." Wells's voice cracked and he spoke his final words through sobs. "Give him back to me! Give him back!" He rushed back to his chair at the head of the defense table, covered his face and then stared at the floor.

At last, it was the turn of Patrick Fitzgerald, the special prosecutor. "Madness! Madness!" he shouted, waving his arms. "Outrageous! The government has brought a case about two witnesses, two phone calls. And they just want you to speculate. The defense wishes that were so. Saying it loudly, pounding the table, doesn't change the facts. Let's talk about the facts. Let's get busy."

"It's not he said, she said," Fitzgerald declared. On the courtroom screen appeared the eight people with whom Libby had discussed Plame nine times. "It's he said, he said, he said, she said, she said, she said, he said, he said. Is this the greatest coincidence in the world?"

"One of the myths is that Wilson's wife is not important." For Cheney and Libby "she wasn't a person. She was an argument. She was a fact to use against Wilson."

The defense left virtually untouched the many witnesses corroborating that Libby sought Plame's identity and spread it. Now Fitzgerald reviewed their unimpeached testimony. Point by point, Fitzgerald deconstructed Cathie Martin's talking points dictated by Cheney, getting down to the irreducible nub of Cheney's obsession, handwritten on a copy of Wilson's *New York Times* op-ed article: "Or did his wife send him on a junket?"

Speaking rapidly in order to fit all his facts into the hour allotted to him, Fitzgerald did not slow his clipped delivery as he came to the most dramatic statement of the trial. "You just think it's coincidence that Cheney was writing this?" he asked rhetorically, before answering his own question. "There is a cloud over the vice president. He wrote on those columns. He had those meetings. He sent Libby off to the meeting with Judith Miller where Plame was discussed. That cloud remains because the defendant obstructed justice. That cloud is there. That cloud is something that we just can't pretend isn't there."

"That cloud" was like the sudden appearance of a thunderhead over the proceedings and the administration. In no uncertain terms, in his most public statement, Fitzgerald made clear that he believed that Cheney was the one behind the crime for which he was prosecuting Libby. It was Cheney who was the boss, Cheney who gave the orders, and Cheney to whom Libby was the loyal soldier, and it is Cheney for whom Libby is covering up.

There was more: Fitzgerald on why Cooper was credible and Russert was "a devastating witness," and Libby remembering "Rove's conversation with Novak better than Novak." More: The uniqueness with which the witnesses recalled their conversations with Libby on Plame. And more: The importance of the Wilson matter to him and Cheney. Yet more: Witness after witness recalling Libby's anger, irritation, and agitation. "We all know, when you're angry at someone, you remember . . . He was angry about Wilson. What Wilson said is that the country got lied into war. One of the people he blamed was the defendant—and the vice president."

For his final words, Fitzgerald transformed Wells' lachrymose closing ("Give him back to me!") into a challenge about the truth and the rule of law. "He stole the truth from the judicial system," Fitzgerald told the jury. "If you return a guilty verdict, you give the truth back." Thus the closing statements ended, first with a whimper and then with a bang.

On Wednesday Judge Reggie Walton gave his instructions to the jury, and it is now deliberating.

February 22, 2007

United States v. I. Lewis Libby: The Verdict

The conviction of I. Lewis "Scooter" Libby, Vice President Dick Cheney's former chief of staff, on criminal charges of obstruction of justice and perjury brings only a partial conclusion to the sordid political tragedy that is the Bush presidency. Yet the judgment on this matter goes to the heart of the administration.

Foreign policy was and is the principal way of consolidating unchecked executive power. In the run-up to the Iraq war, professional standards, even within the military and intelligence agencies, were subordinated to political goals. Only information that fit the preconceived case was permitted. Those who advanced facts or raised skeptical questions about sketchy information were seen as deliberate enemies causing damage from within. From the beginning, the White House indulged in unrestrained attacks on such professionals. Revealing the facts, especially about the politically driven method of skewing policy, was treated as a crime against the state.

For questioning the undermanned battle plan for the invasion of Iraq, Army Chief of Staff Eric Shinseki was publicly humiliated by neoconservative Deputy Secretary of Defense Paul Wolfowitz and then cashiered. For disclosing negligence on terrorism before the September 11 attacks, counterterrorism chief Richard Clarke was accused by then National Security Advisor Condoleezza Rice of acting purely out of motives of personal greed to promote his recently published memoir. For exposing the absence of rational policymaking in economics as well as foreign policy, Secretary of the Treasury Paul O'Neill was threatened with an investigation for allegedly abusing classified material. Once he was intimidated into silence, the probe was dropped.

In the aftermath of former ambassador Joseph Wilson's revelation that the most explosive reason given for war against Iraq—that Saddam Hussein was seeking yellow cake uranium in Niger to fuel nuclear weapons had no apparent basis in fact, the Bush White House revved into high gear against the critic. Wilson, however, was even more dangerous than the others because he was a witness to the false rationale for the war.

As Libby's defense counsel insisted, Scooter was merely one of many in the White House assailing Wilson's integrity. Others, including Bush's political strategist Karl Rove, were involved. To a degree, the smear campaign was for a time successful, fueled by the Republican-controlled Senate Intelligence Committee and elements of the Washington press corps. But the trial exhibits—documents entered by the special prosecutor—knocked down every single one of their falsehoods.

Libby's defenders argued that there was no underlying crime. He was not charged with revealing the identity of Valerie Plame, Wilson's wife, as a covert CIA agent, which was a charge raised by the White House gang in an effort to prove she sent Wilson on his Niger mission—another of the lies spread about him.

But Libby committed his crimes to cover-up the role of his boss and to protect his own position in the attack on Wilson. At base, then, the reasons for war were the scandal.

Libby was no mere factotum. He was a central member of the neoconservative cast of characters, who began as a protégé of Wolfowitz and was elevated to the role of Cheney's indispensable man.

Libby's conviction not only indelibly stains neoconservatism. It is a damning condemnation of the Bush White House belief that the ends justify the means and its aggrandizement of absolute power. Ultimately, this is a verdict that can never be erased from the history of the Bush presidency.

March 5, 2007

The History Book Club

As witnesses were trooping to the stand in the federal courthouse in Washington to testify in the case of *United States v. I Lewis Libby*, and the *Washington Post* was publishing its series on the squalid conditions that wounded Iraq war veterans suffer at the Walter Reed Army Medical Center while thousands more soldiers were surging into Baghdad, President Bush held one of his private book club sessions that Karl Rove organizes for him at the White House. Rove picks the book, invites the author and a few neo-conservative intellectual luminaries, and conducts the discussions. For this Bush book club meeting, the guest was Andrew Roberts, the conservative historian and columnist and the author of *The Churchillians* and, most recently, *A History of the English-Speaking People Since 1900.*

The subject of Winston Churchill inspired Bush's self-reflection. The president confided to Roberts that he believes he has an advantage over Churchill, a reliable source with access to the conversation told me. He has faith in God, Bush explained, but Churchill, an agnostic, did not. Because he believes in God, it is easier for him to make decisions and stick to them than it was for Churchill. Bush said he doesn't worry, or feel alone, or care if he is unpopular. He has God.

Even as Scooter Libby sat at the defendant's table silently wearing his fixed, forced smile, and Vice President Dick Cheney was revealed by witnesses as the conductor of the smear campaign against former ambassador Joseph Wilson, Bush and Rove felt free to hold forth in their salon, removed from anxiety. Rove had narrowly escaped the fate of Libby by changing his grand jury testimony just before he might have been indicted for perjury. Bush, who proclaimed that he would fire any leaker found in his administration, is apparently closer to Rove than ever. The night before the Libby verdict, the president had dinner at Rove's house, and Rove sent to the reporters shivering outside a doggie bag filled with sausage and quail wings.

"Where's Rove? Where's, you know, where are these other guys?" wondered a juror, Denis Collins, standing on the courthouse steps after the Libby verdict was delivered. Collins said that he and other jurors came to think of Libby as a "fall guy," someone who had certainly committed the crimes of which he was accused but who also was hardly acting on his own.

The opening statement of Libby's attorney seemed to augur a presentation of the "fall guy" scenario. "They're trying to set me up. They want me to be the sacrificial lamb," Theodore Wells said, recalling Libby's words to Cheney. "I will not be sacrificed so Karl Rove can be protected." Rove, after all, had disclosed the identity of Wilson's wife, covert CIA operative Valerie Plame, to two reporters, conservative columnist Robert Novak, who first put her name into print, and Matthew Cooper of *Time* magazine. Rove told

MSNBC *Hardball* host Chris Matthews that Plame was "fair game." And he offered as his motive for attacking Wilson to another reporter: "He's a Democrat."

In a note entered as a trial exhibit, Cheney expressed his concern that his chief of staff was being thrown to the wolves while Rove was being protected. "Not going to protect one staffer and sacrifice the guy that was asked to stick his neck in the meat grinder," the note read. Despite the dramatic opening, Libby's defense made no reference to the note during the trial. In yet another mysterious lapse, although Libby's lawyers repeatedly gave every indication to Judge Reggie Walton that both Libby and Cheney would testify, neither did. In a perjury trial, if the defendant does not look the jury in the eye and say he did not lie or that he made an honest error, it's difficult to win. But Libby never appeared as a witness on his own behalf; Cheney was not called; and the defense rested on the thin reed of Libby's weak memory and the supposed impeached credibility of journalists. The feeble defense amounted to a verdict foretold.

But why was Libby virtually passive? If Libby knew he was going to offer the barest defense, why didn't he do as Rove did, amending his grand jury testimony to reflect the truth? Why didn't Libby do as former White House press secretary Ari Fleischer did, turning state's evidence and being granted immunity in exchange for his testimony? What stopped Libby from risking indictment? What prevented him from making more than a minimal defense that invited conviction?

Libby could not plead the Fifth Amendment against self-incrimination. Had he done so he would not have been able to continue in his position as Cheney's chief of staff; he would have been compelled to resign. But why didn't he testify? Why didn't he make the case of Rove's perfidy that his lawyer suggested?

Libby and Rove's falsehoods in front of the grand jury, in which they blamed reporters for telling them about Plame, were a cleverly contrived coverup. They did not believe that the prosecutor would be able to break through the curtain of the First Amendment or untangle the tale as told by journalists. Both Libby and Rove relied on the same alibi, hiding behind the press corps that they had manipulated for years and whose erratic habits they knew well. But prosecutor Patrick Fitzgerald was not about to be confounded by this device. He knew the law was on his side, and he received a judicial decision forcing the reporters to testify.

Just as Fitzgerald was about to indict Rove for perjury and obstruction of justice, Rove got a lucky break. A reporter for *Time* magazine, Viveca Novak, a colleague of Cooper's and privy to his conversation with Rove, became consumed with an overwhelming desire to be an important inside dopester, and she rushed to inform Rove's lawyer, Robert Luskin, about Cooper's information. Suddenly, Rove retrieved an e-mail from Cooper that he had not produced to the prosecutor for a year, refreshed his memory, altered his testimony, and was off the hook. (Novak did not tell her editors or Cooper of her freelancing, and she was forced to resign, in effect sacrificing her career to save Rove by the skin of his teeth.) Libby was left to take the fall alone.

What bearing might this have on Libby's weak defense? Why didn't Libby and Cheney testify? Observing the trial as it developed, Cheney may have decided Libby would lose and that his becoming a witness was beside the point. Ultimately, did Cheney's self-protective calculation trump loyalty to his loyalist?

Did something change in the defense after its opening statement about Rove (Libby "will not be sacrificed so Karl Rove can be protected") that led to its refusal to follow up during the trial? Did the prosecutor have new information that has not yet been made public about Libby and Cheney? If so, that evidence would have been irrelevant to the precise charges against Libby but might have come into play if Libby and Cheney testified. Their appearances might have made them vulnerable to additional perjury and obstruction charges if they were found to have lied on the stand. But who might have proved that?

The missing piece in the extensive evidence and testimony that detailed the administration's concerted attack on Wilson, orchestrated by Cheney, is the conversations among Libby, Cheney—and Rove. Rove had made a deal with Fitzgerald. Rove changed his testimony, escaped prosecution, and went back for a fifth time before the grand jury. Fitzgerald owned Rove.

Only if Libby and Cheney appeared could Fitzgerald cross-examine them about their discussions with Rove, which presumably Rove had already testified about before the grand jury. Rove was the hostile witness against Cheney whom the prosecution had waiting in the wings, the witness who was never called. If Libby had come to the stand in his own defense, and summoned Cheney as well, Fitzgerald might have been prompted to call Rove from the deep to impeach Libby's and Cheney's credibility and reveal new incriminating information about them. Instead, Libby remained silent, Cheney flew off to Afghanistan, and Rove never appeared. Rove was the missing witness for the prosecution.

Now Libby's only hope is a presidential pardon. He has already offended Rove and perhaps by extension Bush. Libby cannot afford to offend Cheney. His pardon depends on Cheney's importuning of Bush. Thus Libby's final plea is to Cheney—and his cover up continues. Back at the White House, Rove makes the next selection for the book club.

March 8, 2007

The Assassination of Dick Cheney

Was the suicide bomber attack at Bagram Air Base in Afghanistan on February 27 an attempted assassination of Vice President Dick Cheney or a horse's head in his bed?

The day before, Cheney had delivered a stinging message to Pakistani President Pervez Musharraf—U.S. aid would be withheld unless Pakistan supported strikes against Taliban and Al-Qaeda forces that have nestled in Pakistan as a sanctuary, where they have gathered strength in anticipation of a spring offensive against the Afghan government. Musharraf's official response via a spokesman was immediate: "Pakistan does not accept dictation from any side or any source." Then came the bombing. Was it another form of reply? The Taliban claimed credit. But was only the Taliban involved?

The Pakistani Inter-Services Intelligence (ISI) agency was present at the creation of the Taliban, which it has deployed to give it strategic depth in its long war with India. The ISI has lent clandestine support to other terrorist groups against India. And ISI agents have also been deeply involved with Al-Qaeda. ISI operatives continue to aid and advise the Taliban and Al-Qaeda resurgence in Afghanistan.

Musharraf, a former army chief of staff who took power in a military coup in 1999, has been a rival of ISI influence and has never succeeded in securing control over it. The circumstances surrounding the two assassination attempts against him, using suicide bombers within eleven days in 2003, remain unsolved, though experts believe they are linked to his tough policy toward the Taliban and Al-Qaeda. Soon after September 11, 2001, encouraged and aided by the U.S., Musharraf waged an unsuccessful military campaign against the Taliban and Al-Qaeda in the remote tribal province of Waziristan, bordering Afghanistan. Last spring, Musharraf withdrew Pakistani troops from south Waziristan, ceding it to the Taliban and its allies. Last September, Musharraf surrendered north Waziristan, agreeing to a formal truce with Taliban representatives and even returning seized weapons. Taliban and Al-Qaeda flags fly side by side throughout the region. From 2001 to the present, the Pakistanis reportedly have not arrested a single Taliban leader. The Taliban operate their headquarters unimpeded out of Quetta, the capital of Pakistan's Baluchistan province, the gateway to Kandahar in southern Afghanistan.

Musharraf's retreat was an acceptance of political reality and an act of self-protection. He believed that U.S. backing for his appeasement policy was critical to maintenance of his power, which he must assume is the larger mutual goal. Cheney's recent ultimatum, however, puts him in a precarious spot, especially with parliamentary elections scheduled this year and the popularity of Bush at its nadir among Pakistanis. The questions pressing upon Musharraf are the degree of control he has over his own government and country and his survival at the sufferance of the ISI and its clients.

The questions raised by the would-be assassination of Cheney highlight the counterproductive incoherence and impotence of administration policy. Before the bombing, Cheney was gleefully using his foreign travels as a platform for partisan strafing. After he declared that House Speaker Nancy Pelosi's criticism of the administration's Iraq policy aided and abetted Al-Qaeda, she called President Bush to register her objection to having her patriotism smeared. Cheney's remark, she said, was "beneath the dignity of his office." On February 26, a reporter from ABC News asked Cheney if he stood by his statement. Cheney was only too happy to repeat it. "If we adopt the Pelosi policy, then we will validate the strategy of Al-Qaeda. I said it and I meant it," he said. The pool reporter noted that Cheney "looks pretty chipper, near the end of a weeklong odyssey." But after the bombing, Cheney fell uncharacteristically silent.

Since September 11, Bush and Cheney have proclaimed a Manichaean struggle in which, as Bush said, "you're either with us or with the terrorists." This formula has been applied at home and abroad. It is a distillation of Bush's foreign policy and his domestic politics. In his "war on terror," he is leading the forces of "freedom" against "evil" because it is "part of God's plan," and that "God is not neutral." Then Palestinian Foreign Minister Nabil Shaath told the BBC in 2005 that Bush had confided in him and Mahmoud Abbas, former prime minister and now Palestinian president: "I'm driven with a mission from God. God would tell me, 'George, go and fight those terrorists in Afghanistan.' And I did, and then God would tell me, 'George, go and end the tyranny in Iraq,' and I did."

At Cheney's direction, intelligence was skewed to suggest links between Saddam Hussein and Al-Qaeda. Over the past year, as that intelligence was exposed as false and, worse, as disinformation, Cheney has defended the conflation of threats through a contrivance of illogic, also routinely repeated by Bush: "We were not in Iraq on September 11th, 2001, and the terrorists hit us anyway."

Cheney's implication that the U.S. presence in Iraq cannot possibly be an inspiration for terrorism is simply not shared at the highest levels of the senior military, including commanders on the ground in Iraq. I have learned that they are privately reading, circulating, and in agreement with a new article written by terrorism experts Peter Bergen and Paul Cruickshank, senior fellows at the New York University Center on Law and Security. (Bergen is also a fellow at the New America Foundation. For purposes of full disclosure, I am also a senior fellow at the NYU Center.) Their article, "The Iraq Effect: War Has Increased Terrorism Sevenfold Worldwide," published in *Mother Jones*, provides empirical evidence for careful conclusions:

> Our study yields one resounding finding: The rate of terrorist attacks around the world by jihadist groups and the rate of fatalities in those attacks increased dramatically after the invasion of Iraq. Globally there was a 607 percent rise in the average yearly incidence of attacks (28.3 attacks per year before and 199.8 after) and a 237 percent rise in the average fatality rate (from 501 to 1,689 deaths per year). A large part of this rise occurred in Iraq, which accounts for fully half of the global total of jihadist terrorist attacks in the post–Iraq War

period. But even excluding Iraq, the average yearly number of jihadist terrorist attacks and resulting fatalities still rose sharply around the world by 265 percent and 58 percent respectively.

Draining military and economic resources from Afghanistan in the run-up to invading Iraq contributed to Afghanistan's current crisis. While money and materiel were siphoned to Iraq, Afghanistan was starved. "Aid per capita to Afghans in the first two years after the fall of the Taliban was around a tenth of that given to Bosnians following the end of the Balkan civil war in the mid-1990s," Bergen noted in testimony on February 15 before the House Foreign Affairs Committee. Former U.S. ambassador to Afghanistan James Dobbins has said, "Afghanistan was the least resourced of any major American-led nation building operation since the end of World War II." But the Iraq policy has had other ricochet effects, according to Bergen and Cruickshank:

> Since the invasion of Iraq, Afghanistan has suffered 219 jihadist terrorist attacks that can be attributed to a particular group, resulting in the deaths of 802 civilians. The fact that the Taliban only conducted its first terrorist attacks in September 2003, a few months after the invasion of Iraq, is significant. International forces had already been stationed in the country for two years before the Taliban began to specifically target the U.S.–backed Karzai government and civilians sympathetic to it. This points to a link between events in Iraq and the initiation of the Taliban's terrorist campaign in Afghanistan. True, local dynamics form part of the explanation for the resurgence of the Taliban in Afghanistan. But the use of terrorism, particularly suicide attacks, by the Taliban is an innovation drawn from the Iraqi theater.

The bombing at Bagram silenced Cheney's bombast, at least for the moment. His mission to Musharraf and the subsequent assassination attempt, if it was that, also exploded his simplistic ideological sloganeering. Rather than waging a grand battle of good vs. evil, he and Bush are dependent upon an ambiguous Pakistani leader with a tenuous grasp on power, whose untrustworthy intelligence service is crucial in directing the Taliban.

Rather than approaching a climactic struggle against free-floating sects of "Islamofascism," the administration has been a party since September 11 to regional conflicts in which not only were economic, social, and diplomatic instruments ignored but international military help was also rejected. Belatedly, in Afghanistan, circumstances of the administration's own making have forced it to concede the necessity of getting assistance from allies. Yet the movement of 1,400 British troops there is a direct result of the disintegration of the "coalition of the willing" in Iraq. Those very troops are being redeployed from southern Iraq, the British sector now being ceded to control of Muqtada al-Sadr's Mahdi Army, which Bush's "surge" is supposedly intended to suppress.

Rather than returning home a conquering hero, Cheney slinks back from his trip having revealed how the failure of administration policy has validated the strategy of the Taliban and Al-Qaeda. That harsh conclusion, moreover, is not mere punditry. It is the considered view of senior military commanders.

March 1, 2007

All Roads Lead to Rove

The Bush administration's first instinct was to shield Karl Rove from scrutiny when Congress began inquiring about the unusual firings of eight U.S. attorneys. Among the replacements, the proposed new U.S. attorney for Arkansas happened to be one of Rove's most devoted underlings, his head of opposition research, Tim Griffin, who boasted during the 2000 presidential election about the effectiveness of the negative campaign against Al Gore: "We make the bullets!" Griffin also posted a sign in his department at Bush headquarters: "Rain hell on Al!" A letter written by the Department of Justice in late February informed Congress: "The department is not aware of Karl Rove playing any role in the decision to appoint Mr. Griffin." Despite this categorical disavowal, a sheaf of internal Justice Department e-mails released this week to Congress under subpoena revealed Kyle Sampson, Attorney General Alberto Gonzales's chief of staff, writing in mid-December 2006, "I know getting him appointed was important to Harriet, Karl, etc." Harriet, of course, was Harriet Miers, then the White House legal counsel.

The Justice Department's statement on Karl Rove was simply one part of its coverup. The department's three top officials—Attorney General Alberto Gonzales, Deputy Attorney General Paul J. McNulty, and William E. Moschella, principal associate deputy attorney general—all testified before Congress under oath that the dismissed U.S. attorneys had been removed for "performance" reasons, not because they had been insufficiently partisan in their prosecution of Democrats or because they would be replaced by those who would be. Yet another Sampson e-mail, sent to Miers in March 2005, had ranked all ninety-three U.S. attorneys on the basis of being "good performers," those who "exhibited loyalty" to the administration, or "low performers," those who "chafed against Administration initiatives, etc."

The day before the e-mails were made public Sampson resigned, offering a classic fall-guy statement, claiming that he was the one who failed to inform Gonzales and other officials about the firings. Sampson, who was Gonzales's closest aide, accompanying him from the White House Counsel's Office to the Justice Department when Gonzales was appointed attorney general, had sought to become a U.S. attorney himself through the purge. And Sampson was considered to be politically adept enough to be considered a stand-in for the supposedly indispensable Rove. When it was rumored that Rove might be indicted in the Valerie Plame case, the *Washington Post* reported that Sampson was likely to replace him.

Sampson's abrupt departure was followed by Gonzales's bizarre press conference on Wednesday. Speaking in a passive voice that "mistakes were made," he pleaded ignorance of "all decisions" at his department, explained that it has 110,000 employees, appealed to his modest origins, and promised to oversee the investigation of his own misfeasance. His defense was the very grounds used to fire the U.S. attorneys: poor performance. He used his failure as a shield.

But the day before, Gonzales's ignorance defense had already been punctured. A White House spokeswoman, Dana Perino, acknowledged that the U.S. attorneys' dismissals were preceded by a conversation between President Bush and Gonzales last October in which Bush complained that some prosecutors were not pursuing voter fraud investigations. These were, in fact, cases that Rove thought were especially important to Republicans.

Rove was the conduit for Republican political grievances about the U.S. attorneys. He was the fulcrum and the lever. He was the collector of information and the magnet of power. He was the originator, formulator, and director. But, initially, according to the administration, like Gonzales, he supposedly knew nothing and did nothing.

Even after the administration alibis had collapsed, the White House trotted out Dan Bartlett, the cool and calm communications director, to engage in a bit of cognitive dissonance. There was no plot, and maybe Rove was involved in the thing that didn't happen. "You're trying to connect a lot of dots that aren't connectible," Bartlett said, adding, "It wouldn't be surprising that Karl or other people were receiving these complaints." Thus the "dots" are invisible and Rove is at their center.

To the extent that the facts are known, Rove keeps surfacing in the middle of the scandal. And it is implausible that Sampson, the latest designated fall guy, was responsible for an elaborate bureaucratic coup d'état. Nor is it credible that Gonzales—or Harriet Miers, who has yet to be heard—saw or heard no evil. Neither is it reasonable that Gonzales or Miers, both once Bush's personal attorneys in Texas, getting him out of scrapes such as his drunk driving arrest, could be the political geniuses behind the firings. Gonzales's and Miers's service is notable for their obedience, lack of originality and eagerness to act as tools. The scheme bears the marks of Rove's obsessions, methods, and sources. His history contains a wealth of precedents in which he manipulated law enforcement for political purposes. And his long-term strategy for permanent Republican control of government depended on remaking the federal government to create his ultimate goal—a one-party state.

"We're a go for the US Atty plan," White House deputy counsel William Kelley notified the Justice Department on December 4, 2006, three days before seven of the eight U.S. attorneys were dismissed. "WH leg[islative affairs], political, and communications have signed off . . ."

From the earliest Republican campaigns that Rove ran in Texas, beginning in 1986, the FBI was involved in investigating every one of his candidates' Democratic opponents. Rove happened to have a close and mysterious relationship with the chief of the FBI office in Austin. Investigations were announced as elections grew close, but there were rarely indictments, just tainted Democrats and victorious Republicans. On one occasion, Rove himself proclaimed that the FBI had a prominent Democrat under investigation—an investigation that led to Rove's client's win. In 1990, the Texas Democratic Party chairman issued a statement: "The recurring leaks of purported FBI investigations of Democratic candidates during election campaigns is highly questionable and repugnant."

A year later, Rove received a reward. Gov. Bill Clements, a Rove client, appointed him to the East Texas State University board of regents. Appearing before the state Senate's Nominations Committee, a Democratic senator asked Rove about how long he had known the local FBI chief. "Ah, Senator," replied Rove, "it depends. Would you define 'know' for me?"

Rising to the White House as Bush's chief political strategist, Rove well understood the power of U.S. attorneys to damage Democrats and protect Republicans, and he paid close attention to their selection. When U.S. senators, who recommend the U.S. attorneys for their districts, wanted a more independent-minded professional, Rove leaned on them. In 2001, he instructed Senator Peter Fitzgerald, R-Illinois, to sponsor a safe choice from within Republican state circles. Rove "just said we don't want you going outside the state. We don't want to be moving U.S. attorneys around," Fitzgerald told the *Chicago Tribune* on March 12. But Senator Fitzgerald would not relent, and his nominee, Patrick Fitzgerald, an assistant U.S. attorney from New York, became the U.S. attorney in Illinois, where he successfully prosecuted Republicans, including the incumbent governor, George Ryan, for corruption, and went on to be appointed special prosecutor in the Plame case. "That Fitzgerald appointment got great headlines for you, but it ticked off the base," Rove told Senator Fitzgerald.

In 2002, the first midterm elections of the Bush presidency, Republicans systematically raised charges of voter fraud involving Native Americans in the hotly contended U.S. Senate race in South Dakota. Though the accusations were never proved and the GOP failed to depose the Democratic senator, Tim Johnson, the campaign served as a template.

By the election of 2004, Rove became a repository of charges of voter fraud across the country, from Philadelphia to Milwaukee to New Mexico, all in swing states. In the campaign, unproven voter fraud charges, always aimed at minority voters, became a leitmotif of Republican efforts.

In Washington state, when the Democrat won the governorship by 129 votes, the state Republican Party chairman, Chris Vance, demanded that U.S. Attorney John McKay tell him the status of his investigation. At that time, Vance was in constant contact with Rove. "I thought it was part of my job, to be a conduit," Vance told the *Seattle Times*. "We had a Republican secretary of state, a Republican prosecutor in King County and a Republican U.S. attorney, and no one was doing anything." McKay refused to have any conversation about an investigation. And he found no basis for charging anyone with voter fraud. In a September 13, 2006, e-mail, Kyle Sampson identified McKay as one of those "we should now consider pushing out"—and he was among the eight attorneys fired.

In 2006, Rove addressed the Republican Lawyers Association on the "growing problem," as he put it, of voter fraud. Every instance he cited was in a swing state. New Mexico was one of them.

Rove had heard complaints from the New Mexico Republican Party chairman, Allen Weh, about David Iglesias, the state's U.S. attorney, for his supposed refusal to indict Democrats for voter fraud. Iglesias appeared to be a dream figure for local Republicans—the model for the movie "A Few Good Men," Hispanic and evangelical. "Is anything ever going to happen to that guy?" Weh asked Rove at a White House Christmas party. "He's gone," Rove replied. Indeed, Iglesias's firing was already a done deal.

In California, it was time for payback against U.S. attorney Carol Lam, who had prosecuted Rep. Randy "Duke" Cunningham in the most flagrant corruption case involving a member of Congress. Her probe was expanding to encompass the dealings of Representative Jerry Lewis, another California Republican. On May 11, 2006, Sampson e-mailed the White House Counsel's Office regarding "the real problem we have right now with Carol Lam." Soon, she was axed, one of the eight.

Those fired were not completely "loyal," as Sampson's e-mails emphasized. But to what policies should a prosecutor be "loyal"? Two academics, Donald C. Shields of the University of Missouri and John F. Cragan of Illinois State University, studied the pattern of U.S. attorneys' prosecutions under the Bush administration. Their conclusions in their study, "The Political Profiling of Elected Democratic Officials," are that "across the nation from 2001 through 2006 the Bush Justice Department investigated Democratic office holders and candidates at a rate more than four times greater (nearly 80 percent to

18 percent) than they investigated Republican office holders and seekers." They also report, "Data indicate that the offices of the U.S. Attorneys across the nation investigate seven times as many Democratic officials as they investigate Republican officials, a number that exceeds even the racial profiling of African Americans in traffic stops." Thus what the 85 U.S. attorneys who were not dismissed are doing is starkly detailed.

If the Democrats hadn't won the midterm elections last year there is no reason to believe that the plan to use the U.S. attorneys for political prosecutions—as they have been used systematically under Bush—wouldn't have gone forward completely unimpeded. Without the new Congress issuing subpoenas, there would be no exposure, no hearings, no press conferences—no questions at all.

The replacement of the eight fired U.S. attorneys through a loophole in the Patriot Act that enables the administration to evade consultation with and confirmation by Congress is a convenient element in the well-laid scheme. But it was not ad hoc, erratic, or aberrant. Rather, it was the logical outcome of a long effort to distort the constitutional framework for partisan consolidation of power into a de facto one-party state.

This effort began two generations ago with Richard Nixon's drive to forge an imperial presidency, using extralegal powers of government to aggrandize unaccountable power in the executive and destroy political opposition. Nixon was thwarted in the Watergate scandal. We will never know his full malevolent intentions, but we do know that in the aftermath of the 1972 election he wanted to remake the executive branch to create what the Bush administration now calls a "unitary executive." Nixon later explained his core doctrine: "When the president does it, that means it's not illegal." Karl Rove is the rightful heir to Nixonian politics. His first notice in politics occurred as a witness before the Senate Watergate Committee. From Nixon to Bush, Rove is the single continuous character involved in the tactics and strategy of political subterfuge.

March 15, 2007

Law and Disorder

Leave aside the unintentional irony of President Bush asserting executive privilege to shield his aides from testifying before the Congress in the summary firings of eight U.S. attorneys because the precedent would prevent him from receiving "good advice." Leave aside also his denunciation of the Congress for the impertinence of requesting such testimony as "partisan" and "demanding show trials," despite calls from Republicans for the dismissal of Attorney General Alberto Gonzales. Ignore as well Bush's adamant defense of Gonzales.

The man Bush has nicknamed "Fredo," the weak and betraying brother of the Corleone family, is, unlike Fredo, a blind loyalist, and will not be dispatched with a shot to the back of the head in a rowboat on the lake while reciting his Ave Maria. (Is Bush aware that Colin Powell refers to him as "Sonny," after the hothead oldest son?) But saving "Fredo" doesn't explain why Bush is willing to risk a constitutional crisis. Why is Bush going to the mattresses against the Congress? What doesn't he want known?

In the U.S. attorneys scandal, Gonzales was an active though second-level perpetrator. While he gave orders, he also took orders. Just as his chief of staff, Kyle Sampson, has resigned as a fall guy, so Gonzales would be yet another fall guy if he were to resign. He was assigned responsibility for the purge of U.S. attorneys but did not conceive it. The plot to transform the U.S. attorneys and ipso facto the federal criminal justice system into the Republican Holy Office of the Inquisition had its origin in Karl Rove's fertile mind.

Just after Bush's reelection and before his second inauguration, as his administration's hubris was running at high tide, Rove dropped by the White House legal counsel's office to check on the plan for the purge. An internal e-mail, dated January 6, 2005, and circulated within that office, quoted Rove as asking "how we planned to proceed regarding the U.S. attorneys, whether we are going to allow all to stay, request resignations from all and accept only some of them, or selectively replace them, etc." Three days later, Sampson, in an e-mail, "Re: Question from Karl Rove," wrote: "As an operational matter we would like to replace 15-20 percent of the current U.S. attorneys—the underperforming ones . . . The vast majority of U.S. attorneys, 80-85 percent I would guess, are doing a great job, are loyal Bushies, etc., etc."

The disclosure of the e-mails establishing Rove's centrality suggests not only the political chain of command but also the hierarchy of coverup. Bush protects Gonzales in order to protect those who gave Gonzales his marching orders—Rove and Bush himself.

"Now, we're at a point where people want to play politics with it," Rove declared on March 15 in a speech at Troy University in Alabama. The scene of Rove's self-dramatization as a victim of "politics" recalls nothing so much as Oscar Wilde's remark about Dickens's *Old Curiosity Shop*: "One must have a heart of stone to read the death of little Nell without laughing."

From his method acting against "politics," Rove went on to his next, more banal talking point: There can be no scandal because everyone's guilty. (This is a variation of the old "it didn't start with Watergate" defense.) "I would simply ask that everybody who's playing politics with this, be asked to comment on what they think of the removal of 123 U.S. attorneys during the previous administration and see if they had the same, superheated political rhetoric then that they're having now." Instantly, this Rove talking point echoed out the squawk boxes of conservative talk radio and through the parrot jungle of the Washington press corps.

Indeed, Presidents Clinton, George H. W. Bush, and Reagan replaced the ninety-three U.S. attorneys at the beginning of their administration as part of the normal turnover involved in the alternation of power. A report issued on February 22 from the Congressional Research Service revealed that between 1981 and 2006, only five of the 486 U.S. attorneys failed to finish their four-year terms, and none were fired for political reasons. Only three were fired for questionable behavior, including one on "accusations that he bit a topless dancer on the arm during a visit to an adult club after losing a big drug case." In brief, Bush's firings were unprecedented, and Rove's talking point was simply one among several shifting explanations, starting with the initial false talking point that those dismissed suffered from "low performance."

"Administration has determined to ask some underperforming USAs to move on," wrote Sampson in a December 5, 2006, e-mail to associate attorney general Bill Mercer. Yet the Associated Press reported on Tuesday, March 20: "Six of the eight U.S. attorneys fired by the Justice Department ranked in the top third among their peers for the number of prosecutions filed last year, according to an analysis of federal records. In addition, five of the eight were among the government's top performers in winning convictions."

When the scandal first broke, Rove personally offered a talking point on one of those fired, claiming on March 8 that the U.S. attorney for San Diego, Carol Lam, "refused to file immigration cases . . . at the direction of the Attorney General, she was asked to file, and she said I don't want to make that a priority in my office." Though there was pressure on Lam to pursue more immigration cases, a heated issue for Republicans, three months before she was dismissed, the Justice Department had sent a letter to Senator Dianne Feinstein, D-California, noting that Lam's office had devoted "fully half of its Assistant U.S. Attorneys to prosecute criminal immigration cases."

Nor was the U.S. attorney for Washington state, John McKay, dismissed for "low performance." On August 9, 2006, Sampson recommended him for a federal judgeship, writing in an e-mail: "re: John, it's highly unlikely that we could do better in Seattle." Yet, less than a month later, on September 13, Sampson placed McKay on a list titled: "[U.S. Attorneys] We Now Should Consider Pushing Out." McKay was removed from favored status, according to his own sworn testimony before the Congress, because of his refusal to prosecute Democrats on nonexistent charges of voter fraud after the Democratic candidate for governor won by a razor-thin margin in 2004. McKay said he received telephone calls from Ed Cassidy, chief of staff to Representative Doc Hastings, R-Washington, and state Republican Party chairman Chris Vance pressuring him to open a probe. Now, McKay has called for a special prosecutor to investigate the firings.

McKay's case parallels that of David Iglesias. As Iglesias wrote in *The New York Times* in an article titled "Why I Was Fired":

> Politics entered my life with two phone calls that I received last fall, just before the November election. One came from Representative Heather Wilson and the other from Senator [Pete] Domenici, both Republicans from my state, New Mexico. Ms. Wilson asked me about sealed indictments pertaining to a politically charged corruption case widely reported in the news media involving local Democrats. Her question instantly put me on guard. Prosecutors may not

legally talk about indictments, so I was evasive. Shortly after speaking to Ms. Wilson, I received a call from Senator Domenici at my home. The senator wanted to know whether I was going to file corruption charges—the cases Ms. Wilson had been asking about—before November. When I told him that I didn't think so, he said, "I am very sorry to hear that," and the line went dead. A few weeks after those phone calls, my name was added to a list of United States attorneys who would be asked to resign—even though I had excellent office evaluations, the biggest political corruption prosecutions in New Mexico history, a record number of overall prosecutions and a 95 percent conviction rate.

Domenici and Wilson have both hired lawyers, given that they could potentially face prosecution for obstruction of justice. Their possible legal vulnerability and that of other Republicans across the country suggests a major reason why Bush is fighting to keep Rove from testifying before the Congress under oath.

McKay's and Iglesias's cases, as they explain them, involve efforts to pressure U.S. attorneys to launch investigations solely for political motives. The U.S. attorneys decided that evidence was lacking for such probes, and they were accordingly punished. Meanwhile, four of those fired were guilty of offenses of commission, not omission, having begun legitimate public corruption investigations of Republican officials.

Lam, who had successfully prosecuted Representative Randy "Duke" Cunningham, was following the trail by investigating his associates, defense contractor, and Republican fund-raiser Brent Wilkes, and Wilkes's best friend, Dusty Foggo, the number three ranking official at the CIA, the chief of contracting; and Representative Jerry Lewis, a California Republican.

Daniel Bogden, the U.S. attorney for Nevada, was investigating whether Governor Jim Gibbons "accepted unreported gifts or payments from a company that was awarded secret military contracts when Mr. Gibbons served in Congress," according to *The Wall Street Journal.*

H. E. "Bud" Cummins, the U.S. attorney for Arkansas, was investigating conflict-of-interest corruption involving state contracts that Missouri governor Matt Blunt granted to Republican contributors. In October 2006, Cummins announced he would not seek indictments. But his statement just came four weeks before the election for the U.S. Senate seat in Missouri that the Democratic candidate, Claire McCaskill, won narrowly. Cummins told the *Los Angeles Times*, "You have to firewall politics out of the Department of Justice. Because once it gets in, people question every decision you make. Now I keep asking myself: 'What about the Blunt deal?'"

Paul Charlton, the U.S. attorney for Arizona, was investigating Representative Rick Renzi, R-Arizona, for allegedly corrupt land deals and introducing legislation to benefit a major campaign contributor. Charlton was curiously accused of not filing obscenity cases, which, in fact, he did pursue.

In each of these public corruption cases, it is reasonable to assume that the relevant Republican political figures either themselves complained or complained through surrogates about the U.S. attorneys to Rove, the matrix of national GOP politics. But which officials—instead of foolishly making direct calls to the U.S. attorney, like Domenici and Wilson—went through Rove to stymie the investigations (or rush them, if they were targeting Democrats)? Then, what did Rove say about the individual U.S. attorneys to the White House Office of Legal Counsel and officials in the Justice Department?

Bush's resistance to having Rove placed under oath or even having a transcript of his testimony appears to be a coverup of a series of obstructions of justice. The e-mails hint at the quickening pulse of communications between the White House and the Justice Department. But only sworn testimony can elicit the truth.

On Wednesday, the House Judiciary Committee issued five subpoenas, including one for Rove, and on Thursday the Senate Judiciary Committee plans to follow suit. With these subpoenas, a constitutional battle is joined. "The moment subpoenas are issued, it means that they have rejected the offer," said White House press secretary Tony Snow. Bush is barricading his White House against the Congress to prevent its members from posing the pertinent question that might open the floodgate: What did Karl Rove know, and when did he know it?

March 22, 2007

The Passion of the Judas

As he tells it, Matthew Dowd's conversion from true believer in George W. Bush to disenchanted critic is a chapter in a "Pilgrim's Progress" through the wilderness of this world. His long quest for agape, as related to a *New York Times* reporter, begins about a decade ago with Dowd in the Slough of Despond, "frustrated about Washington, the inability for people to get stuff done and bridge divides," when suddenly a great-hearted figure appears who lights a candle in the darkness. "It's almost like you fall in love," Dowd professed. But his dream turns to dross and his faith into doubt. Bush is not the deliverer but the deceiver. "I had finally come to the conclusion that maybe all these things along do add up. That it's not the same, it's not the person I thought." But Dowd is unsure whether Bush is a changed man or a captive. "He's become more, in my view, secluded and bubbled in."

Whether Bush has strayed or been led astray, the fellowship he promised is lost. Dowd does not offer to save Bush, but only claims to seek salvation himself. His trials and tribulations—"one of Mr. Dowd's premature twin daughters died, he was divorced, and he watched his oldest son prepare for deployment to Iraq as an Army intelligence specialist fluent in Arabic," according to the *Times*—have seared his soul. But these are elements of a story, in which the afflicted Dowd appears utterly passive—not the full story.

He contemplates writing a public confession, an op-ed piece, that a man he has wronged, Senator John Kerry, is virtuous. He would title his article of atonement "Kerry Was Right," but decides not to submit it. He considers joining the protesters in a march against the Iraq war, but once again cannot bring himself to put his foot forward. Yet the pilgrim continues on his upward path. "I'm a big believer that in part what we're called to do—to me, by God; other people call it karma—is to restore balance when things didn't turn out the way they should have." Following his inner map guides him away from world-weary vanity. "I wouldn't be surprised if I wasn't walking around in Africa or South America doing something that was like mission work," Dowd told the *Times*.

As the pollster who helped bring Bush to power and sustained him there, Dowd is expert in framing stories, and he has framed his own as a classic conversion narrative. But the political consultant cleanses his story of politics, so it is hardly surprising that there are gaps in the telling and characters missing. Dowd does not offer any explanation of why Bush has changed, only how he, Dowd, perceives the changes. Bush has become remote and untouchable, but he is not the hidden God, *Deus Absconditus*. Who has seduced Bush into his seclusion? Who has absconded with him? His Satanic Majesty, almost always present in conversion stories, is absent here. Dowd says nothing about Karl Rove, for to bring Rove into the narrative would alter it. Dowd attempts to blot out the politics with the personal, his soul-searching obscuring his poll taking. Yet he provided the diagrams for Rove's machinations, the bright signs for Rove's dark wonders.

The political man's refusal to explain the politics behind his turnabout has given his former friends the opening to assign him even deeper personal motives to drain it of political sting. White House counselor Dan Bartlett, appearing on CBS's *Face the Nation* on April 1, described Dowd as someone on "a personal journey" and consumed with "personal turmoil." Rather than burn him as a heretic in an auto-da-fé, the White House dismisses him as a head case—Dowd's "Pilgrim's Progress" turned into *One Flew Over the Cuckoo's Nest*.

A more mundane version of Dowd's story begins with a little-known pollster in a state capital, laboring for a political party headed for seemingly perpetual minority status. Attached to the conservative wing of the Texas Democrats, Dowd was a partner in the Austin-based Public Strategies P.R. firm. Along with one of his partners, media consultant Mark McKinnon, he seamlessly shifted into the presidential campaign of Governor Bush.

Dowd has given a couple of accounts of this painless conversion, attributing it variously to the shining impression made by Bush and the persuasive skills of Rove, whom he came to know well in the hothouse atmosphere of Austin. McKinnon told his friends he wasn't a Republican, but a "Bush guy," while Dowd, for his part, simply left it at that he had become a "Bush Republican." Had they not jumped at the main chance that materialized, they would have been mired as provincial losers. Instead, they chose fame and fortune. Observers viewed their leap as symbolic of Bush's unusual capacity for bipartisanship.

Bush's loss of the popular majority by 543,895 votes in the 2000 election was a shock to his political advisors and prompted an internal rethinking of his strategy. During the Florida contest and before the Supreme Court delivered the presidency to Bush, Dowd wrote a confidential memo to Rove that analyzed data from the recent vote and argued that there was no significant center in the electorate. "Dowd's analysis destroyed the rationale for Bush to govern as 'a uniter, not a divider,'" wrote Thomas Edsall in his book *Building Red America*. Bush's confected campaign persona as a "compassionate conservative" was suddenly discarded. The "architect," as Bush called Rove, had an architect. Bush's brain had an outsourced brain. Rove's and Bush's radical imperatives derived from Dowd's conclusions.

With Bush as president, Dowd was put on the Republican National Committee payroll and became an intimate participant in White House strategy sessions. Bush and the Republicans now exploited divisive wedge issues and tactics with a vengeance. After September 11, 2001, fear was bundled with loathing, the terrorist threat from abroad conflated with the gay menace within. By 2004, relying on Dowd's numbers, Republicans made gay marriage the most salient social issue, exceeding abortion and gun control in its inflammatory potential to mobilize conservatives. Dowd prescribed the strategy for targeting of Republican base voters' "anger points," as GOP consultants called them, for maximum turnout.

The "war on terror" was the glue that held the Bush message together. In the political rinse cycle, Dowd transformed the disinformation justifying the Iraq war into platitudinous Republican talking points. In the interviews he granted, Dowd repeated them effortlessly. "Events in Iraq," he told National Public Radio during the Republican Convention in September 2004, "and removing Saddam Hussein is all part of the war on terror. You can't separate out removing a brutal dictator from a place that harbored terrorists from the war on terror." One plus one equals three; the clock struck 13.

Dowd packaged his vicious tactics as nothing more than the application of basic advertising technique. His slicing and dicing of wedge issues was no such thing, he explained. He was, he said, just creating a new Republican "brand." After Rove executed Dowd's carefully calculated targeting to produce Bush's narrow victory in 2004, Dowd was triumphant.

"Issues don't matter in presidential campaigns," he exulted in 2005, "it's your brand values that matter." For Dowd, facts didn't matter either, only "brand" identity.

Contaminating his rival's brand was as vital as enhancing his own. Dowd had been central in formulating the 2002 midterm campaign that zeroed in on the Democrats' patriotism. In 2004, he and Rove crafted the negative attack on Kerry as a "flip-flopper." Asked about the TV ads ripping Kerry, Dowd said on September 22, 2004, on CNN, "I think it's totally tasteful. And the American public is going to be fine with it." He also blithely defended the Swift Boat Veterans for Truth's defamation of Kerry's sterling Vietnam War record. "I think the Swift boat ads were part of that dialogue," he said in a 2005 PBS *Frontline* documentary, "but it was more important in that they pointed out something about John Kerry, which is, all this guy's talking about is his Vietnam record. What does that have to do with the war on terror?"

Dowd believed he was designing a permanent Republican majority, but, working alongside Rove, his short-term winning tactics built enormous pressure that produced an implosion. During the 2006 midterm campaign that lost the Republicans control of Congress, Dowd worked as a consultant for California Governor Arnold Schwarzenegger, a Republican running as a virtual liberal Democrat. "I think we should design campaigns that appeal not to 51 percent of the people," Dowd told the *Times*, "but bring the country together as a whole."

But Dowd neither detailed nor did the *Times* mention his consulting work in the campaign last year of Richard DeVos, billionaire heir of the Amway fortune, for governor of Michigan. DeVos is a zealous follower of and major donor to the most extreme organizations of the religious right. His campaign against incumbent Democratic Governor Jennifer Granholm was marked by nasty ads falsely stating: "Under Governor Granholm's administration, you can stay on welfare as long as you want." These weren't a new paradigm but old racial code words.

Dowd is perhaps the most peripheral member of the original Texas inner circle that brought Bush to power. (The nimble McKinnon is now working for John McCain's presidential campaign, not as a Republican, of course, but as a McCain guy.) Unlike Attorney General Alberto Gonzales, who is Bush's creature pure and simple, Dowd is both creature and creator. His self-involved and tortuous explanation of his disillusionment helps cast light on the banality of his motives in his original defection from Democrat to Bush Republican.

However traumatic his private drama, he appears fundamentally the same opportunist, a point subtly driven home by those who know him well.

"I've known him for a while," said President Bush, asked at his press conference on Tuesday about Dowd. Bush stayed on message, reducing Dowd's defection to being overwrought about his son's shipping out to Iraq: "I understand his anguish over war. I understand that this is an emotional issue for Matthew." The *Washington Post* added: "Dowd, contacted later by e-mail, chose not to engage in a debate. He had said his piece. 'I don't have anything to add,' he wrote."

Dowd can have no riposte to the White House insinuation that he is a troubled person unless he breaks through his own rigidly constructed tale of conversion. There is also the danger that he could be seen as handling himself like one of his clients. His corporate communications firm, ViaNovo—"new way" in Latin, like the Christian religion itself—advertises on its Web site that it specializes in "high-stakes positioning."

Dowd has much to add to history as an eyewitness. What was Rove's involvement in the independent expenditure negative campaign against Senator John McCain in the Republican South Carolina primary of 2000? White House chief of staff Andrew Card said in 2002 about the propaganda campaign for the Iraq war, "From a marketing point of view, you don't introduce new products in August." What was the marketing done to hone various rationales for the invasion of Iraq? In the 2004 campaign, exactly how was homosexuality targeted? What were the links between the Bush campaign and the Swift Boating of John Kerry? What polling was performed to determine how to discredit Kerry's war record? After the indictment of Vice President Cheney's chief of staff, Scooter Libby, what polls did Dowd take to inform White House positioning? These are only a few of the questions that Dowd can illuminate with his special knowledge. But so far, his conversion lacks a confession.

As Dowd acts out his spiritual crisis, he maintains his silence about what he knows, a strange kind of post-betrayal omertà. It's more than a little late for the turncoat to continue playing the loyalist, wanting it both ways, unless Dowd truly means what he says about "mission work," and he is preparing to disappear for the next ten years in Africa for the HIV/AIDS initiative of the Clinton Foundation.

April 5, 2007

The Republican Grand Experiment

On January 26, J. Scott Jennings, the White House deputy political director working for Karl Rove, delivered a PowerPoint presentation to at least forty political appointees, many participating through teleconferencing, at the General Services Administration, which oversees a $60 billion budget to manage federal properties and procure office equipment. Jennings's lecture featured maps of Republican "targets" for the House of Representatives and the Senate in the 2008 election. His talk was one of perhaps dozens given since 2001 to political appointees in departments and agencies throughout the federal government by him, Rove, and Ken Mehlman, the former White House political director and Republican National Committee chairman. Rove and Co. drilled polling data into the government employees and lashed them on the necessity of using federal resources for Republican victory. "Such intense regular communication from the political office had never occurred before," *Los Angeles Times* reporters Tom Hamburger and Peter Wallsten wrote in their book, *One Party Country: The Republican Plan for Dominance in the 21st Century.*

At the GSA presentation, the agency's chief, Lurita Alexis Doan, according to a witness, demanded of her employees, "How can we use GSA to help our candidates in the next election?" But when the House Oversight and Government Reform Committee held a hearing on March 28, Doan's short-term memory loss grew progressively worse as she spoke. "There were cookies on the table," she said. "I remember coming in late—honestly, I don't even remember that." At a break, she ordered an assistant to remove her water glass, unaware that the microphone in front of her was still on. "I don't want them to have my fingerprints," she said. "They've got me totally paranoid!"

The Oversight Committee is investigating multiple charges against Doan—her attempt to grant a no-bid contract to a friend; her effort to thwart contract audits, and to cut funds of the GSA Office of the Inspector General, which she called "terrorists" after it began a probe into her conduct; and her potential violation of the Hatch Act, which forbids the use of government offices for partisan activity. A major Republican contributor who made a fortune as a military and homeland security contractor, Doan had held no previous government posts before being appointed last year to head the GSA. Like the fabled ("heck of a job, Brownie") Michael Brown, the former head of the Federal Emergency Management Agency, Doan is another stellar example of the culture of cronyism that has permeated the federal government under George W. Bush.

But Doan's instant incompetence and wackiness under pressure disclose more than the price of patronage. "To the victor belong the spoils" has been the rule since Andrew Jackson. And every administration has displayed cases of abuse. But the Bush administration's practices are more than the common and predictable problems with patronage. Bush has not simply filled jobs with favorites, oblivious to their underhanded dealings, as though he were a blithering latter-day version of Warren Harding. Bush has been determined to turn the entire federal government, every department and agency, into an instrument of a one-party state. From the GSA scandal to the purging of U.S. attorneys, Bush has engaged in a conscious, planned and systematic assault on the professional standards of career staff, either subordinating them or replacing them with ideologues.

Doan and Brown are on a continuum of officialdom that runs to Monica Goodling—until recently the number three official in the Department of Justice, an evangelical graduate of Messiah College and Pat Robertson's Regent Law School, and a true believer in Bush as political messiah. Doan and Brown are cronies, but Goodling is a cadre. Within the Bush administration, there are hundreds of Monica Goodlings, and she was their ideal. A zealot for the cause, she apparently divides the world into good and evil, sacred and profane. She interprets criticism and debate as a mortal threat to all that is good and holy. She sees any institution of American life that is not devoted to the flag and cross to which she pledges and worships as twisted, biased and infernal. (To Goodling, CNN is "a force of the left.") She cannot distinguish between her absolute beliefs and their political instrumentality. She considers objective and professional analysis a ruse, an ideology in itself, a false faith. She sees those who adhere to standards of professionalism as agents of deception, hiding their real agendas. She was enthusiastic in weeding out Justice Department employees and replacing them with true believers like herself. Goodling's refusal to testify before the Senate investigation into the firing of U.S. attorneys and her assertion of the Fifth Amendment because the Senate operates in "bad faith" casts her as martyr and saint, warrior and crusader.

While Vice President Dick Cheney and former Secretary of Defense Donald Rumsfeld installed neoconservative ideologues throughout the national security apparatus, sidelining the senior military, diplomatic corps, and intelligence community, and creating parallel operations to avoid assessment by professionals, Rove was handed the rest of the executive branch to arrogate for political purposes.

Consider the reports surfacing only within the past month: that scientists at the Fish and Wildlife Agency and the National Oceanic and Atmospheric Agency have again been forbidden to discuss climate change; that nine newly appointed U.S. attorneys are political cadres; that the new U.S. attorney for Minnesota, Rachel Paulose, cites Bible verses in the office, harshly orders underlings around and, according to one of four assistant U.S. attorneys in her office who voluntarily demoted themselves, treats disagreement as "disloyalty"; that the Election Assistance Commission last year, giving credence to Republican talking points of widespread voter fraud, ignored experts' testimony to the contrary; that between 2001 and 2006, the Civil Rights Division of the Justice Department has purged 60 percent of its professional staff and not filed a single voting discrimination case on behalf of African American or Native American voters; and that after the state Republican Party complained to Rove that the U.S. attorney in Wisconsin, Steven Biskupic, was not attacking voter fraud, Biskupic kept his job by filing corruption charges against an aide to the incumbent Democratic governor on the eve of the 2006 elections. (The 7th Circuit Court of Appeals recently ruled the aide was "wrongly convicted" on evidence that was "beyond thin.")

On the one hand, Rove has sought to forge a permanent Republican majority. On the other hand, that project might not be completed in just two Bush terms. In either case, Rove's strategy has depended on subjecting the federal government to political objectives. He is not trying to achieve any abstract goal, such as reaching the conservative nirvana of limited government. The endless scandals revealed are not a random compendium of corruption and incompetence, though they are that, too. They are evidence of Rove's—and Bush's—larger strategy of hollowing out the federal government in the interest of building a political state.

In 2002, a University of Pennsylvania professor and earnest conservative named John DiIulio, who had been appointed a White House domestic policy advisor to Bush's faith-based initiative (the essence of Bush's claim to being a "compassionate conservative"), resigned, becoming the first person to quit the administration in disgust. As DiIulio told reporter Ron Suskind, writing in *Esquire* magazine, the tone was set from the top. He overheard Rove shouting about some poor object of his anger, "We will fuck him. Do you hear me? We will fuck him. We will ruin him. Like no one has ever fucked him." DiIulio was shocked to discover not only that Rove was placed in charge of domestic policy but also that Bush had no interest in it except as a political tool. "On social policy and related issues, the lack of even basic policy knowledge, and the only casual interest in knowing more, was somewhat breathtaking," DiIulio said.

Possessed with a sense of history, the disillusioned professor's remarks of five years ago have proved prophetic: "There is no precedent in any modern White House for what is going on in this one: a complete lack of a policy apparatus. What you've got is everything—and I mean everything—being run by the political arm. It's the reign of the Mayberry Machiavellis."

In all his machinations Rove did not calculate that he would ever create an opposing force that might stop him. The Republican Congress had long shielded the administration from oversight and investigation, protecting Rove's handiwork. Now the Democratic Congress has begun to uncover seemingly endless series of abuses. In this respect, the clash of the legislative and executive branches is not over a difference in policy, as in the conflict over the Iraq war. Rather, Congress's effort is even more fundamental: to salvage the executive branch—its capability of functioning in the public interest in the future—from Rove's radical experiment to transform it forever.

April 12, 2007

Dances with Wolfowitz

Paul Wolfowitz's tenure as president of the World Bank has turned into yet another case study of neoconservative government in action. It bears resemblance to the military planning for the invasion of Iraq, during which Wolfowitz, as deputy secretary of defense, arrogantly humiliated Army chief of staff Eric Shinseki for suggesting that the U.S. force level was inadequate. It has similarities to the twisting of intelligence used to justify the war, in which Wolfowitz oversaw the construction of a parallel operation within the Pentagon, the Office of Special Plans, to shunt disinformation directly to the White House, without its being vetted by CIA analysts, about Saddam Hussein's alleged ties to Al-Qaeda and his weapons of mass destruction, and sought to fire Mohamed ElBaradei, director of the United Nations' International Atomic Energy Agency, for factually reporting before the invasion that Saddam had not revived his nuclear weapons program. Wolfowitz's regime also uncannily looks like the occupation of Iraq run by the Coalition Provisional Authority, from which Wolfowitz blackballed State Department professionals—instead staffing it with inexperienced ideologues—and to whom Wolfowitz sent daily orders.

Wolfowitz's World Bank scandal over his girlfriend reveals many of the same qualities that created the wreckage he left in his wake in Iraq: grandiosity, cronyism, self-dealing, and lying—followed by an energetic campaign to deflect accountability. As with the war, he has retreated behind his fervent profession of good intentions to excuse himself. The ginning up of the conservative propaganda mill that once disseminated Wolfowitz's disinformation on WMD to defend him as the innocent victim of a political smear only underlines his tried-and-true methods of operation. The hollowness of his defense echoes in the thunderous absurdity of Monday's *Wall Street Journal*: "Paul Wolfowitz, Meet the Duke Lacrosse Team."

Superficially, Wolfowitz's arrangement for his girlfriend of a job with a hefty increase in pay in violation of the ethics clauses of his contract and

221

without informing the World Bank board might seem like an all-too-familiar story of a man seeking special favors for a romantic partner. Wolfowitz has tried to cast the scandal as a "painful personal dilemma," as he described it in an April 12 e-mail to outraged employees of the World Bank, who have taken to calling the neoconservative's girlfriend his "neo-concubine." He was, he says, just attempting to "navigate in uncharted waters." But the fall of Wolfowitz is the final act of a long drama—and love or even self-love may not be the whole subject.

Wolfowitz's girlfriend, Shaha Ali Riza, is a Libyan, raised in Saudi Arabia, educated at Oxford, who now has British citizenship. She is divorced; he is separated. Their discreet relationship became a problem only when he ascended to the World Bank presidency. Riza had floated through the neoconservative network—working at the Free Iraq Foundation in the early 1990s and the National Endowment for Democracy—until landing a position in the Middle East and African department of the World Bank. The ethics provisions of Wolfowitz's contract, however, stipulated that he could not maintain a sexual relationship with anyone over whom he had supervisory authority, even indirectly.

Back in 2003, Wolfowitz had taken care of Riza by directing his trusted Pentagon deputy, Undersecretary of Defense Douglas Feith—who had been in charge of the Office of Special Plans and had been Wolfowitz's partner in managing the CPA—to arrange for a military contract for her from Science Applications International Corp. When the contract was exposed this week, SAIC issued a statement that it "had no role in the selection of the personnel." In other words, the firm with hundreds of millions in contracts at stake had been ordered to hire Riza.

Riza was unhappy about leaving the sinecure at the World Bank. But in 2006 Wolfowitz made a series of calls to his friends that landed her a job at a new think tank called Foundation for the Future that is funded by the State Department. She was the sole employee, at least in the beginning. The World Bank continued to pay her salary, which was raised by $60,000 to $193,590 annually, more than the $183,500 paid to Secretary of State Condoleezza Rice, and all of it tax-free. Moreover, Wolfowitz got the State Department to agree that the ratings of her performance would automatically be "outstanding." Wolfowitz insisted on these terms himself and then misled the World Bank board about what he had done.

Exactly how this deal was made and with whom remains something of a mystery. The person who did work with Riza in her new position was Elizabeth Cheney, then the deputy assistant secretary of state for Near Eastern affairs. And Riza's assignment fell under the purview of Karen Hughes, undersecretary of state for public diplomacy. But these facts raise more questions than they answer.

The documents released by the World Bank do not include any of the communications with the State Department. How did Elizabeth Cheney come to be involved? Did Wolfowitz speak with Vice President Dick Cheney, for whom he had been a deputy when Cheney was secretary of defense in the elder Bush's administration?

Riza, who is not a U.S. citizen, had to receive a security clearance in order to work at the State Department. Who intervened? It is not unusual to have British or French midlevel officers at the department on exchange programs, but they receive security clearances based on the clearances they already have with their host governments. Granting a foreign national who is detailed from an international organization a security clearance, however, is extraordinary, even unprecedented. So how could this clearance have been granted?

State Department officials familiar with the details of this matter confirmed to me that Shaha Ali Riza was detailed to the State Department and had unescorted access while working for Elizabeth Cheney. Access to the building requires a national security clearance or permanent escort by a person with such a clearance. But the State Department has no record of having issued a national security clearance to Riza.

State Department officials believe that Riza was issued such a clearance by the Defense Department after SAIC was forced by Wolfowitz and Feith to hire her. Then her clearance would have been recognized by the State Department through a credentials transmittal letter and Riza would have accessed the State Department on Pentagon credentials, using her Pentagon clearance to get a State Department building pass with a letter issued under instructions from Liz Cheney.

But State Department officials tell me that no such letter can be confirmed as received. And the officials stress that the department would never issue a clearance to a non-U.S. citizen as part of a contractual requisition. Issuing a national security clearance to a foreign national under instructions from a Pentagon official would constitute a violation of the executive orders governing clearances, they say.

Given these circumstances, the inspector general of the Defense Department should be ordered to investigate how Shaha Ali Riza was issued a Pentagon security clearance. And the inspector general of the State Department should investigate who ordered Riza's building pass and whether there was a Pentagon credentials transmittal letter.

Wolfowitz's willful behavior, as though no rules bound him or facts constrained his ideas, should not have surprised anyone. At the Pentagon, Wolfowitz was an insistent force behind an invasion of Iraq, bringing it up at the first National Security Council meeting of the Bush administration, months before September 11. For years he had been a firm believer in the crackpot theories of Laurie Mylroie, a neoconservative writer, who argued that Saddam was behind the 1993 World Trade Center bombing and even the 1995 Oklahoma City bombing. After September 11, Wolfowitz pursued his obsession by sending former CIA Director James Woolsey on a secret mission to attempt to confirm the theory. Woolsey came back with nothing, but Wolfowitz continued to believe. His beliefs are stronger than any evidence.

Surrounded by his Praetorian Guard, Wolfowitz insulated himself at the World Bank from the career staff. There, as at the Pentagon, Wolfowitz pushed aside the professionals and replaced them with a small band of politically reliable assistants. Wolfowitz rewarded them, too, on his own authority, with enormous tax-free salaries. Consider Kevin Kellems, his public affairs officer at the Pentagon, who had guided conservative media from that perch and is known as "keeper of the comb," for having been the person to hand Wolfowitz the infamous comb he licked before slicking down his hair in the Michael Moore film "Fahrenheit 9/11." Kellems was given a salary of $240,000, at least equal to what World Bank vice presidents with years of service earn.

Wolfowitz had spent his career staging neoconservative insurgencies against what he considered to be liberal establishments. But at the World Bank he tried to model himself after Robert McNamara, who had turned his presidency at the bank into his vehicle for redemption for his part in the Vietnam War. Wolfowitz, the chief intellectual and policy advocate for the Iraq war, no longer mentioned it. Now he pleads to the World Bank board that his corrupt dealings be overlooked for the greater good of his crusade against corruption. His refusal to resign discredits and paralyzes the institution he had hoped would vindicate him.

April 19, 2007

Torture Kitsch

Having written extensively on the Bush administration's torture policy, I concluded, in light of the shocking photographs from Abu Ghraib, that the visual medium was the most powerful and penetrating way to communicate the policy. More than two years ago, I brought the idea of making a documentary on the Bush policy to Alex Gibney, the director of *Enron: The Smartest Guys in the Room*. Alex shared my sense of urgency, and *Taxi to the Dark Side* premieres April 27 at the Tribeca Film Festival. (Alex is the director; I am executive producer. And at Tribeca, *Taxi* won the prize for best documentary.)

Through the film runs the story of an Afghan taxi driver, known only as Dilawar, completely innocent of any ties to terrorism, who was tortured to death by interrogators in the U.S. prison at Bagram Air Base in Afghanistan. *Taxi to the Dark Side* traces the evolution of the Bush policy from Bagram (Dilawar's interrogators speak in the film) to Guantánamo (we filmed the official happy tour) to Abu Ghraib; its roots in sensory deprivation experiments decades ago that guided the CIA in understanding torture; the opposition within the administration from the military and other significant figures (the former general counsel of the Navy, Alberto Mora, and former chief of staff to Secretary of State Colin Powell, Lawrence Wilkerson, explain how that internal debate went, while John Yoo, one of its architects, defends it); the congressional battle to restore the standard of the Geneva Convention that forbids torture (centered on John McCain's tragic compromise); and the sudden popularity of the Fox TV show *24* in translating torture into entertainment by means of repetitious formulations of the bogus ticking-time-bomb scenario.

Yet *Taxi to the Dark Side* is more than an exposé of policy. Its irrefutable images are the counterpoint to the peculiar aesthetics propagated in the age of George W. Bush, in which, through the contradictory styles of softening nostalgia and hardening cruelty, the president and his followers seek to justify their actions not only to the public but also to themselves.

The notion that there might be an aesthetic that informs the Bush presidency would seem to be an unfair and artificial imposition on a man who prizes his intuition ("I'm a gut player") and openly derides complication ("I don't do nuance")—that is, if Bush himself did not insist on the connection. Indeed, he appears on the official White House Web site, conducting a tour of the art and artifacts he has chosen to decorate the Oval Office, assuming the duty of docent himself. He holds forth on the large windows and the rug with rays of the sun emanating from the seal of the president and the provenance of his desk before getting to the artwork. (On April 19, Bush recounted to a crowd in Tipp City, Ohio, a story he has told many times, of how he commissioned his wife, Laura, to design the rug and then in defense of his Iraq policy simply remarked, "Remember the rug?")

"Each president can put whatever paintings he wants on the wall. I've chosen some paintings that kind of reflect my nature," Bush says in his video tour. He points to portraits of Abraham Lincoln ("The job of the president is to set big goals for the country") and George Washington ("You couldn't have the Oval Office without George Washington on the wall"), and pats busts of Lincoln ("You can tell he's one of my favorites"), Dwight Eisenhower ("steady"), and Winston Churchill ("gift of the British prime minister . . . Churchill was a war leader . . . resolute, tough").

Bush takes special pride in pointing out two paintings he has hung that highlight his motives and legacy. He consciously placed these pictures in the Oval Office at the beginning of his tenure to serve as prescient cultural markers. "The Texas paintings are on the wall because that's where I'm from and where I'm going," he says.

One of them, by little known painter and illustrator William Henry Dethlef Koerner, titled *A Charge to Keep*, depicts a hatless cowboy followed by two other riders galloping up a hill. Their faces are intent as they pursue some quarry in the distance that cannot be seen by others. Or are they being chased? "I love it," Bush said, further explaining his intimate feeling for the painting to reporters and editors of the *Washington Times*, a conservative newspaper. He offered his interpretation: "He's a determined horseman, a very difficult trail. And you know at least two people are following him, and maybe a thousand." Bush added that the painting is "based" on an old hymn. "And the hymn talks about serving the Almighty. So it speaks to me personally." When he was governor of Texas and the painting hung in his office, Bush wrote a note of explanation to his staff: "This is us."

W. H. D. Koerner, born in 1878, was a German immigrant who settled with his family in Iowa. After an early stint as a rapid-hand illustrator for the *Chicago Tribune* before photographs became commonplace in newspapers, he studied at the Howard Pyle School of Art, in Delaware, led by the leading illustrator in the country. Koerner then became a regular illustrator for *The Saturday Evening Post*, a mass magazine that appealed to small-town sentimentality and mythology in an age before the spread of radio. The magazine's trademark was its hundreds of covers produced by Norman Rockwell, a commercial artist whose ubiquitous work in advertising and his glossy but homey kitsch for *The Saturday Evening Post* gained him a reputation as one of the definers of everyday Americana.

The magazine used Koerner especially to provide pictures to accompany short stories about cowboys. In 1912, it gave Koerner the choice assignment of illustrating Zane Grey's "Riders of the Purple Sage." The Koerner painting that now hangs in the Oval Office first appeared as an illustration for a cowboy story called "The Slipper Tongue" in the June 3, 1916, issue. The next year, the magazine reprinted the illustration to accompany another cowboy story, "Ways That Are Dark." (Both of the writers of these short stories were forgettable figures in the Western pulp fiction tradition, originated in the late nineteenth century by Ned Buntline, inventive publisher of Wild West dime novels and mythologizer of "Buffalo Bill" Cody and "Wild Bill" Hickok, who in the process became the wealthiest author of his time.) Two years after his illustration was first printed, Koerner resold it to *Country Gentleman* magazine, to go with another Western called "A Charge to Keep." The editors of *Country Gentleman* didn't seem to mind that the picture had been used twice before by another publication.

In 1995, at Bush's inaugural as governor of Texas, his wife, Laura, selected an eighteenth-century Methodist hymn, written by Charles Wesley, titled "A Charge to Keep." Its words in part are:

A charge to keep I have,
A God to glorify,
A never-dying soul to save,
And fit it for the sky.
To serve the present age,
My calling to fulfill:
O may it all my powers engage
To do my master's will!

After the ceremony, one of Bush's childhood friends, Joseph I. "Spider" O'Neill, managing partner of his family's oil and investment company, told him that he owned a painting, remarkably enough titled *A Charge to Keep*, and that he would happily lend it to the governor. O'Neill and his wife, who attended Southern Methodist University with Laura, as it happened had also played Cupid in arranging the first date between George and Laura. Presented with the cowboy painting, Bush enthusiastically displayed it at the Governor's Mansion and now the White House.

The idea of Bush as a Christian cowboy, dashing upward and onward to fulfill the Lord's commandments, inspired him to title his campaign auto-biography (written by his then communications advisor, Karen Hughes) *A Charge to Keep: My Journey to the White House*. Sample: "I could not be gover-nor if I did not believe in a divine plan that supersedes all human plans."

On the White House Web site, Bush continues his tour of his favored art-work, drawing attention to an additional painting, by regional Texan artist Julian Onderdonk, which portrays in soft beige tones one of the most iconic and historic places in the state—the Alamo. The painting features indistinct Mexican women making tortillas in the plaza of the mission that the Mexican army besieged in the Texas war of independence of 1836. Nearly every man was killed, a massacre that became symbolic of a heroic last stand and a rallying cry for revenge. As everyone knows who has ever read one of the many histories or novels about the conflict or seen the TV series of the 1950s, *Davy Crockett*, or any of the movies titled *The Alamo*, such as the one featuring John Wayne as Davy Crockett, the ragtag defenders knew they were doomed but decided to fight the overwhelming Mexican army. In an incident that may be apocryphal, the commander, William Travis, drew a line in the ground, urging those who wished to leave to cross it; none did. Thus dying for the cause became the red badge of courage. Dying was "never dying," as the old hymn said, but gave birth to the republic of Texas.

Studying the racing cowboy, Bush gleans a moral lesson to stay the course, even if its end cannot be seen; his certainty that he is followed, not just by two men but also by "thousands"; and his conviction that his hot pur-suit is divinely guided. As he gazes at the Alamo he is reminded that doubt and skepticism are equivalent to cowardice and capitulation, that battling to the end will lead to redemption and resurrection.

In his private study off the Oval Office, Bush displays another artifact, but one that is not featured on the Web site tour—Saddam Hussein's pistol, seized after U.S. soldiers captured him in December 2003. "It's now the property of the U.S. government," Bush announced at a press conference shortly afterward. The president has had the gun mounted like a trophy. "He really liked showing it off," a visitor told *Time* magazine. In his fortress of solitude, surrounded by images of the rider and the Alamo, the determined pursuer and the last stand, the gun has become a token of Bush's inevitable victory.

Bush understands his war in Iraq through his Western artifacts—a West, by the way, without any manifestation of Native Americans. The more resistant the reality in Iraq, the tighter he clings to the symbolism of the West. And so do those who support him. "America has a vital interest in preventing the emergence of Iraq as a Wild West for terrorists," Senator John McCain declared on April 11. But there is a dark side to the Wild West show of the conservative mind (just as there was to the Wild West). "We have to work the dark side," said Vice President Dick Cheney a week after the September 11 terrorist attacks.

One week after Cheney's statement, on September 25, 2001, the Department of Justice sent the White House a memo titled "The President's Constitutional Authority to Conduct Military Operations Against Terrorists and Nations Supporting Them." The memo declared that there were "no limits" on the president's powers to wage a war without any known end and that the president was invested with powers to stage "preemptive" strikes against any target he designates at any time without consulting Congress.

On August 1, 2002, another memo, cowritten by the chief of the Office of Legal Counsel of the Justice Department, Jay Bybee, and his deputy assistant, John Yoo, who had been the author of the earlier September 25, 2001, memo, laid out the rationale for a new policy on torture.

On January 25, 2002, White House legal counsel Alberto Gonzales stated in a memo to President Bush that the Geneva Conventions Common Article Three to which the U.S. is a signatory and that forbids torture was obsolete: "In my judgment, this new paradigm renders obsolete Geneva's strict limitations on questioning of enemy prisoners and renders quaint some of its provisions."

Now, Bybee and Yoo redefined torture. In their memo they recast techniques illegal under the Geneva Conventions as acceptable: "Physical pain amounting to torture must be equivalent in intensity to the pain accompanying serious physical injury, such as organ failure, impairment of bodily function, or even death." Bush promptly ordered implementation of the new policy. Thus the decision whose grotesque consequences were enacted at Abu Ghraib began at the top of the chain of command. When the Bybee memo was exposed the administration declared that it had been rescinded. But the "coercive interrogation techniques," as Bush calls them, continued. "This program won't go forward if there's vague standards applied like those in the Geneva Conventions," he said on September 15, 2006. He assailed Congress for trying to legislate against torture and reiterated that Article Three is "so vague."

An obsession with torture has not been restricted to the White House. It has spread into the larger culture, especially through a popular TV series, on Rupert Murdoch's Fox entertainment channel, called *24*. Every week, a fictional hero named Jack Bauer, an agent for a fictional government Counter Terrorist Unit, races the clock, in fantastic ticking-time-bomb scenarios, to thwart terrorist plots. Bauer's favored method is torture. Agent Bauer has shot one suspect's wife, staged a fake execution of another's child, electrocuted another bad guy, and even tortured his own brother. Bauer is also tortured from time to time, fostering an impulse for vengeance. From 2002 through 2005, the Parents Television Council, a watchdog group, counted sixty-seven torture scenes on *24*.

In March 2006, in Washington, the Heritage Foundation, a right-wing think tank, sponsored a panel discussion devoted to *24*, titled "America's Image in Fighting Terrorism: Fact, Fiction, or Does It Matter?" Lending verisimilitude to the celebration of the fictional TV series, Secretary of Homeland Security Michael Chertoff was the first speaker. "Frankly," he said about the program, "it reflects real life." He expressed a wish that terror investigations could be more like those on TV. "I wish we could have a rapid execution of tasks within 24 hours," Chertoff said. Howard Gordon, the show's executive producer, conceded, "When Jack Bauer tortures, it's in a compressed reality."

The moderator, right-wing talk show host Rush Limbaugh, boasted, "Everybody I've met in the government that I tell I watch this show, they are huge fans. Vice president's a huge fan. Secretary [of Defense Donald] Rumsfeld is a huge fan." In fact, on the same day as the Heritage Foundation event the producer and director of *24* were feted at a private lunch at the White House. Jane Mayer of *The New Yorker* reported: "Among the attendees were Karl Rove, the deputy chief of staff; Tony Snow, the White House spokesman; Mary Cheney, the Vice-President's daughter; and Lynne Cheney, the Vice-President's wife, who, [Joel] Surnow [the show's director] said, is 'an extreme '24' fan.'"

But *24* is more than the return of the repressed. Administration officials seem to view it as the war on terror in its ideal form, utterly without "quaint" restraints or actual frustrations. *24* is torture without excuses or embarrassment. Bush administration fans apparently project themselves onto Agent Bauer, whose methods are always cheered and whose own suffering ends within the hour. For them it is all more real than real life.

John Yoo, in his book justifying torture, *War by Other Means*, published in 2006, even cited *24* as a legitimate intellectual proof for the policy he helped put into place: "What if, as the popular Fox television program '24' recently portrayed, a high-level terrorist leader is caught who knows the location of a nuclear weapon?" he writes about the most grandiose of ticking-time-bomb plots. This sort of scenario invariably prompts agent Bauer's remorseless threat to terrorist suspects: "You are going to tell me what I want to know. It's just a question of how much you want it to hurt." Thus the lines between fact and fiction, reality and kitsch, and policy and entertainment are blurred.

The distance between the cowboy paintings Bush proudly displays in the Oval Office and the secret-agent torture porn that his administration officials not so secretly watch with envy reflects a yawning chasm in the sensibility of kitsch. Koerner's Western pictures depict an idealized past, where never is heard a discouraging word. At *The Saturday Evening Post*, he joined with Norman Rockwell to create the brush strokes of a warming nostalgia.

These enduring images infused Reaganism with its emotional culture. Ronald Reagan, after all, had been raised at the turn of the century in small-town Illinois and became a contract player in Hollywood's dream factory. Communicating kitsch was second nature to him. The perfect representation came in the TV commercial for his reelection campaign in 1984. As an American flag was raised in a small town, the voice-over intoned: "It's morning again in America." The past was present and all was right with the world.

Now, kitsch has been radically remade. No longer evoking nostalgic utopianism, kitsch releases the compulsions of fear. Under Bush, kitsch has been transformed from sentimentality into sadomasochism.

April 26, 2007

Spooked

If former CIA director George Tenet's *At the Center of the Storm* were an intelligence operation, it would have to be assessed as achieving precisely the opposite of the results intended. Tenet hoped that his elaborate apology for his government service would cast him as honest, prudent, and professional; his admission of his own mistakes would shine a light on his integrity; his disclosures of the machinations of Vice President Dick Cheney and the neoconservative cabal would show him as a truth teller; and his refusal to say nary a bad word about President Bush would demonstrate his respect for the presidency.

But Tenet's sketchy book, devastating in patches, is glaringly misleading about many decisive events in which he played an important role. By depicting himself as a spook for all seasons, moreover, he has simply exposed himself as a self-serving poseur. Tenet, after all, never served as an intelligence agent and was never posted overseas. For years he was the staff director of the Senate Select Intelligence Committee, until then CIA director John Deutch chose him as deputy director, in great part on the strength of his congressional ties. When Deutch self-immolated for downloading classified files onto his personal computer, Tenet was promoted by President Clinton to the directorship and retained by President Bush, who seemed to appreciate his chameleon-like quality of adapting to any environment.

Despite this résumé as a consummate bureaucratic player, Tenet has shown himself to be politically impaired. He appears unable to perceive what he has done or what he is doing. He has only the dimmest sense of the moment into which he has inserted himself. Rather than being hailed for bravery, he finds himself in a hail of fire. He seems strangely oblivious that his supposed self-defense is shredding the remains of his reputation. His promotional performances on TV reveal an angry man careening out of emotional control, attempting to deflect difficult questions by demanding deference to his departed and tarnished authority. "Now you see what we've had to deal with," a former high CIA official told me. "And I like George."

Tenet's version of his notorious statement assuring the president that the intelligence reports that Saddam Hussein possessed weapons of mass destruction were a "slam-dunk" may clarify the historical record, but his account only reveals his poor judgment. In an Oval Office meeting on December 21, 2002, Tenet did not use the phrase as Bob Woodward reported in his book *Plan of Attack* but, as he tells it, "Instead, I told the president that strengthening the public presentation was a 'slam dunk.'" If true, Tenet is confessing that as director of the CIA he engaged in free-wheeling political strategy meetings on the propaganda campaign to the American public to sell them the Iraq war, skirting close to the edge of violating the CIA's charter against involvement in domestic affairs. Unaware of the egregious inappropriateness of his revelation, Tenet is consumed with rage against the source that "later described the scene to Bob Woodward," making him the scapegoat for bad intelligence. "It's the most despicable thing that ever happened to me," Tenet said on CBS's *60 Minutes*. But he is blind that his alternative account is equally undermining.

In his TV appearances, Tenet proclaims his devotion to the professionalism of the men and women of the agency he once headed, but his book depicts him as feckless in defending them from the intimidation of Cheney and the neoconservatives. He acknowledges that Cheney and his former chief of staff, I. Lewis "Scooter" Libby, frequently turned up at the Langley, Virginia, headquarters to browbeat analysts into accepting their disinformation that there were direct links between Saddam and Al-Qaeda. Tenet describes how analysts, in response to the pressure, produced a study, "Iraq and al-Qa'ida: Interpreting a Murky Relationship," which "made clear that there were no conclusive signs between Iraq and al-Qa'ida with regard to terrorist operations" but indicated there were signs "to at least require us to be very concerned." In fact, there were no such ties, and the "murky" conclusion was a middle ground between the utter absence of any solid evidence and the falsehoods that Cheney and Co. were pushing. Libby and then Deputy Secretary of Defense Paul Wolfowitz rejected the paper out of hand.

Trying to produce a more "comprehensive paper," the parallel intelligence operation at the Pentagon, the Office of Special Plans, set up to counter the CIA's vetting process, was churning disinformation straight into the White House. Tenet attended a meeting for one of its slide show presentations on August 15, 2002, "Iraq and al-Qa'ida—Making the Case." "It is an open-and-shut case," said a member of the Pentagon team. "No further analysis is required."

Tenet never confronted Cheney or Secretary of Defense Donald Rumsfeld. While Tenet was eager to offer his opinion to the president on political propaganda—"slam-dunk"—he never told him of the attack on the integrity of the intelligence process. Tenet never shielded his analysts from Libby. His passivity fed the momentum of the neocons. Then he lent his weight to the National Intelligence Estimate on WMD, presented to Congress only days before it voted in October 2002 on the Authorization for Use of Military Force Against Iraq: "Baghdad has chemical and biological weapons as well as missiles with ranges in excess of UN restrictions; if left unchecked, it probably will have a nuclear weapon during this decade." Tenet admits now that the conclusions of the NIE were "not facts and should not have been so characterized." Nonetheless, he briefed members of Congress at the time that they were indeed facts. Even Democratic senators who voted against the authorization in their floor speeches gave credence to the supposedly indisputable fact that Saddam had WMD.

Tenet confesses that he believed the information from an Iraqi source called "Curve Ball." Only later, he claims, did he learn that Curve Ball was a complete fraud. But Tyler Drumheller, former chief of CIA operations in Europe, has emerged to brand Tenet's account as false. In fact, says Drumheller, he had communicated the reports from German intelligence that Curve Ball was a fabricator, and in November and December 2002 debated the issue inside the agency. (Drumheller's version appears in his recent book, *On the Brink: An Insider's Account of How the White House Compromised American Intelligence.*) But Tenet brushed off those serious concerns and approved disinformation based on Curve Ball that served as the heart of Secretary of State Colin Powell's February 5, 2003, speech to the United Nations Security Council. Tenet now writes, "It was a great presentation, but unfortunately the substance didn't hold up." One principal reason it did not is that Tenet had carefully failed to perform his due diligence, all the while assuring Powell that he had.

Tenet's account of the July 20, 2002, meeting of CIA officials and British intelligence officers in Washington is also misleading, according to a former high CIA official with firsthand knowledge, who described it to me as "total bullshit." That meeting was important as the basis of the subsequent briefing of Prime Minister Tony Blair that took place at Downing Street three days later, summarized in the famous so-called Downing Street memo. In the memo, Sir Richard Dearlove, chief of MI6, is quoted: "Military action was now seen as inevitable . . . Bush wanted to remove Saddam, through military action, justified by the conjunction of terrorism and WMD." Even more ominously, Dearlove warned that "the intelligence and facts were being fixed around the policy."

Tenet writes that Dearlove told him he was misquoted and that Tenet "corrected it to reflect the truth of the matter." "Tenet doesn't say what the truth of the matter is," the former CIA officer told me. "Dearlove just didn't want to be blamed." Dearlove, the former CIA official emphatically insists, claiming direct knowledge, was accurately relating what Tenet had personally told him.

The former CIA official explains that the Washington meeting was an annual U.S.–U.K. event, usually held in Bermuda. But in 2002, as the drums of war were beating, Tenet wanted to blow off the British. British intelligence officials threatened that if they were not briefed with the latest material, they would have Blair call Bush and force the meeting to happen. Still, Cofer Black, the State Department chief of counterterrorism, tried to block it. The overwhelming factor working in the Brits' favor was the figure of Blair. "They could deliver Tony Blair, and he was important as the one major international figure who supported Bush and was popular with the American public," the former official told me. So the meeting was held at Langley. After a daylong briefing in the director's conference room and private dining room, Tenet took Dearlove into his office. According to the CIA source, "That's where Dearlove asked where the intelligence was going, was it heading to war, did it matter what the intelligence was. Tenet said, that's the way things are heading, they are looking for intelligence to fit into this." Dearlove's "fix" was simply the British version of "fit." He was not misquoted; he was spot on.

In his interview with *60 Minutes*, Tenet echoed Bush's refrain, "We do not torture." Tenet used the word like the Red Queen in *Alice in Wonderland*. It means whatever he says it means. Torture becomes "not torture" by saying so.

Tenet has written his book as an act of self-exculpation to distance himself from Cheney and Co. But the controversies he has revisited entangle him even deeper in the making of the false case for war. His book underlines his failure to protect his agency. And in his hollow defense of torture he has lashed himself to Bush and Cheney.

May 3, 2007

Royal Crush

President Bush greeted Queen Elizabeth in Washington on May 7, 2007, as a royal distraction from polls showing him as the most unpopular president since Richard Nixon resigned in disgrace. Bush has held the fewest number of state dinners of recent presidents, only four previous ones, but for the queen he staged a white-tie affair and even forced himself to stay up past his usual nine o'clock bedtime.

The queen's events began with a welcoming ceremony on the south lawn of the White House. "You've dined with ten presidents," Bush read from his speech. "You helped our nation celebrate its bicentennial in 17— in 1976," he said, quickly recovering. He turned to the queen, smirked, winked, paused, and then said to the crowd: "She gave me a look that only a mother could give a child."

Confronted with a dignified white-haired woman failing to participate in his shenanigans, Bush instantly equated her with his mother and her silence with disapproval. In his experience the most common look that a mother gives a child is censorious. The queen's presence instinctively prompted him to declare himself a naughty little boy.

Indeed, the queen and the president have had a mother-and-child-like history. During the queen's 1991 visit, then first lady Barbara Bush, anxious about her ne'er-do-well eldest son, instructed him not to speak to the queen. "The family never knows what he'll say in polite society," the *Washington Post* commented at the time. "Are you the black sheep of the family?" Queen Elizabeth asked him. "I guess that might be true," he said. "Well, I guess all families have one," she replied. He asked her who the black sheep was in her family. "Appearing from out of nowhere," the *Post* reported, Barbara Bush swooped from across the room to save the queen, shouting, "Don't answer that!" The queen maintained her regal silence and walked away from the impertinent prince.

After presiding at a lunch for the queen at Blair House, across Pennsylvania Avenue, President Bush, walking back, heckled a *Newsweek* photographer, demanding that he admit it was "a special day" at the White House, and then berating him: "Then why didn't you wear something other than hand-me-down clothes?" The photographer, however, had not received the white-tie invitation.

That afternoon, the queen attended a garden party at the British embassy. Knots of neo-conservatives surged toward the canapés. Neocon *New York Times* columnist David Brooks, in his best imitation of Uriah Heep, wrote of the event: "Although as a child I had turtles named Disraeli and Gladstone, I was never invited to sip champagne with the queen until yesterday." Around a tent-pole clustered the remnants of the Georgetown set that had once dominated Washington. Queen Elizabeth, attired in salmon from hat to shoes, parted the sea of notables, stopping to speak to a short elderly man, his jacket bedecked with medals—Mickey Rooney. "What does one say upon being introduced to Mickey Rooney?" I wondered to an Georgetowners standing near me. "How was Ava Gardner?" he replied.

The state dinner enabled Bush to bestow grace and favor in a time of cholera. Here came three former secretaries of state—Henry Kissinger, George Shultz, and Colin Powell; Texas oilmen (including T. Boone Pickens who funneled $3 million to the Swift Boat Veterans for Truth smear campaign against Senator John Kerry in 2004); Lynne Cheney's brother; and one James Click, owner of the Jim Click Ford dealership of Tucson, Arizona, representing the Rangers (the highest rank of Bush-campaign fundraisers).

Laura Bush, a former librarian, who has made reading her special cause, invited not a single American writer. Perhaps she feared that men and women of letters might use the occasion to protest the Iraq War. (On April 25, she remarked about the war: "No one suffers more than their president and I do when we watch this.") Also absent from the guest list were American artists, filmmakers, and musicians, except violinist Itzhak Perlman, who performed after dinner.

Instead, Calvin Borel, the jockey who had just won the Kentucky Derby, seventy-eight-year-old golfer Arnold Palmer, football quarterback Peyton Manning (not related to British ambassador David Manning), and retired football player Gene Washington (Condoleezza Rice's escort) were summoned to embody American culture. The *Washington Post*, without the slightest ironic tone, described the dinner as the "most elegant Washington evening in a decade," or at least since Warren G. Harding played poker.

May 10, 2007

Loyalty and Betrayal

Loyalty has always been the alpha and omega of George W. Bush's presidency. But all the forms of allegiance that have bound together his administration—political, ideological and personal—are being shredded, leaving only blind loyalty. Bush has surrounded himself with loyalists, who fervently pledged their fealty, enforced the loyalty of others, and sought to make loyal converts. Now Bush's long downfall is descending into a series of revenge tragedies in which the characters are helpless against the furies of their misplaced loyalties and betrayals. The stage is being strewn with hacked corpses—on Monday, former Deputy Attorney General Paul McNulty; imminently, World Bank president Paul Wolfowitz; tomorrow, whoever remains trapped on the ghost ship of state. As the individual tragedies unfold, Bush's royal robes unravel.

Loyalty to Bush is the ultimate royal principle of the imperial presidency. The ruler must be unquestioned and those around him unquestioning. Allegiance to Bush's idea of himself as the "war president," "the decider," and "the commander guy" is paramount. But the notion that the ruler is loyal to those loyal to him is no longer necessarily true. While he must be beheld as the absolute incarnation of kingly virtue, his sense of obligation to those paying homage has become perilously relative.

Those who feel compelled to tell the truth rather than stick to the cover story are cast in the dust, like McNulty. Those Bush defends as an extension of his authority but who become too expensive become expendable, like Wolfowitz. And those who exist solely as Bush's creations and whose survival is crucial to his own are shielded, like Attorney General Alberto Gonzales.

On Tuesday, James Comey, the former deputy attorney general, disclosed a story that might have been written by Mario Puzo, and it explained the rise of Gonzales as attorney general. On March 10, 2004, Comey was serving as acting attorney general while John Ashcroft was in an intensive-care unit being treated for pancreatitis. After an "extensive review" by the Justice Department's Office of Legal Counsel, which concluded that Bush's warrantless domestic surveillance program was illegal, Comey refused to sign its reauthorization. An aide to Ashcroft tipped Comey off that White House legal counsel Gonzales and chief of staff Andrew Card were headed to Ashcroft's hospital to get him to sign it. Comey rushed to the darkened room, where he briefed the barely conscious Ashcroft. Gonzales and Card entered minutes later, demanding that Ashcroft comply. He refused, pointing to Comey, saying he was the attorney general. "I was angry. I had just witnessed an effort to take advantage of a very sick man," Comey testified.

Gonzales and Card then summoned Comey to the White House, where they attempted to intimidate him by telling him that Vice President Dick Cheney and his counsel, David Addington, were in favor of the reauthorization. Comey still refused. And the program went forward without the legal Justice Department approval. Comey and other high Justice Department officials prepared their resignation letters. The next day, having heard about the planned mass resignations, President Bush met alone with Comey, who briefed him on what needed to be done to bring the program under the law. Several weeks later Comey signed the authorization for a legal program. But during that period it was conducted outside the law.

Then, after Bush's reelection, Ashcroft was not reappointed. In his place Bush sent a new name to the Senate for confirmation—Alberto Gonzales. Every position he had held was the result of his undying loyalty to Bush. The confrontation in Ashcroft's hospital room had been a turning point in his rise. Comey, who Bush privately derided as "Cuomo," quit. In his confirmation hearing before the Senate Judiciary Committee, Gonzales was asked about domestic surveillance, and he blithely misled the senators, acting as if he would always uphold the existing law, even though he had pressured Ashcroft and Comey to approve the illegal program. "The government cannot do that without first going to a judge," he said. "Government goes to the FISA [Foreign Intelligence Surveillance Act] court and obtains a warrant to do that." Gonzales spoke those lines knowing he had done precisely the opposite. His lie demonstrated his higher loyalty to his patron.

At the moment that Comey was finishing his testimony about the drama at Ashcroft's sickbed, Gonzales was delivering a speech at the National

Press Club blaming his former deputy for the political purge of eight U.S. Attorneys. "You have to remember," said Gonzales, "at the end of the day, the recommendations reflected the views of the deputy attorney general. The deputy attorney general would know best about the qualifications and the experiences of the United States attorneys community, and he signed off on the names." Gonzales had previously accepted generic "responsibility," claimed he didn't know anything about the dismissals and also blamed his former chief of staff, D. Kyle Sampson.

McNulty had, in fact, testified truthfully before the Senate, which reportedly infuriated Gonzales. Though ostensibly in charge of the U.S. attorneys, McNulty was kept out of the loop of the detailed planning for the purge, informed only in outline and briefed to give false testimony about the reasons for the firings by Sampson and others at his February appearance before the Senate Judiciary Committee. After McNulty conveyed his talking points about the U.S. attorneys being dismissed for "performance related" problems, he conceded under questioning that one had been replaced in order to fill his post with one of Karl Rove's protégés. That revelation blew up the scandal. McNulty's scapegoating and resignation were inevitable.

McNulty was tainted as a betrayer for telling the truth. He had been an operator for two decades within the Republican Party, but his loyal service could not protect him. A graduate of the Capital University Law School in Columbus, Ohio, he had striven upward as a faithful party man, making a career of political networking. His adherence to the principles of the Federalist Society lent him an imprimatur as a reliable conservative. He served as counsel to the House Judiciary Committee during the impeachment of President Clinton. His partisanship was considered so solid that he was named head of the Bush transition team for the Justice Department. He received the plum appointment as U.S. attorney for Northern Virginia, the so-called rocket docket, used for high-profile terrorism cases after 9/11, like that of John Walker Lindh. With Comey's departure, he rose to deputy attorney general.

In the end, McNulty suffered Comey's fate. His loyalty to party did not extend beyond the boundaries of the law. Thus he became a betrayer and a fall guy. His reputation was tarnished while Gonzales remained. Gonzales carried out his shameless finger-pointing at McNulty without the slightest hesitation. The destruction of trust within his department seemed to bother him not at all. His instinct for self-preservation easily triumphed over his desire for self-respect. Bush's loyalty to Gonzales is a monument to his vulnerability if he were to resign.

Monica Goodling, the former number three ranking Justice Department official, presents another version of loyalty, that of the religious fanatic. Her refusal to testify before the Senate, invoking the Fifth Amendment, was brushed aside last week by a federal court that granted her limited immunity. Her equation of loyalty is to faith, a complete commitment in which her political agenda is part of a destined plan for salvation. Goodling sees Bush as the crusader king and herself as loyal vassal. Within this administration, she is not deluded, and her rise without visible credentials was proof that she was well prepared by Pat Robertson's Regent University to serve Bush as the Lord Ruler.

As Gonzales maintained his grip on his office while his deputy and aides were tossed into the inferno, the Wolfowitz drama inexorably moved to its final act. Wolfowitz, intellectual architect of the Iraq War as deputy secretary of defense, and even before, had had a long career before receiving Bush's patronage. Bush, indeed, is not his patron, but Cheney, for whom Wolfowitz was an aide when Cheney was secretary of defense in the elder Bush's administration, is. Wolfowitz's career precedes that period, too, as one of the most fully formed neoconservatives in Washington. Unlike Gonzales, he is not Bush's creature. But Bush's policy is his. In being loyal to Wolfowitz, Bush is tacitly acknowledging his debt, not his majesty. He should feel compelled to defend Wolfowitz not because he is his appointee as president of the World Bank, but because Wolfowitz formulated the central purpose of the Bush presidency in the invasion of Iraq.

In his loyalty to his own ideas, Wolfowitz exhibits his loyalty to the man of ideas—himself. From abstraction to abstraction, he has bullied his cause and career forward. His loyalty to Bush is contingent on Bush's embrace of Wolfowitz's schemes. Wolfowitz has never shown allegiance to the institutions where he served: not to the Defense Department, which was an instrument for his notions, nor to the World Bank. He surrounded himself with ill-qualified ideological aides, whose loyalty was above all to him and through him to his ideas. The professional staffs at both the Pentagon and the World Bank seethed at Wolfowitz's highhanded managerial style, a combination of arrogance and incompetence.

At the World Bank, he entangled himself in a scandal involving his girlfriend, Shaha Riza, personally arranging for the bank to pay her a large salary increase to move her to a State Department foundation, then blaming the bank's staff for having approved the decision. According to the World Bank report issued this week, Wolfowitz muttered a malediction to the head of the bank's human resources department: "If they fuck with me or Shaha, I have enough on them to fuck them too." Thus Wolfowitz posed as Tony Soprano and depicted the World Bank as the Bada Bing. Loyalty would be forthcoming, or else.

The report described Wolfowitz as a person of "questionable judgment and a preoccupation with self-interest" who "saw himself as the outsider to whom the established rules and standards did not apply." His insistence that he had been requested by the bank to arrange Riza's job "simply turns logic on its head."

On Tuesday, Wolfowitz defended himself by blaming his girlfriend, saying of the bank staff, "Its members did not want to deal with a very angry Ms. Riza." He added that her "intractable position" forced him to give her a large salary increase. With that, the honorable gentleman attributed his rule breaking to his emotionally volatile girlfriend. In short, the bitch set him up.

In a final letter of defense, Wolfowitz pleaded that he was the victim of "unfair" treatment, maligned as being described as a "boyfriend" and that Riza was also denigrated as a "girlfriend." He reminded the bank board of his dear children.

Meanwhile, Cheney, demonstrating his loyalty, called Wolfowitz "a very good president of the World Bank," adding, "I hope he will be able to continue." As part of the salvage effort, Treasury Secretary Henry Paulson, the former chief of Goldman Sachs, was enlisted to telephone finance ministers to urge them to support keeping Wolfowitz. A recent appointee, with no history of involvement with Wolfowitz, Paulson lent his reputation to the scandal-ridden neocon as an act of loyalty to the administration as though it were just a business matter. He simply nicked him as part of the damage. Paulson, too, was left out to dry when White House press secretary Tony Snow announced that insofar as Wolfowitz's future was concerned "all options are open," a formula applied also to Iran.

The root of "loyal" is *loi*, or French for law. Under Bush, loyalty has become a law unto itself. Bush is loyal to those who break the rules but adhere to him. Avowing loyalty for the administration becomes a substitute for making difficult ethical and moral decisions. Yet the less Bush and his loyalists are willing to engage the harsh realities they have created, the more comfort they draw from loyalty. Once loyalty is no longer reciprocal, as in the McNulty case, the leader becomes more isolated as those beneath him become increasingly insecure and paranoid about their status. Demonstrations of loyalty cease being effective as displays of power and greatness. Instead, they are seen as stonewalling or sandbagging, more like the levees of New Orleans that will be inevitably breached. Loyalty to Bush has become loyalty to his self-image and, in the case of Gonzales, loyalty above the law, betraying the meaning of the word itself.

May 17, 2007

Wolfowitz's Tomb

Paul Wolfowitz's doctrines are a summa of numerous failed political dogmas of the twentieth century. His notion of politics was essentially Bolshevik, but less democratic in practice than Lenin's. Wolfowitz had no concept of mass politics. Nor did he have an idea of democratic centralism, the core of Leninism, by which the vanguard led the cells of the party. Wolfowitz believed only in the vanguard. The dutiful student of obscurantist authoritarian philosopher Leo Strauss operated as a solitary intellectual at the head of a single cell, the lone Wolfowitz. His view of international political dynamics was a strange concoction of the most heated, impassioned idea of Leon Trotsky—the permanent revolution—admixed with the most rigid, Manichaean metaphor of John Foster Dulles—the domino theory of the Cold War. Dulles's idea, applied to Southeast Asia, was a reaction to his mistaken understanding of Communist expansion as Trotskyist in conception. From this thesis and antithesis came the synthesis of Paul Wolfowitz. Welcome to the dustbin of history.

The squalid ending of Wolfowitz's glittering career, bickering over lies about payments to his girlfriend, submerged his grandiosity. Wheedling with the World Bank board, he appeared as a shadow of his former self, the intellectual field marshal pulverizing the opposition with the artillery of his arguments, reduced to using a Washington lawyer to make fine points. His class enemies—the CIA and the Baathists, the State Department, and the McGovernites—had retreated under his barrages, but he found himself at last whining of persecution at the hands of the sort of bureaucrats he had brushed aside throughout his long rise.

Wolfowitz's vision promised nothing less than a rupture with the entire world order. By one decisive act of will, all that existed—all—would be transformed. After a brief, very brief, interval, collective happiness and universal harmony would be ushered in. With shock and awe, change would roll in mighty waves, pounding all with its unceasing force.

He was a good boy, not a rebel. Unlike some neoconservatives who had begun on the left and swerved right, his path was straight. His mathematician father's only complaint about him was that he had not become a mathematician. Instead, young Wolfowitz fell under the spell of one of his father's friends, Albert Wohlstetter, an old Trotskyist turned Cold War nuclear theologian. Wolfowitz was a pupil in the most exclusive school. (Richard Perle was another acolyte of Wohlstetter's.) Wolfowitz's study of nuclear policy was more than a higher mathematics; it was a kind of mystical Kabbalah. Strauss's influence on him at the University of Chicago was decidedly minor. His connection at the University of Chicago with Ahmed Chalabi, the Iraqi exile, and Zalmay Khalilzad, another neocon later to be U.S. ambassador to Iraq, was more significant than having Strauss as a teacher. His true master was Wohlstetter, master of throw-weights. Wolfowitz's doctoral thesis was on why Israeli development of a nuclear weapon threatened Middle Eastern and world stability.

Wolfowitz's recruitment onto the "B Team" in the late 1970s, created under the Ford administration through conservative pressure in order to discredit the CIA's assessments of the Soviet Union's nuclear capabilities, signaled his entrance into the sanctum sanctorum of nuclear theologians and Republican policymaking. The factual rebuttal of the B Team's assertions was not a black mark. Conservatives were on the ascendancy, and Wolfowitz was a rare young man among them with a first-class mind and education.

With the end of the Cold War the cold warrior without a mission fastened onto a new idée fixe. As the undersecretary of defense for policy in the first Gulf War, serving under Secretary Dick Cheney, Wolfowitz had concurred in the decision not to pursue Saddam Hussein to Baghdad after expelling him from Kuwait. He had been present at the February 21, 1991, meeting where that policy was approved and uttered not a skeptical or contrary word. But when the elder Bush was defeated, Wolfowitz in exile became the champion of regime change. He developed an elaborate utopian scheme based on the overthrow of Saddam—instant democracy in Iraq, inciting democratic revolutions throughout the Middle East, accompanied by the equally sudden quiescence of the Palestinians, creating peace for Israel while doing away with any negotiations involved in a peace process. And he imagined Saddam, a brutal enough tyrant, as an octopus, his tentacles manipulating nearly every horror. Even after every available piece of evidence and trials proved otherwise, he continued to insist that Saddam was behind the Oklahoma City and 1993 World Trade Center bombings.

By now Wolfowitz had compiled a distinguished foreign policy résumé marking his upward mobility—from the Arms Control and Disarmament Agency to director of State Department policy planning, from deputy assistant secretary of defense to ambassador to Indonesia—and then, as the dean of the Johns Hopkins School of Advanced International Studies, he was paired with Condoleezza Rice as tutor to Governor George W. Bush. Unlike Rice, however, Wolfowitz did not intuitively grasp the mind of his new student. He did not have a natural facility for the art of stroking. He sought to impress through his brilliance. Being acknowledged as the smartest aide in the room was how he had gotten ahead before. His breadth of detail and depth of concepts had gained him a series of patrons, from George Shultz to Cheney, who knew how to harness his cerebral talents. But Wolfowitz was not a man for nicknames and locker-room jokes. Despite his privileged proximity to the candidate, Bush did not take to him. And between administrations Wolfowitz was almost lost in the shuffle.

Originally, Wolfowitz aspired to be deputy secretary of state. But the newly named secretary, Colin Powell, had observed Wolfowitz as a Cheney aide during the Gulf War opposing his various positions, and rejected him. Instead, he deployed Washington lawyer and former Reagan chief of staff Kenneth Duberstein, acting as his representative, to offer Wolfowitz the consolation prize of ambassador to the United Nations. Leaving the cockpit of action for a place despised by neoconservatives would have been a cruel punishment. Wolfowitz was suspended in a void. The Kremlin-like politics of the Bush transition determined his fate.

Senator Dan Coats of Indiana, staffed by a close Cheney friend, favored by social conservatives for his hostility to gays in the military as a member of the Armed Services Committee, emerged as the first choice for secretary of defense. He was to be part of a two-for-one package. Richard Armitage, armed with Pentagon experience, would be his deputy and run the department. But after Powell eclipsed Bush in the press conference where his nomination as secretary of state was announced, Cheney immediately understood that the Coats scenario threatened his intention to become the most powerful vice president in history. While Coats was dim, Armitage was adept. And this combination empowered Powell, potentially giving him dominion over not only State but also Defense. Once this prospect loomed, Cheney, whose clashes with Powell went back to the Gulf War, sought an alternative. Meanwhile, the neoconservative press sounded the alarm. *The Weekly Standard* ran an article headlined "The Long Arm of Colin Powell: Will the Next Secretary of State Also Run the Pentagon?" Coats cooperated by undermining himself. His interview with President-elect Bush was a combustible mix of bad chemistry. The dreary Coats didn't laugh at Bush's jibes and instead declared his skepticism about "Star Wars" missile defense and complained about Powell. Instantly, he fell through the trapdoor, shipped to Germany as ambassador.

Donald Rumsfeld, who had been secretary of defense under Gerald Ford, wanted to be director of the CIA. His longtime rival, the elder Bush, opposed his appointment to the position he himself had once held. Bad blood had flowed through their relationship since the Ford years, when Rumsfeld had systematically sidelined Bush. In 1988, Rumsfeld endorsed Senator Bob Dole for the Republican presidential nomination against Vice President Bush. When he won, Bush cut Rumsfeld out of the administration. At dinner parties in Chicago, where Rumsfeld worked as a corporate executive, he entertained with vicious derision of Bush as a hopeless wimp, according to someone who was at several of these affairs.

With Coats out, Cheney, Rumsfeld's former deputy, moved him in as secretary of defense, establishing a broad basis for Cheney's empire. Rumsfeld did not want to accept Armitage as his deputy because he was Powell's best friend, and Powell snapped up Armitage for himself. The lines were being drawn for the internal Cold War that would play out over the first term between Powell and Cheney. But where did that leave Wolfowitz?

Wolfowitz thought that he ought to be director of the CIA. But as soon as he advanced himself, his estranged wife, Clare, wrote a private letter to

President-elect Bush saying that he could not be trusted. This embittered letter remained a closely guarded secret, although a former high official of the CIA told me about it. Chris Nelson also reported it on April 16 in his widely respected, nonpartisan foreign policy newsletter:

> A certain Ms. Riza was even then Wolfowitz's true love. The problem for the CIA wasn't just that she was a foreign national, although that was and is today an issue for anyone interested in CIA employment. The problem was that Wolfowitz was married to someone else, and that someone was really angry about it, and she found a way to bring her complaint directly to the President. So when we, with our characteristic innocence, put Wolfowitz on our short-list for CIA, we were instantly told, by a very, very, very senior Republican foreign policy operative, "I don't think so." It was then gently explained why, purely on background, of course. Why Wolfowitz's personal issues weren't also a disqualification for DOD we've never heard.

The *Daily Mail* of London also reported on his wife's letter at the time that Wolfowitz was appointed president of the World Bank in 2005. Asked about it by the newspaper, Clare Wolfowitz did not deny it, saying, "That's very interesting but not something I can tell you about."

President-elect Bush summoned George Tenet, the holdover CIA director. "I guess this is the end," Tenet told a colleague as he headed out the door, that colleague told me. When he returned, a surprised Tenet said, "He wants me to stay until he can find someone better."

Cheney and Cheney's chief of staff, I. Lewis "Scooter" Libby, who had been Wolfowitz's Wolfowitz before he became Cheney's Cheney—his student when Wolfowitz taught at Yale and his assistant when Wolfowitz served under Cheney at the Pentagon—intervened. Cheney guided Wolfowitz to a safe harbor as deputy to Rumsfeld. But Rumsfeld was unenthusiastic and hesitated. Wolfowitz told him to decide on the spot or he would go to the United Nations, so Rumsfeld took him.

Once in place, Wolfowitz became an indispensable node of the neoconservative cell. He brought in his coterie of neocons to staff an intelligence operation, the Office of Special Plans, outflanking the CIA by circulating its own reports around regular channels to the office of the vice president (run by Libby). Now Wolfowitz was at the center of an embedded Team B.

Despite their shared views, Rumsfeld came to distrust Wolfowitz. "Rumsfeld considered himself fully qualified to supervise the grander themes, and had no intention of ceding the role to Wolfowitz," writes Andrew Cockburn in his biography, *Rumsfeld: His Rise, Fall, and Catastrophic Legacy.* "The net result was that neither man paid the requisite attention to routine tasks of management and decision making, although Wolfowitz did make an effort to perform both." Always a disorganized manager, Wolfowitz handled things badly. Meanwhile, he had to call Armitage to find out what was going at Principals Committee meetings because Rumsfeld wouldn't tell him.

Wolfowitz set to work at once to implement his master plan. He brought up overthrowing Saddam in the first National Security Council meeting with the president, eight months before 9/11. In the immediate aftermath of the terrorist attacks, Wolfowitz hammered on the idea of striking at Iraq.

Less than a month before the invasion, for which his intelligence operation had provided the justifications (later all disproved as sheer disinformation), Wolfowitz was approaching an ecstatic state of being. He could see the shape of things to come through the fog of war. On February 19, 2003, in an interview with National Public Radio, he held forth on the new dawn: "But we're not talking about the occupation of Iraq. We're talking about the liberation of Iraq . . . Therefore, when that regime is removed we will find one of the most talented populations in the Arab world, perhaps complaining that it took us so long to get there. Perhaps a little unfriendly to the French for making it take so long. But basically welcoming us as liberators . . . There's not going to be the hostility . . . There simply won't be."

Five months later, on July 23, 2003, after his trip to Iraq, Wolfowitz was still in an elevated state. "There is no humanitarian crisis," he said. "There is no refugee crisis. There is no health crisis. There has been minimal damage to infrastructure—minimal war damage . . . So, fortunately, much of what . . . we planned for and budgeted for has not proved necessary."

Wolfowitz's girlfriend, Shaha Riza, a Libyan-Tunisian-Saudi British citizen, London School of Economics educated, Arab feminist, neoconservative, and intimate of the circle of favored Iraqi exile Chalabi, was his perfect partner. He had her detailed at one point to a defense contractor, SAIC, and she reported back to the World Bank, where she said that conditions were just fine in Iraq for bank loans.

But when Wolfowitz leaped to the bank presidency she could not remain there under the World Bank rules. As he drew up elaborate blueprints for the bank, he handled her transfer and compensation ineptly. Thus his usual managerial failings extended to his girlfriend problem, which proved fatal.

Bush, Cheney, and the rest of the administration were left standing on the monument of Wolfowitz's legacy in Iraq. Atop Wolfowitz's tomb they reviewed the troops and issued brave statements about the future.

On the day Wolfowitz agreed to resign, the sedate employees of the bank surged into the corridors, celebrating the day of liberation by hoisting champagne glasses and bursting into song: "Nah, nah, nah, nah, hey, hey, hey, goodbye!"

May 24, 2007

The Libby Lobby

Those who served most closely with him described their feelings with persuasive intensity. One after another they used the same words: "Raymond Shaw is the kindest, bravest, warmest, most wonderful human being I've ever known in my life." Gradually, however, Major Ben Marco breaks through his brainwashing to discover that Raymond Shaw is a sleeper agent programmed to install the Manchurian candidate as president.

One after another, in nearly the same language, in letters that General Peter Pace, chairman of the Joint Chiefs of Staff acknowledged had been prompted by I. Lewis "Scooter" Libby, in his attempt to mitigate a harsh sentence for his conviction for perjury and obstruction of justice, dozens of people described the former chief of staff to the vice president with the warmest feelings.

"I know Mr. Libby to be a patriot, a dedicated public servant, a strong family man, and a tireless, honorable, selfless human being," wrote Donald Rumsfeld, the former secretary of defense.

"Mr. Libby was one of the most dedicated public servants I have known in my career," wrote Eric Edelman, the undersecretary of defense for policy.

"I can say, without hesitation, that Scooter was among the finest and most selfless public officials with whom I have ever worked," wrote John Hannah, Vice President Cheney's national security advisor.

"Scooter Libby is one of the most genuine, kind, hardworking and patriotic people I know," wrote Elizabeth Denny, Cheney's social secretary.

One after another, the letter writers declare that Libby's "character" is "inconsistent" with the jury's verdict. These same words—"character" and "inconsistent"—appear dozens of times.

"The Scooter Libby I have known for a number of years now is someone about whom such crimes as perjury and obstruction of justice seem as improbable to me as life on Mars," wrote Midge Decter, the neoconservative writer. Her husband, Norman Podhoretz, the neoconservative editor emeritus of *Commentary* magazine, wrote: "Like everyone else who knows him, I find it inconceivable that a man of his sterling character, who is also famous for his lawyerly scrupulousness, could deliberately have told lies to a grand jury, or for that matter to anyone else." (Decter and Podhoretz's son-in-law, Elliott Abrams, convicted of lying to Congress in the Iran-Contra scandal and subsequently pardoned, is a deputy national security advisor.)

Unmoved by these letters, Judge Reggie Walton imposed a sentence of two and a half years and a $250,000 fine, and told Libby, "Your lies blocked an extremely serious investigation, and as a result you will indeed go to prison." Almost immediately, Cheney praised Libby's "personal integrity," and added his wish that the sentence will be overturned on appeal: "Speaking as friends, we hope that our system will return a final result consistent with what we know of this fine man." Thus, Cheney encouraged his former chief of staff to maintain his steadfast refusal to implicate his former boss in the crimes Libby felt compelled to cover up with his lies to the grand jury.

To be sure, others convicted of crimes often submit similar testimonials before sentencing. But most of those who throw themselves on the mercy of the court express sorrow at what they have done. Libby, however, refused to show remorse. He offered no contrition, only an exercise in victimhood. Like the child who has killed his parents and demands mercy for being an orphan, Libby tried to murder the truth and then got dozens of people to plead for leniency based on his good character.

The act of procuring these letters is further evidence of Libby's stove-piping of disinformation. Libby could not reasonably have expected to sway the judge, but there is a higher authority to which he is appealing. These letters constitute the beginnings of the Libby Lobby's pardon campaign.

Ironically, the longest, most detailed, and among the most personal letters supporting Libby is also the most damaging. In "Re: Character Reference for I. Lewis Libby," Paul Wolfowitz writes, "I am currently serving, until June 30 of this year, as President of the World Bank." Either obtusely or obliquely, Wolfowitz's opening line emphasizes the symbiotic nature of their careers, both men having fallen from grace within weeks of each other after years of collaboration. "It is painful for me to reflect on the fact that his life would have been very different if we had never met. He would almost certainly now be a successful attorney in Philadelphia." Wolfowitz describes their thirty-five-year association, going back to when he was an assistant professor at Yale and Libby was his assistant, and how he recruited Libby to serve as his assistant in the State Department and then in the Defense Department. According to Wolfowitz's account, Libby was an indispensable man in ending the Cold War, winning the Gulf War, and waging the "global war on terror." But he was also, Wolfowitz writes, of "service to individuals."

The leading example he offers is a stunning revelation, which does not reflect on Libby's charity, compassion, and sympathy as Wolfowitz might imagine. The story about Libby "involves his effort to persuade a newspaper not to publish information that would have endangered the life of a covert CIA agent working overseas. Late into the evening, long after most others had left the matter to be dealt with the next day, Mr. Libby worked to collect the information that was needed to persuade the editor not to run the story."

Unintentionally and foolishly, Wolfowitz has hanged the guilty man again. Wolfowitz's defense of Libby is composed with the same care and skill that Wolfowitz brought to the invasion and occupation of Iraq, creating the opposite effects of what he desired. In this bizarre disclosure, rather than exculpating Libby, Wolfowitz incriminates him; for this story is damning evidence of Libby's state of mind—that he knew he was engaged in wrongdoing in leaking the identity of a CIA covert operative, Valerie Plame

Wilson, to two reporters, Judith Miller of *The New York Times* and Matt Cooper of *Time* magazine, and in vouchsafing it to White House press secretary Ari Fleischer for the purpose of his leaking it to the press, which he promptly did.

In their filings and sentence pleading, Libby's lawyers argued repeatedly that he did not know that Plame was covert, that he did not "knowingly disclose classified material," and, as his lead attorney, Ted Wells, told the jury in his closing statement, that Libby acted in "good faith," always believing that he was operating within the law. On October 30, 2006, his lawyers filed a claim denying that "any damage to the national security, the CIA, or Ms. Wilson herself was, or could have been, caused by the disclosure of that status."

Once again, Wolfowitz has blundered. Just as he has undone himself at the World Bank, this time he has inadvertently exposed Libby's "good faith" for bad faith. Indeed, the Wolfowitz letter shows that Libby knew the consequences of revealing the "status" of a CIA operative. As evidence introduced in the CIA leak case proved, Cheney had confided the secret to him and ordered him to spread it. But Libby has never mentioned the previous incident of apparently trying to protect a covert CIA operative. If Wolfowitz remembers the story, and it's credible, so Libby must recall it too. Therefore, he must also have known that his defense was based on false premises contrary to what he understood to be right and how he had acted in the past. He sent his attorneys to court to make a case he consciously knew was wrong from his own prior experience of having protected a national security asset from exposure. One can only wonder if Libby ever told his lawyers the story that Wolfowitz has recounted or whether he misled them, too.

The sentencing letters in support of Libby are a treasure trove of ironies and hypocrisies, pointing to the past actions of the epistolary authors or Libby. Seeking to arouse sympathy for his former disciple, Wolfowitz writes, "Harriet and Scooter Libby are both deeply loving parents and the suffering of their children has been a torture for them both." The word "torture" is an especially artless choice. Libby, in fact, was instrumental in Bush's torture policy, even browbeating and isolating administration officials who raised questions about it, as one of them who was subject to Libby's scorn told me.

Yet Douglas Feith, a former undersecretary of defense, wrote in a letter, "Scooter showed an admirable concern for preserving civil liberties." In the Pentagon, Feith oversaw the Office of Special Plans, constructed as a parallel intelligence operation apart from the regular channels to give a stamp of approval to what turned out uniformly to be disinformation about Saddam Hussein's weapons of mass destruction and supposed links to terrorism. These falsehoods, collected almost exclusively from the neo-conservatives' favorite Iraqi exile, Ahmed Chalabi, were siphoned from the OSP to the OVP (Office of the Vice President), where Libby was in charge of packaging them. Libby and Cheney appeared at CIA headquarters numerous times, occasions on which Libby forced analysts to respond to his relentless interrogatories in order to get them to give their stamp of authority that the information was true. Within the CIA, the analysts even began to prepare for these visits with "murder boards," according to former CIA director George Tenet's memoir, *At the Center of the Storm.* He quotes a senior analyst: "Were they trying to push us and drive us? Absolutely." Secretary of State Colin Powell rejected one of Libby's lengthy briefs out of hand as a basis for his February 5, 2003, speech before the United Nations Security Council on Saddam's WMD and Al-Qaeda connections, but nonetheless still delivered a speech replete with disinformation. (Powell and Tenet were not among those who wrote letters on Libby's behalf.)

Another letter writer, John Bolton, defended Libby's perjury merely as a lapse of "perfect recall." He also offered opinions on the handling of intelligence. "With classified information, it was frequently hard to know who was cleared to see what or what could be discussed with whom. If there is anyone who fully understands our 'system' for protecting classified information, I have yet to meet him." Bolton, the former U.N. ambassador and undersecretary of state for arms control, was Cheney and Libby's ally within the State Department, blocking and spying on Powell. Bolton gamed the "system" to keep information from Powell, sought to intimidate State Department Intelligence and Research Bureau analysts into accepting his skewed views, and tried to reassign them when they did not bend. Libby, for his part, was also crucial in blackballing Foreign Service officers, experienced in nation building, who were involved in Powell's elaborate "Future of Iraq" project.

Kenneth Adelman, a neoconservative former member of the Pentagon's Defense Policy Board, who had declared that the war in Iraq would be a "cakewalk," wrote a letter for Libby, too. "Your Honor," he wrote, "this is punishment enough. Hence I ask that this decent man not be subjected to time in jail, and allowed to cope with his conviction as best as anyone could in these circumstances. After all, Scooter Libby is a good person."

A neoconservative is a Bush administration official who has mugged reality and claims he's the victim. Neoconservatism has now been reduced to a clemency plea.

June 7, 2007

Fugue State

I returned from Europe a week before President Bush departed for the G8 summit in Germany. In Rome and Paris I met with Cabinet ministers who uniformly said the chief issue in transatlantic relations is somehow making it through the last eighteen months of the Bush administration without further major disaster. None of the nonpartisan think tanks in Washington can organize seminars on this overriding reality, but within the European councils of state the trepidation about the last days of Bush is the number one issue in foreign affairs.

One of the ministers with whom I met, who had supported the invasion of Iraq and had been an admirer of outgoing British Prime Minister Tony Blair, ruefully cited Blair's remark about Iraq at his joint press conference with Bush on May 17 at the White House: "This is a fight we cannot afford to lose." "Cannot? Cannot lose?" mocked the minister. "Should not have lost."

High officials of European governments describe U.S. influence as squandered and swiftly eroding (one minister went down a list of Bush administration officials, rating them according to their stupidity), the country's moral authority nil. Lethal power vacuums are emerging from Lebanon to Pakistan, and Europeans are incapable on their own of quelling the fires that burn far closer to them than to the United States through their growing Muslim populations and proximity to the Middle East. They have no illusions that they will be treated seriously as real allies or that there will be a sudden about-face by the Bush administration. Their faint hope—and it is only a hope—is that they have already seen the worst and that it is not yet to come. Even worse than Bush, from their perspective, would be another Republican president who continued Bush policies and also appointed neoconservatives. That would toll, if not the end of days, then the decline and fall of the Western alliance except in name only, and an even more rapid acceleration of chaos in the world order.

Bush's procession through Europe was a pageant of contempt, disdain, delusion, provocation, and vanity masquerading as a welcome respite from his troubles at home. In Albania he landed at last in a place where he was hailed as a conquering hero. His demolition derby of U.S. influence was presented as a series of bold moves, but it confirmed the fears of the other world leaders at the G8 summit (and elsewhere) that the rest of Bush's presidency will be an erratic series of crashes. His performance ranged from King Nod, issuing proclamations oblivious to and even proud of their negative effect, to King Zog (the last king of Albania). No president has had a more disastrous European trip since President Reagan placed a wreath on the graves of SS soldiers in the Bitburg cemetery. Yet Reagan's mistake was unintentional and symbolic, a temporary and superficial setback, doing no real damage to U.S. foreign relations, while Bush's blunders not only reinforced counterproductive policies but also created a new one with Russia that has the potential of profoundly undermining U.S. national security interests for years to come.

Bush's foreign policy has descended into a fugue state. Dissociated and unaware, the president and his administration are still capable of expressing themselves as if it all makes complete sense, only contributing to their bewilderment. A fugue state should not be confused with cognitive dissonance, the tension produced when irreconcilable ideas are held at the same time and their incompatibility is overcome by denial. In a fugue state, a trauma creates a kind of amnesia in which the sufferer is incapable of connecting to his past. The impairment of judgment comes in great part from a denial of distress. Bush's fugue state involves the reiteration of a failed formula as though nothing has happened. So he proudly reasserts the essence of his Bush doctrine: Our acts are independent of other countries' interests. And he adds new corollaries: Other nations must forgive our unacknowledged mistakes even if we threaten their national security. To this, Bush overlays cognitive dissonance: Our policy is working; it just needs more time. Thus the incoherent becomes coherent.

Bush's amusing gaffes should not divert attention from the gravity of his underlying decline. Though his verbal hilarity has been present since the beginning, his miscues, misstatements, and mistakes now highlight a foreign policy in utter disarray.

Upon meeting Pope Benedict XVI at the Vatican last weekend, Bush presented him with a gift of a wooden cane carved with English words. When the pope asked the president what they were, Bush told His Holiness, "The Ten Commandments, sir." To *sir*? With love?

In Rome, on June 9, a reporter asked Bush about setting a deadline for Kosovo independence. "What? Say that again?" *"Deadline for the Kosovo independence?"* "A decline?" *"Deadline, deadline."* "Deadline. Beg your pardon. My English isn't very good." Bush then declared, "In terms of the deadline, there needs to be one. This needs to come—this needs to happen." The next day, asked when he would set a deadline, he replied, "I don't think I called for a deadline." Reminded of his previous statement, Bush said: "I did? What exactly did I say? I said, 'Deadline'? OK, yes, then I meant what I said."

Before offering that tongue twister, Bush quite deliberately upset German Chancellor Angela Merkel's proposal for climate change at the G8. She put before the summit a program for carbon limits and an emissions trading system supported by, among others, Tony Blair, as his final gesture to burnish his reputation before he leaves office on June 27. Bush countered with a proposal for voluntary limits that would have to be approved by China, India, and other major industrial countries that would not agree. In short, Bush's program was no program at all, except as a gambit to push aside Merkel's. With that, Bush demolished the possibility of any positive plan emerging from the summit. He also deprived Blair of a last achievement. Were it not for his relationship with Bush and support for his Iraq policy, Blair would not be leaving Downing Street. He has sacrificed his career to Bush's fiasco. His advice on the reconstruction of Iraq ignored, his advocacy grew more passionate. From whom much has been asked, nothing has been given.

While Bush was undermining traditional allies, Russian President Vladimir Putin was making child's play of him. Bush's proposal to put tracking stations for a missile defense system in Poland and the Czech Republic gave Putin his opening. In response, he offered a radar site in Azerbaijan to be jointly operated by the United States and Russia. Bush had deployed the wrong tactic on behalf of the wrong strategy. Bush's missile shield has not been proved to work, has cost hundreds of billions of dollars, and has an uncertain purpose. Is the plan meant to reassure eastern European nations of the former Warsaw Pact, Donald Rumsfeld's "new Europe," against Russia, or is it a short-term ploy to rally support in the one region in the world that still likes Bush because of deep residual pro-Americanism? If Bush intended to persuade Putin to temper his authoritarianism, he only succeeded in antagonizing the Russian leader. As Bush's "freedom" agenda has collapsed, he has reverted to a Plan B for a new ersatz Cold War. His ham-handed move allowed the adroit Putin to change the subject and corner him. Meanwhile, the engagement of Russia in areas of mutual interest—containing Iran—languishes.

In Iraq, Bush's policy is now to arm all sides in the sectarian civil war between Shiites and Sunnis. He claims to be devoted to nation building, which he previously dismissed, while he presides over a mass exodus of 2 million Iraqis, upholds law and order while holding tens of thousands of prisoners without due process, and conducts a "surge" of troops to secure the capital city of Baghdad whose main effect has been to facilitate its ethnic cleansing. The Iraqi government, for its part, has not met any of the benchmarks in reforming its laws demanded by the United States as the sine qua non of continuing support.

And where in the world is Condoleezza Rice? While Bush was in Europe, the secretary of state was at home. Instead of attending the summit, she delivered a speech at the Economic Club of New York, announcing that the new doctrine of the administration henceforth should be called "American realism." Until that moment, we were supposed to refer to it as "transformational diplomacy." Rice, the former realist turned neoconservative fellow traveler, seemed to have come full circle. But what was it exactly that she was doing with her rhetorical adjustment?

Rice's frenetic but feckless diplomacy in the Middle East has been fruitless. She is unwilling or unable to break beyond the bounds that Bush establishes, forbidding relations with Syria, for example, and thus guaranteeing her failure.

As she shuttles endlessly and meaninglessly, neoconservatives within the White House undermine her foredoomed initiatives. Elliott Abrams, the deputy national security advisor for policy, in briefing a meeting of Jewish Republicans, said that Rice's "talks are sometimes not more than 'process for the sake of process,'" the Israeli newspaper Haaretz reported on May 14.

According to Haaretz, "Those attending the meeting of Jewish Republicans understood Abrams's comments as an assurance that the peace initiative promoted by Secretary of State Condoleezza Rice doesn't have the full backing of President George W. Bush." As she engages in an academic exercise to rebrand empty rhetoric with new empty rhetoric, the neocons continue to create a parallel foreign policy.

Rice contradicts herself but forgets that she has. Bush continues to prattle about "freedom" but cannot remember his benchmarks. Only Dick Cheney remains consistent. The new mission statement is the old mission statement. The new scenarios are the old delusions. Time marches on.

June 14, 2007

Null and Void

In private, Bush administration sub-Cabinet officials who have been instrumental in formulating and sustaining the legal "war paradigm" acknowledge that their efforts to create a system for detainees separate from due process, criminal justice, and law enforcement have failed. One of the key framers of the war paradigm (in which the president in his wartime capacity as commander in chief makes and enforces laws as he sees fit, overriding the constitutional system of checks and balances), who a year ago was arguing vehemently for pushing its boundaries, confesses that he has abandoned his belief in the whole doctrine, though he refuses to say so publicly. If he were to speak up, given his seminal role in formulating the policy and his stature among the Federalist Society cadres that run it, his rejection would have a shattering impact, far more than political philosopher Francis Fukuyama's denunciation of the neoconservatism he formerly embraced. But this figure remains careful to disclose his disillusionment with his own handiwork only in off-the-record conversations. Yet another Bush legal official, even now at the commanding heights of power, admits that the administration's policies are largely discredited. In its defense, he says without a hint of irony or sarcasm, "Not everything we've done has been illegal." He adds, "Not everything has been ultra vires"—a legal term referring to actions beyond the law.

The resistance within the administration to Bush's torture policy, the ultimate expression of the war paradigm, has come to an end through attrition and exhaustion. More than two years ago, Vice President Dick Cheney's then chief of staff I. Lewis "Scooter" Libby and then general counsel David Addington physically cornered one of the few internal opponents, subjecting him to threats, intimidation, and isolation. About that time, the tiny band of opponents within approached Karen Hughes, newly named undersecretary of state for public diplomacy, hoping that the long-time confidante of President Bush, now assigned responsibility for the U.S. image in the world, might be willing to hear them out on the damage done by continuation of the torture policy. But she rebuffed them.

Two weeks ago, Hughes unveiled her major report, extolling "our commitment to freedom, human rights and the dignity and equality of every human being," but making no mention of detainee policy. The action part consists of another of her campaign-oriented rapid-response schemes, this one a Counterterrorism Communications Center, staffed by military and intelligence officers, to rebut the false claims of terrorists. Asked whether the administration's policies might be a factor contributing to the problem, Sean McCormack, the State Department spokesman, replied, "You're always going to get people criticizing policy."

General David Petraeus's declaration on May 10 against torture reflected less the ringing authority of an order than the impotence of a personal credo. "Beyond the basic fact that such actions are illegal, history shows that they also are frequently neither useful nor necessary," he said. But his moral sentiment had been dismissed long before he had uttered it. The commander's strongly worded statement, putting him by implication in the category of "people criticizing policy," had no effect on the elaborate system of "enhanced interrogation techniques," black site prisons, maintenance of Guantánamo, or the twenty thousand Iraqi prisoners incarcerated on U.S. military bases without due process. Petraeus has no more influence over the president who says he listens to his military commanders than the commanders who have opposed the policy since its inception.

In the year since the Supreme Court ruled (on June 29, 2006) in *Hamdan v. Rumsfeld* that the Bush administration's military commissions for detainees violated the Uniform Code of Military Justice and the Geneva

Conventions—and Bush promptly got the Republican-led Congress to legislate approval of the illegal commissions as well as suspend habeas corpus—further court decisions have thrown his "war paradigm" into a legal twilight zone.

In February, a Cheney protégé, Susan J. Crawford, was appointed as the convening authority for military commissions. An armed forces appeals court judge, she had been Cheney's special counsel when he was secretary of defense under the elder Bush and had become a family friend. She has long been close to Libby and Addington. She facilitated the unusual transfer of David Hicks, a former kangaroo skinner from Australia, captured in Afghanistan as a fighter with the Taliban and held at Guantánamo. Charged with a host of crimes, including murder, Hicks filed an affidavit alleging torture. When the Hamdan decision was handed down, the charges against him were dropped, but after passage of the Military Commissions Act he was newly charged with providing material aid to terrorism. His five-year detention in Guantánamo provoked a public outcry in Australia. Cheney flew there to confer with Prime Minister John Howard, who wanted to defuse the issue. Soon afterward, a deal was worked out: Hicks pleaded guilty to the lesser charge of providing material aid, he was released to Australian authorities, and he is serving a reduced nine-month sentence.

Crawford's appointment, however, did not prevent military commission judges at Guantánamo from ruling on June 4 that the commissions had no jurisdiction over enemy combatants who were not designated as "unlawful." In effect, this decision threw the commissions into a void. According to the judges' decision two prisoners, Omar Kadhr, captured as a fifteen-year-old child soldier and accused of killing a U.S. Special Forces medic on the battlefield, and Salim Hamdan, one of Osama bin Laden's former drivers, did not fall under the category that would enable them to be tried by the commissions.

On June 11, the U.S. Court of Appeals for the 4th Circuit, the most conservative in the country, issued a decision striking at the heart of Bush's conception of the presidency. In *al-Marri v. Wright*, the court ruled that Ali Saleh Kahlah al-Marri, a resident of Qatar, arrested as a student at Bradley University in the United States, accused of aiding Al-Qaeda, could not be held in indefinite detention as an "enemy combatant" and must be remanded to the civilian criminal court system. (Al-Marri, in an affidavit, claimed to have been tortured.) The decision acknowledged that al-Marri might have committed serious crimes. But the government's assertion that the president has "inherent constitutional authority," rooted in his "war-making powers," is a "breathtaking claim" contrary to U.S. constitutional law and history.

"The President," the court said, "claims power that far exceeds that granted him by the Constitution." This extraordinary decision, citing the Framers, declared Bush's actions—and his imperial presidency—null and void. It is worth quoting at some length:

> Put simply, the Constitution does not allow the President to order the military to seize civilians residing within the United States and detain them indefinitely without criminal process, and this is so even if he calls them "enemy combatants" . . . Of course, this does not mean that the President lacks power to protect our national interests and defend our people, only that in doing so he must abide by the Constitution. We understand and do not in any way minimize the grave threat international terrorism poses to our country and our national security . . . The Court has specifically cautioned against "break[ing] faith with this Nation's tradition"—"firmly embodied in the Constitution"—"of keeping military power subservient to civilian authority." Reid, 354 U.S. at 40. When the Court wrote these words in 1957, it explained that "[t]he country ha[d] remained true to that faith for almost one hundred seventy years." Id. Another half century has passed but the necessity of "remain[ing] true to that faith" remains as important today as it was at our founding.

Then, the court delivered the coup de grâce to Bush's "war paradigm." Having cited the Framers, it now cited the example of Abraham Lincoln.

> In an address to Congress at the outset of the Civil War, President Lincoln defended his emergency suspension of the writ of habeas corpus to protect Union troops moving to defend the Capital. Lincoln famously asked: "[A]re all the laws, but one, to go unexecuted, and the government

itself to go to pieces, lest that one be violated?" Abraham Lincoln, Message to Congress in Special Session (July 4, 1861), in Abraham Lincoln: Speeches and Writings 1859-1865 at 246, 254 (Don E. Fehrenbacher ed., 1989). The authority the President seeks here turns Lincoln's formulation on its head. For the President does not acknowledge that the extraordinary power he seeks would result in the suspension of even one law and he does not contend that this power should be limited to dire emergencies that threaten the nation. Rather, he maintains that the authority to order the military to seize and detain certain civilians is an inherent power of the Presidency, which he and his successors may exercise as they please. To sanction such presidential authority to order the military to seize and indefinitely detain civilians, even if the President calls them "enemy combatants," would have disastrous consequences for the Constitution—and the country. For a court to uphold a claim to such extraordinary power would do more than render lifeless the Suspension Clause, the Due Process Clause, and the rights to criminal process in the Fourth, Fifth, Sixth, and Eighth Amendments; it would effectively undermine all of the freedoms guaranteed by the Constitution. It is that power—were a court to recognize it—that could lead all our laws "to go unexecuted, and the government itself to go to pieces." We refuse to recognize a claim to power that would so alter the constitutional foundations of our Republic.

Few, if any, presidents have ever been the subject of such a devastating legal decision. While presidential actions have been ruled illegal or unconstitutional in the past, they were individual acts. But in the case of Bush, the al-Marri decision not only discredits Bush's position but denies his idea of his presidential legitimacy in the American tradition. The decision also declares that Bush's idea is a mortal threat to the Constitution. And this ruling was issued by the most conservative court in the land.

And yet, nothing changes. After such a stinging rebuke as the decision handed down by the 4th Circuit a reasonable president might well contemplate changing his approach. Instead, Bush digs in, doubles down, surges. As with his other discredited policies, Bush attempts to salvage them through willpower and extra effort, throwing more resources down black holes. Ultimately, his position is losing its cloak of legality. Piece by piece, case by case, the courts are exposing it as ultra vires.

The impulse for supporting the policy, on one level, remains visceral and virulent. Stephen Holmes, professor at the NYU School of Law, describes the concept of "mirror imaging" in his new book, *The Matador's Cape: America's Reckless Response to Terror*: "If our enemies have renounced the laws of civilization, so will we. If they organized a sneak attack, then we will respond with a dirty war. If they terrorized us, we will terrorize them."

For some, this vengeance—"We need to humiliate them," according to Henry Kissinger—requires something more; it involves upholding faith that transcends law. On June 16, Associate Justice Antonin Scalia of the Supreme Court, at an international conference on torture and terrorism in Ottawa, Ontario, sought to resolve the question on a moral basis. His disquisition consisted of a defense of Jack Bauer, the fictional hero of the torture-porn Fox TV series *24*. "Are you going to convict Jack Bauer? Say that criminal law is against him? 'You have the right to a jury trial?' Is any jury going to convict Jack Bauer? I don't think so. So the question is really whether we believe in these absolutes. And ought we believe in these absolutes." Thus, for this conservative jurist, torture, dramatized through popular entertainment, remained the same obsession with "absolutes" as it had been during the Inquisition, which after all developed the enhanced coercive techniques used today.

By contrast, Bush's stance is merely political, a raw assertion of unaccountable and unlimited power. Yet the political idea he seeks to defend—a presidency operating by fiat above the rule of law—finds itself increasingly in conflict with the American system of justice, and not only on the question of detainees and torture.

June 21, 2007

The Imperial Vice Presidency

When Huey P. Long left the governorship of Louisiana in 1932 to become a U.S. senator, he filled the position with a childhood friend named Oscar Kelly Allen, known as O.K., who gave the OK to whatever the Kingfish wished. The story is still told, perhaps apocryphal, that one day a leaf wafted through an open window and landed on O.K.'s desk and, without hesitation, he signed it.

Two months after 9/11, on the day of the fall of Kabul, Afghanistan, November 13, 2001, Vice President Dick Cheney appeared in the Oval Office with a four-page executive order designating terrorism suspects as enemy combatants to be held indefinitely, with no right to have their detention reviewed by any court except newly created military commissions, where they would not be permitted to learn the accusations or evidence against them, or be represented by counsel, or even know that their case had been heard and decided.

The secretary of state and the national security advisor were deliberately kept uninformed as the White House staff secretary prepared the order for signature. According to a four-part series published this week in the *Washington Post* on the extraordinary power of the vice president, "When it [the order] returned to the Oval Office, in a blue portfolio embossed with the presidential seal, Bush pulled a felt-tip pen from his pocket and signed without sitting down. Almost no one else had seen the text." Colin Powell was stunned when he learned of the fait accompli. "What the hell just happened?" he asked. Condoleezza Rice was described as "incensed." But neither of them, then or later, effectively challenged Cheney's usurpation of executive authority. And, as can be gathered inferentially, Bush never bothered to ask Cheney about their opinions on the executive order or to call them; nor did he seem to care.

The *Washington Post* series, written by Barton Gellman and Jo Becker, is an acknowledgment, after more than six years, of the hardly secret scope of

Cheney's unprecedented influence. The articles provide fresh detail of his elaborate network within the federal government and how he pulls its strings. On principle, Cheney and his aides are hostile to regular lines of authority set up to enforce professional standards and a responsible chain of command. Having served as President Ford's chief of staff, he understood intimately how control of the paper flow meant control of the decision making. In 1999, the *Post* reported, Cheney explained to a conference of presidential historians: "The process of moving paper in and out of the Oval Office, who gets involved in the meetings, who does the president listen to, who gets a chance to talk to him before he makes a decision, is absolutely critical."

Cheney has crushed the normal interagency process that permitted communication, cross-fertilization, and cooperation at the sub-Cabinet level through all previous modern administrations. At the same time, he has isolated Cabinet secretaries, causing them to be fired when they contradicted him, as he did with Christine Todd Whitman, former head of the Environmental Protection Agency, and former Secretary of the Treasury Paul O'Neill.

Cheney thrives in darkness, operating by stealth within the government, and makes a cult of secrecy. None of these insights are new, except for additional telling details. Reports the *Post*: "Man-size Mosler safes, used elsewhere in government for classified secrets, store the workaday business of the office of the vice president. Even talking points for reporters are sometimes stamped 'Treated As: Top Secret/SCI.'"

The *Post*'s series appeared just as Cheney refused to provide his office's documents to the National Archives and Records Administration as provided by law. He then attempted to abolish the specific agency within the Archives to punish it for its impudence. Cheney's chief of staff and former counsel, David Addington, floated the novel doctrine that the vice president is not "an entity within the executive branch." He claimed that the Archives had no authority and that therefore it "is not necessary in these circumstances to address the subject of any alternative reasoning." Only when Rep. Rahm Emanuel, D-Ill., proposed cutting off the vice president's $4.8 million in executive-branch funding did Cheney concede.

Despite the absurdity of Addington's argument, Cheney has a point, though not a constitutional one. He has transformed an office that Franklin D. Roosevelt's first vice president, John Nance Garner, said was "not worth a bucket of warm piss" into one of vast power. Cheney has acted as the Stalin of the Bush administration, the master of the bureaucracy, eliminating one rival after another, ruthlessly and unscrupulously concentrating power, the culmination of a more-than-thirty-year career. The *Post* articles are based on information provided by dissidents who have suffered at Cheney's hand and have given *Post* reporters stories proving that Cheney's whole point is power.

Rather than transcending the executive, Cheney has deranged it in his effort to remake it into a branch of government of unlimited, unaccountable power. The head of the search committee who chose himself to be the experienced vice president to a callow president saw in George W. Bush his opportunity to radically alter the place of the executive within the federal government, which he had been straining to do since he served as Donald Rumsfeld's assistant in the Nixon White House. Cheney has viewed recent American history as a struggle between the imperial presidency necessary in a brutish world and the naive, undependable, and in some cases disloyal constraints of Congress, the press, and the judiciary. Under Bush, Cheney has shaped the presidential prerogative, acting as "an entity within the executive branch." Secrecy is essential to the protection of presidential prerogative. Follow the paper trail to the Mosler safe.

Even as the spotlight shines on the opaque Cheney, the light reflects on others as well. By shielding Bush from alternatives, Cheney has locked in certain decisions that Bush stubbornly defends as his own. The president's plight is not that of a removed ruler tragically kept from knowing what his government is doing in his name. He has had time to observe the consequences. He is aware of what Cheney says to him. The Decider decides that Cheney will decide what the Decider decides. This is not a case of if-only-the-czar-knew. In the seventh year of his presidency, Bush's decision making consists of justifying his previous decisions.

Of the Bush Cabinet secretaries, former Attorney General John Ashcroft most strenuously confronted Cheney about his seizures of power. Ashcroft was perhaps the most conservative member of the Cabinet, and it was out of a sense of his own constitutional obligation that he objected. When Ashcroft discovered that John Yoo, the deputy assistant in the Justice Department's Office of Legal Counsel, had been recruited by the Cheney operation to write memos on detainee policy that would deny any role in the new legal process to the Justice Department, he was outraged. At the White House he confronted Cheney and Addington. "According to participants [at the meeting]," the *Post* reported, "Ashcroft said that he was the president's senior law enforcement officer, supervised the FBI and oversaw terrorism prosecutions nationwide. The Justice Department, he said, had to have a voice in the tribunal process." But Cheney did not relent. Ashcroft received no meeting to discuss the matter with Bush. Cheney was the gatekeeper—the decider for the Decider.

The narrative of Powell's internal struggle with Cheney remains largely unknown. From conversations I have had with former senior CIA officials, it is clear that Powell himself does not fully understand all the ways he was misled, manipulated and abused in order to get him to make the case for the invasion of Iraq. To this day, Powell still does not really know what the CIA and the White House knew about weapons of mass destruction and when they knew it, largely because Cheney was so successful in his rigging of the intelligence process.

Powell's performance on NBC's *Meet the Press* on June 10 demonstrated his continuing confusion. He wondered why the CIA didn't tell him before his speech to the United Nations on February 5, 2003, that the intelligence on mobile weapons laboratories wasn't solid, even now unaware that CIA director George Tenet had been informed by CIA officers but dismissed their information because it ran counter to the case the administration wished to make for going to war.

Powell was caught between his diminished self-image as a loyal aide and good soldier indebted to a coterie of Republicans who had promoted him eventually to secretary of state, and his grandiose self-image as the most respected and popular public man in the country, and his influence imploded. He was strangely incapable of gaining political traction to hold his ground. Now the record cannot be changed. He can only learn how easily Cheney toyed with him.

Curiously absent in the lengthy *Post* articles, except in one brief passing scene, is Cheney's ubiquitous shadow in his shadow presidency—his former chief of staff, I. Lewis "Scooter" Libby. Obsessed with secrecy, Cheney ordered Libby to ensure that one national security secret became public—the identity of Valerie Plame Wilson as a covert CIA officer. Now convicted on four counts of perjury and obstruction of justice, Libby awaits word from the federal appeals court on whether he will be able to stay his 30-month prison sentence. Steadfastly refusing to cooperate with the prosecutor, he continues his obstruction, protecting his principal. "There is a cloud over the vice president," said Patrick Fitzgerald, the special prosecutor, in his closing remarks to the jury. "And that cloud remains because this defendant obstructed justice."

Despite the recent round of punditry that Cheney's influence has waned, he remains a formidable force. These are Cheney's final days; this is his endgame. He will never run again for public office. He is freed from the constraints of political consequences. He now has no horizon. He lives only in the present. He is nearly done. There are only months left to achieve his goals. Mortality impinges. Next month, he will have his heart pacemaker replaced. He disdains public opinion. He does not care who's next. "We didn't get elected to be popular," he said on *Fox News* on May 10. "We didn't get elected to worry just about the fate of the Republican Party."

To the last minute, Cheney refuses to loosen his grip on power. Meanwhile, his former aides pump up pressure for a presidential pardon— a pardon that would enshrine Libby's obstruction of justice and shield Cheney forever, "an entity in the executive branch" who would be above the law. A breeze is blowing a leaf toward an open window of the Oval Office.

June 28, 2007

"The Administration of Justice"

In the Plame case, as in nearly every matter, Vice President Dick Cheney controlled and directed the flow of information that shaped the decision making of President George W. Bush. When Nicholas Kristof, *The New York Times* columnist, published "Missing in Action: Truth," on May 6, 2003, referring to but not mentioning by name former Ambassador Joseph Wilson as the one who conducted a mission to Niger, where he found no evidence of Saddam Hussein seeking to purchase yellowcake uranium for nuclear weaponry, Cheney furiously launched the effort to discover Wilson's identity and to discredit him. He ordered I. Lewis "Scooter" Libby, his chief of staff, to head the operation. Libby's frenetic activity triggered a secret State Department investigation and memo that identified Wilson's wife, Valerie Plame, as a covert CIA operative.

Cheney aroused President Bush to the danger from Wilson. A handwritten note by Libby that surfaced in his trial revealed that Bush raised his concern about the Kristof column in a subsequent June 9 meeting. The next day, the State Department memo "Niger/Iraq Uranium Story" began circulating within the administration. On June 12, Cheney identified Plame to Libby, and Libby went hard to work. Within three days, he discussed Plame with five officials. On July 6, after Wilson published a *New York Times* op-ed disclosing that the rationale the president gave for the war was premised on false information, an enraged Cheney ordered Libby into high gear. Cheney also secured Bush's concurrence for Libby to leak selected parts of the still-classified National Intelligence Estimate on Saddam's weapons of mass destruction to *New York Times* reporter Judith Miller on July 8. Bush, therefore, was deeply involved. But what did the president know, and when did he know it?

Bush's commutation of Libby's thirty-month prison sentence for four counts of perjury and obstruction of justice was as politically necessary to hold his remaining hardcore base for the rest of his eighteen months in office as it was politically damaging to his legacy and to the possibility of a Republican succession. It was also essential in order to sustain Libby's cover-up protecting Cheney and perhaps Bush himself.

The sole reason that Bush offers for the commutation—that Judge Reggie Walton's sentence was "excessive"—is transparently false. Indeed, the sentence meets the normal guidelines for such a crime. "The sentence in this case was imposed pursuant to the laws governing sentencings which occur every day throughout this country," said Patrick Fitzgerald, the special prosecutor. "In this case, an experienced federal judge considered extensive argument from the parties and then imposed a sentence consistent with the applicable laws." Nothing is irregular or extraordinary about the length of the sentence, except the person receiving it.

It was not the judge who exceeded the sentencing guidelines; it is the president who ignored federal standards for commutations, by which it is customary that the convicted person serves some time before being eligible. Dishonestly appealing to the letter of the law, Bush's spirit of impunity is masked as benevolence and mercy.

Even as Bush attacked the judgment of Walton, his own appointee to the federal bench, he acknowledged Libby's guilt, declaring: "I respect the jury's verdict." Even as Bush engages in juridical nullification, he does not seek jury nullification. By confessing that Libby was engaged in a cover-up—after all, that was the verdict—Bush establishes his own motive. In brief, Bush's act ratifies Libby's cover-up. The "cloud over the vice president" that the prosecutor decried will never be dispelled. Cheney—and Bush—walk, too.

Libby had to have understood, without a word ever being passed, that leniency of some sort would be granted. His steadfast cover-up was encouraged by his intimate knowledge of the methods of Cheney and Bush. The fine he must pay—$250,000—is meaningless because he will certainly not be paying it himself. His legal defense fund, supported by the friends of the president and vice president, boasts a treasury of $5 million. He has been well taken care of.

The pardon is the one monarchical power that the framers of the Constitution assigned the presidency. But they placed one restriction, that it could not be exercised for impeachment. In other words, the president could not use his power to pardon himself. Bush is entirely within his narrow right to use the pardon power in the Libby case. But it violates the spirit, if not the letter, of the law governing that power because it is a consummate gesture of self-exoneration, at least if the vice president is an "entity within the executive branch." Bush rewards Libby's cover-up, thwarting the investigation into Cheney's and perhaps his culpability. Bush's commutation is the successful culmination of the obstruction of justice.

Since 1776, on every July Fourth, the Declaration of Independence has been posted in public places, published in newspapers and read aloud. Its bill of particulars contains these two passages defining royal tyranny and justifying revolution:

> He has obstructed the Administration of Justice by refusing
> his Assent to Laws for establishing Judiciary Powers. . . . For
> taking away our Charters, abolishing our most valuable Laws
> and altering fundamentally the Forms of our Governments.

Happy Fourth.

July 3, 2007

Marketing, Muslims, and Methodists

One of the more memorable and revealing statements explaining the nature of the Bush administration buildup to the invasion of Iraq was offered in September 2002 by then White House chief of staff Andrew Card. "From a marketing point of view," he said, "you don't introduce new products in August." Five years later, a period longer than the Civil War and World War II, the administration is preparing to present its case for continuing the surge in Iraq. But rather than waiting for September, when General David Petraeus is scheduled to deliver his report, the administration has moved up the marketing to July.

The familiar props are rolled out, like the well-worn and peeling painted backdrop for a production of a traveling Victorian theatrical troupe, and members of the audience are expected to watch with rapt fascination, as though they had never seen this show before. The negative response to the preview does not alter the same old script.

The usual atmospherics are pumped up—sudden panic and fear, an elusive and ubiquitous enemy that assumes many guises and shapes, cherry-picked information to provide a patina of verisimilitude to the danger, followed by a march of authority figures to rescue us. Michael Chertoff, the secretary of homeland security, held a press conference on July 11 to announce that he had a "gut feeling" that the terrorist threat was dire. General Peter Pace, the outgoing chairman of the Joint Chiefs of Staff, on his final tour of Iraq Tuesday, proclaimed a "sea change." Meanwhile, Secretary of State Condoleezza Rice frantically telephoned moderate Republican senators, urging them not to defect from support of the president's position.

Even Rosencrantz and Guildenstern supporting players wander through, like Frances Townsend, President Bush's homeland security advisor, who, Tuesday, entered right into the White House press room to declaim about the terrorist threat, only to confirm the administration's failure to destroy Al-Qaeda and expose her own bafflement: "You're assuming it's a zero-sum game, which is what I don't understand."

General Petraeus is promised as the dramatic hero who will stride to triumph in the last act. The author of a recent study of counterinsurgency who has not previously fought such a war, he has been thrust into the spotlight partly because his halo is yet untarnished. Bush's unpopularity disqualifies him from the "Mission Accomplished" moment. So he pushes out his handpicked general and walks behind his chariot, hoping the cheering of the crowd will be also for him. In his July 12 press conference, Bush mentioned Petraeus eleven times, his name flourished as a talisman for "victory." The generals with the greatest experience with the Iraq insurgency, who opposed Bush's surge, such as General John Abizaid, an Arabic speaker, have been discharged or reassigned. The burden on the ambitious general to produce a military solution is unbearable and his breaking inevitable. But for now, Petraeus's tragedy foretold is being cast as the first dawn of a happy ending.

At his July 12 press conference, Bush elevated Al-Qaeda to enemy number one in Iraq and mentioned it thirty-one times, asserting that not supporting his policy would lead to "surrendering the future of Iraq to Al-Qaeda." Asked about the soon to be released National Intelligence Estimate on Al-Qaeda, Bush claimed it would state, "There is a perception in the coverage that Al-Qaeda may be as strong today as they were prior to September the 11th. That's just simply not the case."

One day later, on July 13, Bush held a meeting at the White House for a small group of conservative pundits, giving them a glimpse into his state of mind. David Brooks of *The New York Times* described his "self-confidence." Fred Barnes of *The Weekly Standard* quoted him saying, "I'm optimistic," even though he also said, "I understand the polls. This is an unpopular war!" At his press conference, Bush had said, "There is a war fatigue in America." And he pointed to his head. "It's affecting our psychology." During his meeting with the conservative writers, he mocked his critics. Kate O'Beirne and Rich Lowry of *National Review* quoted him as saying: "How can he possibly do this? Can't he see? Can't he hear?" The son of a president explained that no one could really understand what it meant to be president. "You don't know what it's like to be commander in chief until you're commander in chief," he said, according to participants. His critics could not possibly understand him. But he was obviously peeved. Washington, he complained, was filled with "a lot of talkers." Yet Bush pledged, unbidden, that he would not listen to these critics. "I'm not on the phone chatting up with these people writing these articles, ascribing motives to me." Such are the reflections of the so-called self-confident president.

On Tuesday, the executive summary of the new NIE on Al-Qaeda was made public. But it did not fit the administration's marketing campaign. Al-Qaeda, the report stated, has "protected or regenerated" itself in the northern provinces of Pakistan. It also said that the terrorist group would "probably leverage" its contacts with the group known as Al-Qaeda in Iraq, an "affiliate," and "the only one known to have expressed a desire to attack the Homeland."

The next day, Wednesday, the U.S. military made a timely announcement of the capture of Khalid Abdul Fatah Daud Mahmoud Mashadani, a courier for Al-Qaeda in Iraq. After two weeks in detention, he confessed to hand delivering messages from Al-Qaeda leaders Ayman al-Zawahiri and Osama bin Laden, suggesting that the so-called enhanced interrogation techniques vociferously defended by the administration indeed work.

The latest NIE, however, is a strange product. According to highly reliable sources in the intelligence community, no new intelligence at all is reflected in the NIE. Its conclusions, on one level, are a rehash of obvious facts that anyone who reads a daily newspaper could glean, such as the protected status of Al-Qaeda in frontier regions of Pakistan. Other conclusions lack contextual analysis, partly because of the continuing pressure from the administration to politicize information and cherry-pick intelligence. The NIE, for example, does not explain that Al-Qaeda in Iraq, while lethal, is a very small part of the Sunni insurgency, and that a number of Sunni insurgent groups are its sworn enemies. Nor did the NIE note how few foreign fighters are in Iraq and what a small percentage of insurgents they constitute. (A *Los Angeles Times* story published on July 15 reported that of the 19,000 Iraqi prisoners held by the U.S. military there, only 135 are foreign fighters, and nearly half are Saudis.) The NIE is utterly devoid of political analysis.

According to intelligence sources, CIA director Michael Hayden has been under attack within the administration from Dick Cheney and the neoconservatives since testifying frankly to the Baker-Hamilton Iraq Study Group that urged a strategic redeployment of U.S. forces and new diplomatic efforts in the region, which were rejected by President Bush. A virtual paralysis is setting in within the intelligence community. Analysts are even anxious about putting their names on their reports. While they are homogenizing information, the administration is still unhappy with the result, as it was with the new NIE.

For the embattled president, filled with "self-confidence," the "motives" he doesn't wish critics to examine turn out to be far more utopian than the military success of the surge, as he explained to his conservative interlocutors. "There is such a thing as the universality of freedom. I strongly believe that Muslims desire to be free just like Methodists desire to be free." Beneath the seething chaotic violence, beyond the tribal and religious strife, past the civil war, the Iraqis, according to the president, under their robes are no different from American Methodists. There's nothing more to understand. If only we can prevail, they can be just like us. The rest is marketing.

July 19, 2007

Stab in the Back

President Bush's political strategy at home is an implicit if unintended admission of the failure of his military strategy in Iraq and toward terrorism generally. Betrayal is his theme, delivered in his speeches, embroidered by his officials, and trumpeted by the brass band of neoconservative publicists. The foundation for his stab-in-the-back theory was laid in the beginning.

"Either you are with us or you are with the terrorists," Bush said in his joint address to Congress nine days after the September 11, 2001, attacks. And in the weeks that followed he repeated variations of his formula, reducing it to "for or against us in the war on terrorism." At the Charleston, South Carolina, Air Force Base on Tuesday, Bush resumed his repudiated habit of conflating threats, suggesting a connection between 9/11 and the Iraq war, and intensified his blaming of domestic critics for the shortcomings of his policy. His story line depends upon omitting his own part in the calamity. "The facts are," insisted Bush to his captive audience, "that Al-Qaeda terrorists killed Americans on 9/11, they're fighting us in Iraq and across the world, and they are plotting to kill Americans here at home again."

But how did it happen that Al-Qaeda in Iraq, sworn enemy of Saddam Hussein and his secularism, operating in isolation prior to 9/11, though almost certainly with the connivance and protection of Kurdish leader and current Iraqi President Jalal Talabani, has come to thrive under the U.S. occupation? And since AQI represents perhaps 1 percent or less of the insurgent strength, how can it be depicted as the main foe, capable of seizing state power? The other Sunni insurgent groups increasingly view it as an impediment to their own ambitions and have marked it for elimination. Rather than address these problematic complexities, Bush points the finger of blame at U.S. senators who dare to question his policy. "Those who justify withdrawing our troops from Iraq by denying the threat of Al-Qaeda in Iraq and its ties to Osama bin Laden ignore the clear consequences of such a retreat."

Bush's accusation of betrayal anticipates the September report of General David Petraeus on the progress of the "surge" in Iraq. The absence of victory inspires a search for an enemy within. Bush's stab-in-the-back theory is the latest corollary to the old policy that military force will create political success. Bush is a vulgar Maoist: "Political power comes from the barrel of a gun," said Chairman Mao. But the surge is simply an endlessly repetitive reaction to the failure of the purely military. Somehow, in the political vacuum, additional U.S. troops are supposed to quell the civil war, compel the sects and factions to lie down like lambs, and destroy AQI. U.S. ambassador Ryan Crocker who last week begged that the Iraqi government not be held accountable for meeting political benchmarks, none of which have been realized; and at the same time he requested exit visas for his Iraqi staff, who obviously have no confidence in the Bush policy and do not wish to leave via the embassy roof. Crocker's actions speak louder than his words—and louder than Bush's.

Bush, however, clings to the rhetoric of conventional warfare, of "victory" and "retreat." The collapsed Iraqi state, proliferation of sectarian warfare and murderous strife even among Shiite militias bewilder him; clear-cut dichotomies are more comforting, producing deeper confusion. The friend of his enemy is his friend; the enemy of his enemy is not his friend. Meanwhile, Bush seeks to displace responsibility for the potentially dire consequences of his policy on others.

Neoconservative publicists spread the calumnies that critics of Bush's policy are against the troops and that these critics will be responsible for genocide if they and not Bush are followed. William Kristol, editor of *The*

Weekly Standard—whose July 15 article in the *Washington Post*, "Why Bush Will Be a Winner," Bush has recommended to his White House staff—has published a new piece in the latest issue of his magazine, "They Don't Really Support the Troops." "Having turned against a war that some of them supported, the left is now turning against the troops they claim still to support," he writes. His combination of nuance and crudity is ideologically deft. By pointing out that "some of them supported" the war at the start, his intention is not to draw distinctions but to lump all critics together as now undifferentiated and discreditable—"the left." Then he ascribed a common motive: fear that Bush will succeed and a hatred of the soldiers. "They sense that history is progressing away from them—that these soldiers, fighting courageously in a just cause, could still win the war, that they are proud of their service, and that they will be future leaders of this country." But this is not enough for Kristol. "The left slanders them. We support them. More than that, we admire them." Slander?

Jonah Goldberg, a columnist for the *Los Angeles Times*, writes in an article Tuesday that "liberals" are the ones responsible for a coming "genocide" in Iraq. "But if genocide unfolds in Iraq after American troops depart, it would be hard to argue that we weren't at least partly to blame. Yes, the mass murder would have more immediate authors than the United States of America, but we would undeniably be responsible, at least in part, for giving a green light to genocide." Having initially adopted a vague "we," he quickly dispenses with this rhetorical strategy, blaming "liberals" and one person in particular for "mass murder." Barack Obama "offers precisely that green light," he writes.

On July 16, the Associated Press reported on a letter from Undersecretary of Defense for Policy Eric Edelman to Senator Hillary Clinton, condemning her for deigning to request in her capacity as a member of the Armed Services Committee information on Pentagon contingency plans for withdrawal. "Premature and public discussion of the withdrawal of U.S. forces from Iraq reinforces enemy propaganda that the United States will abandon its allies in Iraq, much as we are perceived to have done in Vietnam, Lebanon and Somalia," Edelman replied. Even asking about such plans aids and abets the enemy, tantamount to treason. Edelman added the suggestion of a massacre if we "abandon" the "allies," and said its responsibility would fall on those who raised questions.

In response to a letter from Sen. Clinton, asking if Edelman's statement "accurately characterizes your views as Secretary of Defense," Robert Gates in effect repudiated it. "I have long been a staunch advocate of congressional oversight, first at the CIA and now at the Defense Department," he wrote on July 20. "I have said on several occasions in recent months that I believe that congressional debate on Iraq has been constructive and appropriate. I had not seen Senator Clinton's reply to Ambassador Edelman's letter until today."

Gates's note is extraordinary not only for its open acknowledgment of a breach with his undersecretary but also for its revelation that he was unaware of Edelman's vitriolic letter. Edelman is a longtime neoconservative with deep ties to Dick Cheney. Like John Bolton, who served as a counterintelligence agent for Cheney when he was undersecretary of state under Colin Powell, Edelman does not truly serve his immediate superior in the chain of command. His ultimate allegiance is pledged to an ideological network. Given the incendiary nature of his letter to a Democratic presidential candidate, which could only be conceived and interpreted as supremely political, it's hard to imagine that as seasoned an operator as Edelman would act entirely on his own. But if he did not brief and receive approval from Gates—and Gates has gone out of his way to distance himself from any involvement—then whom did Edelman discuss his letter with before he sent it?

Edelman is a rare Foreign Service officer long aligned with neoconservatives. As he explained in his letter of April 21 to Judge Reggie Walton requesting clemency in sentencing for I. Lewis Libby, Cheney's former chief of staff, he has known Libby, "a deeply dedicated public servant," for twenty-six years. Edelman first served with Libby, he wrote, during the Reagan administration, followed by service as Libby's deputy in the Defense Department during the elder Bush's administration, under Secretary of Defense Cheney, and most recently as Libby's deputy on Cheney's staff.

Edelman, in fact, was the first person on Cheney's staff to sound the alarm against former ambassador Joseph Wilson after reading the May 6, 2003, column by Nicholas Kristof in *The New York Times* that described Wilson but did not name him. Edelman urged Libby to leak information to rebut Wilson's disclosure that it was a request from the vice president's office that initiated his mission to Niger in search of the phantom yellowcake uranium Bush claimed Saddam was purchasing—a major rationale for the Iraq war.

This year, Edelman leaped to the defense of the prewar disinformation campaign operated out of the Pentagon through a small unit called the

Office of Special Plans and run by Edelman's predecessor in his current post, the neoconservative Douglas Feith. When the Defense Department's inspector general, Thomas Gimble, issued a report in February calling Feith's operation "inappropriate" and urging that new controls be established to prevent officials from conducting rogue "intelligence activities," Edelman countered with a heated fifty-two-page memo calling the I.G. "egregious," charging that he "does not have special expertise" on an issue that is "fraught with policy and political dimensions." Edelman's blast succeeded in forcing the I.G. to drop his recommendations and, as *Newsweek* reported, "shows how current and former Cheney aides still wield their clout throughout the government."

The degree to which Edelman has been rewarded for his ideological affinities is apparent not only in his appointments but also in monetary emoluments. According to State Department records, in 2005 and 2006, he received Senior Foreign Service performance awards of $10,000 and $12,500, respectively, both standard for someone of his rank. However, in June of this year he received a Presidential Rank Award of $40,953, an amount described as "amazing" by a former senior State Department professional who has administered such awards. Indeed, the Office of Personnel Management cautions against granting Presidential Rank Awards for appointments requiring Senate confirmation and for those in their positions for less than three years. Gates signed off on this award, but Cheney loomed as Edelman's sponsor, having personally reviewed his performance evaluations from 2001 to 2003.

In addition to the accusations of betrayal involving aiding "enemy propaganda," stabbing our troops in the back just as they are about to succeed, and acting as the architects of genocide, neoconservatives also argue that if only their initial advice had been followed in installing their favorite exile, Ahmed Chalabi, as leader of Iraq, none of the subsequent problems would have occurred. Thus it would all have been a "cakewalk" as projected, if not for the occupation, for which they were not responsible. The only error the neoconservatives admit is not being vigilant against compromise and insisting on the seamless political correctness of their plan, such as it was.

The latest personage to take up this neoconservative argument is none other than Cheney himself. "I think we should have probably gone with the provisional government of Iraqis," he says. "I think the Coalition Provisional Authority was a mistake." The vice president's remark appears in a new, authorized biography, *Cheney: The Untold Story of America's Most Powerful and Controversial Vice President*, by Stephen F. Hayes, *The Weekly Standard* writer best known for his effort to bolster the case for a link between Al-Qaeda and Saddam before the invasion of Iraq and for defending Cheney's pressure on the intelligence community to put its imprimatur on such views.

"I always felt that he was an ally," Hayes quotes an obviously perplexed L. Paul Bremer, who served as the head of the CPA. Bremer ought to have grounds for being confused by Cheney's odd comment. According to his 2005 memoir, *My Year in Iraq*, he was first contacted to serve by "Scooter" Libby and Paul Wolfowitz, the neoconservative deputy secretary of defense. Cheney had already blocked State Department participation in the Office of Reconstruction and Humanitarian Assistance, the CPA's predecessor organization. The CIA had flown Chalabi, a principal source of the false intelligence used to justify the war, later a self-proclaimed "hero in error," from his base in Iran to Iraq with several hundred of his "Free Iraqi Fighting Forces." (Chalabi was long on the payroll of the Iranian intelligence service.) Chalabi and his forces eagerly led the looting of Iraqi ministries. His advice to disband the Iraqi army and fire Baath Party members that ran the government bureaucracies was accepted by Wolfowitz and Feith—and ratified by Bremer.

In his account, Bremer writes that the Principals Committee meeting of the National Security Council that gave Bremer his marching orders decided that the Iraqi exiles were too weak and unrepresentative to establish authority in the country. Bremer cites his notes from that meeting: "Here's the vice president . . . 'We're not at a point where representative Iraqi leaders can come forward. They're still too scared. We need a strategy on the ground for the postwar situation we actually have and not the one we wish we had.' This didn't sound like an open endorsement of the exiles."

Cheney's seeming confession of error is little more than belated historical revisionism to obscure his own part in the fiasco. It is his first step toward walking away from responsibility through self-denial, not least about the reality that the Iranians played him and the neoconservatives as stooges.

Cheney prides himself on his skill as a hidden-hand master manipulator of politics through control of bureaucracies. Hayes's hagiography is a shabby, tendentious work, of the sort that used to be produced in the Soviet Union, impossible to grasp without independent knowledge or access to samizdat. Nonetheless, there are a few shiny objects that can be retrieved from this dump.

Cheney granted Hayes a series of interviews that provide insight into the development of his cynical politics, his view of unaccountable executive power, and his penchant for secrecy. One can almost hear Cheney chuckle as he tells his Boswell how the credulous Washington press corps got him wrong all these years, to his everlasting advantage. "The press never looked at my voting record" as a congressman, he says. "They thought I was all warm and fuzzy and they never looked to see."

Cheney also reveals how as President Gerald Ford's chief of staff he learned to undermine and destroy Vice President Nelson Rockefeller, the last unabashed moderate Republican in the White House. Cheney described how he would put "sand in the gears," claiming "we'll staff it out," to kill Rockefeller's projects. Cheney gloats over humiliating Rockefeller at the 1976 Republican Convention, where during Rockefeller's last moment on the public stage, giving the nomination speech for his successor, the microphone suddenly went dead. Cheney recalls that Rockefeller blamed him and that they had "shouting matches." Yet Cheney doesn't deny the accusation. Instead, he snickers. "You've got to watch vice presidents. They're a sinister crowd."

Hayes also recounts Cheney's confrontation with Senator Patrick Leahy, Democrat of Vermont, on the floor of the Senate on June 21, 2004, when, having heard of Leahy's critical comments about Halliburton's contracts in Iraq, he told him, "Go fuck yourself." Hayes quotes a "fishing buddy" of Cheney's, Merritt Benson, recalling that afterward Cheney told him of his regret: "You never, ever let those people get to you. Or then they win." Of course, Cheney was paraphrasing Richard Nixon, the first president he served, who said on the day he resigned his office, "Always remember that others may hate you, but those who hate you don't win unless you hate them. And then you destroy yourself."

But that Nixon citation is not the end of Cheney's reflections on what he calls "the F-bomb." "It was out of character from my standpoint, I suppose," he confesses. "But what can you say . . . It was heartfelt." Cheney unleashed is Nixon without regrets. If it feels good, do it—and it feels so good to drop the bomb.

July 26, 2007

The Code of Silence

Omertà (or a code of silence) has become the final bond holding the Bush administration together. Honesty is dishonorable; silence is manly; penitence is weakness. Loyalty trumps law. Protecting higher-ups is patriotism. Stonewalling is idealism. Telling the truth is informing. Cooperation with investigators is cowardice; breaking the code is betrayal. Once the code is shattered, however, no one can be trusted and the entire edifice crumbles.

If Attorney General Alberto Gonzales were miraculously to tell the truth, or if he were to resign or be removed, the secret government of the past six years would begin to be unlocked. So long as a Republican Congress rigorously engaged in enforcing no oversight was smugly complicit through its passive ignorance and abdication of constitutional responsibility, the White House was secure in enacting its theories of the imperial presidency. An executive bound only by his self-proclaimed fiat in his capacity as commander in chief became his own law in authorizing torture and warrantless domestic wiretapping and data mining. Following the notion of the unitary executive, in which the departments and agencies have no independent existence under the president, the White House has relentlessly politicized them. Callow political appointees dictate to scientists, censoring or altering their conclusions. Career staff professionals are forced to attend indoctrination sessions on the political strategies of the Republican Party in campaigns and elections. And U.S. attorneys, supposedly impartial prosecutors representing the Department of Justice in the states, are purged if they deviate in any way from the White House's political line.

Last week, for example, the *Washington Post* reported that William R. Steiger, director of the Office of Global Health Affairs in the Department of Health and Human Services, suppressed the 2006 "Call to Action on Global Health" report of U.S. Surgeon General Richard Carmona, which explained the connection of poverty to health and urged that attacking diseases become a major U.S. international commitment. Steiger, who has no credentials in the field, is the son of a former congressman who was Vice

President Cheney's earliest patron, giving Cheney his first congressional job as a staff intern. At the White House's behest, Steiger acts as a micromanaging political commissar. His insistence on approving every single overseas appointee of the Centers for Disease Control and Prevention has left many of its posts empty. "Only 166 of the CDC's 304 overseas positions in 53 countries are filled," the *Atlanta Journal-Constitution* reported in April. "At least 85 positions likely will remain unfilled until 2008." Such is the theory of the unitary executive in action.

Just this week, Jeffrey Toobin wrote in *The New Yorker* about the suspicion that fell on the U.S. attorney in Washington State, John McKay, who was fired in the wholesale purge because of his interest in devoting full resources to an investigation of the murder of an assistant U.S. attorney, Tom Wales, who had been a prominent local advocate of gun control. On July 31, the U.S. attorney in Roanoke, Virginia, John Brownlee, testified before the Senate Judiciary Committee that the night before a guilty verdict was delivered in his case against the drug manufacturing company that produced OxyContin, he received a call from a Justice Department official asking him to slow down his prosecution.

On Wednesday, Bush prepared to invoke executive privilege to protect his senior political aide, Karl Rove, and Rove's deputy, J. Scott Jennings, from testifying before Congress on the firing of the U.S. attorneys. Bush has already covered his chief of staff, Josh Bolten, and former counsel Harriet Miers with executive privilege to prevent their testimony. The House Judiciary Committee responded by citing both for contempt of Congress, which requires action by the U.S. attorney of the District of Columbia. But the Justice Department has declared that it will thwart that process, in effect rendering the nation's system of justice a political arm of the executive.

Bush has steadfastly refused to fire Attorney General Gonzales, even though Gonzales's former chief of staff, Kyle Sampson, directly contradicted Gonzales's testimony before the Senate Judiciary Committee that he knew nothing about the purge of U.S. attorneys and by documentation that Gonzales's claim that they were dismissed for "performance" was a politically contrived excuse. In protecting Gonzales, Bush is shielding the true author of the purge—Rove, who informed and received the approval of Bush himself.

Last week, after Gonzales had testified for the second time before Congress that there was no internal dissent against the authorization of warrantless domestic spying, FBI Director Robert Mueller testified before

Congress that Gonzales's statement was false and offered himself as proof of someone who had opposed the program that Gonzales said had won universal support. James Comey, the deputy attorney general in Bush's first term, had described the now-infamous "Enzo the Baker" scene of March 2004, when Comey, serving as acting attorney general, and Mueller rushed to a Washington hospital to intercept then White House counsel Gonzales, who tried to browbeat Attorney General John Ashcroft, drugged and in pain after emergency surgery, into signing his approval of the wiretapping. Ashcroft refused. Comey confronted President Bush on the program's illegality and it was modified. Yet, in his latest testimony, Gonzales not only contradicted Comey's version but also claimed that the operation was about "other intelligence activities."

Gonzales's unashamed performance prompted senators to demand that the second-ranking Justice Department official, Solicitor General Paul Clement, appoint a special prosecutor to investigate Gonzales's potential perjury, and members of the House to file a resolution asking the Judiciary Committee to launch impeachment proceedings.

The mystery surrounding Gonzales's position deepened with the bizarre attempted defense of Gonzales offered by Michael McConnell, director of national intelligence, who sent a letter Tuesday to Sen. Arlen Specter, Republican of Pennsylvania, explaining that the warrantless wiretapping was part of a much larger surveillance program authorized by a single executive order of the president. If this is true, then Gonzales's past efforts to describe the policy as narrow and relatively small are false. This defense, therefore, provided grist for further incrimination and failed to shine any light on Gonzales's patently misleading testimony.

Gonzales is a unique figure of disrepute in the history of the Justice Department, a cipher, enabler, and useful idiot who was nonetheless indispensable in the rise of his patron and whose survival is elemental to that of the administration. Warren G. Harding's attorney general, Harry Daugherty, trailing accusations of bribery for which he was never indicted, resigned after Harding's death. Daugherty had been one of Harding's creators as the Republican Party chairman of Ohio. Two of Richard Nixon's attorneys general resigned in disgrace during the Watergate scandal, both significant political men: John Mitchell, Nixon's former law partner and campaign chairman, and Richard Kleindienst, an important player in the Barry Goldwater wing of the Republican Party of Arizona.

Gonzales earned the gratitude and indebtedness of Bush in 1996, when he enabled him to escape jury duty in Travis County, Texas, on the attenuated argument that as governor he might find himself in a conflict of interest in the future when considering a clemency or pardon. In fact, Bush's worry was filling out the juror's form that required listing arrests. By avoiding acknowledgement of his drunken-driving violation, Bush maintained his political viability. Grants of clemency and pardons never bothered Bush again. Of the 152 people condemned to execution in Texas during his tenure, the most under any governor in modern American history, he indulged in not a single act of clemency. His counsel, Alberto Gonzales, briefed him on fifty-seven of these cases, and "repeatedly failed to apprise the governor of crucial issues in the cases at hand: ineffective counsel, conflict of interest, mitigating evidence, even actual evidence of innocence," according to a study published by *The Atlantic.*

As White House counsel, Gonzales served as a figurehead and rubber stamp for the radical views of Cheney and the legal neoconservatives on questions of executive power ranging from torture to domestic spying. Gonzales routinely signed the memos written by John Yoo and other ideologues and pushed the executive orders drawn up by Cheney's counsel, David Addington, on to the president for his signature.

Though Gonzales has nary a shred of credibility, even among Republican senators, his continued existence as attorney general is necessary to the preservation of the Bush White House. He is the firewall for Rove—who issued his ultimate marching orders in the U.S. attorney firings—and Bush. So Bush adamantly stands by him, covering Rove and the others with executive privilege.

Bush can ill-afford to have Gonzales resign or be removed. Gonzales's leaving would ratchet up the administration's political crisis to an intense level. Bush could not nominate a replacement without responding to the Senate Judiciary Committee's inevitable request for information on matters that he has attempted to keep secret. On unresolved and electrified issues the Senate would demand documents—the cache on the development of policy since 2001 on torture, the gutting of the Civil Rights Division, the U.S. attorneys, and much more. Only Gonzales's perpetuation in office holds back the deluge.

Yet there is still another opening for Congress to explore that only became apparent in an editorial published in *The New York Times* on July 29.

After observing that in March 2004 "the Justice Department refused to endorse a continuation of the wiretapping program because it was illegal," the *Times* revealed, almost in passing, "Unwilling to accept that conclusion, Vice President Dick Cheney sent Mr. Gonzales and another official to Mr. Ashcroft's hospital room to get him to approve the wiretapping."

"Cheney sent Mr. Gonzales . . ."

This disclosure had not previously appeared anywhere else in print, including the news pages of the *Times*. Yet the *Times*'s editorial page published it as indisputable fact. On Tuesday, the guest on CNN's *Larry King Live* was none other than Vice President Cheney. King asked Cheney about the *Times*'s report about his order to Gonzales. "I don't recall," replied Cheney in a classic nondenial denial. "That would be something you would recall," King continued. "I would think so," said Cheney. "But certainly I was involved because I was a big advocate of the Terrorist Surveillance Program."

But under what authority did the vice president give this order to the then White House counsel? That is not a matter for editorial writers, but for Congress.

The Office of the Vice President has the most limited legal and constitutional power over the Justice Department. It can have input on an extremely narrow range of political policies, but absolutely none in operational matters. Yet the *Times* reports that Cheney sent Gonzales to pressure the attorney general to sign off on warrantless wiretaps. Why would a White House counsel act on a vice president's orders? And what else did Cheney's office do to influence the Justice Department over the past six years? Nothing is known beyond that one line in the *Times*.

We know nothing about the domestic wiretapping program, especially if it is as extensive as National Intelligence Director McConnell suggests. Only a congressional investigation can settle suspicions. When he was a congressman, Cheney notoriously defended the conduct of Oliver North in the Iran-Contra affair as an aspect of executive power of which he approved. After North testified before the joint congressional committee investigating the scandal, Cheney declared that he was "the most effective and impressive witness certainly this committee has heard." In the minority report on Iran-Contra written under Cheney's aegis, the congressional role in overseeing foreign policy was contemptuously dismissed: "If they interfere with the core presidential foreign policy functions, they should be struck down." In the theoretical discussion of his view of the executive, it may be forgotten that North, whom he so passionately defended, had gotten the Washington field office of the FBI to wiretap the sources of the congressional investigators who were probing his activities. Fawn Hall, North's secretary, at his March 1989 trial delivered a line that summarized the entire affair and presciently anticipated certain Bush administration policies. "Sometimes you have to go above the law."

Now, in light of the *Times*'s revelation of Cheney's order to Gonzales, the relevant committees of Congress are justified in requesting or subpoenaing documents from the Justice Department about the intrusion of the Office of the Vice President into domestic legal matters. The trail of what happened from 2001 to the present will be visible, to the extent it remains a record, embedded in e-mail communications and memorandums from the OVP to the Justice Department or in internal memos referring to such communications. Requesting them from the department rather than the White House makes any claim of executive privilege hollow regarding departments or agencies outside the White House itself. The Justice Department has already cooperated with Congress in turning over documents. Why would it suddenly now refuse?

If executive privilege were to be applied in this instance to the Justice Department, then the unitary theory of government in which all power resides in a single vessel, a great Decider, would render the Constitution's grant of powers to three branches of government defunct.

Even Nixon, in asserting executive privilege in the heat of the Watergate scandal, did not claim that it applied to decisions made in the Justice Department. Attorney General John Mitchell, found guilty of perjury and obstruction of justice, could not be protected from prosecution for his part in what he called the "White House horrors."

Dick Cheney, the greatest exponent of the Nixonian concept of the presidency, more successful than Nixon, has usurped in his grasp of executive power even command of domestic legal policy. But we have seen only a flicker of a shadow of his power. And Bush knows that Rove, too, has played puppet master. Losing Gonzales would raise the curtain on this era's "White House horrors." So Bush throws executive privilege over everyone he can. The yes man has become the indispensable man.

August 2, 2007

•

Colin Powell's Ghost

Every movement, gesture, and tic of the Bush administration is shadowed by its past. When National Intelligence Director Michael McConnell was deployed politically to overawe timorous legislators into approving unlimited and warrantless domestic surveillance, he was acting in the shadow of former CIA Director George Tenet, whose presence was used to lend credibility to intelligence being fixed to suit arguments for the invasion of Iraq. As General David Petraeus prepares to deliver his report in September on the "surge" in Iraq, he is elevated into the ultimate reliable source, just as former Secretary of State Colin Powell's sterling reputation was exploited for his delivery of the case for invasion before the United Nations Security Council on February 5, 2003, a date that will live in mendacity, for every statement he made was later revealed to be false; Powell regretted publicly that it was an everlasting "blot" on his good name. Meanwhile, during the dog days of August, the president's aides are preparing the fall public relations campaign to envelop Petraeus's report. On cue, neoconservative organs spew out good news of "progress on the ground" and thrash critics as "defeatist." "Defeatists in Retreat" trumpets William Kristol's latest screed in *The Weekly Standard,* repackaging old themes once again.

Behind the display of bravado, the West Wing is seized with anxiety. Any rustle in the brush, any sudden noise, upsets the president's aides. As they try to regain their composure and confidence, recalling the glory days when they constituted themselves as the White House Iraq Group, or WHIG, a P.R. juggernaut before the invasion, they know who and what they have buried along the way and fear their return.

The release of a documentary on the administration's failures in Iraq, *No End in Sight,* directed by Charles Ferguson, has the White House spooked. Bush's aides are not worried because the film is brilliantly shot and edited, or because it is compelling, but because of what—or whose appearance—it might augur to upset their September rollout.

The film features three former administration officials speaking on camera as unreserved critics of prewar and postwar planning: Powell's former chief of staff, Colonel Lawrence Wilkerson; Powell's former deputy secretary of state, Richard Armitage; and former U.S. ambassador Barbara Bodine, a senior member of the Office of Reconstruction and Humanitarian Assistance in Iraq, closely aligned with Powell.

Wilkerson and Bodine have spoken out before. But Armitage's debut in particular has the White House fuming and fretting that it somehow signals Powell's emergence as a full-throated critic in the middle of the September P.R. offensive. National Security Advisor Stephen Hadley, according to sources close to him, has voiced anger and concern about whether Powell will step forward and what he might say, and other presidential aides are wondering how to cope with that nightmarish possibility.

Two months ago, Powell declared the surge a near-certain failure. On June 10, on NBC's *Meet the Press*, he declared, "The current strategy to deal with it, called a surge—the military surge, our part of the surge under General Petraeus—the only thing it can do is put a heavier lid on this boiling pot of civil war stew . . . And so General Petraeus is moving ahead with his part of it, but he's the one who's been saying all along there is no military solution to this problem. The solution has to emerge from the other two legs, the Iraqi political actions and reconciliation, and building up the Iraqi security and police forces. And those two legs are not—are not going well. That part of strategy is not going well."

Hadley and others are taking Powell's early skepticism toward the surge and willingness to express it as a potential sign that he will swoop down on them just after Petraeus asks for more forbearance for the president's policy. Powell is the White House's ticking-time-bomb scenario. He was Petraeus before Petraeus, the good soldier before the good soldier, window-dressing before window-dressing. The White House aides' fear of Powell reflects their guilt, if not their stricken consciences, over his disposal. Powell was used, ruined, and tossed overboard. His warnings were ignored, his loyalty was abused, and when he no longer served Bush's purposes he was unceremoniously discarded.

Throughout the excruciating years of his slow destruction, no one served Powell less ably than Powell. To the degree that his abusers and tormentors may be haunted, he is more haunted. Powell's aides are now on the front line of criticism against the administration, while he obviously simmers, pretending to be happily retired. He travels the country delivering motivational speeches, a theater of make-believe, as though he were the same Colin Powell as before Bush. While he preaches his secrets of success, he can see the neo-conservative architects of failure in Iraq who demonized him distributed among the leading Republican candidates for president. There is not one among them who does not boast neocon dominance of his foreign policy circle. Powell's absence cedes the political terrain to those who ousted him from office. Notwithstanding his tarnished reputation, he has a final chance to regain his dignity and at least some of his previous standing by stepping forward at the crucial hour. Does he accept his marginalization as permanent? He is Banquo's ghost, but will he make an appearance at Bush's banquet?

Hadley and Co. worry that Powell may be secretly writing a memoir that would expose their hidden history, though Powell has said he will not produce a sequel to his inspirational autobiography. One of the most significant stories for which Powell would be an ideal narrator is his own mistreatment and misjudgments. Were Powell to decide to stop serving his false friends and instead to serve history, or if he were to decide simply to serve the truth before Bush perpetrates more damage, he would have to start at the beginning.

When did he realize that as secretary of state he was not the principal foreign policy advisor to the president? Was it when he was appointed in December 2000 as secretary-designate?

Being an experienced bureaucrat at the most senior levels of government, having been national security advisor and chairman of the Joint Chiefs of Staff, why did he not make common cause with Brent Scowcroft and other experienced senior personnel with whom he had long relationships to get an alternative point of view to a president whose only policy choices were being filtered through Dick Cheney's neocon structure? As chairman of the President's Foreign Intelligence Advisory Board, Scowcroft was politically isolated, forced to speak out occasionally in op-ed pieces and interviews. When Scowcroft published his op-ed in *The Wall Street Journal* on August 15, 2002, "Don't Attack Saddam," where was Powell and what did he say to Scowcroft?

Why did Powell not join Scowcroft in expressing concern about the rehabilitation of Iran-Contra convicted felon Elliott Abrams, appointed on June 1, 2001, as special assistant to the president and senior director on the National Security Council for Near East and North African Affairs. And why did Powell make no effort to block Cheney's neocon takeover of the administration?

On October 5, 2004, two weeks before he was ousted by Bush as chairman of the President's Foreign Intelligence Advisory Board, Scowcroft objected to Israeli Prime Minister Ariel Sharon's advisor Dov Weisglass's statement in favor of freezing the Oslo peace process. Why didn't Powell step in to help Scowcroft against Abrams's manipulation of information flowing to the president about what Weisglass was saying? Was Powell aware that Abrams was working with Weisglass?

Powell watched as the neocons filled strategic positions throughout the administration. Why did he agree to the appointment of John Bolton as undersecretary for arms control and international security on May 11, 2001, and keep him on instead of firing him for reporting to Cheney rather than to him? Why did he permit Bolton to hire neocon David Wurmser as a special advisor?

On September 17, 2001, one week after 9/11, Bush signed a "top secret" document to begin planning the invasion of Iraq. Powell was later reported to have said at meetings at the time, "Jeez, what a fixation about Iraq." In April 2002, Bush advised Condoleezza Rice that he was prepared to move against Saddam. Did he advise Powell? When did Powell learn what Bush had told Rice? Was he cut out?

In February 2003, Cheney, Secretary of Defense Donald Rumsfeld, and General Richard Meyers briefed Saudi ambassador Prince Bandar on the Iraq war plans. Had they already briefed Powell? If he was cut out, what did he do subsequently?

On May 16, 2004, Powell stated on *Meet the Press* that his February 5, 2003, presentation before the United Nations Security Council on weapons of mass destruction was inaccurate. When he agreed to make the administration's case, why did he take only two personal staffers (Colonel Wilkerson and executive assistant Craig Kelly) to the CIA to review what Cheney, Scooter Libby, and Paul Wolfowitz had prepared and/or distorted, instead of bringing knowledgeable members of his own intelligence service, the State Department Intelligence and Research Bureau (INR), to protect him?

On February 5, 2004, I quoted Greg Thielman, former director of the Strategic, Proliferation and Military Affairs Office of INR, in *Salon*: "He didn't have anyone from INR near him. Powell didn't want to know what was true or not. He wanted to sell a rotten fish. At some point, Powell decided there was no way to avoid war. His job was to go to war with as much legitimacy as we could scrape up." Why did Powell cut out his own people to his own ultimate detriment?

The documentary *No End in Sight* depicts the creation of the multivolume "Future of Iraq" study prepared by Powell's State Department staff for the reconstruction of Iraq after the war. When Rumsfeld and Deputy Secretary of Defense Wolfowitz rejected the study and blackballed Powell's staff, what did he do to counter them, if anything?

Eventually, history will answer these questions. But in September, Bush will attempt to impose his endgame for Iraq, a continuation of his policy, until he hands off the disaster to his successor. Petraeus is Bush's agent, just as Powell had been. Bush and his White House dread the "mockery" of Powell's "horrible shadow." If Powell remains silent in September it will be his last act of acquiescence as a spectral being.

Haunted by Banquo's ghost, Macbeth says, "If charnel-houses and our graves must send/ Those that we bury back, our monuments/ Shall be the maws of kites." And when Banquo's ghost vanishes, still plagued with the guilt of Banquo's murder, Macbeth cries out: "Hence, horrible shadow! Unreal mockery, hence!"

August 9, 2007

Rove's Fall

With the departure of Karl Rove the Bush administration now enters its last throes. As a legacy for his patron, Rove has designed the public relations offensive for the fall presidential campaign to attempt to corner congressional Democrats through a combination of General David Petraeus's forthcoming report on the "surge" in Iraq and presidential budget vetoes; but once those tactics are played the political string runs out. President Bush will be left with the unalloyed counsel of Vice President Dick Cheney, whose endgame transcends Rove's machinations. "I don't worry about the polls," Cheney said on CNN's *Larry King Live* on July 31. One more hypothetical restraint on Cheney has been removed.

Rove's resignation marks a tacit recognition of the failure of his theory of political realignment, though hardly of its consequences. Trailing him out of the West Wing is the cloud of a subpoena from the Senate Judiciary Committee that seeks his testimony about his primary role in purging U.S. attorneys for partisan purposes. But even when Rove leaves government service at the end of August, Bush will extend the protective cover of executive privilege.

Rove's merger of politics and policy was an effort to forge a total one-party state. While he is acclaimed as a political strategist, his true innovation was in governing. He sought to subordinate the entire federal government to his goal of creating a permanent Republican majority. Every department and agency has been subject to an intense and thorough politicization. Indeed, Rove's ambitious plan was tantamount to a proto-Sovietization. Even science has been suppressed in the name of the party line, recalling the Lysenko episode. Cheney and Rove acted as the pincers of the unitary executive. While Cheney sought to concentrate unaccountable power in the presidency, Rove brought down the anvil of politics on the professional career staff.

Rove's radicalization of government was early described by the first member of the administration to quit in disgust, John DiIulio, a University of Pennsylvania professor and the first director of the White House Office of Faith-Based and Community Initiatives. He discovered that "compassionate conservatism," Rove's slogan for Bush's 2000 campaign, was little more than a sham. "What you've got is everything—and I mean everything—being run by the political arm. It's the reign of the Mayberry Machiavellis," said DiIulio.

Rove's saga is a rags-to-riches success story of a political serial killer. His first involvement in a political campaign was to conduct a dirty trick against a candidate running for Illinois state treasurer. After Rove dropped out of the University of Utah, his promise was recognized and he was appointed executive director of the College Republicans. Donald Segretti, ringmaster for the Committee to Reelect the President of a gang of dirty tricksters engaged in what he called "ratfucking," recruited Rove. Rove conducted one session training young Republicans to sift through the garbage of opponents. In the Watergate scandal, Segretti was sentenced to prison for forging campaign literature. The FBI questioned Rove, but dropped its investigation of the small fry. Yet he would become the greatest ratfucker of them all. The new chairman of the Republican National Committee, George H. W. Bush, named Rove chairman of the College Republicans and, even more fortuitously, appointed him as a handler of his obstreperous older son. It was love at first sight, at least from the nerdy Rove's point of view. "Huge amounts of charisma, swagger, cowboy boots, flight jacket, wonderful smile, just charisma—you know, wow," he said later.

Rove weathered rough storms, including being fired in 1992 from the Bush for President campaign by the candidate himself for leaking damaging information to conservative columnist Robert Novak about the elder Bush's close friend and top fundraiser Robert Mosbacher.

In 1981, Rove established a direct-mail firm, Karl Rove & Co., in Austin, Texas, which became his cockpit for the destruction of the state Democratic Party. Over more than the next decade, he was involved in dozens of campaigns marked by dirty tricks, sexual innuendo, and the use of friendly FBI agents and prosecutors to harass Democrats. In Texas and elsewhere, he laid the groundwork for his later efforts. The whispering campaign in 1994 against Governor Ann Richards claiming that she was a lesbian and the rumor-mongering that an esteemed Alabama state judge was really a secret pedophile were harbingers of the smear campaign against Senator John McCain in the South Carolina primary in 2000. Rove's exploitation of prosecutors pioneered his later politicization of U.S. attorneys.

Rove promoted the Bush campaign for president in 2000 as a national extension of his realignment of Texas politics. He cast Bush as William McKinley and by inference himself as the political boss Mark Hanna. Rove's historical analogy was either the autodidact's self-inflated misreading of history or a shrewd manipulation of a gullible and careerist press corps, or both. Whatever Rove's pretension, Bush lost the 2000 election, unlike McKinley in 1896, which was a major victory of the Republican Party. There was no parallel except in the name of the party: One election marked a genuine realignment of Republican support, firmly consolidating its uncertain majority since the Civil War. The other was a gift handed to the loser of the popular majority in a decision not so contrived since Dred Scott. George W. Bush is less William McKinley than Rutherford B. Hayes.

Nonetheless, Bush began governing as if he had a mandate for the most radical presidency ever. The story is told that before the inauguration Bush pollster Matthew Dowd (now another disillusioned and lost soul) wrote a memo to Rove explaining that there was no middle in American politics and that only those who turned out their maximum base through polarization would win. Yet, Dowd memo or not, Bush, Cheney, and Rove were prepared to govern as radicals. The theory helped justify what had been decided already.

Only the attacks of September 11 gave Rove, Bush, and Cheney an atmosphere in which such theories could thrive through the exploitation of fear. Rove became the public exponent of using terror as a political instrument to demonize the Democrats as unreliably soft. Just before the 2002 midterm elections swept by Republicans, Rove held forth on the coming realignment. "Something is going on out there," Rove said. "Something else more fundamental . . . But we will only know it retrospectively. In two years or four years or six years, [we may] look back and say the dam began to break in 2002."

After the Republican victories in 2002, an enraptured press corps celebrated Rove. "Let me disclose my own bias in this matter. I like Karl Rove," wrote David Broder, the lead political columnist for the *Washington Post*, on May 18, 2003. "In the days when he was operating from Austin, we had many long and rewarding conversations. I have eaten quail at his table and admired the splendid Hill Country landscape from the porch of the historic cabin Karl and his wife Darby found miles away and had carted to its present site on their land."

The 2004 election should have been a foregone conclusion, and perhaps it was, based on the momentum from 9/11. Rejecting Bush at that early point, a year after the invasion of Iraq, would have been an extraordinary repudiation not only of him but of the public's recent and continuing support before it had come to the conclusion that his policies had been given a full chance and were not working. The 2004 election also took place before the further radicalization of policy and politics that was to occur in its immediate aftermath—the Terri Schiavo case, "the last throes" in Iraq, and Hurricane Katrina. Bush and Rove also faced a flawed Democratic candidate and campaign that steadfastly refused to respond to the early smears of Senator John Kerry's heroic war record, declined to offer any critique of the administration at the Democratic National Convention, and was tentative and inarticulate on issues concerning the Iraq war. And yet Bush still barely eked out a victory, dependent ultimately on slim margins in swing states reinforced by initiatives against gay marriage.

At the St. Regis Hotel, just blocks from the White House, a week after the election, the panjandrums of the Washington press corps hailed Rove at a lunch held by *The Christian Science Monitor.* "When Rove entered the room, everyone stood up to congratulate him and shake his hand," reports Joshua Green in the September issue of *The Atlantic.*

Once again, Bush and Rove plunged forward. "I earned capital in the campaign, political capital, and now I intend to spend it," Bush proclaimed. "It is my style." Bush's first proposal of the second term, politically devised by Rove, was to privatize the great achievement of the New Deal—Social Security. But it never even reached a single congressional hearing room. Soon the winds and water of Katrina washed away the façade. Bush named Rove reconstruction czar for New Orleans. He did little except for the permanent removal of about a quarter million black voters who held the political balance of power in Louisiana.

As the aftereffects of fear from 9/11 receded, Rove's strategy of using terror as the main political weapon against Democrats dulled. Rove himself was engulfed in the investigation into the White House's outing of a covert CIA operative, Valerie Plame Wilson, in order to damage her husband, ambassador Joseph Wilson, for having revealed that the rationale for the invasion of Iraq was based on bogus claims about Saddam Hussein. Rove escaped indictment for perjury and obstruction of justice only by the skin of his teeth, amending his grand jury testimony at the last minute after a helpful journalist at *Time* magazine told his lawyer that Matthew Cooper, a correspondent there, had evidence of Rove's involvement.

On the eve of the 2006 midterm elections, the press corps continued to salute Rove's genius. "The emphasis, for those who want to understand the world, should be on 'genius' and not 'evil' (as in Rove is an 'evil genius')," wrote Mark Halperin, then political editor of ABC News, in *Slate.* He went on: "People who live in Bethesda, Chevy Chase, and Manhattan should understand that in much of red America, Rove is beloved and respected, and they should ask themselves why that is."

After the Republicans lost Congress, Rove blamed the disaster on one wayward homosexual Republican member, Representative Mark Foley of Florida, not on the administration's policies. Still treated as an oracle, Rove was invited to the Aspen Institute's Idea Festival two years in a row. On July 9, he told the assembled eminences, intellectuals, and corporate executives that conditions were fine in the Guantánamo prison camp for detainees. "Our principal health problem down there is gain of weight, we feed them so well," he said. Next, he predicted that the Iraq war would not be a defining issue in the 2008 presidential campaign. "I think it's likely not to be the dominant issue because I think, because of my assumptions about where it is—where it is likely to be."

Perhaps Rove quit because he wishes to cash out, securing corporate contracts, lecture fees, and a book advance, as the sun begins to set on the Republican White House. Perhaps he will act as an unofficial go-between for Bush and advisor to the Republican candidate in 2008. Whatever his gambits, he will remain protected by executive privilege for the duration and beyond. "We've been friends for a long time, and we're still going to be friends," Bush said as he hugged Rove. "I would call Karl Rove a dear friend."

We now take leave of "the Architect," "Turdblossom," and the "Mayberry Machiavelli," his grand experiment in political realignment collapsed, and remember him as he wants to be remembered, rapping onstage as MC Rove at the 2007 Radio and Television Correspondents Association dinner as members of the Washington press corps bopped and shimmied as his backup dancers.

August 13, 2007

The War of Memory

Even before the date of his resignation from the White House took effect, Karl Rove furiously launched himself on his legacy tour. Appearing on three Sunday morning TV shows on August 19 he was intent on demonstrating the range of his political, military, and literary mastery. Rove rattled off statistics of minority group voting patterns for President Bush in the 2004 election as if the moment were the apotheosis of the Republican Party. He cited Napoleon in order to justify the Iraq war—"Look, Napoleon said that your battle plan doesn't survive the first contact with the enemy, but you still have to have a plan"—but not Napoleon's remark after the retreat from Moscow: "There is only one step from the sublime to the ridiculous." And Rove thrashed around in search of an appropriate character from fiction to describe his ineffable and immortal being. "I'm Moby Dick," he began, but dissatisfied with identifying himself as the great white whale drew upon his wellspring of literature for yet other self-projections. "Let's face it. I mean, I'm a myth, and they're—you know, I'm Beowulf. You know, I'm Grendel. I don't know who I am. But they're after me." Hunted and hunter, beast and warrior, author of his own tale nonetheless suffering an identity crisis, a figure transcendent beyond history still pursued down dark alleys, Rove finally rested on a note of paranoia. If the demons were after him, what would he not do to punish them?

When questioned about his indisputable part in the outing of covert CIA operative Valerie Plame Wilson, Rove did what came easiest to him, distorting reality, mangling facts, and baldfaced lying—"dissembling, to put it charitably," as Matthew Cooper, the former *Time Magazine* reporter, said on NBC's *Meet the Press* after observing Rove's interview there. Rove's performance included not only petulantly refusing to apologize to Plame ("No!"); repeating various canards about former ambassador Joseph Wilson; claiming that he had not told MSBNC *Hardball* host Chris Matthews, as Matthews had reported, that "Wilson's wife is fair game"; but also mimicking word for word the perjured testimony of Vice President Cheney's former chief of staff, I. Lewis "Scooter" Libby, who had falsely insisted that he had not planted stories about Plame with reporters but after learning of her identity from them had replied, "I've heard that, too." "I remember saying, 'I've heard that, too,'" said Rove brightly. "To imply that he didn't know about [Plame's identity], or that he heard it in some rumor out in the hallways, is nonsense," commented Cooper.

Rove, however, was not alone in burnishing his standing as statesman. Michael Gerson, former chief Bush speechwriter, specialist in faith-based rhetoric, now a columnist for the *Washington Post* and *Newsweek*, joined his latest campaign. "I found Rove to be the most unusual political operative I have ever known; so exceptional he doesn't belong in the category," wrote Gerson on August 17 in the *Post*. "His most passionate, obsessive love—after his wife—is American history." Thus fervor equals omniscience equals omnipotence. Rove the secret Heathcliffe is also the second coming of Abraham Lincoln. Gerson's proof is located not only in Rove's ability to quote Lincoln on political technique and his unique collection of artifacts—"carefully archived pictures of President William McKinley's funeral, original ballots from the 1860 election"—but in Rove's "ideas." Neither the realities of Bush's policies nor Bush's current abysmal poll ratings, Gerson argues, reflect on them. "The complications of Iraq have obscured Rove's victories, not undone them," he writes. Contrary to Matthew 7:20, "Wherefore by their fruits ye shall know them," belief and acts do not meet in Gerson's doctrine. Through faith alone the spirit—and the Bush administration's reputation—shall be reborn.

As Gerson preached to pagan Washington on behalf of Rove's virtue, he found himself defending his own. Like Rove, he stood accused of grandiosity, dishonesty, and hypocrisy. But while gladiatorial combat in the arena is routine for Rove, for the evangelical Gerson, cast as a saint by a press corps guided by its penchant for stereotype—"deeply religious," according to the *Washington Post*; the "president's spiritual scribe," in the *Time*'s version—the assault came as a surprise.

Michael Gerson was credited with writing Bush's most memorable lines, his momentous speeches and inaugural addresses, infusing them not only with religious uplift but also with ideological intensity. The character of Gerson has served as earthly evidence of Bush's spiritual calling. In numerous journalistic accounts, Gerson was depicted as selfless and pure of heart. But the article about him appearing in the September issue of *The Atlantic*, written by Matthew Scully, a speechwriter who served with him, portrays Gerson less as St. Francis than Tartuffe, less Joan of Arc than Sammy Glick. "For all of our chief speechwriter's finer qualities, the firm adherence to factual narrative is not a strong point," writes Scully. "The artful shaping of narrative and editing out of inconvenient detail was never confined to the speechwriting. (The phrase *pulling a Gerson,* as I recently heard it used around the West Wing, does not refer to graceful writing.)"

Scully describes how Gerson carefully crafted his own image as Bush's voice and conscience, conveniently airbrushing the other speechwriters out of the picture. Scully recalls being at a crowded meeting on September 13, 2001, with Bush, at which the president declared, "We're at war." In the version appearing in the *Washington Post*, under the byline of Bob Woodward and two other reporters, "the rest of us have vanished, and the president declares, 'Mike, we're at war.'"

The White House tick-tock story (or detailed, minute-by-minute account), a favorite of the prestige newspapers, showing their superior access, is always fraught with manipulation. And the versions that appear are invariably a tale agreed upon by those selected or volunteering to tell the tale. Gerson was a master of the genre and the whole Washington press corps was his keyboard, but especially Bob Woodward.

"Woodward's trilogy about the Bush years is a tale of speechwriting glory that Mike himself could hardly improve upon," writes Scully. "Remember those powerful and moving addresses the president gave after September 11? According to Woodward's *State of Denial*, Mike wrote all of those speeches by himself . . . How do I break the news to Bob Woodward that his high-placed source wrote not a single one of the lines quoted above, at best a third of any of the speeches he mentions, and that the National Cathedral address was half-written before Mike even entered the room?"

Michael Gerson emerged as a perfect hothouse flower of the religious right and conservative infrastructure. After graduating from Westminster Christian Academy, he majored in theology at the evangelical Wheaton College, and was immediately recruited as a ghostwriter for Charles Colson, the Watergate dirty trickster and felon who had become a religious-right leader of the Prison Fellowship Ministries. Gerson has called Colson his mentor, an example of "tremendous personal integrity." Gerson was soon appointed a "senior policy advisor" at the Heritage Foundation, though expert in no particular policy, and served as a speech-writer for a succession of Republicans, from Senator Dan Coats of Indiana to Senator Bob Dole. After Gerson's brief stint at *U.S. News & World Report* Karl Rove signed him up for the presidential campaign of George W. Bush. From there, the rest is mythology.

"The narrative that Mike Gerson presented to the world is a story of extravagant falsehood," writes Scully. "He has been held up for us in six years' worth of coddling profiles as the great, inspiring, and idealistic exception of the Bush White House. In reality, Mike's conduct is just the most familiar and depressing of Washington stories—a history of self-seeking and media manipulation that is only more distasteful for being cast in such lofty terms. There are rewards for such behavior, and in Mike's case the Washington establishment has raised him up as one of its own—a status complete with a columnist's perch at *The Washington Post*."

Scully's memoir is unusual in the annals of Washington tell-alls. Typically, the disillusioned narrator wishes to distance himself from failure, assign blame to others, or expiate his guilt. Scully, however, desperately wants to claim his proper share of credit for the Bush catastrophe. While he accuses the devout Gerson of bad faith, he never quite recognizes why

Gerson's credit hogging has seemed so plausible. Whether or not Gerson wrote what he claimed to have written, the orotund, purple prose that is his style is completely consistent with Bush's high-flown rhetoric. Phrases like "axis of evil" mark Bush's language as a torrent of incoherence, arrogance, and fanaticism. But the stupidity of the ideas is no hindrance to the fight over pride of authorship. Taking credit for the disaster is better than anonymity, a Washington version of the Hollywood P.R. truism that there's no such thing as bad publicity.

The conflict between Matthew Scully and Michael Gerson is a clash between two cardinal sins: The bearer of envy meets the bearer of false witness. Scully is transparently envious of the rewards bestowed on Gerson by the Washington Post Corp.—both *Post* and *Newsweek* columns—suggesting a payoff to a source, an unreliable one at that. He neglects the complicating possibility of an ecumenical blessing bestowed on a suddenly socially acceptable right-wing evangelical—Colson ghostwriter ascendant as *Post* columnist—another bizarre twist in the twilight of the Bush period in Washington.

But Scully's sua culpa is the *Boys' Life* version of the Bush presidency. He can't get over his infatuation with Bush. The worst charge he levels against Gerson is that his self-promotion "diminishes" Bush's "achievement." In contrast, Scully presents himself as a paragon of good faith, the real true believer. "Six years later, with all that has gone wrong in Iraq, I know one is now supposed to sigh with regret at how mistaken we all were about Bush in those days, how foolish of us to think the man had greatness in him . . . And yet I think I recognize greatness when it steps before me, and the sight of George W. Bush in those days left an impression that has never worn off."

Still mesmerized by his heroic conception of Bush, Scully does not see in Michael Gerson a representative figure of Bush's presidency. In his inability to connect his words (whichever they were) to Bush's deeds, moreover, Scully is little different from Gerson or Rove—or Bush—promoting a legacy that ignores the realities of their history and instead takes a leap of faith into myth.

August 22, 2007

Fredo's End

When Alberto Gonzales swiftly turned heel on the stage at the Department of Justice without answering questions about his resignation as attorney general he left behind yet another lingering cloud of mystery. What is he not telling about his resignation?

The true story may be something like the denouement of Edgar Allan Poe's "The Purloined Letter," which was in plain sight all along, a solution that can, as Poe wrote, "escape observation by dint of being excessively obvious; and here the physical oversight is precisely analogous with the moral inapprehension by which the intellect suffers to pass unnoticed those considerations which are too obtrusively and too palpably self-evident." To be excessively obvious, Gonzales's resignation, following Karl Rove's exactly by two weeks, is the shadow of the first act.

Under investigation by the House and Senate Judiciary committees for his part in the political purge of U.S. attorneys and warrantless domestic surveillance, Gonzales wandered through his appearances down winding paths of dissembling. On the U.S. attorneys, his former deputies—his former chief of staff, Kyle Sampson, and former deputy attorney general, Paul McNulty—contradicted him. On domestic spying, the former acting attorney general, James Comey, described then White House counsel Gonzales's attempted coup on behalf of a program Comey considered illegal through Gonzales's securing the signature of the ailing Attorney General John Ashcroft, barely able to lift his head in his hospital bed after surgery. After Gonzales offered a different account, FBI Director Robert Mueller appeared before the Senate on July 27 to corroborate Comey's version, staking his position against Gonzales's credibility. Senators called for the appointment of a special prosecutor.

In the weeks leading up to his resignation, Gonzales was undoubtedly aware of the various investigations into his activities, the avenues being pursued, and the witnesses questioned, not all of them in public. As a practiced attorney, he knew that once he left government service he would become less interesting to investigators and that whatever revelations were unearthed would have less political impact. The logic of his resignation became indisputable from his own narrow interest and the larger interest of the administration. But the resignation of Rove severed his lifeline to his political control agent. Without Rove, Gonzales was adrift.

From the beginning of his rise with George W. Bush until the day of his abrupt resignation, Alberto Gonzales was anointed, directed, and protected by Karl Rove. At the Department of Justice, Gonzales served as Rove's figurehead. In the real line of authority, the attorney general, a constitutional officer, reported to the White House political aide. Bush did not nickname Gonzales "Fredo," after the weak brother in *The Godfather*, without reason.

As White House counsel and attorney general, Gonzales operated as the rubber stamp of the two great goals of the Bush presidency—the concentration of unaccountable power in the executive and the subordination of executive departments and agencies to partisan political imperatives. Vice President Cheney directed the project for the imperial presidency, while Rove took charge of the top-down politicization of the federal government. Gonzales dutifully signed memos abrogating the Geneva Conventions against torture, calling them "quaint," and approved the dismissal of U.S. attorneys for insufficient partisan zeal.

Rove ran the Department of Justice like a personal fiefdom as Gonzales reigned there as his vassal lord. The civil rights division was gutted, more than 60 percent of its professional staff forced out; and since 2001, not a single discrimination case was filed. The antitrust division became a favor bank. Rove granted dispensations to companies, including those seeking to override laws involving foreign purchases of U.S. assets with national security implications, a former government official involved in such a case told me.

Typical of the political interference was the 2005 federal racketeering case against big tobacco companies in which government witnesses were suddenly withdrawn, suggested penalties lessened and lawyers ordered to read a weak closing statement prepared for them. Sharon Y. Eubanks, the twenty-two-year veteran federal prosecutor in the case, revealed to the *Washington Post* in March 2007 that the chain of command ran directly through the attorney general's office. "The political people were pushing the buttons and ordering us to say what we said," Eubanks said. "And because of that, we failed to zealously represent the interests of the American public . . . Political interference is happening at Justice across the department. When decisions are made now in the Bush attorney general's office, politics is the primary consideration . . . The rule of law goes out the window."

Rove's interest in tobacco cases was hardly new. From 1991 through 1996, while guiding the ascent of Bush to the Texas governorship and during his early years in that office, Rove worked as a $3,000-a-month consultant to Philip Morris. In 1996, when Texas Attorney General Dan Morales filed a suit against tobacco companies seeking compensation for state Medicaid funds spent on workers who fell ill because of smoking, Rove conducted a dirty trick against him—a push poll spreading smears about him.

Rove vetted and approved every important appointment made by Governor Bush. Like Bush, Rove saw the political possibilities in having a prominent Hispanic as part of the entourage. The son of immigrants, from the town of Humble, Texas, no less, was perfect casting.

From 1982 to 1994, Gonzales worked as a partner at the Houston-based Vinson and Elkins law firm, which handled the legal affairs of Enron and Halliburton. Enron was the single biggest financial supporter of Bush's political career in Texas; and Cheney, of course, was the CEO of Halliburton, for which Gonzales performed legal services.

In 1994, for Bush's run for governor, Rove got tobacco firms, Enron, and Halliburton, among other interests, to siphon funds into various front groups on the issue of "tort reform." Through these funding sources, Rove also managed a flow of donations to candidates for the Texas Supreme Court, whom he handled as a consultant. (Rove was among the biggest owners of Enron stock among White House staffers, holding between $100,000 and $250,000. His influence with Enron extended to arranging a lucrative Enron consulting contract for Republican operative Ralph Reed, an old associate from College Republicans days, while Reed simultaneously worked on Bush's 2000 campaign.)

Upon Bush's election, Gonzales was named his legal counsel. In 1996, he successfully argued that Bush should not serve on a Travis County jury because of a potential conflict of interest given his powers of pardon and clemency. The real reason was that Bush did not want to disclose his past drunken-driving arrest, which would have threatened his political viability as he began planning his presidential campaign.

Having proved his loyalty, Gonzales was made Texas secretary of state and then appointed to the Texas Supreme Court. Rove guided him every step of the way. In 2000, Gonzales had to win election to his appointed judgeship. Even as he was running Bush's presidential effort, Rove handled Gonzales's campaign, just as he managed the campaigns of all Republican candidates for the state high court. Once again, Rove drew upon his deep sources of campaign funding. Enron and its law firm, Vinson and Elkins, were the principal financiers of Gonzales's race, kicking in $35,450.

Once elected president, Bush immediately named Gonzales his White House counsel. To the extent that Gonzales was pliable he was useful. But his "remarkable journey," as he called it today in his resignation statement, was remarkable only for his unwavering subservience.

From the start, Rove and Gonzales were secret sharers. But one was "the Architect" and the other was "Fredo." With Rove's resignation, Gonzales lost the political and policy hand that had guided him all along. When the puppet master departed, the puppet collapsed in a heap.

August 27, 2007

Top Secret

On September 18, 2002, CIA director George Tenet briefed President Bush in the Oval Office on top-secret intelligence that Saddam Hussein did not have weapons of mass destruction, according to two former senior CIA officers. Bush dismissed as worthless this information from the Iraqi foreign minister, a member of Saddam's inner circle, although it turned out to be accurate in every detail. Tenet never brought it up again.

Nor was the intelligence included in the National Intelligence Estimate of October 2002, which stated categorically that Iraq possessed WMD. No one in Congress was aware of the secret intelligence that Saddam had no WMD as the House of Representatives and the Senate voted, a week after the submission of the NIE, on the Authorization for Use of Military Force in Iraq. The information, moreover, was not circulated within the CIA among those agents involved in operations to prove whether Saddam had WMD.

On April 23, 2006, CBS's *60 Minutes* interviewed Tyler Drumheller, the former CIA chief of clandestine operations for Europe, who disclosed that the agency had received documentary intelligence from Naji Sabri, Saddam's foreign minister, that Saddam did not have WMD. "We continued to validate him the whole way through," said Drumheller. "The policy was set. The war in Iraq was coming, and they were looking for intelligence to fit into the policy, to justify the policy."

Now two former senior CIA officers have confirmed Drumheller's account to me and provided the background to the story of how the information that might have stopped the invasion of Iraq was twisted in order to justify it. They described what Tenet said to Bush about the lack of WMD, and how Bush responded, and noted that Tenet never shared Sabri's intelligence with then Secretary of State Colin Powell. According to the former officers, the intelligence was also never shared with the senior military planning the invasion, which required U.S. soldiers to receive medical shots against the ill effects of WMD and to wear protective uniforms in the desert.

Instead, said the former officials, the information was distorted in a report written to fit the preconception that Saddam did have WMD programs. That false and restructured report was passed to Richard Dearlove, chief of the British Secret Intelligence Service (MI6), who briefed Prime Minister Tony Blair on it as validation of the cause for war.

Secretary of State Powell, in preparation for his presentation of evidence of Saddam's WMD to the United Nations Security Council on February 5, 2003, spent days at CIA headquarters in Langley, Virginia, and had Tenet sit directly behind him as a sign of credibility. But Tenet, according to the sources, never told Powell about existing intelligence that there were no WMD, and Powell's speech was later revealed to be a series of falsehoods.

Both the French intelligence service and the CIA paid Sabri hundreds of thousands of dollars (at least $200,000 in the case of the CIA) to give them documents on Saddam's WMD programs. "The information detailed that Saddam may have wished to have a program, that his engineers had told him they could build a nuclear weapon within two years if they had fissile material, which they didn't, and that they had no chemical or biological weapons," one of the former CIA officers told me.

On the eve of Sabri's appearance at the United Nations in September 2002 to present Saddam's case, the officer in charge of this operation met in New York with a "cutout" who had debriefed Sabri for the CIA. Then the officer flew to Washington, where he met with CIA deputy director John McLaughlin, who was "excited" about the report. Nonetheless, McLaughlin expressed his reservations. He said that Sabri's information was at odds with "our best source." That source was code-named "Curve Ball," later exposed as a fabricator, con man, and former Iraqi taxi driver posing as a chemical engineer.

The next day, September 18, Tenet briefed Bush on Sabri. "Tenet told me he briefed the president personally," said one of the former CIA officers. According to Tenet, Bush's response was to call the information "the same old thing." Bush insisted it was simply what Saddam wanted him to think. "The president had no interest in the intelligence," said the CIA officer. The other officer said, "Bush didn't give a fuck about the intelligence. He had his mind made up."

But the CIA officers working on the Sabri case kept collecting information. "We checked on everything he told us." French intelligence eavesdropped on his telephone conversations and shared them with the CIA. These taps "validated" Sabri's claims, according to one of the CIA officers. The officers brought this material to the attention of the newly formed Iraqi Operations Group within the CIA. But those in charge of the IOG were on a mission to prove that Saddam did have WMD and would not give credit to anything that came from the French. "They kept saying the French were trying to undermine the war," said one of the CIA officers.

The officers continued to insist on the significance of Sabri's information, but one of Tenet's deputies told them, "You haven't figured this out yet. This isn't about intelligence. It's about regime change."

The CIA officers on the case awaited the report they had submitted on Sabri to be circulated back to them, but they never received it. They learned later that a new report had been written. "It was written by someone in the agency, but unclear who or where, it was so tightly controlled. They knew what would please the White House. They knew what the king wanted," one of the officers told me.

That report contained a false preamble stating that Saddam was "aggressively and covertly developing" nuclear weapons and that he already possessed chemical and biological weapons. "Totally out of whack," said one of the CIA officers. "The first paragraph of an intelligence report is the most important and most read and colors the rest of the report." He pointed out that the case officer who wrote the initial report had not written the preamble and the new memo. "That's not what the original memo said."

The report with the misleading introduction was given to Dearlove of MI6, who briefed the prime minister. "They were given a scaled-down version of the report," said one of the CIA officers. "It was a summary given for liaison, with the sourcing taken out. They showed the British the statement Saddam was pursuing an aggressive program, and rewrote the report to attempt to support that statement. It was insidious. Blair bought it." "Blair was duped," said the other CIA officer. "He was shown the altered report."

The information provided by Sabri was considered so sensitive that it was never shown to those who assembled the NIE on Iraqi WMD. Later revealed to be utterly wrong, the NIE read: "We judge that Iraq has continued its weapons of mass destruction (WMD) programs in defiance of UN resolutions and restrictions. Baghdad has chemical and biological weapons as well as missiles with ranges in excess of UN restrictions; if left unchecked, it probably will have a nuclear weapon during this decade."

In the congressional debate over the Authorization for the Use of Military Force, even those voting against it gave credence to the notion that Saddam possessed WMD. Even a leading opponent such as Senator Bob Graham, then the Democratic chairman of the Senate Intelligence Committee, who had instigated the production of the NIE, declared in his floor speech on October 12, 2002, "Saddam Hussein's regime has chemical and biological weapons and is trying to get nuclear capacity." Not a single senator contested otherwise. None of them had an inkling of the Sabri intelligence.

The CIA officers assigned to Sabri still argued within the agency that his information must be taken seriously, but instead the administration preferred to rely on Curve Ball. Drumheller learned from the German intelligence service that held Curve Ball that it considered him and his claims about WMD to be highly unreliable. But the CIA's Weapons Intelligence, Nonproliferation, and Arms Control Center (WINPAC) insisted that Curve Ball was credible because what he said was supposedly congruent with available public information.

For two months, Drumheller fought against the use of Curve Ball, raising the red flag that he was likely a fraud, as he turned out to be. "Oh, my!

I hope that's not true," said Deputy Director McLaughlin, according to Drumheller's book *On the Brink*, published in 2006. When Curve Ball's information was put into Bush's January 28, 2003, State of the Union address, McLaughlin and Tenet allowed it to pass into the speech. "From three Iraqi defectors," Bush declared, "we know that Iraq, in the late 1990s, had several mobile biological weapons labs . . . Saddam Hussein has not disclosed these facilities. He's given no evidence that he has destroyed them." In fact, there was only one Iraqi source—Curve Ball—and there were no labs.

When the mobile weapons labs were inserted into the draft of Powell's United Nations speech, Drumheller strongly objected again and believed that the error had been removed. He was shocked watching Powell's speech. "We have firsthand descriptions of biological weapons factories on wheels and on rails," Powell announced. Without the reference to the mobile weapons labs, there was no image of a threat.

Colonel Lawrence Wilkerson, Powell's chief of staff, and Powell himself later lamented that they had not been warned about Curve Ball. And McLaughlin told the *Washington Post* in 2006, "If someone had made these doubts clear to me, I would not have permitted the reporting to be used in Secretary Powell's speech." But, in fact, Drumheller's caution was ignored.

As war appeared imminent, the CIA officers on the Sabri case tried to arrange his defection in order to demonstrate that he stood by his information. But he would not leave without bringing out his entire family. "He dithered," said one former CIA officer. And the war came before his escape could be handled.

Tellingly, Sabri's picture was never put on the deck of playing cards of former Saddam officials to be hunted down, a tacit acknowledgment of his covert relationship with the CIA. Today, Sabri lives in Qatar.

In 2005, the Silberman-Robb commission investigating intelligence in the Iraq war failed to interview the case officer directly involved with Sabri; instead its report blamed the entire WMD fiasco on "groupthink" at the CIA. "They didn't want to trace this back to the White House," said the officer.

On February 5, 2004, Tenet delivered a speech at Georgetown University that alluded to Sabri and defended his position on the existence of WMD, which, even then, he contended would still be found. "Several sensitive reports crossed my desk from two sources characterized by our foreign partners as established and reliable," he said. "The first from a

source who had direct access to Saddam and his inner circle"—Naji Sabri—
"said Iraq was not in the possession of a nuclear weapon. However, Iraq was
aggressively and covertly developing such a weapon."

Then Tenet claimed with assurance, "The same source said that Iraq was
stockpiling chemical weapons." He explained that this intelligence had
been central to his belief in the reason for war. "As this information and
other sensitive information came across my desk, it solidified and reinforced the judgments that we had reached in my own view of the danger
posed by Saddam Hussein and I conveyed this view to our nation's leaders."
(Tenet doesn't mention Sabri in his recently published memoir, *At the
Center of the Storm*.)

But where were the WMD? "Now, I'm sure you're all asking, 'Why
haven't we found the weapons?' I've told you the search must continue and
it will be difficult."

On September 8, 2006, three Republican senators on the Senate Select
Committee on Intelligence—Orrin Hatch, Saxby Chambliss, and Pat
Roberts—signed a letter attempting to counter Drumheller's revelation
about Sabri on *60 Minutes*: "All of the information about this case so far
indicates that the information from this source was that Iraq did have
WMD programs." The Republicans also quoted Tenet, who had testified
before the committee in July 2006 that Drumheller had "mischaracterized"
the intelligence. Still, Drumheller stuck to his guns, telling Reuters, "We
have differing interpretations, and I think mine's right."

One of the former senior CIA officers told me that despite the certitude
of the three Republican senators, the Senate committee never had the original memo on Sabri. "The committee never got that report," he said. "The
material was hidden or lost, and because it was a restricted case, a lot of it
was done in hard copy. The whole thing was fogged up, like Curve Ball."

While one Iraqi source told the CIA that there were no WMD, information that was true but distorted to prove the opposite, another Iraqi source
was a fabricator whose lies were eagerly embraced. "The real tragedy is that
they had a good source that they misused," said one of the former CIA officers. "The fact is there was nothing there, no threat. But Bush wanted to
hear what he wanted to hear."

September 6, 2007

The General Testifies

Two years ago the Sunni sheiks leading the insurgency in Iraq's Anbar province approached the United States, offering to end the violence in exchange for a timetable establishing that U.S. forces would withdraw from the country, a senior official at the highest level of the British government told me. Without some sort of negotiated deal that the Sunni leaders could brandish, they explained, they would not have the essential political justification for quelling the conflict. The British believed that the Sunni offer was being made in good faith and urged that it be accepted.

But according to the senior British source, President Bush rejected it out of hand, still certain that he could achieve a military victory. He saw any agreement with the Sunnis as tantamount to defeat, the British official said. And yet, even as the Sunnis were rebuffed, Bush continued to invest trust in the Shi'a-dominated Iraqi government to forge a political conciliation.

On September 13, 2007, in a nationally televised address from the Oval Office, billed officially as "The Return on Success," President Bush announced the withdrawal of 5,700 troops by Christmas and an additional 21,700 by July 2008, leaving the U.S. force at the level it was before the "surge," through the presidential-election year, proving "sustainable security," according to Bush. As General David Petraeus did in his congressional testimony, Bush pointed to the turning of Sunni tribes against Al-Qaeda in Iraq in Anbar province as the key evidence of the surge's triumph, "a good example of how our strategy is working." But he did not discuss how he discarded the earlier Sunni offer to negotiate and dismissed the advice of the British government as he pursued the chimera of "victory."

He also carefully neglected to observe that the Sunni action against Al-Qaeda in Iraq began independently before the surge, that it was never foreseen as part of the surge, that the Sunnis politically are more estranged than ever from the Shi'a-run government of Nouri al-Maliki, or that the U.S. arming of the Sunnis may be a perverse preparation for the next phase of the Iraqi sectarian civil war in the likely absence of political power-sharing. Yet the assassination of the Sunni sheikh Abdul Sattar Abu Risha on the day of Bush's speech compelled him to acknowledge it: "Earlier today, one of the brave tribal sheikhs who helped lead the revolt against Al-Qaeda was murdered."

Bush's progress report, moreover, contradicted other realities. He claimed, "Iraq's national leaders are getting some things done," such as "sharing oil revenues with the provinces," and allowing "former Ba'athists to rejoin Iraq's military or receive government pensions." But these assertions were wishful thinking; neither of these events has happened. In fact, the deal on sharing oil revenue had collapsed that week. Bush went on to praise "the thirty-six nations who have troops on the ground in Iraq," despite the State Department's most recent weekly report on Iraq observing that the remnant of the "coalition of the willing" consists of twenty-five countries supplying 11,685 troops—about a 7 percent augmentation of the U.S. forces. Bush also simply glided over the contradiction between his withdrawal of these 30,000 troops and his doomsday scenarios that withdrawing U.S. forces will presage genocide on the scale of Cambodia.

The appearance of General Petraeus was staged to coincide with the sixth anniversary of the terrorist attacks of September 11, 2001. Yet the emotional impact of the memorials has been overshadowed by the fresh casualty lists from Iraq. The day before this September 11, two U.S. soldiers from the 82nd Airborne, who had joined five others in writing an op-ed article for *The New York Times* saying that the surge was not working, were killed in action. Yet Bush still sought to wring political gain out of the tragic memories of 9/11 as though his paradise lost—the national unity after 9/11—could be regained.

Artillery barrages of TV commercials seeking to soften public opinion preceded Petraeus's report. A new front group, Freedom's Watch, created at the instigation of the White House, funded by Bush's political financiers (including prominent members of the Scooter Libby defence fund) and directed by Dan Senor (former press secretary for the catastrophic Coalition Provisional Authority), launched a series of ads that were a pastiche of past Republican themes. Children in small-town America were depicted raising a flag, a scene plagiarised from Ronald Reagan's 1984 "Morning Again in America" commercial. Then fragments of Bush's 2004 campaign washed up like messages in bottles. Soldiers who had lost limbs in Iraq segued into pictures of the burning World Trade Center as words appeared on the screen: "They attacked us." A soldier said, "We're winning on the ground in Iraq. It's no time to quit." A bereaved woman whose uncle died as a fireman in the twin towers and whose husband was killed in Iraq spoke as words flashed on the screen: "More attacks." "Surrender is not an option." In another ad, a marine in a wheelchair said, "To hear Congress talk about surrendering really makes me angry." After these poisons were injected into the atmosphere, Petraeus emerged from behind the curtain as the sober voice of reason.

Seated side by side, Petraeus and U.S. ambassador to Iraq Ryan Crocker presented less a united front than the antipodes of Bush's strategy. Both men were great stone faces, droning and dull, their lack of affect serving as masks for their onerous tasks. Instead of complementing each other, the men's testimonies made plain the surge's strategic incoherence. Deploying the classic euphemisms and misdirections of diplomacy, Crocker demolished, intentionally or not, whatever Petraeus sought to achieve with his dazzling display of dubious statistics. Then, in response to a single pointed question, Petraeus conceded the emptiness of his performance. He aimed friendly-fire at himself.

"War is the extension of politics by other means," wrote the great military strategist Carl von Clausewitz. As a military operation the surge was intended to produce political power sharing and reconciliation. But Crocker disclosed that the military had not achieved these ends. Not only are the political benchmarks that the Iraqi government and the Bush administration established unmet, but they may never be realized. Crocker could attach no period of time to these goals. He could only suggest that there should be no benchmarks. "Some of the more promising political developments at the national level," Crocker said, "are neither measured in benchmarks nor visible to those far from Baghdad." In other words, the evidence is anecdotal, scattered, and uncertain. Asked when political reconciliation might occur, he replied, "I could not put a timeline on it or a target date . . . How long that is going to take and, frankly, even ultimately whether it will succeed, I can't predict." Crocker's version of Bush's policy was *Waiting for Godot*.

Petraeus, meanwhile, meticulously unveiled an array of metrics attempting to demonstrate that the surge had succeeded in lowering the level of sectarian violence and civilian casualties. But his effort to gain empirical ground was greeted with widespread skepticism because his statistics were in dispute. The National Intelligence Estimate released on August 23 stated: "The level of overall violence, including attacks on and casualties among civilians, remains high." The Government Accountability Office (GAO) report of September 4 stated that the aim of "reducing the level of sectarian violence in Iraq and eliminating militia control of local security" was "not met," and that "there was no clear and reliable evidence that the level of sectarian violence was reduced and that militia control of local security was eliminated."

GAO comptroller general David Walker testified before the Senate Foreign Relations Committee that "there are several different sources within the administration on violence, and those sources do not agree" and that "part of the problem that we had in reaching a conclusion about sectarian violence is there are multiple sources showing different levels of violence with different trends." And the Independent Commission on the Security Forces of Iraq, chaired by retired General James L. Jones and created by Congress, reported: "The Iraqi Police Service is incapable today of providing security at a level sufficient to protect Iraqi neighborhoods from insurgents and sectarian violence."

Petraeus's presentation relied on the power of PowerPoint, but it was less than overwhelming. He had to plead that his statistics were valid even as he refused to reveal his full methodology. As it was, the strangeness of his categories—a bullet to the back of the head entitled the victim to be registered as a civilian casualty, but a bullet to the front of the head did not, putting the victim into an insurgent casualty category—suggested arbitrary classification, political willfulness, and subjectivity.

In any case, Crocker's description of the Iraqi political void made Petraeus's claim of progress appear absurd. Petraeus was left dangling, flourishing numbers about tactics unrelated to the strategy. The ambassador consigned the general to a Clausewitzian twilight zone.

The highly credentialed and qualified Petraeus has a doctorate from Princeton and has written a recent report on the history of counterinsurgency. But he has apparently not studied the case of Colin Powell, whose sterling reputation and military expertise were appropriated by Bush for political purposes and who, after his utility was exhausted, was abandoned on the side of the road. The real frontline where Petraeus found himself was more political than military.

If the surge has no connection to political goals in Iraq, it still has strategic political goals, just not in Iraq. The surge is the military means to Bush's political ends at home. "So now I'm an October-November man," Bush told his authorized biographer, Robert Draper, in *Dead Certain*. "I'm playing for October-November." The rollout of the Petraeus report is the last major political offensive of the Bush administration. Petraeus's reputation is the token for buying precious time for an unpopular president. The Democratic Congress lacks sufficient majorities to alter Bush's policy. Petraeus's show is staged to keep Republicans, on the edge of sheer panic, from defecting en masse.

Through Petraeus, Bush is locking in the congressional leaders and the Republican presidential candidates behind his policy. The general has been wound up as a mechanism for Bush's endgame—perpetuating the president's Iraq policy until the conclusion of his term and assigning responsibility for "victory" or "defeat" to his successor. In his address, Bush made explicit his goal to hand off the Iraq war to the next president, describing it as an "engagement that extends beyond my presidency." In his analogizing to the Vietnam war, Bush has begun to lay the basis for a stab-in-the-back, who-lost-Iraq debate, a poisonous legacy.

Senator John Warner, the Virginia Republican who announced his retirement on August 31 and who has called for disengaging from Iraq, asked Petraeus a simple and obvious question about Bush's policy, one that Bush likes to answer: "Do you feel that that [strategy] is making America safer?" Unexpectedly, Petraeus paused. "I believe this is indeed the best course of action to achieve our objectives in Iraq," he finally replied, carefully sidestepping a direct response. So Warner repeated his question: "Does the [Iraq war] make America safer?" Again Petraeus paused before answering, "I don't know, actually. I have not sat down and sorted it out in my own mind."

In the end, Petraeus could not convince even himself. Petraeus has lost his battle. Crocker has revealed the strategy as hollow. But the policy goes on.

September 17, 2007

Sidney Blumenthal

The Many Victories
of George W. Bush

There has never been a moment when we were not winning in Iraq. Victory has followed victory, from "Mission Accomplished" to the purple fingers of the Iraqi election to, most recently, President Bush's meeting at Camp Cupcake in Anbar province with Abdul-Sattar Abu Risha, the Sunni leader of the group Anbar Awakening (who was assassinated a week later). Turning point has followed turning point, from Bush's proclamation two years ago of his "National Strategy for Victory in Iraq" to his announcement last week of his "Return on Success." "We're kicking ass," he briefed the Australian deputy prime minister on September 6 about his latest visit to Iraq. In his quasi-farewell address to the nation on September 13, Bush assigned any possible shortcomings to General David Petraeus and bequeathed his policy "beyond my presidency" to his successor.

After Bush pretended to deliberate over whether he would agree to his own policy as presented by his general in well-rehearsed performances before Congress—"President Bush Accepts Recommendations" read a headline on the White House Web site—he established an ideal division of responsibility. Bush could claim credit for the "Return on Success," whenever that might be, while Petraeus would be charged with whatever might go wrong.

One week after Petraeus flashed his metrics, a whole new set of facts on the ground suddenly emerged: an admission (previously denied) by Petraeus that the United States was arming the Sunnis, who might use those weapons in the next phase of Iraq's civil war; the release of a Pentagon report that there is "an increase in intra-Shi'a violence through-out the South" (a report conveniently withheld as Petraeus was testifying); the Iraqi government's expulsion of Blackwater, a private security firm with close ties to the administration, after a band of its guards gunned down Iraqi civilians; the restriction of all nonmilitary U.S. personnel in Iraq to the Green Zone; a report by the Iraqi Red Crescent that about 1 million people are internal refugees as a result of ethnic cleansing (apart from the

315

more than 2 million refugees who have fled the country); and the announcement by the House Committee on Oversight and Government Reform of an investigation into the State Department's inspector general for quashing scrutiny and embarrassing studies of fraud in the construction of the U.S. Embassy in Baghdad, among other projects.

As these events played out, Petraeus was detailed as Bush's Willy Loman to preside over the cooling of the special relationship with America's most important ally in the coalition of the willing. The general traveled to London to meet with Prime Minister Gordon Brown on the policy from which he is rapidly disengaging, already having withdrawn British forces in Basra to its airport before final evacuation. Such is the face of victory ten days after Petraeus's march through Capitol Hill.

In his semiretirement, Bush engaged in appeals to history, which he now says on nearly every occasion will absolve him. Early on and riding high, he expressed contempt for history. "History, we'll all be dead," he sneered to Bob Woodward in an interview for *Bush at War*, a panegyric to Bush the triumphant after the Afghanistan invasion and before Iraq. Now Bush cites history as justification for everything he does. "You can't possibly figure out the history of the Bush presidency—until I'm dead," he told Robert Draper, his authorized biographer, in an interview for *Dead Certain*. The use of the words "history" and "dead" between the Woodward and Draper interviews makes for a world of difference—the difference between a president who couldn't care less and one who cares desperately but can't admit it.

Bush incessantly invokes a host of presidents past—Truman, Lincoln, and Washington—as appropriate comparisons, and also talks of Winston Churchill. Frederick Kagan, the neoconservative instigator of "the surge," refers to it as "Gettysburg," a leap of historical imagination that transforms Bush into the Great Emancipator. In his unstoppable commentary about himself, Bush has become as certain of his exalted place in history as he is of his policy's rightness. He projects his image into the future, willing his enshrinement as a great president. History has become a magical incantation for him, a kind of prayerful refuge where he is safe from having to think in the present. For Bush, history is supernatural, a deus ex machina, nothing less than a kind of divine intervention enabling him to enter presidential Valhalla. Through his fantasy about history as afterlife—the stairway to paradise—he rationalizes his current course.

Draper's biography has the feel of a lengthy feature magazine article wrapped in a dust jacket. It lacks any serious discussion of the influence of Dick Cheney, the rise of the neoconservatives, Karl Rove's attempt to create a one-party state, the government's torture policy, splits within the senior military, the scapegoating of the CIA, or the evisceration of federal departments and agencies. Nonetheless, Draper's unusual access enabled him to collect valuable anecdotes as well as to put a microphone in front of a president who, when interrupted by an aide, told him not to worry because the interview was "worthless." Letting down his guard, Bush does not understand what he reveals.

In his interviews with Draper, he is constantly worried about weakness and passivity. "If you're weak internally? This job will run you all over town." He fears being controlled and talks about it relentlessly, feeling he's being watched. "And part of being a leader is: people watch you." He casts his anxiety as a matter of self-discipline. "I don't think I'd be sitting here if not for the discipline . . . And they look at me—they want to know whether I've got the resolution necessary to see this through. And I do. I believe—I know we'll succeed." He is sensitive about asserting his supremacy over others, but especially his father. "He knows as an ex-president, he doesn't have nearly the amount of knowledge I've got on current things," he told Draper.

Bush is a classic insecure authoritarian who imposes humiliating tests of obedience on others in order to prove his superiority and their inferiority. In 1999, according to Draper, at a meeting of economic experts at the Texas governor's mansion, Bush interrupted Rove when he joined in the discussion, saying, "Karl, hang up my jacket." In front of other aides, Bush joked repeatedly that he would fire Rove. (Laura Bush's attitude toward Rove was pointedly disdainful. She nicknamed him "Pigpen," for wallowing in dirty politics. He was staff, not family—certainly not people like them.)

Bush's deployed his fetish for punctuality as a punitive weapon. When Colin Powell was several minutes late to a Cabinet meeting, Bush ordered that the door to the Cabinet Room be locked. Aides have been fearful of raising problems with him. In his 2004 debates with Senator John Kerry, no one felt comfortable or confident enough to discuss with Bush the importance of his personal demeanor. Doing poorly in his first debate, he turned his anger on his communications director, Dan Bartlett, for showing him a tape afterward.

When his trusted old public relations handler, Karen Hughes, tried gently to tell him, "You looked mad," he shot back, "I wasn't mad! Tell them that!"

At a political strategy meeting in May 2004, when Matthew Dowd and Rove explained to him that he was not likely to win in a Reagan-like landslide, as Bush had imagined, he lashed out at Rove: "KARL!" Rove, according to Draper, was Bush's "favorite punching bag," and the president often threw futile and meaningless questions at him, and shouted, "You don't know what the hell you're talking about."

Those around him have learned how to manipulate him through the art of flattery. Former Secretary of Defense Donald Rumsfeld played Bush like a Stradivarius, exploiting his grandiosity. "Rumsfeld would later tell his lieutenants that if you wanted the president's support for an initiative, it was always best to frame it as a 'Big New Thing.'" Other aides played on Bush's self-conception as "the Decider." "To sell him on an idea," writes Draper, "aides were now learning, the best approach was to tell the president, This is going to be a really tough decision." But flattery always requires deference. Every morning, Josh Bolten, the chief of staff, greets Bush with the same words: "Thank you for the privilege of serving today."

Draper reports a telling exchange between Bush and James Baker, one of his father's closest associates, the elder Bush's former secretary of state and the one the family called on to take command of the campaign for the 2000 Florida contest when everything hung in the balance. Baker's ruthless field marshaling safely brought the younger Bush into the White House. Counseling him in the aftermath, Baker warned him about Rumsfeld. "All I'm going to say to you is, you know what he did to your daddy," he said.

Indeed, Rumsfeld and the elder Bush were bitter rivals. Rumsfeld had scorn for him, and tried to sideline and eliminate him during the Ford administration because he wanted to become president himself. If George W. Bush didn't know about it before, he knew about it then from Baker, and soon thereafter he appointed Rumsfeld secretary of defense. Draper does not reflect on this revelation, but it is highly suggestive.

Quoted in an August 9 article in *The New York Times* on the lachrymose father, Andrew Card, aide to both men, lately as White House chief of staff, and a family loyalist, spoke out of school. "It was relatively easy for me to read the sitting president's body language after he had talked to his mother or father," Card said. "Sometimes he'd ask me a probing question. And I'd think, Hmm, I don't think that question came from him."

The elder Bush assumed that the Bush family trust and its trustees—James Baker, Brent Scowcroft, and Prince Bandar—would take the erstwhile wastrel and guide him on the path of wisdom. In this conception, the country was not entrusted to the younger Bush's care so much as Bush was entrusted to the care of the trustees. He was the beneficiary of the trust. But to the surprise of those trustees, he slipped the bonds of the trust and cut off the family trustees. They knew he was ill-prepared and ignorant, but they never expected him to be assertive. They wrongly assumed that Cheney would act for them as a trustee.

Cheney had worked with and for them for decades and seemed to agree with them, if not on every detail then on the more important matter of attitude, particularly the question of who should govern. The elder Bush had helped arrange for Cheney to become the CEO of Halliburton, making him a very rich man at last. But Bush, Baker, Scowcroft, et al. didn't realize that Cheney's apparent concurrence was to advance himself and his views, which were not theirs. When absolute power was conferred on him, the habits of deference lapsed, no longer necessary. ("Thank you for the privilege of serving today.") Cheney was always more Rumsfeld oriented than Bush oriented. The elder Bush knew that Rumsfeld despised him and that Cheney was close to Rumsfeld, just as he knew his son's grievous limitations. But the obvious didn't occur to him—that Cheney would seize control of the lax son for his own purposes. The elder Bush committed a monumental error, empowering a regent to the prince who would betray the father. The myopia of the old WASP aristocracy allowed him to see Cheney as a member of his club. Cheney, for his part, was extremely convincing in playing possum. The elder Bush has many reasons for self-reproach, but perhaps none greater than being outsmarted by a courtier he thought was his trustee.

Through his interposition of Petraeus, Bush has bound his party to his fate. Of the Republicans, only Newt Gingrich, former speaker of the House, leader of the 1994 self-styled radical "revolution" that captured Congress, is willing to speak publicly about the danger Bush poses to the future of the party. "I believe for any Republican to win in 2008, they have to have a clean break and offer a dramatic, bold change," he told a group of reporters on September 14. "If we nominate somebody who has not done that . . . they're very, very unlikely to win it."

But repudiating Bush would also mean repudiating Gingrich's legacy, too. Draper reports that Bush loves claiming Ronald Reagan, not his father, as his role model. But Gingrich, more than Reagan, is Bush's forerunner. It was Gingrich who heightened the politics of polarization to a level of personal attack and unscrupulousness unlike any seen since the underside of Richard Nixon's operations was exposed in the Watergate scandal. Reagan was free of such dishonest and vicious politics. Bush, Cheney, and Rove ("Pigpen") picked up where Gingrich left off. Republicans can no more return to the halcyon days of Reagan than magic carpets can be used in Iraq. For the Republicans to recover, they would have to extirpate their entire recent history, root and branch.

"History would acquit him, too. Bush was confident of that, and of something else as well," writes Draper. "Though it was not the sort of thing one could say publicly anymore, the president still believed that Saddam had possessed weapons of mass destruction. He repeated this conviction to Andy Card all the way up until Card's departure in April 2006, almost exactly three years after the Coalition had begun its fruitless search for WMDs."

Bush grasps at the straws of his own disinformation as he casts himself deeper into the abyss. The more profound and compounded his blunders, and the more he redoubles his certainty in ultimate victory, the greater his indifference to failure. He has entered a phase of decadent perversity, where he accelerates his errors to vindicate his folly. As the sands of time run down, he has decided that no matter what he does, history will finally judge him as heroic.

The greater the chaos, the more he reinforces and rigidifies his views. The more havoc he wreaks, the more he insists he is succeeding. His intensified struggle for self-control is matched by his increased denial of responsibility. Hence Petraeus.

Bush's unyielding personality would have been best suited to the endless trench warfare of World War I, as a true compatriot of the disastrous British General Douglas Haig. His mind is geared toward a static battlefield. For low-intensity warfare, such as in Iraq, "an authoritarian cast of mind would be a crippling disability," wrote British expert Norman F. Dixon in his classic work, *On the Psychology of Military Incompetence.* "For such 'warfare,' tact, flexibility, imagination and 'open minds,' the very antithesis of authoritarian traits, would seem to be necessary if not sufficient."

Bush's ever-inflating self-confidence hides his gaping fear of failure. His obsession with deference demands exercises of humiliation that never satisfy him. His unwavering resolve is maintained by his adamant refusal to wade into the waters of ambiguity. "You can't talk me out of thinking freedom's a good thing!" he protests to his biographer. For Bush, even when he is long out of office, presiding at his planned library's Freedom Institute—"I would like to build a Hoover Institute"—victory will always be just around the corner.

September 20, 2007

A Republic, If You Can Keep It

Under crisis conditions of an extraordinary magnitude political leadership of the highest level will be required in the next presidency. The damage is broad, deep and spreading, apparent not only in international disorder and violence, the unprecedented decline of U.S. prestige, and the flouting of our security and economic interests but also in the hollowing out of the federal government's departments and agencies, and their growing incapacity to fulfill their functions, from FEMA to the Department of Justice.

The more rigid the current president is in responding to the chaos he has fostered, the more the Republicans still supporting him rally around him as a pillar of strength. His flat learning curve, refusal to admit error and redoubling of mistakes are regarded as tests of his strong character. Whatever his low poll ratings of the moment, his stubborn adherence to failure is admired as evidence of his potency.

The patently perverse notion that weakness is strength is the basis of Bush's remaining credibility within his party. His abuse of presidential power is seen as his great asset rather than understood as his enduring weakness. But when the president assumes all the responsibility, he also receives all the blame, which becomes unitary and unilateral. Supreme Court Justice Robert Jackson stated the constitutional principle in the 1952

Youngstown Steel case: "When the President takes measures incompatible with the expressed or implied will of Congress, his power is at its lowest ebb. Presidential claim to a power at once so conclusive and preclusive must be scrutinized with caution, for what is at stake is the equilibrium established by our constitutional system."

In his waning year, Bush is pointedly indifferent to the predictable consequences of his collapse. According to those who have met with him recently, he envisions himself as a noble idealist having made moral decisions that will vindicate him generations from now.

Despite the obvious shortcomings of his policies, he has startlingly succeeded in reshaping the executive into an unaccountable imperial presidency. And Bush's presidency is now accepted as the only acceptable version for major Republican candidates who aspire to succeed him. All of them have pledged to extend its arbitrary powers. Their embrace of the imperial presidency makes the 2008 election a turning point in constitutional government.

This campaign pits two parties running on diametrically opposite ideas of the presidency and the Constitution. There has not been such a sharp divergence on the foundation of the federal system since perhaps the election of 1860.

Two models of the presidency are at odds, one whose founding father was George Washington, the other whose founding father was Richard Nixon. Under the aegis of Dick Cheney, who considered the scandal in Watergate to be a political trick to topple Nixon, the original vision has been entrenched and extended. Cheney is the pluperfect staff man, beginning as Donald Rumsfeld's assistant in the Nixon White House, and was aptly code-named "Backseat" by the Secret Service when he pulled the strings in the Ford White House as chief of staff. For Cheney and the president under his tutelage, eagerly acting as "The Decider" on decision memos carefully packaged by "Backseat," the Constitution is a defective instrument remedied by unlimited executive power.

Like Nixon, Bush and Cheney act on the idea that the more they operate outside the constitutional system, the stronger they are. But, unlike Nixon, they are willfully contemptuous of facts and evidence, believing that unfettered power gives them the authority to create or impose their own. Bush and Cheney have refined and simplified Nixon's concept, purging it of his realism and flexibility. There will be no opening to Iran as there was an opening to China. In Bush's imperial presidency, neoconservatism meets Nixonianism, the ideology providing the high concept of low politics.

In ways that Nixon did not achieve, Bush has reduced the entire presidency and its functions to the commander in chief in wartime. And in order to sustain this role he has projected a never-ending war against a distant, faceless foe, ubiquitous and lethal. Fear and panic became the chief motifs substituting for democratic persuasion to engineer the consent of the governed, as Jack Goldsmith, Bush's former director of the Office of Legal Counsel in the Justice Department, explains in *The Terror Presidency*. He writes, "Why did the administration so often assert presidential power in ways that seemed unnecessary and politically self-defeating? The answer, I believe, is that the administration's conception of presidential power had a kind of theological significance that often trumped political consequences."

The imperial president must by definition be an infallible leader. Only he can determine what is a mistake because he is infallible. Stephen Bradbury, the acting director of OLC in the Justice Department who wrote secret memos justifying the torture policy in 2005, defined this Bush doctrine in congressional testimony in 2006: "The president is always right." Placing his statement in context, Bradbury explained that he was referring to "the war paradigm," the neoconservative idea of the Bush presidency, "the law of war," wherein the president is a law unto himself. This notion seems medieval, but it is central to the new radical Republican notion of the presidency. When Bradbury uttered his extraordinary remark, he did not think he was saying anything unusual. His statement, after all, was only a corollary of Nixon's infamous one made in his post-resignation interview with David Frost, "When the president does it, that means it's not illegal." Bush exceeds Nixon in his claim of divine inspiration from the Higher Father.

Every executive policy does not exist on its own merit but as part of an overarching plan to establish an executive who rules by fiat. Enforcing these policies is intended to break down resistance to aggrandizing unaccountable power for the presidency. Warrantless domestic surveillance is a case in point.

Torture is the linchpin of the new Republican argument on presidential power. Abuse of detainees is the metaphor for beguiling the public into supporting abuse of the presidency. The sadomasochistic ecstasy of torture and the thrill of vengeance are the ultimate appeal of the party of torture. Projecting violence against accused terrorists in an endless war is a deep political strategy to forge and fortify a new regime. This novel form of government, never before installed in the U.S., despite precursors from Nixon's planned seizure of powers, is being cemented into place so that its penetrability and removal will become extraordinarily difficult. Those who undertake the task of rebuilding the structure will be vulnerable to harsh political attacks as unpatriotic and subversive. Thus restoring American constitutional government after Bush demands the most strategic political and bureaucratic genius.

So vital is torture to the imperial presidency that Bush staked the nomination of his new attorney general, Michael Mukasey, on his refusal to oppose a ritual designed during the Spanish Inquisition to purge sinful heresy: waterboarding. Were Mukasey to have called waterboarding torture, as it surely is, he would have been obligated to prosecute those responsible for war crimes.

Mukasey's testimony was symptomatic of the new constitutional order forged by Bush. Even more insidious, the secretive process to which the administration subjected Mukasey to get him to toe the line underlines that the radical changes Bush has made in the presidency are not merely for one administration, but intended for all that follow.

On October 25, Senator Dick Durbin of Illinois received written responses from Mukasey to questions he had submitted. In one question, Durbin asked about a report that Mukasey had met with unnamed conservative figures to discuss his legal views and allay any misgivings they might have.

The list of names extracted from Mukasey by Durbin passed by unnoticed in the controversy. Mukasey revealed that on order of "officials within the White House" he sat down with six prominent right-wing leaders, whose gathering constituted a de facto subcommittee of the "Inner Party" of the conservative movement. Those present were Reagan's attorney general, Edwin Meese III; former Reagan and Bush I legal officials Lee Casey and David Rivkin; the executive vice president of the Federalist Society, Leonard Leo; the president of the Ethics and Public Policy Center, Edward Whelan; and the chief counsel for the American Center for Law and Justice (founded by Pat Robertson), Jay Sekulow.

Mukasey's meeting with this group at the insistence of the White House amounted to a supra-official confirmation hearing. The incident demonstrates that the Bush imperial presidency is a central tenet of the permanent elite of the party extending beyond his administration. Politicizing paranoia, subsuming intelligence by ideology, purging and deputizing prosecutors, dismissing law by fiat (signing statements), and holding in contempt checks and balances are not temporary measures. It is no accident, as the Marxists (or neoconservatives) say, that President Bush will address the 25th anniversary gala of the Federalist Society on Thursday.

All major Republican candidates for president have embraced Bush's imperial presidency, but none has surpassed in his fervor Rudy Giuliani. The possibility of holding unaccountable power and conducting a presidency on the footing of what one of his closest advisors, the literary critic as foreign policy expert manqué Norman Podhoretz, has called "World War IV" has wildly excited him. Giuliani time, indeed.

Whether Giuliani becomes the nominee or not, he has defined more clearly than the others the coming themes of the Republican campaign for 2008. His political premise in running for mayor of New York was that the city was under siege, overrun by crime and chaos. His answer to crime was his new police commissioner: Bernard Kerik, the lawless lawman.

Giuliani's image of New York then is transformed now into an image of the country besieged from within and without. As mayor he stoked inflammatory racial confrontation and basked in demagogy. His heated and cynical paranoid style has gone international. (For cynicism, few episodes exceed his showdown in 1999 with the Brooklyn Museum over an African artist's painting of a portrait of the Virgin Mary using elephant dung as a material when Giuliani was slipping in the polls against his prospective opponent for the U.S. Senate, Hillary Clinton. When the chips are down, Giuliani always looks for the elephant chip.) Whether he becomes the Republican candidate or not, he has helped consolidate Bush's authoritarian model as the only acceptable one for Republicans.

November 15, 2007

Acknowledgments

The Strange Death of Republican America culminates my reporting and analysis of an entire era in which the Republican Party, even while Democrats held the White House, remained the dominant influence, controlling and limiting public policy and political agendas. For decades, after the Democratic debacle of 1968, the prevalence of Republicanism has held sway. Now, with this book, I chronicle week-by-week, month-by-month, from the spring of 2006 through the fall of 2007, the decisive historical disintegration of the Republican Party. Built up since the presidency of Richard Nixon, reaching its apex with Ronald Reagan, and extended through George H.W. Bush, this version of the Republican Party reached its fiery apotheosis under George W. Bush.

The sections of *The Strange Death of Republican America* mark the phases of its progress, or more accurately, morbid decline. "Implosion" describes the chain reaction of self-generated catastrophe. "Repudiation" records the voters' revulsion against Bush's policies and revolt at the ballot box, overthrowing the Republican Congress. "Delusion" captures the president's astounding denial of reality in his refusal to come to terms with the consequences of his actions, including the lasting damage to his party.

In one sense, this book can be read seamlessly as volume two of my previous work, *How Bush Rules: Chronicles of a Radical Regime*, published in 2006, which documents and deconstructs the Bush presidency and its doctrine of an unfettered executive from its zenith of hubris to the beginning of its self-inflicted collapse. But, in another sense, *The Strange Death of Republican America* is the final chapter of the work I began in *The Rise of the Counter-Establishment*, published in 1986, at the height of Reagan's presidency, when I was on the national staff of the *Washington Post*. While that book illuminates the rise of the conservative movement and era, this one shines a light on its fall. Conceived shortly after Reagan's election, this project has consumed a quarter-century of my life. Whatever its imperfections or omissions, this entire story encompasses an age that is near to its close.

I am grateful to *Salon*, the online magazine that first published the articles and essays in this book, especially Joan Walsh, *Salon's* editor, and Michal Keeley, whose sharp eye and precise pen have made my words as clear as possible. I am also grateful to *The Guardian* of London, especially Alan Rusbridger, Seumas Milne, and Georgina Henry, and OpenDemocracy.net of London, especially Isabel Hilton and David Hayes, for publishing these pieces.

I am indebted to Philip Turner, director of Union Square Press, for his acuity, determination, and brilliant idea of reissuing *The Rise of the Counter-Establishment* to accompany this volume, thereby providing bookends for the theme of the Republican rise and fall. I owe thanks to Peter Dougherty, director of Princeton University Press, for encouraging us to collaborate.

This book is dedicated to Sean Wilentz, the greatest American historian of our generation, but of greater importance a dear friend. Our conversations have gone on for years and I hope this moveable feast continues for years to come.

Finally, this book, as with all the others, would not have been possible without the support, intelligence, and forbearance of my wife, Jackie. Our endless dinner table talk and telephone calls with our sons, Max and Paul, who have emerged as figures in their own right in journalism and public policy, make this work a genuine family enterprise.

Index

ALSO AVAILABLE

The Rise of the Counter-Establishment:
The Conservative Ascent to Political Power
By Sidney Blumenthal

Since its publication in 1986, Sidney Blumenthal's *The Rise of the Counter-Establishment* has been regarded as a seminal book of contemporary politics—the parent volume for *The Strange Death of Republican America.*

The Rise of the Counter-Establishment explores how the Republican Party built up its infrastructure in the years following what seemed like a cataclysmic moment after Barry Goldwater's electoral 1964 defeat, through Nixon's election in 1968, to the culminating and triumphant Reagan years. Based on hundreds of interviews with key policy makers, Blumenthal shows how conservatives orchestrated and magnified their influence to change American politics, endowing academic chairs, funding think tanks, and subsidizing a political infrastructure.

For this edition of his classic, Blumenthal has written a new introduction, tracing the party's steady ascent over several decades, up to its precipitous decline as George W. Bush's presidency nears its end, while also charting the path of Dick Cheney's career. Blumenthal demonstrates that, "early on, Cheney's notions for an imperial presidency and his relationships with the neoconservatives merged on to a single track." Reaching back to the beleaguered Ford White House, when Cheney served as Chief of Staff, Blumenthal argues that the vice-president has been a primary architect of the neoconservative movement, making possible its rise, while also pre-ordaining the fall with his over-reaching grab at executive power.

Taken together, *The Rise of the Counter-Establishment* and *The Strange Death of Republican America* masterfully chart the rise and fall of a political party.

"An excellent history of modern American conservatism . . . thoughtful and fair-minded." —*New York Times Book Review*

"We have long needed an anatomy of Reaganism as an intellectual movement, and at last Sidney Blumenthal has filled the gap in this incisive, illuminating and enlivening work."—Arthur Schlesinger, Jr.

"Skillful, extensively researched and unfailingly interesting... The people and institutions Blumenthal so skillfully and intelligently describes have had an incalculable impact on public life." —*Boston Sunday Globe*

Union Square Press / 368 pages / ISBN 978-1-4027-5911-6 / $12.95 / April 2008
Available at fine bookstores everywhere